HISTORICAL ESSAYS AND STUDIES

MACMILLAN AND CO., Limited
LONDON · BOMBAY · CALCUTTA
MELBOURNE

THE MACMILLAN COMPANY
NEW YORK · BOSTON · CHICAGO
ATLANTA · SAN FRANCISCO

THE MACMILLAN CO. OF CANADA, Ltd.
TORONTO

HISTORICAL
ESSAYS & STUDIES

BY

JOHN EMERICH EDWARD DALBERG-ACTON
FIRST BARON ACTON
D.C.L., LL.D., ETC. ETC.
REGIUS PROFESSOR OF MODERN HISTORY IN THE UNIVERSITY OF CAMBRIDGE

EDITED BY

JOHN NEVILLE FIGGIS, M.A.
SOMETIME LECTURER IN ST. CATHARINE'S COLLEGE, CAMBRIDGE

AND

REGINALD VERE LAURENCE, M.A.
FELLOW AND LECTURER OF TRINITY COLLEGE, CAMBRIDGE

MACMILLAN AND CO., LIMITED
ST. MARTIN'S STREET, LONDON

1907

PREFATORY NOTE

WITH the exception of the hitherto unprinted paper entitled " The Causes of the Franco-Prussian War," this volume consists of articles reprinted from the following periodicals : *The Quarterly Review*, *The English Historical Review*, *The Nineteenth Century*, *The Rambler*, *The Home and Foreign Review*, *The North British Review*, *The Bridgnorth Journal.* The Editors have to thank Mr. John Murray, Messrs. Longmans, Kegan Paul, Williams and Norgate, and the proprietors of *The Bridgnorth Journal* for their kind permission to republish these articles.

Acton and Simpson collaborated in writing the two articles on Buckle's *History of Civilisation* (which it was impracticable to separate) ; the former of them is very largely Simpson's work.

J. N. F.

R. V. L.

August 24, 1907.

CONTENTS

WOLSEY AND THE DIVORCE OF HENRY VIII.[1]

HALF a century ago a writer of great authority delivered the opinion that few things in history were better known than the divorce of Catharine of Aragon. Since that time the archives have been explored, and the old story which satisfied Hallam will never be told again. Mr. Brewer has done more than any other man to dispel the dark tradition, and to pour light upon an epoch which will always interest every description of educated men. After all that has been already gathered from Rome and Venice and Simancas, from Brussels and Vienna, his volume on the last and most momentous years of Wolsey's ministry embraces seven thousand letters, of which a large proportion are important and new. The most competent of his foreign critics, Dr. Pauli, reviewing the earlier part of the Calendar, declared that no other country possesses a work so satisfactory and complete ; and this is not exaggerated praise, although even Mr. Brewer's analysis cannot be accepted as a substitute for the full text of documents. He has not aimed so high ; and his readers will not seldom find that there is something still to learn in earlier and humbler publications.

If the Calendar does not utterly supersede all previous collections, the introduction in which Mr. Brewer has gathered up the innumerable threads, and has woven them into a consistent picture, so far surpasses all former narratives of the same events as to cause regret that he

---

[1] *The Quarterly Review*, January 1877.

has not chosen rather to write a life of Wolsey, which everybody would have read, than to bury the fruit of so much study in prefaces to bulky and not very accessible volumes. With little additional labour he would have enjoyed greater freedom in the management of materials and in the use of colour, and literature would have been endowed with a popular masterpiece. Mr. Brewer has thought it a duty to devote the whole of his accumulated knowledge and power to the public work which has occupied so large a portion of his life. So few men are capable of extracting for themselves and digesting all the information his Calendar contains, that the elaborate introductions by the editor add immeasurably to its permanent utility and value. But it is impossible not to feel and to regret the generosity of so great a sacrifice.

Many of the problems that have agitated and perplexed ten generations of men are still unsolved. Yet, although we have not reached the fulness of knowledge that sates curiosity, it is not likely that much more will be learnt Some progress may be looked for in biography ; for the early lives of Gardiner, Tunstall, and Cromwell have not been studied ; nobody has taken the pains to restore the true text of the original Life of Fisher ; and not one of More's fifteen biographers has worked from manuscripts. The Vatican continues to yield priceless additions to the works of Raynaldus, of Theiner, and of Lämmer ; part of the correspondence of Charles V. lies unused at Brussels ; and the papers of Campeggio may yet, perhaps, be found in the place where Sigonius saw them. But whatever the future may reveal, we now possess, in Mr. Brewer's pages, an account of the Divorce, to the fall of Wolsey, which is eminently trustworthy and intelligible.

That which distinguishes the whole reign of Henry VIII., both in Wolsey's happier days and during the riotous tyranny of later years, the idea of treating ecclesiastical authority not as an obstruction, but as a convenient auxiliary to the Crown, was anticipated by the example of his father-in-law Ferdinand. The Norman conquerors of Sicily established a form of government in which the spiritual power was more completely subdued by the civil than in any other place beyond the Byzantine boundary. In the struggle for the inheritance of the Suabian emperors, the Sicilians resisted for centuries the anathemas and the arms of Rome, and the kings of the House of Aragon maintained themselves in defiance of excommunications which were almost perpetual, and of an interdict which lasted seventy years. In a country which had endured ecclesiastical isolation so long, the Papacy could not recover its influence when the dynastic strife was ended. The Kings of Sicily acknowledged no superior, but exercised all jurisdiction themselves, allowing no appeals, and holding under strict control the intercourse between Rome and the Church within the island. This system of undivided power, consolidated and codified under Ferdinand the Catholic, became known by the significant designation of the Sicilian Monarchy. It was established without a conflict, and without ostensibly derogating from the papal dignity, by the instrumentality of the fiction that the King was, in his own dominions, hereditary Legate of the Pope. The combination of legatine authority with the highest political office in the person of Wolsey was an expedient that bore close practical resemblance to this institution.

It was in 1515 that Ferdinand proclaimed himself the virtual head both of Church and State in Sicily—*cujus tam in spiritualibus quam in temporalibus curam gerimus.* In the following year Henry VIII. demanded that Leo X. would appoint his favourite minister Legate *a latere.* For three years he made the demand in vain. It was granted at length, and the appointment was justly described as the keystone of the Cardinal's position. Henry had too much of the instinct and of the passion of power to surrender willingly the advantage which it gave him. That advantage could be preserved only by close union with Rome, or by the exclusion of its authority. The intimate alliance with the Papacy through every vicissitude of political fortune which is characteristic of Wolsey's administration, actually prepared the way for separation after his disgrace.   It was so essential an element in his scheme of government that it was not disturbed when Henry imputed to Leo, and bitterly resented, his failure to obtain the Imperial crown.

The elevation of his rival, the King of Spain, suddenly raised England to an important position in the politics of Europe.   An auction began, at which Francis I. sought to purchase her friendship with gold ; whilst Charles V. not only offered the same sums as his competitor, but increase of territory at his competitor's expense.   France was still our hereditary enemy.   England remembered that an English King had been crowned in the French capital ; and Calais was an irritating memorial of the lost inheritance, and of conquests that had ended in defeat. The nation adopted with joy the alliance with the House of Burgundy, and Parliament voted supplies for war against France.

To make sure of Wolsey, Charles promised that he should be made Pope ; and the compact was scarcely concluded when the See of Rome fell vacant.   The Cardinal summoned the Emperor to employ his army in securing his election.   Charles assured him that he would not shrink from force if it was needed ; but the choice of the conclave fell so speedily on Adrian VI. that his sincerity was not tested.   Wolsey waited, without discouragement, for another chance.   In less than two years Adrian died, and Wolsey was again a candidate. His ambition was not unreasonable.   He was the foremost of ecclesiastics and of statesmen ; and it had been said of him long since that he was seven times greater than the Pope.   In the conclave of 1522 six cardinals had paid him the compliment of inscribing his name on their votes.[1] The traditional aversion of the College for men from the barbarous North had been put aside in favour of one who, in point of public service and political reputation, bore no

---

[1] They were probably split votes, involving little more than a compliment or a warning ; for a voting paper sometimes contained six or eight names.   On the 3rd of January 1522 thirty-nine Cardinals gave more than sixty votes.   Volterra had twelve, De Monte seven, Ancona seven, Medici, Santa Croce, Della Valle, Aegidius of Viterbo, Wolsey, six each ; Adrian of Utrecht, eight.

comparison with the Cardinal of York; and when it was
first reported that a foreigner was elected, people supposed
that it must be Wolsey. He now tempted his colleagues
with enormous bribes, and he appealed once more to the
Emperor. Charles acknowledged his engagements, and
even exhibited a copy of the orders sent to his ambassador to procure Wolsey's election. But he caused the
original to be detained, and took care that no effort
should be spared to ensure the elevation of Medici; or,
failing Medici, of Colonna or Farnese.

This time the disappointment was final, and no hope
remained. It could not escape the sagacity of the
Cardinal that the new Pontiff, who was younger than himself, had been raised to the throne by him whose support
he had so painfully striven to secure, that his own claim
had not been seriously put forward, and that he had been
fooled with false professions. He at once prepared to
withdraw from the warlike alliance against France.

In the year 1523, while Suffolk ingloriously harried
Picardy, Wolsey already manifested his disbelief in the
project for recovering the lost dominions of the English
Crown, and opposed the attempt to push the frontier
beyond the Somme. His moderate counsels were encouraged by the new Pope, Clement VII., whose minister,
the famous *Datario* Giberti, revolving vast schemes for
the expulsion of foreigners from Italy, solicited in secret
the co-operation of England, and began by proposing a
suspension of arms. Just then the French were expelled
from Lombardy; and Bourbon, on the point of invading
France, bound himself by the most sacred oaths to depose
Francis, and to acknowledge no King but Henry.
Richard Pace, the successor of Colet at the Deanery of
St. Paul's, a respectable scholar, but a negotiator of un-
sound judgment, who was destined, in the imagination of
the Imperialists, to supplant Wolsey, followed the invaders
over the Maritime Alps, and witnessed the easy conquest
of Provence. He persuaded himself that the whole
kingdom would speedily be overrun, and that Bourbon
would be faithful to his oath. The Constable was a

traitor and a deserter, yet Pace declared that it would be folly to doubt his word, and that it would be Wolsey's fault if he did not seat his master on the throne of the Valois. The prospect that dazzled Pace, and attracted the ambitious King, did not disturb the Cardinal's clearer vision. He supplied the Imperial generals with some money and much advice, reminding them of the first axiom of military science, that the object of war is the destruction of the enemy's forces in the field. When Pescara turned aside from the campaign to besiege Marseilles, he refused to send a single English soldier into France. That Bourbon and Pescara should employ their victorious troops in making the Emperor master of the coast that connected his Spanish dominions with his Italian conquests, was reasonable. But it was not to be believed that they would risk destruction by plunging into the heart of France, from a chivalrous desire that a foreign potentate, who refused to help them, should be made, in spite of himself, as powerful as their master. Wolsey warned Pace that he had allowed himself to be made a dupe ; and Pace protested that the ruin of the expedition was due to the malice of Wolsey.

For many months a discreet agent of the French King had been concealed at Blackfriars, and he was followed, before the end of 1524, by an envoy of great distinction. As the tide of fortune turned, and the besiegers of Marseilles were shut up in Lodi and Pavia, Wolsey drew nearer to France, without renouncing his claims on Spain. The rivalry that subsisted like a permanent force of nature between the two Powers, gave him hope that he would be able, by his skill in negotiation, to derive profit, and to incur no risk, from the success of either. Whilst the issue was undecided, he would not commit England irrevocably. But the spirit of the Burgundian alliance gradually changed to resentment, and in February 1525 the seizure of the Imperial agent's papers disclosed the secret animosity that was parting the allies. The French envoys were on the way to their first audience, when they were met by the news from Italy that their King was taken, and his army destroyed. The calculations founded on the balance of power were overthrown. No advantage could be extracted from the keenness of a competition which had come to an end. The men who in the previous year had denounced the backwardness of Wolsey, were triumphant ; and in Spain, in Italy, in the Low Countries, the English agents clamoured for the immediate partition of France.

If the policy of the last four years was worth anything, the time had come to prove it. The allies were victorious ; Charles had gained the object for which he had associated himself with England ; it was now to be shown what English purpose that association had served. Henry sent Tunstall to Madrid to demand the Crown of France. At the same time he attempted to raise money for the French war by a method of coercion which was termed an Amicable Grant.

Charles V. refused everything. He would fulfil no engagement. He would not keep his promise to marry Henry's daughter, unless she was sent to be educated in Spain. Instead of paying his debts, he asked for more money. At the same time the Amicable Grant was met by a general and indignant resistance. Henry could obtain no help at home or abroad towards the conquests which had formed so long the ruling purpose of his actions. The political system which had been constructed on the friendship and the pledges of Charles V. had ended in disastrous and dishonourable failure. England had spent much, and had acquired nothing. The Emperor, who had undertaken to continue the payments and pensions formerly made by France, had repudiated his obligation, and had solicited the Pope to release him from it. When he wanted the help of England, he had obtained it for nothing. He contemptuously refused to pay for it now that he required it no more.

Wolsey had long prepared for this. Whilst, with seeming confidence, he invited Charles to redeem his bond, he was making his bargain out of the extreme necessity of France. The Regent, Louise of Savoy, could cede no territory; but she was willing to pay a heavy price for the only succour that could avail, and Wolsey exacted a sum of money equal to the ransom for which Charles afterwards released his captive. Gold was in his eyes a surer gain than the expensive chances of conquest; but it was hard for Henry to content himself with a sordid equivalent for glory. The Emperor Maximilian, whose capricious and ingenious fancy was so little satisfied with things as they were that he wanted to be Pope, and talked of making Henry Emperor in his stead, had also suggested that he should be King of France. Down to the battle of Pavia Henry pursued this idea. What Henry V. had done with the slender resources of his time seemed not impossible now, with the aid of the most powerful of the French vassals, and of those alliances which displayed Wolsey's imperial art. To relinquish so hopeful an enterprise without a shadow of political or military success, whilst the hearts of his people were hardened against him, and his confederate defied him at the division of the spoil, was an impotent and ignominious end of Henry's aspiring schemes. The author of all this humiliation was Wolsey. It was his policy that had been brought to ruin by the subtler art of the Imperial Chancellor Gattinara. His enemies at home had their opportunity, and they were the whole nation. Detested by the nobles for his influence over Henry, by the clergy for his use of the powers delegated by Rome, and, in spite of his profuse beneficence, by the people of England, as the oppressor of the nobility, he had hardly a friend except the King, whose pride he had brought so low.

Yet Wolsey withstood the shock, and his credit remained unshaken. Henry adopted his inglorious policy, bowed his own imperious will before the resistance of London citizens and Kentish monks, and, at the moment when the crown of France seemed near his grasp, abandoned without a struggle the cherished hope of rivalling the Plantagenets. Wolsey was able to bring these things about because of an important change that had come over the domestic life of the King.

Catharine of Aragon was little past forty; but the infirmities of age had befallen her prematurely, and her husband, though he betrayed it by no outward sign, had become estranged from her since the end of the year 1524.[1] As long as she was fair and had hope of children, and as long as the Austrian alliance subsisted, her position was unassailed. But when her eldest children died, people had already begun to predict that her marriage would not hold good;[2] and now that she had lost the expectations and the attractiveness of youth, a crisis came in which England ceased to depend on the friendship of her family, and was protected against their enmity by a close union with France and Rome.

The motives that impelled Wolsey to take advantage of the change were plausible. For a quarter of a century the strength of the Tudors had been the safety with which the succession was provided for; but when it became certain that Catharine would have no son to inherit the crown, the old insecurity revived, and men called to mind the havoc of the civil war, and the murders in the Royal House, which in the seven preceding reigns had seven times determined the succession. To preserve the Tudor dynasty, the first of the English nobles had suffered death; but nothing was yet secure. If a Queen could reign in England, Henry VII., who had no hereditary claim except through his mother, who survived him, was not the rightful king. Until the birth of Elizabeth no law enabled a woman to wear the crown; no example justified it; and Catharine's marriage contract, which provided that her sons should succeed, made no such provision for her daughters. It was uncertain whether Mary would be allowed to reign unchallenged by the Scots or by adherents of the House of York. The White Rose had perished, in the main line, amid the rout of

[1] That is the date given by Henry himself to Grynaeus. His secretary, 4th December 1527, calls the divorce a thing he "hath long tyme desyred." Wolsey writes, 5th December, "longo jam tempore." Campeggio writes, 17th October 1529, "piu di dui anni." But on the 28th, after hearing the Queen's confession, he says, on her authority, "gia molti anni." There is no reason to doubt the report of Grynaeus.

[2] Rawdon Brown, 1st September 1514.

Pavia ; yet Catharine tortured herself with misgivings as
to her daughter's claim.   The Earl of Warwick, a helpless
and unoffending prisoner, had been put to death, that her
wedding might be auspicious.   His sister Margaret, the
Countess of Salisbury, was living, and directed the
Princess's education.   Catharine vowed that she could
not die in peace unless the crimes of her husband's family
against the House of York had been atoned by the
marriage of Mary with the Countess of Salisbury's son.

It was not unreasonable to apprehend that Henry,
who had been unfaithful to the Queen in earlier years,
would not be true to her now ; that he would fall under
the dominion of favourites put forward and prompted by
the Cardinal's enemies, and that his inheritance would be
disputed by bastards.   The King's soul, the monarchy,
and Wolsey's own position were in jeopardy.   It might
well be difficult to distinguish the influence of politics,
interest, and conscience on his choice of the expedient by
which he hoped to avert the peril.

To a man who understood policy better than religion,
the public reasons for dissolving the King's marriage were
better than those which had recommended it to his
father ; and there was a strong inducement, therefore, to
ponder the words of Leviticus, and to regard the almost
immediate death of the King's three sons as the penalty
of his transgression.   In the arbitrary and uncertain
condition of the law, it was seldom difficult to find
excuses for the dissolution of a Royal marriage.   Henry
could expect that nothing would be denied to him that
favour or influence could procure for others.   No man's
marriage was exposed to more obvious objection.

The battle of Pavia had placed Rome at the mercy of
the Emperor.   Giberti appealed to Wolsey to unite with
France in a league for the protection of Italy and of the
Church.   A breach between Spain and Rome was
essential to the success of that which he meditated ; and
nothing could be more welcome than the appearance of
the Pope striving to combine in one confederacy all the
enemies of Spain.   Having embarked in so perilous a

venture, he could assuredly be made to give a heavy
price for English aid.   Wolsey received his proposals
with the promise of hearty assistance.   The Queen, the
Court, every influence in the State and in the nation was
against him.   But he persuaded the King to enter into
the scheme of Clement VII., with the assurance that
he would be rewarded by spiritual favours more than
sufficient to repay all that he gave up to obtain them.
From that moment may be discerned the faint but
suggestive trace of a secret that required the intervention
of the Pope and threatened disturbance at home.

On Easter Sunday, two months after the great turn of
fortune at Pavia, Wolsey first caused it to be known that
he had renounced the expectation of benefit from the
friendship of Charles V.[1]   Just at this time the Primate
Warham reminded him that it was unwise to broach
too many causes of displeasure at once, and advised that
the Amicable Grant be dropped "till this great matter of
the King's grace be ended."[2]   On the 21st of April
Wolsey wrote to Clement a solemn and mysterious letter,
entreating him to listen favourably to a certain matter
which would be submitted to him by Clerk, the Bishop of
Bath, who was the Cardinal's most trusted confidant.
But the secret was one which the Bishop thought it an
unpropitious moment to reveal.   He was recalled in the
summer, and Casale and Ghinucci, the two men whom
Wolsey selected to take charge of the divorce in 1527,
were sent in his place to expose business of great moment
to the Pope.

Clement and his allies did not dare to defy the
Emperor while the King of France remained his prisoner,
for they justly feared that Francis would seek his own
freedom by betraying them.   He proposed to Charles
that they should subjugate Italy together, and should reduce the Pope to the position occupied by the Patriarch of
Constantinople at the Court of the Macedonian Emperors.

[1] Gayangos, *Spanish Calendar*, 20th April 1525.
[2] Brewer, iv. 1263.   A misprint makes it uncertain whether Warham wrote
on the 12th or 19th of April.   Easter fell on the 16th.

But the chief Minister of Charles V., Gattinara, was a Piedmontese, who preserved the love of his country in the service of its oppressor. He distrusted and opposed the plans of Francis. He even imagined a scheme by which his countrymen, having been rescued from the French by the Spaniards, should buy off the Spaniards by a tribute large enough to avert the financial ruin of Spain. Before attempting war, the Italians tried what could be done by treachery. They offered the crown of Naples to Pescara, the ablest of the Imperial Commanders, as a bribe to desert the Emperor. Pescara threw his tempter into prison ; and a year passed without an effort to mend the fortune of Italy. At length Francis was released, and the Italian patriots took heart to avow their warlike purpose. Clement put himself at the head of a Sacred League, which was joined by France, and protected by England. Giberti called upon his countrymen to cast out the invader ; and Sadolet, in State papers, which are perhaps the noblest compositions of the Renaissance, proclaimed the liberty and the independence of Italy.

The moment for which Henry waited had come. Clement had burnt his ships, had refused fair terms of peace, and could not venture to deny the allies who sheltered him from manifest ruin. The secret matter which had slumbered for a year revived. Giberti assured Wolsey that the Pope would do for him all that was within his power.[1] But Clerk, who was again at Rome, reported that all else would be well but for the inauspicious business of the divorce. Henry paid a large sum into the Papal treasury : but his cause made no progress during the autumn of 1526. Six months later the difficulties were overcome, and matters were arranged in a way so satisfactory to Wolsey that he boasted of it as a triumph of skill.[2]

[1] " In iis secretioribus ac majoris momenti tantum sibi polliceri potest D. V. R. de S. D. N. voluntate quantum progredi potest auctoritas S. S." (Brewer, iv. 2579).
[2] " Wherin such good and substancial ordre and processe hathe hitherto been made and used, as the like, I suppose, hath not been seen in any time hertofore" (State Papers, i. 189).

The Pope soon repented of the temerity with which he had challenged the supremacy of Spain. The stronger confederates held back, while the weaker stood exposed to the calculated vengeance of Charles V. Imperial partisans made their way into the Leonine City and plundered the Vatican. The Emperor appealed before the assembled Cardinals to a General Council against the acts of the Pontiff. This threat had power over Clement. He could not, without danger, allow his claim to be disputed before a hostile audience. His right to enjoy the higher honours of the Church had been questioned by reason of his birth, and his election to the Papacy had been accomplished under conditions which gave ground for cavil. He was elected in consequence of a private agreement with Cardinal Colonna, who was his enemy through life, who had tried to exclude him from the conclave, who attempted afterwards to expel him from the throne. Men suspected the secret method which had wrought that surprising change. It was reported that the rivals had made a simoniacal compact by which Medici obtained the tiara, while Colonna received the richest office and the finest palace in the gift of the Pope. But by a recent law of Julius II. an election won by bribes or promises was for ever invalid. The Pope's courage gave way; even Sadolet declared that resistance was unavailing; and Giberti, boiling with indignation and resentment, and bewailing that it was his fate to serve the subtle and vacillating Florentine instead of the resolute English Cardinal, confessed that, without encouragement from France or hope from England, it was necessary to submit to terms dictated by Spanish generals. In a condition so precarious, the Pope could take no active share in a transaction which was an outrage to the Royal family of Spain. But the *Datario's* animosity against the Imperialists was such as to incline him towards measures which would injure them without compromising the Papacy.

Giberti had applied for an English pension, and he long continued to be trusted as a supporter of Henry's

cause.   After the fall of Rome he withdrew to his diocese
of Verona, where the fame which he won as the model of
a perfect bishop has obscured the memory of his political
career.   He confided to the English agents the fact that
he had left the Court because Clement was ungrateful to
those who deserved well of him.[1]   They understood that
Giberti had advised him to concede what Henry asked for
in his matrimonial affairs ; and they induced him to return
to Rome, under a promise that he would use all his
influence in the King's behalf.   What was the measure
of encouragement he gave during the last days of his
ministry, in the spring of 1527, cannot be ascertained.
It probably amounted to no more than this, that the
marriage might be tried in England without the interference of the Pope.   As things then stood, such an
understanding would be sufficient to justify the exultation
of Wolsey.

Up to this time the idea of divorce had occupied the
thoughts of Henry in a vague and languid way.   Neither
aversion for the Queen, nor desire of an heir, nor religious
scruple caused him to pursue it with a fixed determination.
Whilst it was uncertain who was to be his future Queen,
the King displayed no eagerness.   The only power whose
aid was worth seeking, or that could venture to affront
Charles by taking advantage of his kinswoman's disgrace,
was France.   In the House of Valois there were two
princesses.   Renée, the Queen's sister, was ill-favoured
and all but deformed.   Henry was not likely to incur
such risk for such a bride.   On his last journey to France
Wolsey met an envoy from Hungary, who had been sent
to ask the hand of Renée for his master.   He wrote to
the King that the envoy when he saw her had forthwith
renounced his purpose.   He wrote in terms he would not

[1] " He promises, however, to use all efforts in the King's behalf.   He says the
only cause of his leaving the Pope's palace was that the Pope did not attend to
good advice, and was not grateful to those that deserved well of him ; but Wolsey
must take care not to tell this to Campeggio " (Vannes to Wolsey, Brewer, iv.
5344).   " Praecepit etiam Dominus Veronensis Vicario suo non modo favere Maj.
tuae causae, sed etiam in absentia sua convocare et hortari Theologos ut pro Maj.
tua scribant ; sed et se quoque subscripturum pollicitus est " (Croke to Henry,
Pocock's Records, i. 531).

have thought prudent if he had lately designed that she should be Catharine's successor.

The King's sister, Margaret Duchess of Alençon, was richly endowed with talent and beauty, and she became a widow in April 1525, at the moment when England forsook her Burgundian ally. At first it was imagined that she would marry the Emperor; and she visited Spain, hoping, perhaps, in that way to effect her brother's deliverance. In the year 1526 Margaret was again in France: and a widely spread tradition, doubted but not discussed by Mr. Brewer, points to her as the wife intended for the King. The Venetian Falier, the only diplomatist who showed a disposition to accept the Cardinal's account of the divorce, says that he had made proposals for her hand. The testimony of other writers is vitiated by an anachronism; for they assign the divorce to the year 1527, when Margaret was already married to a second husband. Guicciardini and Harpsfield speak of Renée, as if either name was a guess suggested by obvious probability. Du Bellay, the shrewdest of courtiers, conjectured that Renée had been thought of. He cannot have heard that it was Margaret. She herself once reminded Henry, in after-years, that she was to have been his wife. This speech, which would have been ungracious if she had refused him, was an allusion to proposals made by Lewis XII., immediately after Prince Arthur's death, and renewed in vain until 1507. Francis I. was willing to encourage a measure which would perpetuate enmity between his powerful neighbours; but he would have lost his advantage by implicating himself irrevocably on one side of the quarrel. Intermarriage with the House of Tudor was an object of his policy; but before concluding it he gave his sister in marriage to the King of Navarre, and planned a match between Renée and Hercules, Prince of Este.[1] In the spring of 1527 no princess was left who could have taken the place of

---

[1] Margaret was betrothed to Navarre at Christmas, 1526. The proposed match between Renée and the son of the Duke of Ferrara was known 4th April 1527 (Desjardins, *Négoc. avec la Toscane*, ii. 935).

Catharine. The repudiation of his Spanish wife would not enable Henry to compensate himself by closer ties with France. The divorce, promising no political advantage, could only make way for the elevation of an English bride. But though purposeless now as an affair of State, it became an object of passion.

After long preliminaries a treaty of alliance with France was signed in April 1527; and Henry betrothed his daughter Mary to the son of his ally. The event was celebrated on the 4th of May by a ball, at which the French ambassador, Turenne, danced with the Princess. King Henry's partner was Anne Boleyn. At that time she had lived at Court four years, and Henry, though not dissolute according to the standard of contemporary monarchs, had long regarded her with feelings which contributed to make him indifferent to a foreign match. She repelled his suit; and for more than a year he could obtain no sign of requited love. At length he made her an offer of marriage, which was accepted. His letter is undated; but it must have been written about the time when Anne Boleyn first became conspicuous: not later, because the intrigue which was designed to make her Queen stood revealed before the end of May. There is cogent reason to believe that it was not written earlier. Lord Rochford deposed before the Legates at Blackfriars that the conjugal estrangement between the King and Queen had begun in 1527.[1] His evidence is worthless regarding the date of the desertion of Catharine; but it goes far to determine the date of the engagement of Anne, which he must have known. For in the interest of the Boleyns it was essential that the scruples of Henry should have preceded the proposals of marriage to their daughter. If the offer had been made earlier than 1527, it would have ruined their cause to assign to that year the awakening of the King's conscience.

As soon as the Queen had an appointed rival, and the pleas of policy and religion were absorbed in the

---

[1] Speaking on the 15th of July 1529, he said, "about two years since" (*Herbert's Life*, 114).

stronger influences of passion, the divorce was pressed forward with desperate and unrelenting energy. The friendship of France was secured, and there was nothing to be feared from Rome. On the 17th of May, the Archbishops, Warham and Wolsey, responsible in their character of Legates for the observance of public morality and ecclesiastical law, called Henry to justify himself before them, forasmuch as he was living, in defiance of the Levitical prohibition, in wedlock with his brother's widow. The proceedings were secret. Proctors appeared to accuse and to defend the marriage. Both accuser and defender were officers in the household of the King.

The effect of this collusive suit was to put Henry in the position of defendant. He took charge of the Queen's interests as well as his own. He was not a persecutor, but a victim; the protector, not the assailant, of her happiness and honour. It was in his power so to conduct the defence as to ensure his condemnation, and so to contrive his appeal as to ensure its rejection. Instead of putting forward his own suspicious scruples, he would appear to yield, with grief and remorse, to the solemn voice of the Church, reproaching him with involuntary sin, and dividing those whom God had not joined. It was intended that Catharine should know nothing until sentence was given.

At the end of a fortnight Wolsey adjourned the court. So grave an issue required, he said, that he should consult with the most learned prelates. In truth, the plot was marred by the fall of Rome. The Pope was shut up in the castle of St. Angelo. There was no hope that the Emperor's prisoner would confirm a sentence against the Emperor's aunt. There was danger that he might be induced, by fear or calculation, to revoke the Legate's authority, or to visit the fraudulent intrigue with the censures which were never better employed than in protecting the weak, and upholding the sanctity of marriage. That danger neither Henry nor Wolsey had the hardihood to face. No more was heard of the abortive suit until, in our day, Mr. Brewer dragged it into light.

C

Wolsey had already sounded the opinion of the divines. The first consultation was unfavourable. The Bishop of London, the Dean of St. Paul's, Wakefield, the first Hebrew scholar in the country, six learned men sent up to Lambeth by the University of Cambridge, pronounced that the marriage was valid. Pace and Wakefield promptly retracted. Cambridge was partially brought round by Cranmer. It was generally believed in England that Catharine, in her brief union with Prince Arthur, had not, in fact, contracted affinity with her husband's kindred. It was difficult otherwise to understand how Henry VII. could have spoken seriously of making her his Queen. Such things might be in Portugal, where the King could scarcely be prevented from marrying his step-mother. But in England stricter notions prevailed. Tunstall afterwards declared that he had defended the marriage only until he was convinced that the popular belief on this point was wrong.

No English divine enjoyed so high a reputation as John Fisher, the Bishop of Rochester. Of all the works written against Luther in the beginning of the Reformation, his were the most important ; and he was eminent not only in controversy, but as a promoter of that new learning which theologians who were weaker in the faith looked on with detestation and dismay. Fisher's support would have been worth having ; for he was neither subservient to Wolsey, like the Bishops of Lincoln and Bath, nor afraid of him, like the Primate ; and he would have carried with him the whole weight of the school of Erasmus, which constituted the best portion of the English Church. As Wolsey deemed him an enemy, the question was submitted to him in terms so general that Fisher appears to have made answer without suspecting that he was taking the first step on a road ending at the scaffold.

Catharine had been apprised, very early, of all that was done. In the month of March she had taken alarm. She was not allowed to see the Spanish ambassador alone ; but she warned him that she had

need of his protection.[1] On the 22nd of June Henry
informed her that he could regard her no longer as his
lawful wife. In spite of the vigilance of the Government,
Catharine despatched her physician and one of her
attendants to Spain, to instruct the Emperor of the
outrage inflicted on his blood. The remedy she desired
was that he should cause the Pope to revoke the powers
which had been delegated to the Cardinal for life. The
ambassador, Mendoza, reported at the same time that
public animosity was rising against him; that his enemies
were forcing upon him measures by which he would
inevitably work out his own destruction; and that
Tunstall would soon be Chancellor in his stead.

The French alliance afforded Wolsey the means of
recovering his influence, and of becoming once more, for
a short space, the principal personage in Europe. At the
head of the most splendid embassy that ever crossed the
Channel, he went to concert with Francis the measures to
be taken in common defence against their triumphant
enemy. It was necessary to provide, during the abeyance
of the Papacy, for the government of the national
Churches. Wolsey agreed with Francis that they should
administer the ecclesiastical interests of both countries
without reference to the Pope while his captivity lasted,
and should be free to accept his acts or to reject them at
pleasure. A still larger scheme for the government of
the entire Church was proposed by the French. The
suspension of the Papal authority was not so formidable
as the uses to which it might be put by the ambition of
Charles. If he could not compel his prisoner to serve
him as the instrument of his vengeance against France
and England, it was in his power to put a more pliant
and trusty cardinal in his place. This was no visionary
apprehension. Ferdinand of Austria was entreating his
brother not to relax his grasp until the Pope had accomplished all that was wanted for the settlement of Europe ;
and Mendoza, seeking to tempt Wolsey away from the

[1] "Esta muy sospechosa que en ninguna cosa se hablen verdad" (Mendoza
to Charles, 10th March 1527).

connection with France, whispered to him that the Emperor now united the spiritual and temporal power, and was in a position to fulfil his ancient promise, by deposing Clement. Wolsey was proof against such solicitation. The Divorce parted him irrevocably from Charles; and when the Emperor, seriously alarmed by the report that Wolsey was to be made Patriarch of Gaul, and meant to detach the Gallican and Anglican Churches from the See of Rome, offered him a sum which would be now £160,000, even that stupendous bribe was tendered in vain.

Francis I. offered passports to the Italian cardinals, inviting them to assemble at Avignon to consult with Wolsey and with their French colleagues for the welfare of religion. Wolsey urged them to come, in the expectation that he would, at their head, possess a virtual supremacy. The cardinals who were in France joined with him to inform Clement that they held themselves absolved from their obedience, and intended, if he should die in captivity, to elect a Pontiff for themselves. Among the signatures to this momentous declaration are the names not only of the French and English Chancellors, but of the Legate Salviati, who was nearly related to the Pope. It was not entirely unwelcome to Clement himself,[1] as it made it less likely that the Emperor would coerce him. But he refused to permit his cardinals to accept the ominous invitation to Avignon, for Gattinara met it by threatening him with a council to be summoned by Colonna. To meet the resistance of the Italian cardinals, Wolsey devised the boldest of all his manœuvres. He proposed that Clement should sign a protest nullifying all the acts he might perform under pressure of captivity; and should appoint Wolsey his Vicar-General until the moment of his deliverance. He charged Gambara, the Nuncio in England, to obtain these powers by persuading the Pope that Charles would never set him free, and that his Vicar would do his will in all

---

[1] "Gaudeoque nostra in S. D. N. ecclesiasticaeque authoritatis gratiam suscepta consilia, ex his indiciis ab ejus Sanctitate probari, quae exhibuit per nuncium illum clandestinum quem ad Dom Lautrec ab ea nuper missum V. R. D. scribit" (Wolsey to Duprat, 5th October 1527).

things. He was carefully to conceal from him the purpose to which the required authority was to be applied. It would have settled the question of Divorce, by enabling Wolsey to appoint the judges and to hear the appeal. To strengthen his envoy's hands, he proposed to the French Chancellor, Duprat, that Francis should pledge himself to Wolsey to employ all the resources of France in the Pope's service, and not to sheathe the sword until he was delivered. The engagement was to be seen before starting by Gambara. Then Wolsey undertook, by virtue of his special powers, to release the French King from his bond. After it had been described in fitting terms to Clement, and had exalted his confidence and admiration for the Cardinal, it was to become waste paper.

It was the opinion of Henry's advisers that the question of his marriage might still have been settled, as it was begun, within the realm ; and Wolsey's elaborate and demonstrative arrangements for a separation from Rome that might endure indefinitely, confirmed their advice. It was unreasonable that grave ecclesiastical causes should wait the pleasure of the hostile soldiery that guarded the Pontiff; or that an issue of vital consequence to the English crown and nation should be left to the judgment of men who were the helpless prisoners of an interested and adverse party. But on this point Wolsey was resolved to bear down all opposition. Rome supplied the qualification that made him indispensable. To preserve that supply, to maintain his position as Legate against the influence of Charles V., he upheld with a firm and jealous hand the prerogatives of the Papacy ; and he succeeded, with some difficulty, in convincing his master that it would be unsafe to proceed with no better warrant than they possessed already.

The Cardinal was absent during the whole summer ; the ablest men who were engaged in public affairs, Tunstall, More, and Gardiner, were in his retinue, and those who envied his greatness and denied his capacity possessed the King's ear. They disbelieved that the Pope would be willing now to help them against the

Emperor, or would assent to Wolsey's audacious plans for assuming his place. He might succeed, without any profit to the King. He might effect his own exaltation, and might then be intimidated from employing it for the desired end. It was plain that he was using the Divorce for his own aggrandisement. His aggrandisement might, after all, do nothing for the Divorce. When his vast designs were unfolded, a sense that they were outwitted fell upon the cabal that were pushing the fortunes of Anne Boleyn. Wolsey had been ready in May to go all lengths, and he now declined to go further without the cognisance of Rome, or to question the plenitude of the dispensing power. It seemed that he was betraying the King to the Pope. He defended himself in a remarkable letter, and fancied that he had dispersed the gathering storm. When Henry expressed a wish to see Gardiner, he replied that he could not spare him.

Then, for a season, his adversaries prevailed. They persuaded Henry that he could reach his end by a shorter road; and he sent his Secretary Knight to Rome, with instructions which were unknown to Wolsey. For the delicate mission of inducing the Pope to abdicate his supreme functions in Wolsey's hands, he had chosen to employ none but Italians. The Nuncio Gambara, supported by letters from Cardinal Salviati, was to open the matter. Gambara was to be followed by Casale and Ghinucci. Stafileo, Bishop of Sebenico and Dean of the Rota, promised his assistance; for Wolsey had found him in France, and had no difficulty in moulding his opinion. Ghinucci and Casale were the most respectable of all the agents engaged in these transactions. But Gambara was a man steeped in Italian intrigue; and Stafileo obtained the promise of a French bishopric and a Cardinal's hat, and died in the following summer, claiming his reward with a vigour injurious to the credit of his legal advice. Clement afterwards accused Stafileo of having been the author of the mischief His adhesion was a notable event, for he presided over the supreme tribunal by which, in the last instance, the validity of marriages was decided ; and it was a significant circumstance that the King's cause was at once taken up and pleaded by the official agents of the Papacy.

But the artful machinery which Wolsey had contrived was thrust aside, the management was wrested from his hands, and he was obliged to recall his instructions ; while Knight proceeded to execute orders which were studiously concealed from his knowledge. During the interval in which his adversaries pursued the matter in their own way, and laboured to rob him of the merit of success, Clement made terms with his conquerors. The Protest and the Vicariate became words without a meaning, and Wolsey's dream of superseding the Pope was dissolved.

The substance of Knight's mission was to procure a dispensation for bigamy. The original intention was only to seek a dispensation for marriage within the forbidden degrees when the first should be dissolved. It could be requisite only because the King had been the lover of the mother or sister of Anne Boleyn. He declared that it was not the mother. The dispensation demanded would, in some measure, have confirmed the right to try the cause in London. But the Nuncio advised that it should be unconditional, and should not be made to depend on the divorce of Catharine. This petition was not brought before the Pope. Knight was overtaken on the way by Lord Rochford's chaplain, bringing an altered draft. Cranmer was chaplain to Lord Rochford. He was so much averse to the theories that were undermining the marriage-law, that he protested vehemently against the later practice of his Lutheran friends, calling them Mohammedans for their encouragement of polygamy. It would appear that he was the author of the altered counsels.

When Wolsey on his return reported himself to Henry, the answer came to him in the shape of an order from Anne Boleyn. He could measure the ground he had lost by his prolonged absence. He regained it in the following winter by his inexhaustible energy and resource ; and the importunities of Anne for some token of attention, were it even a basket of shrimps, confirmed him in the assurance of recovered power. Knight's negotiations with Roman and Tuscan masters of refined diplomacy ended in quick discomfiture. Long before his complacent incompetence was exposed, Wolsey had taken back into his own hands the conduct of affairs. The sharp lesson just administered had taught him caution. His services in promoting the Divorce were certain to increase the exasperation of the people, and could never disarm the hatred or the vengeance of the magnates whom he had humbled. Success was not less dangerous than failure. It became the object of his efforts to transfer from himself the formidable burden of responsibility, and to take shelter behind a higher authority. He applied first for powers for himself, or for Stafileo, to try the validity of the marriage ; but he required that their commission should be couched in terms which implicitly ruled the decision. When he knew that the Pope was about to be released, he tried to give him a larger share of action, by proposing that a Cardinal should be sent over as Legate, in the hope that his Commission would enable him to control the Legate's course, and to dictate the sentence. In a passage which was omitted from the fair copy of this despatch, Wolsey confessed that the dissolution of a marriage which had lasted so long would give too great a shock to public feeling for him to take it upon himself.

Before the day came on which the Imperialists had covenanted to release the Pope, he was allowed to escape, and he made his way to Orvieto, where the emissaries of Henry, bringing to his feet the humble but fervent prayer of their King, taught him that he possessed, as Bishop of Rome, resources more than sufficient to restore the lost sovereignty of Central Italy. He was without the semblance of a Court. Few of the prelates, and not the best of them, had joined him in his flight. His chief adviser in this most arduous conjuncture of his stormy Pontificate was Lorenzo Pucci, Cardinal of Santi Quattro, a Florentine, and an adherent of his house, who, after the death of

Leo, had attempted to raise him, by surprise and acclamation, to the vacant throne. To many sordid vices Pucci added the qualities of energy and intrepidity, which his master wanted. At the storming of Rome he was the only Cardinal seen upon the walls. He was struck down whilst, with his voice and his example, he strove to rally the defenders, and climbed into the Castle through a window after the gates had been closed. He had been Minister under Julius, and, for his extortions under Leo, men said that no punishment was too bad for him. Wolsey had given orders that money must not be spared ; but Pucci, who was noted for cupidity, refused a present of two thousand crowns, and could never be made to swerve in his resistance to the English petitions. He drew up the Commission which Knight asked for, with alterations that made it of no effect ; and he baffled the English envoys with such address that the winter passed away before Henry had obtained any concession that he could use, or that the Pope could reasonably regret.

The dominant purpose was to gain time. The Emperor, on receiving the messages of Catharine and Mendoza, immediately insisted, through his Viceroy at Naples, that Wolsey should be forbidden to act in the matter, and this demand reached Clement whilst still surrounded by the soldiery that had sacked Rome before his face. He had now become free ; but it was the freedom of an exile and a fugitive, without a refuge or a protector from an enemy who was supreme in the Peninsula. The instrument which the skill of Pucci had made innocuous and unavailing, appeared to him charged with dreadful consequences. He begged that it might be suppressed. His dejection made him slow to perceive how much Henry's intense need of his spiritual services improved his political position. He strove to exclude the cause from his own direct jurisdiction. Having consulted with Pucci, and with Simonetta, the ablest canonist in Rome, he exhorted Henry to obey the dictates of his own conscience, and to dismiss the Queen and take another wife, if he was convinced that he could lawfully do it.

Wolsey's Legatine powers, or the Commission lately issued, were ample for the purpose. Once married to Anne Boleyn, Henry had nothing to fear. But if he waited the slow process of law, and gave time for protests and appeals, the Emperor might compel them to give sentence in Rome. Clement deemed that it would be a less exorbitant strain of his prerogative, and less offensive to Charles V., to tolerate the second marriage, than to annul the first.

Henry VIII. consented to be guided by Wolsey against the judgment of his Council, but he had inclined at first to more summary and rapid methods, and the mission of Knight in the autumn of 1527 showed that he was slow to abandon that alternative. That he should, nevertheless, have rejected an expedient which was in the interest of those to whom he habitually listened, which was recommended by his own strong passions, and which the confidential counsel of the Pope invested with exceptional security, is the strangest incident in the history of the Divorce. Wolsey's influence is insufficient to explain it ; for Clement repeated his advice after Wolsey's fall, and yet three years passed before Henry's tenacity yielded. In March 1530, the Pope was at Bologna, holding conference with the newly crowned and reconciled Emperor. Charles V. required him to threaten Henry with anathema and interdict if he should contract a second marriage pending judgment on the first. Clement could not resist the demand, but he yielded reluctantly. He put forth a Bull in the terms which the Emperor required. But in private he expressed a wish that his menace might be vain, and that the King's purpose might be accomplished without involving him in complicity. These words were spoken in secret ; and at Orvieto also Clement had desired that his advice should be attributed to the prelates who were about him. Henry may well have feared that, after taking an irrevocable step, he might be compelled to purchase indemnity by some exorbitant sacrifice ; or he may have apprehended in 1528 what happened five years later, that the Pope, compelled by the Emperor, would excommunicate him for disobeying his injunctions. Having taken his stand, and resolved to seek his end on the safer ground of submission and authority, he refused to abandon it.

All the auspices at first favoured Henry, and every prejudice told against the Emperor, whose crafty policy, while it enabled Lutheranism to establish itself in Germany, had inflicted irreparable injury on the See of Rome. The sympathies of the Roman Court were as decided on one side as they might be now in a dispute between the head of the House of Bourbon and the head of the House of Savoy. Henry VIII. had given, during a reign of eighteen years, proofs of such fidelity and attachment as had never been seen on any European throne. No monarch since Saint Lewis had stood so high in the confidence and the gratitude of the Church. He had varied his alliances between Austria, France, and Spain ; but during four warlike pontificates Rome had always found him at its side. He had stood with Julius against Maximilian and Lewis, with Leo against Francis, with Clement against Charles. He had welcomed a Legate in his kingdom, where none had been admitted even by the House of Lancaster. He was the only inexorable repressor of heresy among the potentates of Europe ; and he permitted the man to whom the Pope had delegated his own authority to govern almost alone the councils of the State.

No testimony of admiration and good will by which Popes acknowledge the services of kings was wanting to his character as the chosen champion of religion. The hat, the sword, and the golden rose had repeatedly been sent to him. Julius, in depriving Lewis XII. of his designation of the Most Christian King, had conferred it upon Henry ; and he bore, before Luther was heard of, the title of Defender of the Faith.[1] His book was not yet written when Leo X. convoked the cardinals in

[1] " Regia etiam Majestas aegre fert quod de titulo defensoris sanctae Fidei nihil adhuc acceperit, quasi ejus sanctitas ea re timuerit Gallos offendere " (Wolsey, Desp., 22nd May 1517. Martene, *Amplissima Collectio*, iii. 1274).

order that they might select a title of honour worthy of
such services and such fame ; and it was suggested in the
Consistory that Henry deserved to be called the Angelic
King.[1]   His bitterest enemy, Pole, averred that no man
had done more for Rome, or had been so much beloved.
Such was his reputation in Christendom that when he
talked of putting away a wife who was stricken in years
to marry a bride in the early bloom of her beauty, the
world was prepared to admire his scruples rather than
to doubt his sincerity.   Clement, though not without
suspicions, suffered them to be allayed.   He spoke of
the case as one which was beyond his skill, but which
no divine was more competent to decide than Henry
himself.   Campeggio declared, even at the Imperial
Court, his belief that Henry's doubts were real.   Cajetan
wrote of him in 1534, Cochlaeus in 1535, with the full
assurance that he had been deceived by others, and that
his own religious knowledge was teaching him to discover
and to repair the error of his advisers.   After the final
condemnation had been pronounced, a prelate engaged
in the affair wrote to him in terms implying that in Rome
it was understood that he had been led astray, not by
passion but by designing men.   Even Paul III. protested
that he had made Fisher a Cardinal in the belief that
Henry would esteem the elevation of his subject a
compliment to himself.

The good faith of Henry was attested by an imposing
array of supporters.   The Nuncio came to Rome to plead
his cause.   Stafileo and Simonetta, the foremost judges of
the Rota, admitted that it was just.   Two French bishops
who had visited England, and who afterwards became
cardinals, Du Bellay and Grammont, persistently supported

---

[1] "Cardinalis de Flisio tunc primus in ordine Card. in Consistorio existentium,
dixit sibi videri quod posset scribi et denominari pius, seu pientissimus.   Papa
dicebat quod forsitan posset denominari Rex Apostolicus.   Nonnulli ex Cardinali-
bus dicebant velle scire causam propter quam dicto regi hujusmodi titulus con-
cederetur, ut melius discuti posset qui titulus ei concedendus foret.   Alius dicebat
denominandum regem Fidelem, alius Angelicum, tanquam ab Anglia, alius Ortho-
doxum, alius Ecclesiasticum, alius Protectorem" (Acta Consistorialia, 10th June
1521).   A slightly different report of this curious debate may be found in
Lämmer's *Meletematum Mantissa*, 199.

it. Cardinal Salviati entreated Clement to satisfy the
English demands. Wolsey, on whom the Pope had
lavished every token of his confidence ; Warham, the
sullen and jealous opponent of Wolsey, who had been
primate for a quarter of a century, and who was now an
old man drawing near the grave ; Longland, the Bishop
of Lincoln,[1] the King's confessor, and a bulwark against
heresy—all believed that the marriage was void. The
English bishops, with one memorable exception, confirmed
the King's doubts. The Queen's advisers, Clerk, Standish,
Ridley, successively deserted her. Lee, the adversary of
Erasmus, who followed Wolsey at York, and Tunstall, the
Bishop of London, who followed him at Durham, went
against her. The most serious defection was that of
Tunstall ; for the school of Erasmus were known to
oppose the Divorce, and of the friends of Erasmus among
the English clergy, Cuthbert Tunstall was the most
eminent. He is the only Englishman whose public life
extended through all the changes of religion, from the
publication of the Theses to the Act of Uniformity. The
love and admiration of his greatest contemporaries, the
persecution which he endured under Edward, his tolerance
under Mary, have preserved his name in honour. Yet we
may suspect that a want of generous and definite
conviction had something to do with the moderation
which is the mark of his career. He reproved[2] Erasmus
for his imprudence in making accessible the writings of
the early Fathers ; and in the deliberations touching the
separation from Rome, in the most important Session of
the Parliament of England, when he was, by his position,
his character, and his learning, the first man in the House
of Lords, he allowed himself to be silenced by an order
from the King. Tunstall informed Catharine that he had
abandoned her cause because he believed that she had
sworn a false oath.

[1] Chapuys calls him : "Principal Promoteur et brasseur de ce Divorce" (Le-
grand, *Lettres à Burnet*, 141).
[2] "Cui etiam si germana sit Origenis, et non ab aemulis addita, veteres omnes
refragantur. Quare optassem magis delituisse non versam" (Tunstall to Erasmus,
24th October 1529. Burscher, *Spicilegium*, xviii. 13).

Nor did the conduct of the most distinguished English laymen confirm the reported unpopularity of the Divorce. It is certain that Sir Thomas More and Reginald Pole were conscientiously persuaded that the Queen was a lawful wife.   Pole had, moreover, an almost personal interest to preserve inviolate Mary's right to the Crown ;[1] and he wrote in its defence with such ability and persuasiveness, that Cranmer thought he would carry the whole country with him if his book became known.   Yet Pole allowed himself to be employed in obtaining the assent of the University of Paris, and accepted his share of merit and responsibility in a success which cost Henry more than a million of francs.

Sir Thomas More had defended divorce in the most famous work that England had produced since the invention of printing.   The most daring innovator of the age, he had allowed his sentiments to be moulded by the official theology of the Court.   Under that sinister influence, More, the apostle of Toleration, who had rivalled Tertullian and Lactantius in asserting the liberty of conscience, now wrote of the Lutherans such words as these :—" For heretykes as they be, the clergy dothe denounce them.   And as they be well worthy, the temporaltie dothe burne them.   And after the fyre of Smythfelde, hell dothe receyve them, where the wretches burne for ever."   Henry supposed that a man whose dogmatic opinions he had been able to modify would not resist pressure on a subject on which he had already shown a favourable bias.   More was steadfast in upholding the marriage, but never permitted his views to be known.   He represented to Henry that he was open to conviction ; that he was incompetent to pronounce and willing to receive instruction.   He promised to read nothing that was written in favour of the Queen.   So reticent and discreet a supporter could not be counted on

[1] " Caterina . . . sentiva rimorso nell' animo, et hebbe a dir che non moriva contenta, se nel sangue della Signora Margarita non ritornava la speranza della successione di quel Regno, significando di volere maritar la figliola con uno delli figlioli di detta Signora, alli quali mostrava grande amore" (Beccadelli, *Vita del Polo*, 280).

her side; and More consented, as Chancellor, to act
ministerially against her. He assured the House of
Commons that Henry was not urging the Divorce for his
own pleasure, but solely to satisfy his conscience and to
preserve the succession; that the opinions of the
Universities had been honestly given, and that those of
Oxford and Cambridge alone were enough to settle the
question. Whilst he remained in power he left the
Queen to her fate, and did his best to put off the hour of
trial that was to prove the heroic temper of his soul.

The Bishop of Rochester, indeed, was faithful and
outspoken to the end; but his judgment was not safe to
trust. Death for the sake of conscience has surrounded
the memory of Fisher with imperishable praise; but at
that time he was the one writer among our countrymen
who had crudely avowed the conviction that there is no
remedy for religious error but fire and steel; and the
sanction of his fame was already given to the Bloody
Statute, and to a century of persecution and of suffering
more cruel than his own. Fisher suspected the attack
on the Dispensation of concealing a design against the
Church; and he therefore based the Queen's defence on
the loftiest assertion of prerogative. His examination
of the authorities was able and convincing. He admitted
that they were not all on his side; but he held that even
if the balance had leaned heavily against him it would
not have injured his client. The interpretation of law,
the solution of doubts pertained to the Pope; and the
Pope had decided this dispute by the undeniable act of
dispensation. The question might have been difficult on
its merits; but there was, in reality, no question at all.

The value of the maxim, that the fact proves the
right, had just then been seriously impaired. The divine
whom Leo X. appointed to encounter Luther had invoked
that principle. It was absurd, he contended, to try the
existing system of indulgences by the rule of tradition,
when it was plainly justified by the daily practice of the
Church. But the argument of Prierias was discredited
by Adrian VI., who readily avowed that there had of

late been grievous abuse of power, and that dispensations
only hold good if they are granted for sufficient cause.
It was a source of weakness in dealing with the first signs
of Protestantism in England to adopt a position which
had been so recently discarded in the conflict with the
Reformation in Germany.   But Fisher went still farther.
The strength of the argument for the Queen was that a
prohibition could not be absolute from which the con-
tingency of a brother dying childless had been specially
excepted.   But her advisers would not trust that plea.
The law was clearer than the exception.   No brother,
in the history of Christianity, had felt bound to obey the
injunction of Deuteronomy.   The prohibition of Leviticus
had been almost universally observed.   This objection
was felt so strongly, that Fisher and the advocates of
Catharine contended that even if the Divine law forbade
the marriage, the Divine law must yield to the law of the
Church.[1]   Clement, however, admitted that the right to
dispense against the law of God was not generally
assigned to him by divines,[2] and, being so little versed
in books himself that he took no offence when men spoke
of his want of learning, he did not insist on it.   The
claim was an unsafe ground for sustaining the marriage ;
for the marriage was the most effective precedent by
which papal Canonists sustained the claim.[3]   The argument was set aside by the more cautious disputants, both
in Rome and in England ; but it had done the work of
a signal of distress, to indicate the insecurity of the cause,

[1] The Belgian canonists employed for Catharine said : "Concedantur omnia
Regi, quod auctoritas praedicta sit juris divini, et quod factum de quo est quaestio,
sit in terminis affinitatis, nullatenus tamen illi concedendum est, quod Pont. non
licuerit etiam hoc casu dispensare. . . . Cum maximo consensu et canonum con-
sulta et prudentum responsa pontifici juris divini declarandi, interpretandi, limi-
tandi, et contra illud dispensandi potestatem concedant."   Fisher, *De Causa
Matrimonii*, p. 42, writes : "Nullis argumentationibus diffiniri potest, sed solius
Pont. interpretatione."
[2] The Pope said to Casale on Christmas Day, 1529, that all the divines are
against the power of the Pope to dispense in such a case (Brewer, iv. 6103).
Gardiner wrote on the 21st of April : "The Pope will hear no disputation as to
his power of dispensing.   He seems not to care himself whether the cause be
decided by that article or no, so he did it not" (5476).
[3] "Quod Papa possit, ex gestis Rom. Pont. patet. . . . Moderna quoque
Regina Angliae consummaverat prius matrimonium cum olim fratre istius Regis
Angliae sui mariti" (Cajetan, *in Summam*, *Sec. Secundae*, 154, 9).

and it had deepened the consciousness of division in the English Church.

The shifts by which several writers defended the marriage betray much perplexity. One divine attributed the matrimonial troubles of Jupiter and Saturn to the want of a Papal dispensation. Another explained that the prohibition to marry a brother's wife had crept into the Pentateuch by the fault of a transcriber. It was commonly believed, by a mistaken application of a pronoun in the works of St. Antoninus, that Martin V., with a view to avoid scandal, had permitted a man to marry his own sister. And there were some who maintained that a man might marry not only his sister, but his grandmother, and even his own mother or daughter.

The reasons submitted on the part of Henry VIII. for suspecting the validity of his marriage were presented with such moderation, and such solicitude to avoid disparaging the Papal power, that they explain, apart from the weighty considerations of interest, the long hesitation of Rome. The maxim that a dispensation, to be good, must be warranted by sufficient reason, was generally admitted by canonists ; and Julius, in excusing his delay, had said that a dispensation opposed to law and good morals can be justified only by necessity. Assuming, therefore, in principle, his right to perform the act, the question raised was, whether necessity had been shown, and whether the motives alleged by the petitioners were adequate and true. The English argued that Henry VII. and Ferdinand V. had deceived the Pope with false statements. Henry had pretended that without the marriage there was danger of war ; yet he made it manifest that no such urgent purpose of public welfare existed. The dispensation had no sooner reached his hands than he confessed that it was not wanted, by causing his son to make a solemn protest that he did not mean to use it. Henry VII. survived four years longer, persisting in his determination to prevent the match. It was said that he was troubled in conscience ; [1] and Erasmus affirms that

---

[1] Lopez to Emanuel, Gairdner, *Letters of Henry VII.*, ii. 147.

D

extraordinary pressure was afterwards required to induce Henry VIII. to recant his protest and to marry Catharine.

Her father, though more deeply interested than Henry VII. in securing her marriage, refused for many years to pay the money, without which, according to the agreement, there was to be no wedding. The plea of political necessity for a dispensation, which was repudiated as soon as received, and was not employed during six years from the date of the first demand, was nothing but a transparent pretence.

To this was added another argument, calculated immeasurably to facilitate the task of the Pope. Ferdinand assured him that Prince Arthur had been too young for marriage, and that Catharine, during her short union with a failing invalid, had not contracted the supposed affinity.[1] The dispensation might therefore be granted easily without the presence of those cogent reasons which, in ordinary circumstances, would be required to make it valid. He was willing, to satisfy English scruples, that the Bull should provide for the opposite conditions ; but he insisted that no such provision was necessary for the security of his daughter's conscience or of her legal position. The Bull was drawn to meet the wishes of the English, but in terms which significantly indicated the influence of the Spanish representations.

Julius had promised it at the eve of his election, and he granted it by word of mouth immediately after. Nevertheless, the Bull was wrung from him with great difficulty after a year's delay, by accident rather than consent. When Isabella the Catholic was dying, she implored him to comfort her last days with the sight of the dispensation which was to secure her daughter's happiness. It was impossible to refuse her prayer. Against the wish of Julius, a copy was sent from Spain to Henry VII., and the authentic instrument could not be withheld. But for this, the Pope would not have

---

[1] " Ahunque en el dicho capitulo dize quel matrimonio de la dicha princesa nuestra hija con el principe de Gales Arthur ya deffunto, que gloria haya, fue consumado, pero la verdad es que no fue consumado. . . . y esto es muy cierto y muy sabido donde ella sta " (Ferdinand to Rojas, 23rd August 1503).

yielded. To the Cardinal Adrian, who was one of those whom he had appointed to advise him in the matter, he expressed a doubt whether such an act lay within his power. The Cardinal assured him that the thing had been done repeatedly by recent Pontiffs.

The contention was that these statements had misled the Pope into the belief that he was doing no more than the facts amply justified, whilst he was in reality exceeding the limits which all his predecessors had observed, on the strength of facts which were untrue. Unless it was certain that neither the imaginary precedents of Adrian, nor the pretended motives of Henry, nor the improbable allegations of Ferdinand, had influenced the decision of Julius II., there was serious ground to question its validity.

It was an issue charged with genuine doubt, and not necessarily invidious in the sight of Rome. Nothing had yet occurred to fix men's minds on the problem, and opinion honestly differed. In the French and English Universities, responses favourable to Henry were obtained with some difficulty, and against strong minorities. Although jurists in Italy could not earn his fee without risk of life, famous teachers of Bologna, Padua, and Sienna, whose names were cited with reverence in the Roman Courts, approved of his cause. The judgments of men in this controversy were not swayed by the position they occupied towards the Papacy. Luther strenuously upheld the rights of Catharine. Sixtus V. declared that Clement had deserved the sorrows that befell his Pontificate by permitting so iniquitous a marriage to endure so long. For the action of Julius was challenged as a judge of fact, not as a judge of law. The English disputed not the plenitude of his authority, but the information which had determined its use ; and it was the opinion of Clement VII. that Julius had not taken due pains to ascertain the truth.[1] The gloss of almost ostentatious

[1] Clement said to Charles V. at Bologna : "The Pope's function is to judge whether such a cause has arisen ; but no such inquiry was made, or judgment given, when the dispensation by Julius was granted" (Brewer, iv. 6103).

respect wore off in the friction of conflict.   But it was essential at first to the position and the tactics of Wolsey. Henry appeared in the character of an affectionate husband, bewildered in conscience by scruples he was anxious to remove.   Nobody could bind him under deeper obligation than by enabling him to live with Catharine undisturbed. As late as the month of May 1529, long after this fiction had become contemptible, Gardiner had the effrontery to say that Henry still lived with the Queen on unaltered terms.[1]   But Wolsey soon put off this pretence ; for if the only difficulty arose from a defect in the dispensation, the Pope could have afforded relief, as the Emperor proposed, by an act in more ample form.

After the failure of Knight, and of his Italian colleagues, Wolsey's tone became peremptory, and he resolved to make his strong hand felt. He despatched the King's almoner, Fox, with his own secretary, Gardiner, a man who had been engaged in the hidden work of the preceding May, and who was fitted to encounter the Roman jurists on their own ground, unswayed by shame or fear. He charged them to make Clement understand that Henry's determination to put away Catharine was founded on secret causes lying deeper than love for Anne Boleyn, causes which neither the removal of his scruples nor any other remedy could touch ; and that it would be executed, if necessary, independently of Rome.   That course would imperil the succession, would overthrow Wolsey, and, in the presence of advancing Lutheranism, would ruin the Church in England.   It was the Pope's interest, therefore, as much as his own, that the thing which could not be prevented should be done with full religious sanction ; that an act of deference on one side should be met on the other by an act of grace. He wrote at the same time to Orvieto that the instruments granted to Knight were little better than a mockery, and that he regarded the hostile influence of the Emperor as the only obstacle he had to overcome.

Gardiner was charged to obtain a Bull for Wolsey, in

[1] Brewer, iv. 5529.

conjunction with a Roman Cardinal, directing them to try
the cause, and if they should be satisfied of certain facts,
which he thought it not difficult to establish, to declare the
marriage null and void. Next to this joint commission,
he preferred one for a Roman Legate alone. In the last
extremity he would accept one for the two English
Archbishops; but he would not act by himself. The
Bull, as Wolsey drafted it, made a defence impossible,
made the trial a mere formality, and virtually dissolved
the marriage. Both Fox and Gardiner declared that it
would be hazardous to rely on powers obtained in so disgraceful a manner. They nevertheless attempted to
obtain the Bull, hoping that it might be useful at least for
the purposes of intimidation and coercion.

The English envoys found the Pope in the dwelling of
Cardinal Ridolfi, Bishop of Orvieto, beneath the shadow
of the gorgeous cathedral, but surrounded by solitude and
desolation, occupying a bare unfurnished chamber, and
eating out of earthenware. At his first step Gardiner fell
into an ambush. Clement inquired after Wolsey, touching a report that he was against the Divorce. Gardiner
eagerly testified to his zeal in its favour. The Pope
replied that, in that case, he would not be accepted as
an impartial judge. During two long interviews he
met the strenuous exertions of the Englishman with im-
perturbable temper and dexterity. He was ready to
appoint Legates, and to confirm their sentence; but it
was impossible to induce him to favour one party to the
detriment of the other, in the manner of the proposed
Bull. Gardiner plied his arguments with extreme vigour.
Addressing the Pope, and the small group gathered round
him, he protested that the King of England asked only
for light to clear his conscience, and would obey the word
of the Church, whatever it might be. He implored them
not to repulse the wanderer who came as a suppliant to a
guide. If he should appeal in vain to the Holy See, the
world would say that they were deprived of wisdom, and
that the Canons which were unintelligible to the Pope
were only fit for the flames. Pucci and the other prelates

listened without emotion, for they were persuaded that Henry had other wishes than to clear up doubts. Clement confessed that he was not a scholar, and that, if it was true, as men averred, that all law was locked in the breast of the Pope, it was a lock to which, unfortunately, he had no key. When Gardiner declared that Henry would help himself, if Rome refused 'to help him, Clement replied that he heartily wished he had done it. Finding that it was useless to ask for the Bull that Wolsey wanted, Gardiner proposed that an act defining the law as desired should be given privately, for fear of Spain, never to be produced unless Clement refused to confirm the sentence. To this the Pope replied that if the thing was just it should be done openly ; and if unjust, not at all.

At length, when the final conference had lasted during many weary hours, Gardiner, believing that he had lost his cause, kindled into anger. Gambara and Stafileo were present, and he exclaimed that they had made themselves tools to deceive and to betray the King. Then he turned fiercely against Clement, and denounced him. It was well, he said, that men should know how Rome treats those who serve her, that she may find no succour in her own extremity, and may fall with the consent and the applause of all the world. At these words the Pope sprang to his feet, and strode about the room, waving his arms, and crying that they might have the Commission as they wished. It was past midnight, on Maundy Thursday morning, when he yielded. The clauses agreed upon were not what Gardiner wished for, but he thought them sufficient. They did not satisfy Wolsey. He feared that the cause might be taken out of his hands, that the rule of law by which he tried it might be rejected, that his judgment might be reversed, by Clement or by his successor.

When the English solicitations reached Clement, in the last days of his captivity and the first of his deliverance, he was weighed down by terror of the Spaniards, and he promised to do more for Henry whenever the approach of his allies made it a safer task. Lord Rochford's priest was sent to accelerate the movements of Marshal Lautrec, who, leaving the Pope to his fate, had wasted precious months in struggling with De Leyva for the possession of Lombardy. At length, by the roads that skirt the Adriatic, Lautrec marched south, and for the last time during many generations the French flag was welcomed in the ancient dominions of the house of Anjou. On the 18th of February the Imperialists evacuated Rome. They were speedily shut up in Naples and Gaeta, and up to the gates of the fortresses the French were masters of the country. In the bloodiest sea-fight of that age, the younger Doria, arming his galley-slaves, destroyed the Spanish fleet in the waters of Salerno. Naples was blockaded. The stream that turned the mills of the garrison was cut off, and it was expected that the city would be starved out before midsummer. It was in the midst of these changes that Clement held anxious conference with the energetic Englishman whose speech was so significant of diminished reverence, who, as Wolsey's successor at Winchester, was soon to lend his powerful aid to the separation of England, and who lived to undo his own work, and to supply history with the solitary example of a nation once separated returning voluntarily to union with Rome. Wolsey had already spoken of going over to Luther when the Papacy obstructed his designs ; but Giberti had received the threat with scornful incredulity. Gardiner's warnings were less impressive than the vast change that was just then occurring in the condition of the Peninsula. From April to July French ascendency seemed to be established ; and the Spanish commanders informed Charles V. that, unless Naples was relieved before the end of August, his dominion over Italy was lost for ever. During those four months Wolsey was able to wring from Clement's unsteady hand every concession he required.

A Commission, dated 13th April 1528, gave him power, in conjunction with any English Bishop he might select, to try the cause, to dissolve the marriage if the dispensation was not proved to be valid, and to do all things that could be done by the Pope himself. A second document of the same tenour was directed to Wolsey alone ; but, as it has not been found in this country, was probably never sent.   The first was not employed, as both Henry and his Chancellor felt that they would not be safe without the intervention of an Italian cardinal.   A third Commission, enabling them to decide jointly or severally, was therefore issued to Wolsey and Campeggio.   Lest these immense concessions should be neutralised by Spanish influence, they were further secured by a written promise.   Clement declared, on the solemn word of a Roman Pontiff, that, considering the justice of the King's cause, whose marriage transgressed divine and human law,[1] he would never revoke the powers he had granted, or interfere with their execution ; and that if he should do anything inconsistent with that promise, the act should be null and void.   He went still further.   He entrusted to Campeggio a Decretal similar to that which he had formerly refused, declaring the dispensation valid only in the event that the assurance given to Pope Julius by Ferdinand of Aragon was true.   This important document was never to leave the Legate's hands, and was to be seen by none but Wolsey and the King.   At the end of July, when the fortunes of Spain were at the darkest, Campeggio, thus provided, set out for England.

Wolsey, relying on their own friendship and on the benefits of Henry, made choice of Campeggio as early as December 1527.   Gardiner was persuaded that the cause would be safe in his hands, and Clement encouraged the belief.   But Casale, who knew the ground better than Gardiner or Wolsey, remonstrated against the choice. The Spaniards reported that the Pope had given Henry leave to have two wives ; and as it was commonly supposed that the Cardinal was sent to enable him to gain his purpose, he was compelled to travel by roads that were safe from the incursions of Imperialists.   Charles V., convinced that the cause was lost if tried in Eng-

---

[1] Gardiner thought the first words of this document, "justiciam eius cause perpendentes," the most decisive of all the concessions made by Clement (Brewer, iv. 5476).

land, wrote that it must be prevented at all costs, and lodged a protest against Campeggio's mission. Contarini, the wisest and best of the Italian public men, saw the Legate at Viterbo, and judged from his conversation that the Emperor's fears were groundless. Another eminent Venetian, Navagero, who met him at Lyons, found that it was not his intention to content the King. The Pope himself wrote to the Emperor that the legates were not to pronounce sentence without referring to Rome; and Charles thereupon assured Catharine that she had nothing to apprehend from Campeggio.[1]

The origin of his elevation had been a successful mission to Austria, to detach Maximilian from the schism of Pisa; and it was by that emperor's influence that Campeggio obtained his mitre and his hat. His conduct in two conclaves caused him to be ranked among the most decided Imperialists, and Clement informed Contarini that he belonged to the Imperial interest. In 1529, when a vacancy was expected, during his absence in England, he was to have been one of the Austrian candidates. After his return he was zealous in the Queen's cause: he was one of the three cardinals who countersigned the Bull threatening Henry with excommunication; and it was he who, in conjunction with Cajetan, procured his final condemnation.

Campeggio foresaw the difficulties awaiting him. He was not eager for the encounter with Henry and Wolsey, and he spent two months on his way. Long before he reached England great changes had occurred. Doria had gone over to the Emperor. Lautrec was dead. The blockade of Naples was raised; and the besiegers had, on the 28th of August, capitulated to the garrison. Five messengers pursued Campeggio, warning him to adjust his conduct to the altered aspect of things, and imploring him to do nothing that could excite the displeasure of

---

[1] Gayangos, 537: "I am certain, because the Pope writes me so, that nothing will be done to your detriment, and that the whole case will be referred to him at Rome, the Cardinal's secret mission being to advise the King, your husband, to do his duty." This was written on the margin in the Emperor's own hand.

the victor.   Clement had resolved to submit, at any sacrifice, to the Imperialists.

When the Emperor learnt how vigorously the English
envoys were labouring to extort the Pope's assent to the
Divorce, he resolved to tempt him by splendid offers.
He would restore his dominions ; he would release his
hostages ; and he proposed an alliance by marriage
between their houses.   Musetola, who brought these
proposals early in June, was well received ; and it soon
appeared that the Pope was willing to abandon the
League.   It had done nothing for him.   There was no
hope for the Papacy in Italy, no prospect of resisting
Lutheranism in Germany, except through Charles V.
No reliance could be placed now in the French, or could
ever have been placed with reason in the Italian confederates.   The people for whom Clement had raised
the cry of national independence, in whose cause, identified with his own, he had exposed the Church and himself
to incalculable risk, and had suffered the extremity of
humiliation and ruin, were making profit out of his disasters.   Venice, his intimate ally, had laid its grasp on
Cervia and Ravenna.   The Duke of Ferrara, a papal
vassal, occupied the papal cities of Modena and Reggio.
Florence, his own inheritance, had cast off the dominion
of his family, and restored the Republic.   One way of
recovering all things remained to him.   He must put
away the ambition of Giberti and Sadolet ; he must accept
Charles as the inevitable master of Italy, and stipulate
with him for restitution and revenge.   Early in September
Clement's resolution was taken.   In October he returned
to Rome.   At Christmas he bestowed the hat and sword
on Philibert, Prince of Orange, the general who took the
command of the Imperialists when Bourbon was struck
down at the foot of the Janiculum, and on whom rested
the responsibility for the unutterable horror of the sack
of Rome.   When Campeggio arrived in London, things
had gone so far that a sentence dissolving the marriage
was not to be thought of.   The problem that taxed his
ingenuity was to avoid the necessity of pronouncing

sentence either way, at least until the Pope should be sufficiently assured of friendship from his detested enemy, to be able to defy the resentment of his ally.

Campeggio's instructions were to elude the difficulty by inducing Henry to desist, or by prevailing on Catharine to retire to a convent. If these resources failed, the Pope relied on his experience to find means to protract the business, and put off the evil day. With Henry there could be no hope. During the summer he was separated from Anne by the sweating sickness. She was taken ill. The King, in great alarm, made ready for the prospect of immediate death. He resorted with fervour to works of religion. He confessed frequently, and practised constant penance for his sins. But his treatment of Catharine was not among the sins of which he was taught to repent. He hailed the Legate's arrival as the signal of his approaching deliverance, and made open preparation for an early marriage. At Campeggio's endeavours to change his purpose by urging the danger of offending Cæsar, he became indignant and vociferous ; and the Legate could do nothing, for his hands were tied by the secret Bull.

When the King and Wolsey saw that document, they insisted that it should be shown to the Council. In their hands it would have served to settle the controversy. It decided the point of law in the manner desired by Henry. The Pope having declared the law, they could judge of the fact without him. They had got from Rome all that they absolutely required ; and the object of Wolsey's policy was attained. To apply to the case in dispute the principle laid down by the supreme ecclesiastical authority, an inferior authority might suffice. Protected by the Bull, they would incur little danger in following Clement's unwelcome counsel to help themselves. The credit of Julius, the consistency of the See of Rome, were sufficiently guarded, when Clement determined under what conditions his predecessor's act was legal, and Wolsey determined, on evidence unattainable at Rome, whether the conditions of legality were fulfilled.

Wolsey sent to Rome to require that Campeggio

should give up the Decretal.   If it had been produced and acted on, the Pope could expect nothing but ruin.   The responsibility of the Divorce and the wrath of the dreaded Spaniard would have fallen not on those who applied the law and were inaccessible, but on him who had laid down the law, and who was within his reach.   Clement understood his danger.   He lost the self-command which had not deserted him in the most distressing emergencies. Laying his hand on Casale's arm, he told him to be silent, and then burst forth in reproaches against the perfidy of Wolsey, at whose urgent prayer and for whose sake alone he had granted the secret Bull.   He detected their object. With the Bull before them, even those who thought the marriage valid would give it up on the Pope's responsibility.   Let them dismiss Campeggio, on the plea that he was slow to act, and accomplish their purpose themselves, without involving Rome.   The Bull ought to have been destroyed, and he would cut off a finger to be able to recall it.

Clement at once despatched an envoy to make sure that the perilous document should remain no longer exposed to accident or treachery.   For this important mission he selected Francesco Campana, a man who long enjoyed the confidence of his family, who, after the fall of Florence, proclaimed to the people the will of the conqueror, that the Medici should reign over the republican city, and who, as Secretary of State, gave efficient aid in building up the intelligent despotism of Cosmo.   Campana travelled slowly ; and when he reached London, with the order to burn the Decretal, Clement was reported to be dying.   To destroy such a document in obedience to a pontiff who was probably dead, on the eve of a conclave, would have been the height of folly. Campeggio resolved to disobey.   In the spring, when Clement had recovered, Campana brought the news that the Legate had yielded,[1] and the most memorable writing in the history of the Divorce disappeared for ever.

[1] Varchi, who had means of informing himself about Campana's journey, says that he brought the Decretal back with him to Rome.   But Mr. Stevenson has

But Henry had seen, under the Pope's sign and seal, that he had never been Catharine's lawful husband. For it was now admitted that, if Julius was deceived, the dispensation was void. No attainable evidence could demonstrate that he was not deceived or could resist the strong presumption in favour of the allegation on which Henry's scruple rested. The uncertainty lay in the legal element of the case, and that uncertainty was now removed. The Pope had been consulted, and the answer he had given was against the Queen. Henry might be right in his facts, or honestly mistaken, or altogether insincere; but right or wrong, true or false, he could not, consistently with his previous conduct, hold himself free to live with Catharine. The nullity of his marriage still required to be publicly declared; but in strictness he was unmarried. It followed that he must consider himself free to marry Anne. Apart from the public sentence, the religious obstacle to the second marriage was removed when Campeggio exhibited the secret Bull.

Mr. Brewer signifies his disbelief in the improbable story which began to be told in Mary's reign, that Rowland Lee solemnised the marriage of Henry with Anne Boleyn at dead of night, in November 1532, in a secret chamber at Whitehall, on being assured that a permission, which could not be fetched at that hour, had arrived from Rome. We trust that, in his next volume, he will determine the true date, and the influence of the Decretal on the event. At Campeggio's coming Anne Boleyn was kept out of the way. She now came to Court, and was treated in public as if she had been Henry's wife. Charles V. afterwards said to Campeggio that even the death of Catharine would be no deliverance, as the harm was done when Henry got possession of his Divorce. Elizabeth assured Parker that her mother's marriage had received the papal approbation.

---

discovered, and Mr. Gairdner has deciphered, two very curious letters of Campeggio, in one of which he says: "Per questo fu mandato il Campano, il quale, ultra alia, quanto a questo proposito mi disse due cose; l' una fu de la decretale, di che è seguito quanto vostra Signoria da lui hara inteso" (Brewer, Introduction, dclxxi).

Three Popes offered to acknowledge her title if she would profess Catholicism, at least, in secret. The secret Bull of Clement VII. made it optional to disregard the claims of Mary Stuart.

Failing to make an impression on Henry, Campeggio addressed himself to the Queen. The Roman divines were, he told her, dubious as to the merits of her cause ; the future was uncertain ; and the Pope consequently desired that she would close her life in a convent. The English bishops recommended the same easy solution. Henry eagerly adopted it, affirming with gross exaggeration, that the Pope had already pronounced against her. Then Catharine tasted the bitterness of the trial that was to come. Had she yielded, as the injured Queen of France had done, she might have averted the schism, until the genuine wave of Protestant thought struck England, when the daughter of her rival had sat for a generation on the throne. But she had no thought of yielding, and displayed, in the evil days that remained to her, the stern and tranquil courage of Isabella. She was alone, for she could not trust her council, and a watch was set on her intercourse with Mendoza. No Spaniard was allowed to approach her. The Belgian lawyers were sent out of the country. The messenger who had apprised Charles of her trouble was dismissed. Vives was put under arrest. Fisher refused to advise her without the King's command. Warham and Tunstall called on her to confess whether she had not practised against her husband's life. In all her solitude and misery she never doubted that her cause was just ; she neglected no chance ; and relied with signal composure on the Emperor alone. Her friends among the common people murmured loudly, and attended her in such crowds that the gates of the palace were closed against them. She acknowledged their cheers with a graciousness she had never shown, and asked for their prayers. Her evident popularity led Catharine into her only serious error. She believed that the Catholic spirit of the country could be roused in her favour, and she forced the Pope, by her importunity and her reproaches, to resort to those extreme measures which, in the end, were fatal to her church.

To gain Campeggio she took the bold step of asking him to hear her confession, when, relieving him of the obligation of secrecy, she declared that her first marriage had never been consummated. Campeggio could not disbelieve her, and the judgment of history, differing somewhat in the estimate of evidence from the judgment of law, must, we think, accept her word.[1] Wolsey was so apprehensive of the effect of such a declaration made upon oath, that he proposed to assail the dispensation on totally different grounds. But Mendoza deemed it a dangerous plea, and difficult to sustain at law. He recommended a safer defence, and he possessed a weapon keen enough to defeat all the art of Wolsey and his master.

Early in the year he had received from Spain a copy of a dispensation in the form of a brief, which expressly excluded the doubt as to the nature of the first marriage. Soon after Campeggio's arrival Catharine sent this paper to the Legates. It contradicted her own statement, and she protested that she had had nothing to do with obtaining it. But it avoided the reproach which had been so damaging to the Bull. Wolsey was taken by surprise. The plan on which he had pursued his operations so long was overthrown in an instant. He could not abandon his system and attack the dispensing power itself. He confessed that the objections taken to the former document did not here apply; but he declared that the Brief was spurious, and set about procuring evidence to prove it. Yet for many months Wolsey remained in doubt whether the paper which frustrated the great undertaking of his life was false or genuine. The reasons for suspecting forgery were stronger than he supposed.

---

[1] To the excellent summary of the evidence in Maurenbrecher's Lectures on the English Reformation, and to the ingenious inquiries of Lorentz, must be added the significant fact that Henry did not persistently deny that he had formerly admitted the truth of the Queen's affirmation. In the *Articuli in Causa Matrimonii Regii* this point is virtually given up: "Quarto nititur probare virginitatem ex confessione Henrici Octavi; circa eandem confessionem possint eadem dici quae dicta sunt circa confessionem Catharinae, videlicet quod testes sunt singulares, et quod confessio omnino est extrajudicialis et parte absente."

The Brief was unheard of until the need for it became apparent. It was unknown to Charles V. when, on the 31st of July 1527, he suggested that the Pope should supply the defects of the Bull.[1]   It was uncertain whether Clement would consent, when, towards the end of the year, the Brief made his consent unnecessary. Its existence was unexplained. It was said to have been obtained about the time of the marriage, in 1509 ;[2] but it was dated 1503. It was obtained by Ferdinand ; yet Ferdinand did not possess a copy. It was sent to England ; but it was admitted that it had left England before the marriage for which it was required. Ferdinand did not want it, for, on his theory, it was quite unnecessary. If he had asked for it, the Brief would have been addressed to him, and a copy would have been treasured up in Spain. It was addressed to Henry VII. But Henry did not want it ; for he was more than content with the original Bull, which he never intended to use, and could never wish to amplify. The Brief was discovered among the papers of the Ambassador De Puebla, who had left England before the marriage, and who was now dead. A list of all his papers relating to the marriage is still extant, and the Brief is not among them.[3]   Two men were living who could have given valuable testimony. De Puebla's heir, Fernandez, had possession of his papers. He was reputed an honest man, and it was desirable to have him examined. It appeared, however, that he had just been sent to one of the few places in Europe which were beyond the reach of Henry and the jurisdiction of Charles—to the dominions of the Earl of Desmond. Accolti, the Cardinal who in the name of Julius had drawn up the dispensation a quarter of a century earlier, was now the most zealous opponent of the Divorce in the Court of Rome. He could have settled the doubt whether a second dispensation had, in fact, been given. Accolti

[1] In a Despatch to Lannoy, Bucholtz, iii. 95.
[2] " In brevi vero quod circiter tempus nuptiarum ut conficeretur ab Ferdinando Rege Catholico procuratum est " (*Philalethae Hyperborei Parasceue*, 1533, p. 30).
[3] Bergenroth, i. 471.

remained impenetrably silent. Though addressed to Henry VII., the Brief was unknown in England. It formed the strongest security for the honour and the legal position of a Spanish Princess : yet it did not exist in the archives of Spain. It constituted the most extreme exertion of the Pope's prerogative known till then : yet Rome preserved no record of its existence. In April 1529, Charles was in doubt as to the value of the Brief.[1] He was willing to submit it to the Pope. His mind would not, he said, be at rest until he knew whether it had been found in the Roman Registers. His doubts were soon satisfied. The Registers were subjected to the scrutiny of Spanish and English agents. They found no trace of the Brief.[2] Errors were detected in the text. A vital flaw was detected in the date. Charles never sent it to Rome for judgment ; it was no longer necessary. The Brief had served to delay action in the Legate's Court until the Pope was reconciled with Spain.

Wolsey knew that delay was ruin. To strengthen himself at Rome he despatched four new ambassadors. He offered to surround the Pope with a guard of two thousand—or even of twelve thousand—men ; and he resorted to expedients which showed that he was desperate. He would resign his Commission and leave judgment to the Pope, with a pledge that judgment would be favourable. He inquired whether, if Henry should take monastic vows to induce the Queen to enter a nunnery, he could be dispensed from them and allowed to marry. Lastly, he desired to know whether the King might have two wives. These proposals were soon dropped, and exerted no influence on the event ; but they show the condition of Henry's mind, and the extremity to which, at the end of 1528, Wolsey was reduced. By the first he surrendered his original

---

[1] "He said also that his mind was not quiet until he knew whether the Brief was found in the Registry at Rome" (Ghinucci and Lee to Wolsey, 5th April 1529. Brewer, 5423).

[2] "Has done all he could to discover in the register books a copy of the Brief, but in vain. Has found instead two other briefs alluding to the affair" (Mai to Charles, 23rd March 1529. Gayangos, 659).

E

position, and actually invited that which he afterwards described as the cause of an inevitable rupture with Rome. The scheme to inveigle the Queen into a convent by simulated vows might possibly be entertained without horror; for it was supposed to be no sin to take an oath intending to be dispensed from it. Francis I. swore to observe the Treaty of Madrid, and bound himself, moreover, on his knightly honour. On the same day he had already declared before a notary that he was resolved to break the oath he was about to take; and his perjury was generally applauded. Cranmer, on becoming Archbishop, closely followed his example. If the desire of liberty excused Francis in deceiving Charles, Henry might plead that he, too, had a justifiable purpose in deceiving Catharine. The right to dispense from vows was not disputed.

It would appear that the proposal of bigamy, which was now made for the second time, never reached the Pope. The idea that the trouble might be healed in that way arose spontaneously in many quarters. The Secretary of Erasmus, writing from his house, made the suggestion that, inasmuch as polygamy was common in the Old Testament, and was nowhere forbidden in the New, Henry might take a new wife without dismissing the first. To Luther and Melanchthon this solution appeared most easy and desirable. They had fought hard to preserve monogamy among their own followers, and had prevailed upon the Landgrave Philip of Hesse to abstain from bigamy. But they found themselves unable to make the prohibition absolute. In Henry's case they thought the marriage originally wrong, but they objected still more to the Divorce. Luther advised that the king should take a second wife rather than put away the first; and Melanchthon thought that the double marriage would be good, and that the Pope would dispense for it. The Landgrave, having discovered this correspondence, renewed his demand, and the Reformers were compelled to sanction his crime. The agony of shame with which they yielded their consent suggests a doubt whether their advice to

Henry might not have been prompted by an idea of embarrassing the Catholics. Twelve months earlier Clement had informed the English agents that one of the cardinals, doubtless Cajetan, had told him that it was in his power to grant a dispensation such as Melanchthon recommended. But he was afterwards advised that it could not be done. Wolsey's proposal was in reality borrowed from the theories put forward in the Queen's behalf, asserting an unlimited power of dispensing.

These extraordinary measures for resisting the Spanish Brief were interrupted, in January 1529, by the dangerous illness of Clement. Once more the early ambition of Wolsey revived; and he caused the Cardinals to be overwhelmed with offers of troops, of money, of political and spiritual benefits. The hand of the spoiler and the oppressor had not departed from the territory of the Church. The Spaniards still detained three Cardinals as hostages, still occupied the papal fortresses, and by their control of the sea, commanded the sources from which Rome drew its supplies. The situation was one to which the French and English protest against an election held under Spanish influence continued applicable. Wolsey urged his friends to leave Rome, to hold the conclave in some city of refuge, and there to make him Pope. One half of the college shrank from the prospect of a Spanish Conclave, and made ready to depart as soon as the Pope should be dead. The imperial agents met the threatening schism with excellent judgment. They released the hostages; they gave up the fortresses, which, indeed, they could have retaken in a week; and they sent to the Tiber vessels laden with grain. They soon received their reward. Clement, in making his farewell to the Cardinals, exhorted them, if he died, to recall Campeggio. He declared that, should he recover, he would visit the Emperor beyond the Mediterranean. He assured the French agent that the fee simple of France would not bribe him now to desert the Spaniards. When at the end of two months he resumed the management of affairs, the reconciliation was accomplished. Charles was supreme in the court of

Rome, by the vivid memory of his irresistible power, and by the immediate sense of the priceless value of his friendship.   The Cardinals had not forgotten the awful time of the siege and the sack of the city.   In February they were still hostile to the Emperor.   In March the Austrian agents at Rome write that they have 448,000 ducats to dispose of ; and the resistance of the hostile Cardinals melted away rapidly.

Clement now regarded Wolsey as a sort of antipope, and as a personal enemy who was seeking to bring instant ruin upon him by employing a writing wrung from his good nature by false promises.   The situation of the year before was reversed.   He had relied on England to rescue him from the clutches of the Imperialists.   The Emperor was now his protector against the machinations of Wolsey.   Gardiner, when he saw him in March, became aware that all his pleas were in vain.   The English had lost as much ground in point of reason and justice, as of influence.   Contrasted with their extravagant demands, the petitions of the Emperor were moderate and just.   Wolsey now required that the Brief should be delivered up to him ; that sentence should be given, if the original was not sent to England ; that the Pope, of his absolute authority, and without inquiry, should declare it a forgery.   He ordered Gardiner to pretend that the paper containing the promises of the Pope had suffered damage, and to procure his signature to a new copy, to be drawn up in stronger terms, by representing that it was unchanged.

The Emperor Charles V., and Catharine herself, in letters conveyed secretly to the hands of the Pope, insisted with unquestionable truth, that a tribunal on which this man sat as judge could not be deemed impartial.   They demanded that the cause should be decided at Rome, where Wolsey himself had so lately proposed to carry it.   Clement doubted no longer what he ought to do.   One course was both safe and just.   He did not indeed believe in the Spanish dispensation : but he refused to condemn it on an *ex parte* argument, if every Spaniard had vanished out of Italy.   He would rather abdicate, he would rather die, than do what Wolsey asked of him.   He made no further attempt to resist the appeals of the Spaniards.   But he was oppressed, at intervals, with a definite expectation of losing the allegiance of England.   His only expedient was delay. Clement was unconvinced by Campeggio's testimony to the innocence of Anne Boleyn.   The King, whose passion had endured for three years, might become inconstant ; or Catharine might be persuaded, as the King had ceased to live with her, to consent that the favourite should occupy her place.   Her health was breaking, and he would have given the riches of Christendom that she should be in her grave.

In April the envoys of the two branches of the House of Austria formally called on him to revoke the powers of the Legates, and to bring the cause before the judgment seat of Rome.   Gardiner thought that it would have been madness to resist.   Clement consented.   On the 9th of May he despatched a nuncio to Barcelona, with full and final powers to conclude a treaty with the Emperor. Until it should be ratified, and the imperial alliance firmly secured, he wished to postpone the inevitable shock which Henry's disappointment would inflict on their long friendship.   An agreement was made between Clement and Casale, that the Commission should not be cancelled, but that the Legates should not proceed to execute it.

When it became certain, in the beginning of May, that there was no more hope from Rome, Wolsey's fall could not be distant.   His obstinate determination, in spite of the general feeling both in Rome and in England, that there should be no divorce without papal sanction, had ended by making the divorce impossible, had brought upon the country the affront of seeing the King's cause removed to a hostile tribunal, and had afforded the Emperor a conspicuous triumph over the influence of England in a matter chiefly of English concern.   At the moment when he was defeated by Spain, he was deserted by France.   The dissolution of the League, and the ruin of his armies compelled Francis to give up the struggle

for supremacy with Charles, and to submit to a dishonourable peace. Wolsey had traded on their rivalry.
It was the obvious and superficial secret of his policy to
sell the help of England to each, as necessity induced one
to outbid the other. Neither of the Powers had an
interest to maintain the statesman who had alternately
betrayed them, and they made peace at his expense.
Francis accused him of having intrigued on his own
account with Rome. His treacherous reports, sent home
by Suffolk, and aided by the certainty that Wolsey had
misled the King, strengthened the constant asseveration
of his enemies that he did not sincerely promote the
Divorce. In truth he had striven for it with incessant
care. But Du Bellay, Mendoza, and Campeggio had
long perceived that his zeal was stimulated only by the
desire to save himself; and he had implored Henry on
his knees to give up his will. When it was announced
that the Commission would be revoked, and that France
was suing for a separate peace, his power was gone. He
besought the King to allow him to attend the Congress at
Cambray. The two men who were thought worthy to
succeed him, More and Tunstall, were sent in his stead;
and an indictment was prepared against him.

It was impossible to doubt that the revocation would
be fatal to Henry's wishes. That which Clement dared
not allow his Legates to do in England, he would not
do himself at Rome, when the Emperor had disarmed
all his enemies, and was coming in triumph to visit his
Italian conquests and to assume the imperial crown. At
first Henry talked of appealing from Clement to the true
Vicar of Christ, to be raised up in his place. But he was
soon made to understand that the potentate who was
feared, having power to coerce and to degrade, was the
Emperor. He resolved to dissemble his anger. Inter-
cepted letters exposed the Pope's intentions, and taught
that nothing would be gained by waiting until Clement
felt himself stronger. Something might, however, be
gained by prompt and strenuous action. Henry resolved
to take advantage of the delay in revoking the Commis-

sion to force on an immediate decision, and summoned Gardiner in all haste to conduct the case.

The Imperialists had consented that the revocation should be postponed in consequence of the pledge obtained by Clement that nothing should meanwhile be done in England. When it was found that the pledge was broken, and that Henry employed the respite to urge on the trial, every voice in Rome called on the Pope to satisfy the just claims of Spain. The English agents confessed that no choice was left him, and bore witness to his good will. Clement protested to them in pathetic terms that the Emperor had him utterly in his power. He made one effort more to get the Imperialists to assent to further delay, but they repulsed him with indignation. They believed that he was seeking an opportunity to deceive them. Even in the following year Charles half expected that Clement would pass over to the English side.

Campeggio had been instructed to create delay by telling Henry that, if he must give judgment, he must give it against him. He replied by asking what he should do in the not improbable event of the judgment being in Henry's favour. Clement's final orders were to proceed with the trial to the last stage preceding sentence, and then to adjourn for the purpose of consulting Rome. Campeggio combined both methods. On the 22nd of July Clement's irrevocable determination was known in London. The pleadings were completed. The parties awaited judgment. Campeggio suddenly adjourned the Court for the vacation, announcing that he must consult the Pope. He strove to comfort Henry by assuring him that the interruption was to his advantage, as the sentence would have been for the Queen.

When the vessel in which the Legate sailed from Dover was boarded by the custom-house officers, he believed that his last hour had come, and called for his confessor. The officers treated him with respect, but they examined his luggage, in the hope either of recovering the secret Bull, or of finding evidence that he had been paid by Catharine. Campeggio returned to Rome with the renown of a successful mission. Men were not blind to the effects which were to follow. But they followed too remotely to disturb the present joy at an immense deliverance. It was observed for the first time after years of anxiety and depression, that Clement VII. held up his head and walked erect.

We have not allowed ourselves space to follow Mr. Brewer's vivid and powerful narrative over another year to the death of Wolsey, with which the volume ends. Before we conclude it is necessary that we should advert to one topic on which we have been unable to accept him for our guide. Touching the great question of the origin of the Divorce, Mr. Brewer wavers between three explanations : King Henry's scruples grew up in the recesses of his own conscience. They were awakened by his inclination for Anne Boleyn. They were suggested by her friends. Mr. Brewer, who adopts the first of these solutions at page 222, prefers the second at page 258, and, forty pages farther, is ready to accept the third.

The idea that the Divorce was instigated by divines of Anne Boleyn's faction was put forward by Pole, apparently with a view to connect Cranmer and the Lutheran influence with the beginning of the troubles. It is supported by no evidence ; and it is in the highest degree improbable that the Boleyns conceived a design which could not have been accomplished without violently subverting the whole system of European politics. The theory which represents the scruple arising involuntarily, almost unconsciously, in the King's mind, is confirmed, no doubt, by his own public declarations; but it is difficult to reconcile with the coarse and candid admission which he made privately of the causes which estranged him from the Queen. Before the Court, at Blackfriars, he spoke only of scruples ; in secret he urged motives of a less spiritual kind. It is quite natural that personal repulsion may have paved the way for scruples. It is much less likely that the idea of separation can have come first, and the unconquerable aversion followed. In

the hypothesis that the whole business took its rise in
the King's passion for Anne Boleyn, there is not the same
inherent improbability. It leaves much unexplained, and
suggests many difficulties ; but it depends mainly on a
question of chronology. If it should ever be possible to
trace the idea of marrying Anne Boleyn farther back
than we can trace the idea of repudiating Catharine of
Aragon, the case would be proved. But with the materials
now available the priority is decidedly with the Divorce.
The latest date to which we can possibly assign the first
steps towards the dissolution of the marriage is the
summer of 1526. We have shown that we are unable
to put the proposal to Anne earlier than 1527. There
is an interval therefore during which the scheme of divorce
is pursued, and is fully accounted for, whilst no trace of
a rival can be detected. We are unable to accept either
of Mr. Brewer's alternative solutions.

There is a fourth explanation to which he shows no
mercy. He absolutely rejects the idea that Wolsey was
the author of the Divorce. Such a report was, he says,
put about by Tyndall and Roper ; but it was contradicted by all those who knew best ; by Henry, by Bishop
Longland, and by the Cardinal himself—while Cavendish
says that when the King first disclosed his intentions to
Wolsey, the latter fell upon his knees and endeavoured to
dissuade him. We regret that Mr. Brewer has not entered
more fully into the evidence which has determined his
judgment on this fundamental point. We will indicate as
briefly as we can the reasons which induce us to attribute
the Divorce of Queen Catharine, with all its momentous
consequences, to the cause he has so pointedly rejected.

Longland never denied that Wolsey was the author
of the King's doubts. It is true that Longland, a persecutor of Lutherans, and an eager and overbearing promoter of the Divorce, when he saw England drifting
towards Lutheranism, in consequence, indirectly, of what
he had helped to do, regretted his share in the transaction, and denied that he was primarily responsible. His
Chancellor, Draycott, conveyed his denial to the historian

Harpsfield, who records it in his Life of Sir Thomas More. But Harpsfield himself was not convinced. In the following year he wrote that Wolsey, " first by himselfe, or by John Langlond, bishopp of Lincolne, and the King's confessor, putt this scruple and doubte into his head." Even if Longland's denial exonerates himself it does not exonerate Wolsey, whom he indicates when he speaks of " others, that weare the cheife setters forth of the divorce beetweene the Kinge and the Queene Catharine."

No serious import belongs to the testimony of Henry and Wolsey, given in open court, to silence just objections to Wolsey's presence there. It was necessary that he should be represented as impartial to justify his appearance on the judgment seat. It would certainly seem that Cavendish meant to say what Mr. Brewer imputes to him, that Wolsey dissuaded Henry from the beginning. But in reality he says no more than he would be justified in saying by the fact that Wolsey did, at various times, dissuade him ; which is all that Wolsey himself has said. Nobody, however, knows better than Mr. Brewer that Cavendish is the author of much of the confusion that has, until the appearance of his work, obscured the history of the Divorce. We cannot allow decisive authority to one ambiguous sentence in an author who, though doubtless sincere, is both partial and inaccurate.

The weight of contemporary testimony is overwhelming against Wolsey. We will say nothing of Polydore Vergil, who was an enemy, or of the Belgian Macqueriau, and the Paris diarist, because they wrote only from rumour. But Jovius was a prelate of the Court of Clement. Guicciardini was connected with Casale, and was the only contemporary writer who knew the secret of Campana's mission. Both Guicciardini and Jovius lay the responsibility on Wolsey. Valdes, who was better informed than either of the Italians, does the same. For in Spain no doubt could subsist. Catharine had written to Charles that Wolsey was the author of her sorrows, and the Emperor never ceased to proclaim the fact.

The tradition of the English Catholics inclined strongly to assign to Wolsey the origin of their misfortunes. If they had any bias it would naturally have been to represent the Reformation in England as springing from an unclean passion. Pole, who was a great authority amongst them, had given the example of this controversial use of Anne Boleyn. But they departed from the example he had set, and preferred an explanation which could serve no polemical purpose. Pole himself once indicated the belief that Wolsey was the author of the King's design. It is firmly maintained by his archdeacon, Nicholas Harpsfield, who was a friend of the Warhams, who had lived with Roper, Rastall, Buonvisi, and the family of More, and in whom were concentrated the best Catholic traditions of that age.

Sir Richard Shelley wrote a history of the Divorce, which is still exant. He was the son of the well-known judge, and was employed both by Mary and Elizabeth in important embassies. He was the English Prior of St. John, and after 1559, swam in the full tide of the Catholic reaction. When the news of the Northern Rising reached Rome, Shelley was one of those whom the Pope consulted before issuing his Bull against the Queen. He attributes all the blame to Wolsey. If any man was more deeply involved than Shelley in the struggle against Elizabeth, it was Nicholas Sanders. Writing history for political effect, he had no scruple about inventing a scene or a fact that served his purpose ; and he had read the works of Rastall and Hiliard, which we possess only in fragments. The evidence which was before him must have implicated Wolsey with a force that was irresistible. Richard Hall, a man who seems to have given proof of sincerity, as he was a Protestant under Mary, and a Catholic under Elizabeth, wrote a life of Fisher, about the year 1580. He had his information from Phillips, the last Prior of the Benedictines at Rochester, who had sat in the Convocation of 1529, and from Thomas Harding, who had been chaplain to Stokesley. Hall is, like the rest, among the Cardinal's accusers. William Forrest, who was a contemporary, and became chaplain to Queen Mary, agrees with Harpsfield and Shelley, Sanders and Hall.

Indeed, without resorting to contemporary foreigners, or to English writers of a later generation, the evidence that Wolsey first moved the idea of divorce appears to us conclusive. The Cardinal himself admitted it to Du Bellay, not speaking under pressing need of deception and excuse, but privately, to one who was his friend, who powerfully supported his policy, who needed no convincing, and had evidently not heard the contrary on any authority worthy of belief. A statement made in these circumstances is not necessarily credible, but it far outweighs a public declaration demanded by the stress of popular suspicion. Wolsey's communication to Du Bellay, confirming what he wrote to Casale,[1] connects the Divorce with the great change in the system of alliances which was made in the spring of 1525, and perfectly explains the tenacious grasp with which he then retained his power in spite of all the sacrifices which the failures of his policy imposed on the King. We cannot reject it without stronger reason than has been yet produced.

After his disgrace, Wolsey constantly declared himself innocent of crime, yet worthy of the royal displeasure. The Divorce, he said, was the cause of his fall, yet he denied that, in that, he had offended. This would be consistent and intelligible language if he was the author of counsels that had proved so pernicious. On his deathbed he delivered to Kingston the lesson of his experience of Henry. He warned him to be cautious what matter he put into his head, as he would never put it out again. He was alluding to what had passed in the affair of Queen Catharine ; and his words had a pregnant as well as a literal significance if he was thinking of a matter which he had himself incautiously put into the King's head.

We are at a loss to find a valid reason for doubting, except the authority of Mr. Brewer. We acknowledge the force of that objection. It is impossible to differ,

[1] 6th December 1527.

without uneasiness and regret, from a historian who has supplied so large and so rich a part of the knowledge attainable on this subject, and who is unsurpassed for accuracy and penetration. But Mr. Brewer's words, in speaking of Wolsey, must be taken with a slight allowance. It is not only because of the dignified liberality, the ceremonious self-restraint, which is due from a divine of the English Church towards a Roman Cardinal, and from an illustrious scholar who is willing to think nobly and generously of the Church of Rome, towards a prelate by whose fault that Church was dishonoured and cast down. For as many years as Wolsey's administration lasted, Mr. Brewer has been employed in investigating his actions. He has hewn him out of the block. He has found much that is new and different from the character which Protestant and Catholic have had so much reason to blacken ; and he has felt the influence not only of disgust for ignorant detractors, but of admiration for the strong man who, when the population of all England did not exceed that of a modern city, when the annual revenue was no more than that which is now received in a single day, when Scotland and Ireland were drains upon her power, when she was without dependencies and without a fleet, raised the kingdom by the force of his solitary genius, to a position among the European nations not inferior to that which it now enjoys.

For Wolsey as a Minister of tyranny, as a pensioner of foreign potentates, as a priest of immoral life, he has an extreme indulgence. The Cardinal attempted to obtain from Parliament a declaration that all things in the land belonged to the Crown—a doctrine which, from the day on which Frederic Barbarossa consulted the jurists of Bologna, until Lewis XIV. caused it to be sanctioned by the divines of the Sorbonne, has been the symbol of despotic power. At the moment when he broke off the alliance with the House of Burgundy and sought the friendship of France, he had for four years been denied his pensions by the Power that he abandoned, whilst he required from the Power that he joined a sum

equal in our money to £285,000. When he exchanged
Durham for Winchester, he asked that the see which he
vacated should be transferred to his son, a youth then
studying at Paris. Mr. Brewer will not admit a doubt
as to Wolsey's integrity. If we remember rightly, he
nowhere mentions the proposed transfer of the great see
of Durham. He is almost unwilling to believe that
Wolsey had a son. That he had a daughter Mr. Brewer
does not dispute. But he thinks that such transgressions
did not necessarily involve any greater impropriety than
the marriage of an English clergyman at the present day.[1]
This view of the age of the Reformation leaves a great
feature in its history unexplained. No influence then at
work contributed more than the private lives of ecclesiastics such as Wolsey to undermine Catholicism, and to
incline men towards a Church which renounced the
hazards of an enforced celibacy. We would undertake,
if necessary, to justify our words by proof which Mr.
Brewer will accept, by the writings of the most eminent
and the most impartial men of the sixteenth century, by
the decrees of twenty synods, by the constitutions of
York itself.

Mr. Brewer's abounding charity defends the Cardinal
as a persecutor. Wolsey had caused Protestants to be
burnt in the day of his power, and in the last hour of his
life, when his speech faltered and his eyes grew dim, he
uttered an exhortation that Henry would not spare the
Lutherans, because they would prove a danger to the
State. Yet even that appalling vision of the dying
Prelate, who, having clothed himself in sackcloth, and
made his peace with God, gathered his last breath to fan
the flames of Smithfield, has no terrors for Mr. Brewer.
No man, he says, was less disposed to persecute; and he
excuses him by the examples of his age, and by the
greater cruelty of More.

---

[1] " Here, as in other Catholic countries at the present day, or at least until
recently, the marriage of the parochial clergy had to be tolerated more generally
than is supposed. . . . In many instances such offences involved no greater
transgression of the moral law than . . . such marriages, for instance, as are
now contracted by the English prelates and clergy " (pp. 639, 640).

The argument which excuses Wolsey by the times he lived in, is a serious fallacy. Christians must be judged by a moral code which is not an invention of the eighteenth century, but is as old as the Apostles. We are no wiser than the contemporaries of Wolsey regarding the rights of conscience. Persecution has indeed become more difficult to carry out ; and the conditions of modern society make toleration easy. But there are, in our day, many educated men who think it right to persecute ; and there were, in the days of Wolsey, many who were as enlightened on that point as Burke or Jefferson. There was a humane and liberal current, both in government and in literature, which the religious conflict that followed checked for generations. Whilst Lollards and Lutherans were burning, in the Chancellorship of Wolsey, the Greeks lived unmolested in Venice, and the Waldenses enjoyed a respite in Savoy ; the Inquisition was forbidden to interfere with the Moriscoes of Granada ; and in Portugal the later laws of Emanuel the Great protected the Judaising heretics from popular fanaticism. No country had suffered so much from religious strife as Bohemia ; but in 1512 Catholics and Utraquists made an agreement in perpetuity that rich and poor of both churches should enjoy freedom unrestrained. In Denmark equal rights were assigned to Catholics and Protestants at the Diet of 1527. Before the close of the fifteenth century the French Inquisition had been shorn of its might ; the bishops refused to prosecute those who were accused of heresy ; the Parliament rescued them ; and Lutheranism was allowed to spread with the connivance of the court, until the long absence and captivity of the King. Many years even then elapsed before the Protestants ceased to regard Francis as their defender. Beneath the sceptre of the Hapsburgs persecution reigned ; yet in 1526 Ferdinand conceded territorial toleration, and Charles himself, in 1532, proclaimed the rights of conscience in language worthy of a better time.

There was a strong body of opinion on the other side, but authorities equally strong may be quoted in favour of murder, not merely among men entangled in the habits of a darker age, but among those who had struggled to emancipate their minds from tradition, and who made it the pride and the business of their lives to resist the vices of the vulgar.   It was no reason for an assassin to escape the gallows that Melanchthon had prayed for a brave man to despatch Henry VIII.; that the brave man who despatched the Duke of Guise was praised by Beza to the skies; that Knox wished the doom of Rizzio to be inflicted on every Catholic; that the Swedish bishops recommended that a dose of poison should be mixed with the King's food.   Nor can we admit that the intolerance of Wolsey is excused by comparison with the greater intolerance of More.   The Cardinal, in his last hours, asked for measures of repression, the nature of which his own example and the statute of Henry IV. left in no kind of doubt.   Sir Thomas More protested before his death, in terms which have satisfied the impartial judgment of one of his latest successors on the woolsack, that no Protestant had perished by his act.

II

THE BORGIAS AND THEIR LATEST HISTORIAN [1]

THE Renaissance is the only epoch of history that has equal charms for idle and for thoughtful men, and stands in visibly intimate connection with the civilisation of the present time, yet beyond the range of its controversies. The interest it awakens is undisturbed by the contests that immediately followed it. Neither religious nor political differences affect the feelings with which men regard the age to which they owe the knowledge of Pagan, of Jewish, and of Christian antiquity, the formation of modern literature, and the perfection of art. The degradation which Italy suffered under native tyrants cannot prevent the pride with which she remembers the days of her national independence and her intellectual supremacy. Stores of new materials continue to be produced in uninterrupted profusion by patriotic scholars ; and the way in which they modify the aspects of the fifteenth century is shown in several recent works. Zeller's *Italie et Renaissance* and Reumont's *Geschichte der Stadt Rom* mark the progress which has been made beyond the range of Roscoe and Sismondi. Both are well-written books, and the authors are perfectly familiar with the spirit of those brilliant times. Burckhardt's *Cultur der Renaissance in Italien* is the most penetrating and subtle treatise on the history of civilisation that exists in literature ; but its merit lies in the originality with which the author uses common books, rather than in actually

---

[1] *The North British Review*, January 1871.

new investigations.   The last traveller over the ground is
Gregorovius.

The seventh volume of his *History of Mediæval Rome*
virtually completes his task, for it reaches the beginning
of the sixteenth century.   Another volume will include
the age of Leo X. and terminate with the siege and
devastation of the city in 1527.   The work gains in
breadth and variety as it proceeds, and at times it is little
less than a history of the Popes.   The treatment is
unequal.   Pius II., the ablest and most interesting pontiff
of the fifteenth century, receives but little attention,
probably because a voluminous life of him appeared only
a few years ago.   But the pontificate of Alexander VI.
is described with elaborate care, and occupies great part
of the volume.   These chapters are amongst the best and
most solid that Gregorovius has written.   Continuous
reports by the envoys of Florence, Venice, and Ferrara at
the court of Rome enable him to emancipate himself from
the trivial diarists on whom every writer since Raynaldus
has been obliged to depend for the secret history of the
Vatican.   He is so well supplied with unpublished documents, and he employs them with so little regard for
purposes of vulgar controversy, that his estimate of
Alexander, which contradicts the unanimous judgment of
all the contemporaries of the Pope, cannot be put aside
at once, and without examination, amongst historical
paradoxes.   Alexander VI. is described by his latest
historian as a man whose everyday mediocrity reflects the
sinfulness of a godless age, whose motives were the love
of pleasure and the advancement of his family, who had
neither political capacity nor serious design, and whose
nature was too frivolous and too passive even for
ambition.[1]

This excessive depreciation of a man whose talents
and success were the admiration of Europe in his time is

[1] In Wahrheit zeigt es sich, wie gewöhnlich und klein dieser Mensch gewesen
ist. . . . Sein ganzer Pontifikat zeigt keine einzige grosse Idee weder in Kirche
noch Staat. . . . Nichts von jenem rastlosen Thatendrange und Herrschersinn
eines Sixtus IV. oder Julius II. erscheint in der wollüstigen und passiven Natur
dieses kleinen Genussmenschen (pp. 500-502).

not due to an irrelevant indignation at his depravity, but to the historian's habit of avoiding the ecclesiastical part of his subject. Looking at secular and profane things only, he does not see that Alexander fills a great space in history, because he so blended his spiritual and temporal authority as to apply the resources of the one to the purposes of the other. The strain which his policy as an Italian sovereign laid on his power in the Church was fruitful of consequences in the next generation, and for all later times. His energy in making the prerogative of the Holy See profitable and exchangeable in the political market was an almost immediate cause of the revolt of Northern Europe. The system which Luther assailed was the system which Alexander VI. had completed and bequeathed to his successors. It was his work and example that Adrian meant to repudiate when he attributed the corruption of the Church to the recent usurpation and immorality of the papacy.[1] And Julius II. attempted to liberate the Church from the responsibility of his acts by declaring that a Pope elected by simony could never become legitimate.[2]

The leading fact that governs his whole pontificate is the notorious invalidity of his election. There had been no hypocrisy in the transaction ; and all Europe was able to learn the exact sums that he had paid or promised to his supporters, and even to their attendants. His seat never became secure. His right was permanently threatened. The shadow of an impending Council darkened his life, and ruined his authority. He was obliged to create for himself the power which belonged in theory to his See. He could not have held his position without perpetual activity and effort.

He was hailed at first with flattery so general and

---

[1] Scimus in hac sancta sede aliquot jam annis multa abominanda fuisse, abusus in spiritualibus, excessus in mandatis, et omnia denique in perversum mutata (Indicat hic optimus Pontifex ea, quae nos in Alexandro VI. deploravimus) ; nec mirum si aegritudo a capite in membra, a summis Pontificibus in alios inferiores praelatos descenderit (Raynaldus, *Annales Ecclesiastici*, 1522, p. 70).

[2] Contra dictum sic electum vel assumptum de simoniaca labe a quocumque Cardinali, qui eidem electioni interfuerit, opponi et excipi possit, sicut de vera et indubitata haeresi (Raynaldus, 1506, p. 1).

excessive that it must have been more than conventional. Men said that he was more than human, that he surpassed all mankind in righteousness, that the splendour of Christ Himself shone forth when he ascended the throne.[1] His very countenance was divine. The golden age came back again ; Astraea returned to earth at his accession. It was really believed that he would be a glorious pontiff.[2] Ferrante of Naples and Ferdinand of Aragon were hostile to him from the beginning ; but in many countries the illusion was not dispelled until the cardinals who had refused his bribes published his iniquity. Julian della Rovere, afterwards Pope Julius II., insisted that a Council should be summoned in order to judge him,[3]

The idea was taken up by the Court of France, when the Pope appointed one of his kinsmen to the archbishopric of Rouen, whilst the Chapter elected George d'Amboise.[4] The ministers boasted that the king

[1] Politian, speaking in the name of Siena, said : " Praestans animi magnitudo, qua mortales crederes omnes antecellere—Magna quaedam de te nobis rara, ardua, singularia, incredibilia, inaudita pollicentur." The Orator of Lucca : " Quid est tuus divinus et majestate plenus aspectus ? " The Genoese : " Adeo virtutum gloria et disciplinarum laude, et vitae sanctimonia decoraris, et adeo singularum, ac omnium rerum ornamento dotaris, quae talem summam ac venerandam dignitatem praebeant, ut valde ab omnibus ambigendum sit, tu ne magis pontificatui, an illa tibi sacratissima et gloriosissima Papatus dignitas offerenda fuerit " (Ciaconius, *Vitae Pont.*, iii. 152, 159). The Venetian Senate rejoiced : " Propter divinas virtutes et dotes quibus ipsum insignitum et ornatum conspiciebamus, videbatur a divina providentia talem pastorem gregi, dominio et sacrosanctae romanae ecclesiae vicarium suum fuisse delectum et praeordinatum " (Romanin, *Storia di Venezia*, v. 10). The Archbishop of Colocza wrote : " Omnes id satis exploratum habent, mitiorem Pontificem nec optari, nec creari potuisse, cui tantum sapientiae, probitatis, experientiae, ac integritatis est, quantum in quovis alio unquam audiverimus" (Petrus de Warda, *Epistolae*, 33). A priest of Parma wrote : " Hominem non dicam, sed divinum hominem, magnanimum pietate gravem ac meritis sapientissimum, ingenio praestantem, consiliis et sententiis probatissimum, omnibus denique virtutibus ornatissimum."
[2] Dicesi che sarà glorioso pontefice (Manfredi to the Duchess of Ferrara, Aug. 17, 1492 ; *Atti e Memorie*, iv. 323).
[3] Quid enim felicis recordationis Alexandro VI. Romano Pontifici praedecessori nostro magis nos odiosos fecit, nisi studium et cura generalis concilii celebrandi? Quid nos terra marique jactavit, cum nobis idem Alexander praedecessor esset infensus? quid toties Alps transcendere transalpinas, Gallias peragrare per aestus, nives et glacies compulit, nisi quod nitebamur, ut a Romano Pontifice concilium indiceretur, convocaretur et celebraretur? (Raynaldus, 1511, 10).
[4] Sdegnati di questa collazione contro del Papa, il Rè tenne il dì medesimo gran consiglio, dove furono proposte e trattate più cose contro del Papa, in riformazione della chiesa (Desp. of Aug. 31, 1493 ; Canestrini, *Négociations avec la Toscane*, i. 249).

possessed an infallible means of subjugating Alexander
by calling a Council.[1]   Charles VIII. claimed the crown
of Naples, and threatened, if investiture should be refused,
to depose the Pope, not by force, but by canonical proof
that he was a heretic and an intruder.[2]   When Alexander
took the side of the house of Aragon, and the French
invaded Italy, his prospects seemed hopeless.   He
expected to be deposed.[3]   The Cardinal of Siena,
whom he sent to mollify the King of France, could not
obtain an audience, and wrote to warn his master of the
approaching danger.[4]   The French intended to summon
a Council at Ferrara to sit in judgment on the Pope,[5]
and they believed that the consciousness of his guilt
would make him pliable.[6]   They occupied Rome without
resistance.   Alexander shut himself up in St. Angelo,
with a small group of faithful prelates ; but the majority
of the Cardinals were urging the king to depose him.[7]
The instrument pronouncing his deposition was drawn

[1] Venetian despatches of the same month of August, in Romanin, v. 33.

[2] Soggiungeva che rifiutando le cose che ricercava, considerasse bene essere a
Carlo cosa libera, poichè adjutato dall' imperatore de' Romani il quale da pochi
giorni s' era seco lui confederato, era per privarlo dalla dignità apostolica, non
solo colle armi colle quali superava tutti gli altri, ma per diritto, radunando
un concilio de prelati, i quali potevano giustamente pronunziare avere egli
comperato la pontificia dignità, di maniera che non si poteva chiamare vero
pastore di Santa Chiesa (Corio, *Storia de Milano*, iii. 525).

[3] Dubitava che il rè lo dimitesse del Papato (Marin Sanuto, in Cherrier,
Hist. de Charles VIII., ii. 61).

[4] Aiunt etiam multo vulgo inter illos iactari, regem Romam venturum et
statum Romanae Ecclesiae reformaturum (Piccolomini to Alexander, Lucca,
Nov. 4, 1494).

[5] Le quali cose sono di qualità, secondo che me concluse dicto oratore (the
French envoy at Florence), che daranno materia al prefato Rè Christ., de fare
praticha con qualche Cardinale, come già se fece, de chiamare Sua Santità a
Concilio, dicendomi che el credeva che non passariano molti giorni che 'l se
ordinaria dicto Concilio, et di farlo a Ferrara, dove pare che se debba fare per
omni rispecto.   Et a questo gli è molto inclinata prefata Regia M^tà (Manfredi
to Duke of Ferrara, Feb. 16, 1495 ; *Atti e Memorie*, iv. 341.

[6] Crediamo che la Santità di nostro Signore, il quale di sua natura è vile e è
conscius criminis sui, ancora de facili si potrebbe ridurre alle cose oneste, per
dubio delle cose di qua (Florentine Desp., Lyons, June 6, 1494 ; Canestrini,
i. 399).   Eulx deux (Borgia and Sforza) estoient a l'envy qui seroit Pape.
Toutesfois je croy qu'ilz eussent consenty tous deux d'en faire ung nouveau au
plaisir du Roy, et encores d'en faire ung françois (Comines, *Memoires*, ii. 386).

[7] Nostre Saint Père est plus tenu au roy qu'on ne pense, car si ledit seigneur
eust voulu obtemperer à la plupart de Messeigneurs les Cardinaulx, ilz eussent
fait ung autre pappa en intention de reffomer l'église ainsi qu'ilz disaient
(Briçonnet to Queen of France, Rome, Jan. 13, 1495 ; De la Pilorgerie, *Campagne
d'Italie*, 135).

up:[1] French cannon were pointed against the fort ; and part of the walls suddenly gave way. When it seemed that nothing could save Alexander, Charles relented and made terms with him. The reforming cardinals quitted Rome, indignant at the failure of their design. As the Pope instantly broke the treaty that had been forced upon him, Briçonnet himself thought that the king would proceed to extremities against him on his return from Naples.[2] Alexander escaped by flight. He afterwards said that Charles had been restrained from acts of violence by the piety of his courtiers ;[3] but the language of Briçonnet and Comines proves that the opinion of the French camp was in favour of a bolder policy, and the king had not courage to attempt it. When he was gone and the danger was over Alexander excommunicated him. Shortly before he died the Sorbonne exhorted him to convoke a Council, and accomplish the reforms which the Pope persisted in refusing.

Under his successor, Lewis XII., the plan was revived. The Cardinal d'Amboise opened negotiations with Ferdinand and Maximilian with a view to a new election.[4] In the summer of the year 1501, Piccolomini,

---

[1] This was stated by Paul IV. : "Sua Santità entro a deplorar le miserie d' Italia et narrò l' historia dal principio che fù chiamato Rè Carlo in Italia da Ludovico Moro et Alfonso d' Aragona, con li particolari del parentado fra questi due, la causa dell' inimicitia, il passar Rè Carlo per Roma, la paura di Papa Alessandro di esser deposto, come publicamente dicevano li Cardinali che vennero co 'l Rè tra quali erano S. Pietro in Vincola, che fù poi Giulio Secondo : che furno fatti li capitoli della privatione da un Vicentino Vescovo di (illegible), al-l' hora auditor della Camera" (Desp. of B. Navagero, Rome, May 21, 1577 ; MS. Foscarini, 6255).

[2] Divinendo in ragionamento col Card. de S. Malo (Briçonnet) del facto del Papa, sua Rev^ma Sig^ria me disse che il Re ch^mo non ne remaneva cum quella bona satisfactione che 'l sperava, havendose portato non troppo bene in queste pratiche de Spagne, etc., concludendo dicto Card^e che 'l dubitava assai, che, finita che fosse questa impresa del Reame de Napoli, la M^tà del Rè non se desponesse a pigliare qualche expediente per reformare la chiesa, parendogli che 'l sia molto necessario, vedendosi come sono gubernate le cose della chiesa et sede apostolica (Manfredi to Duke of Ferrara, Feb. 25, 1495 ; *Atti e Memorie*, iv. 342).

[3] Adducendo su questo proposito quello che accadette al Christianissimo Rè Carlo quando andava in lo reame : che avendo pur contra sua santità malo animo, non solo fù consentito per li Sig^ri francesi che ageret contra eam, ma fù necessitato ad inclinarseli et basarli lo pede, et tenerli la staffa in mezo la fango (Desp. of Saracini to Duke of Ferrara, Rome, Oct. 27, 1501).

[4] Le Gendre, *Vie du Cardinal d'Amboise*, i. 245.

Cardinal of Siena, who became Alexander's successor, proposed to him to call together a Council and undertake reforms himself, lest the thing should be done in spite of him, to the detriment of the papacy, by the cardinals who were living abroad. Alexander entertained the idea for a moment, and then gave it up when he was reminded that Piccolomini was a nephew of Pius II., "un concilionista," whose advice in these matters was open to suspicion.[1] In the following year it was reported in Rome that the French were resolved to depose him. There is a celebrated medal bearing the effigy of Lewis XII., with the lilies, and the words "Perdam Babylonis nomen," which is ascribed to the time of the deadly quarrel between Lewis and Julius II. It belongs to the times of Alexander VI. Constabili speaks of it, and describes the sensation which it made at Rome, in a letter to the Duke of Ferrara, on the 11th of August 1502.

The aspiration of the Councils of Constance and Basel, the hope of honest reforms, had remained unsatisfied, and was kept up by the condition of the Roman Court during several pontificates. It was scarcely worse under Alexander than under his predecessors, and the zeal of the French Government was not attributable exclusively to disinterested motives of conscience. The flaw in his election was too tempting an instrument to be neglected. There was more to gain by practising on his fears than by deposing him. Neither Germany nor Spain was willing to accept a Pope created by the King of France.[2]

King Ferdinand continually impressed on Alexander that he heartily despised him. Gonzalvo of Cordova came to Rome and spoke out the indignation and horror of Europe.[3] A joint embassy was despatched by the Kings of Spain and Portugal to protest against

[1] Constabili to Duke of Ferrara, Rome, Feb. 23, 1502.

[2] Cardinal Perrauld said to the Venetian Ambassador at the Court of Maximilian: "Non se parla de deporre el Pontifice; ma se vol provvedere che el stato della chiesa non sia tirannizzato, ovviar alla simonia, coreger la vita dei prelati et levare le estorsioni che se fano nela cancelaria" (De Leva, *Storia di Carlo V.*, i. 73).

[3] Zurita, *Historia del Rey Don Hernando*, i. 117.

the scandals of the papacy.[1]   Alexander received the envoys in the presence of five cardinals.   They represented the immediate necessity of a thorough reformation ; they demanded that a Council should be assembled at the Lateran ; they informed the Pope that all Italy could bear witness that his election was void.[2] He replied that their king was excommunicated, and that it was well for them that Cæsar Borgia did not hear them.   Later on he made one concession. ' He promised that the Duchy of Benevento should not be alienated from the See of Rome.   He had conferred it on his son, the Duke of Gandia, who was almost immediately murdered ; and the Spanish Ambassador had resisted, and declared that it should not be done.

Grief for the loss of his son roused the conscience of the Pope, and he spoke of abdicating the throne and changing his life.   He would send Cæsar to reside in his diocese of Valencia.   He would resign the Government into the hands of the cardinals.   A commission of six was appointed on the 17th of June 1497, and drew up in the following month a scheme of reform which has not been noticed by Gregorovius.[3]   Their proposals were quickly forgotten ; but two months later they were still acting as advisers of the Pope in the affair of Savonarola.[4]

During the short interregnum over which the promise of improvement lasted, Cardinal Borgia was sent with the powers of a papal legate into Umbria.   His letters to Alexander VI., written in the summer of 1497, are the most eloquent testimony we possess touching the state of

[1] Mores esse profligatos, pietatis studium restinctum, flagitiorum licentiam solutam, res sanctissimis pretio indignissimis addici—remque esse in extremum paene discrimen adductam (Osorius, "De rebus gestis Emanuelis," *Opera*, i. 595).
[2] Italia tutta aviebbe dimostrato lui non esser vero Pontefice (Marin Sanuto, in *De Leva*, 61).   Que eran notorias las formas que se tuvieron en su eleccion, y quan graves cosas se intentaron, y quan escandalosos (Zurita, 159).
[3] Raynaldus, who is his sole authority here, depends upon Zurita, and Zurita gives no particulars.   The plan is in Malipiero (*Annali Veneti*, 494).
[4] Se era deliberato per el Papa et per li sei Cardinali deputati pro reformatione, che ullo pacto non se dasse la absolutione che addimandava questa Signoria per fra Hieronimo nostro, nisi prius pararet mandatis del suo generale et del Papa, non se attendendo alli ragionamenti facti per li antedicte Cardinali de suspendere le censure per duos menses (Manfredi to Duke of Ferrara, Aug. 16, 1497 ; *Atti e Memorie*, iv. 585).

society which the Borgias set themselves to abolish in the
dominions of the Church, and the influences which determined their unrelenting policy.[1]   It was a pacific mission.
The legate went unarmed to try the force of persuasion,
and to test the moral authority of the papacy in a district
where the idea of the State was quenched in feudal strife,
and each man's safety consisted in the terror he was able
to inspire.   In his first letter, on the day of his arrival
at Narni, he announced that he could accomplish nothing
without troops, as the demons he had to deal with were
not to be frightened with holy water.[2]   The presence of
a legate was so little heeded that Alviano, the same who
afterwards commanded the Venetians when their power
was broken at Agnadello, seized a town belonging to the
Pope and sacked it almost before his face.   Borgia sent
for him, and summoned him to keep the peace.   Alviano
replied that he would gladly help the Pope to subdue his
neighbours, but that he would destroy the town rather
than give it up.[3]   It was soon discovered that the legate
was not followed by an army ; and things grew worse.[4]
The country was without police or law.   The inhabitants
of Todi, finding that there was no government to protect them, deserted the town in despair.[5]   Brigands held
unmolested sway, and were only checked by rival bands.
At Perugia the legate caused a murderer to be put to
death.[6]   It was an immense achievement.   Murder was

[1] The originals are among the manuscripts in St. Mark's Library (Lat. Cl.
x. 176).
[2] E molto necessaria la provvisione de le genti d' arme contro questi demonii
che non fugono per acqua sancta (July 16, 1497).
[3] Intendendo che quando l' antique sue rasoni non li siano sopra de quella da
la Sta vostra instaurate, spianarla per modo che dire sepossa, qui fù Lugnano
(July 17).
[4] Solo in la mia prima ionta in provintia cessarono un poco per timore dele
gente d' arme, fo dicto me seguitavano, ma hormai reassicurati comensano nel
primo modo offenderse et non dare loco ad mei commandamenti (July 27).
[5] Ricevo ad ogni hora da quelli proveri loro castelli querele miserabili che le
prede et occisioni se le fanno tutta via maiuri.   Per la qual cosa la S^a V^a po
ben comprendere che tucto lo remedio de questi mali consiste in la venuta de la
gente d' arme, le quali tardando più forniscese el paese de Tode da desolare,
essendo da la partita mia in qua la cita totalmente derelicta et lassata vacua
(July 30).
[6] In questa cita hieri si fecero li bannamenti et con maraviglioso consenso
sonno da tucti posti in observantia, et procedono le cose qui con tanta obedien-
tia et quiete che meglio non si potriano desiderare (July 30). Dopo li Bandi-

common, but legal punishment was a thing almost unknown. Perugia, in consternation, became an altered city. Borgia was proud of his success. He assured the Pope that the rest of the country could be reduced to order and peace by measures of exceeding rigour.

Reigning over subjects unaccustomed to obey, befriended by no Power in Europe except the Turk, surrounded by hostile cardinals, with a flaw in his title which invited defiance and contempt, Alexander found himself in a position of the utmost danger. In the natural course of things, a power so wrongfully acquired, and so ill secured would have fallen speedily ; and the Papacy bearing the penalty of its corruption would have been subjugated. It was only by resorting to extraordinary artifice of policy, by persisting in the unlimited use of immoral means, and creating resources he did not lawfully possess, that Alexander could supply the total want of moral authority and material force. He was compelled to continue as he had begun, with the arts of a usurper, and to practise the maxim by which his contemporaries Lewis XI., Ferrante of Naples, and Ferdinand of Aragon prevailed over the disorganised and dissolving society of feudalism, that violence and fraud are sometimes the only way to build up a State.[1] He depended on two things— on the exchange of services done in his spiritual capacity for gold, troops, and political support ; and on the establishment of principalities for his own family. The same arts had been employed by his predecessors with less energy and profit. It was an unavoidable temptation, almost a necessity of his position, to carry them to the furthest excess.

The theory of the Papal prerogative was already equal to the demands he made on it. Flatterers told him that he was invested with the power of Almighty God on

menti, dui becharini homicidi ho facti pigliar, et son stati senza tumulto et piacer del popolo menati in presione.   Cosa da bon tempo in qua insolita in questa cita, et questa matina ne è stato appichato uno (Aug. 2).

[1] Uno in una città disordinata merita laude, se, non potendo riordinarla altri-menti, lo fa con la violenza e con la fraude, e modi estraordinarii (Guicciardini, in *Opere Inedite*, i. 22).

earth, that he was supreme in the temporal as well as the spiritual order, that no laws or canons could bind him, for he himself was the animated law and the rightful judge over the princes of the world.[1] He made the most of this doctrine, and resolutely applied it in practice. He declared that his authority was unlimited, that it extended over all men and all things.[2] In virtue of this claim he bestowed Africa and America on the kings of Spain, excommunicating beforehand all who would presume to trespass on these regions without licence.[3] The plenitude of power thus exercised was justified by an enlargement of the mediæval theory, which adapted it to the enlarged horizon of the Church. It is the Pope's office, it was argued, to teach the Gospel to all nations, and to compel observance of natural law. But the heathen will not hear the Gospel, and will not keep the law, unless they are made subject to Christians. Conquest, said one of the best writers of the next generation, makes more converts in a few days than mere preaching in three hundred years. Civil rights and authorities cannot lawfully obstruct the propagation of the faith.[4] The Spanish Government

[1] Tibi supremi rerum omnium opificis potestas in terris concessa est. Pontifex est, qui Lege, Canone, et propria constitutione Papali solutus, ea tamen vivere non dedignatur ; qui Canon in terris animatus vocatur : qui denique omnium Principum, Regum et Imperatorum Judex legitimus appellatur. Negabit ergo quispiam, quod gladii potestatem utriusque a vero Deo demandatam non obtineas ? (Ciaconius, 155, 158).

[2] Altissimus, sicut in Beato Petro, Apostolorum Principe, aeternae vitae clavigero, omnes atque omnia, nullo prorsus excepto, ligandi atque solvendi plenariam tribuit potestatem, ita Nos, super gentes et regna constitutos . . . in Prophetam mandavit (to Charles VIII., Aug. 5, 1495).

[3] Auctoritate omnipotentis Dei nobis in Beato Petro concessa, ac vicariatus Jesu Christi qua fungimur in terris. Ac quibuscunque personis cujuscumque dignitatis, etiam imperialis et regalis status gradus ordinis vel conditionis sub excomunicationis latae sententiae poena, quam eo ipso, si contra fecerint, incurrant districtius inhibemus ne ad insulas et terras firmas inventas et inveniendas . . . accedere praesumant.—Auctoritate nobis in B. Petro concessa, de ipsa Africa omnibusque regnis, terris et dominiis illius sine alicujus Christiani principis praejudicio, auctoritate apostolica tenore praesentium . . . plene investimus (Raynaldus, 1493, p. 22 ; 1494, p. 36).

[4] Habet igitur Papa potestatem ubique gentium, non solum ad praedicandum Evangelium, sed etiam ut gentes si facultas adsit, cogat, legem naturae cui omnes homines subjecti sunt, servare. . . . Ut autem infideles Evangelicam praedicationem audire et legem naturae servare cogantur, necesse est ut Christianorum imperio subjiciantur. . . . Hac ratione paucis diebus plures et tutius ad Christi fidem convertuntur, quam fortasse trecentis annis sola predicatione converterentur. . . . Quanquam enim Ecclesiastica potestas, quam Christus tradidit Vicario suo, in iis potissimum rebus versatur, quae religionem attingunt, patet tamen latissime

profited by this sweeping grant, but attached no religious value to it, for they soon after agreed with Portugal to shift the line of partition which the Pope had drawn across the earth.

Alexander VI. employed the terrors of excommunication with a sparing hand. The risk was great and the weapon blunted. His censures against the King of France were effectually suppressed by Cardinal Julian. The Sorbonne declared that his threats might be disregarded with a safe conscience. They were of no avail when unsupported by material force. But in Italy, where they were backed by carnal weapons, men thought of them with awe, and the Venetians dreaded them even when unjust.[1] Accordingly, the Pope used excommunication as a way of declaring war on those whom he was about to attack. The rebellious vassals were assailed with spiritual arms on account of their impiety as a prelude to the arrival of Cæsar's army.[2]

It was by squandering ecclesiastical privileges, by the profusion of graces and dispensations, that he disarmed enemies, made friends, and got money. The Venetians accused him of abetting the Turks against them,[3] and they dreaded extremely the progress of Cæsar Borgia in Romagna. Yet they feared to oppose him, for they required the Pope's aid in taxing the clergy, and in raising money from the people. They gained 120,000 ducats by the Jubilee in 1501.

Marriage dispensations became, by careful manage-

---

in omni terrarum orbe, pertinetque etiam ad imperia civilia et omne genus, si hoc religionis moderandae vel propagandae ratio postulare videatur. . . . Belli parandi classisque mitendae gravissimus auctor fuit Alexander VI. Pontifex Max. cujus Pontificis auctoritas ea est ut ejus legibus atque decretis publice factis obsistere vel contradicere nefas sit, et sacrorum interdicto haereticorumque poenis sancitum (Sepulveda, *Opera*, iv. 334, 335, 340 ; iii. 12, 15).

[1] Perchè giusta vale, ingiusta timenda est. . . . Con veritade il favor d' un Papa è più grande di quello che cadauno può considerare. . . . Perchè l' auttorità sua vale assai, edico grandemente apud Deum et homines (Priuli, May 25, June 10, Aug. 23, 1501).

[2] Alexander to the Magistrates of Bologna, Jan. 28, 1501, in Gozzadini, *Memorie di Bentivoglio*, Doc. 75.

[3] Se la stessa Santità Vostra persuade altrui ci si lasci punire e battere dagli infedeli, convien pur dire si voglia e si desideri che prima noi, e poco dopo l' universa religione cristiana vada in ruina (Council of Ten to the Pope, June 30, 1500 ; De Leva, i. 69).

ment, productive sources of revenue and of political
influence. Charles VIII. wished to marry the betrothed
bride of the King of the Romans, and the Pope was
solicited on either side to permit or to prevent the match.
He informed Valori that he meant to decide in favour of
France, as the stronger and more useful power.[1] But he
said the thing was too scandalous to be done publicly, and
afterwards spoke of the marriage as invalid.[2] Divorce
served him better even than dispensations. Lewis XII.
wished to marry the widow of his predecessor, whose
dower was the duchy of Brittany. He was already
married ; but Cæsar was despatched to France with the
permission for the king to put away his wife. He was
rewarded by a French principality, a French wife, and a
French army wherewith to conquer Romagna. Ladislaus
of Hungary desired to put away his wife, the widow of
Mathias Corvinus. The Pope gave him leave, and
earned 25,000 ducats by the transaction. He twice
dissolved the marriage of Lucretia. The King of Poland
had married a princess of the Greek Church, and had
bound himself by oath not to compel her to change
her religion. The Pope informed him that the oath
was illegal, and not only absolved him from it, but required that compulsion should be used, if necessary, in
order to convert her. But if neither ecclesiastical nor
secular weapons should avail to subdue her obstinacy,
then he commanded that she should be punished by
having her goods confiscated, and by being turned out
of her husband's house.[3]

[1] Lo ricercammo, qual era in secreto la intenzione sua. Rispose che in
ultimo satisfarebbe al Re di Francia, e terrebbe più conto di lui che del Re de'
Romani ; non solo perchè la Francia è più potente, ma anco perchè quella casa
è stata sempre amica e difensora di Santa Chiesa (Desp. Rome, March 31,
1493 ; Canestrini, i. 486).
[2] Publicava que la dispensacion que el Rey Carlos tenia, con la qual casò con
la duquesa de Bretaña, era de ningun efecto . . . y dezia, que en publico no
queria concenderla, por el escandalo (Zurita, 27).
[3] Pollicitus es, quod eciam iuramento forte dictorum oratorum sub nomine tuo
confirmatum extitit, nunquam eandem compulsurum ad ritum Romane ecclesie
suscipiendum : sed si sponte sua ad eandem Romanam ecclesiam venire vellet,
libertati sue in hoc eam dimitteres, que tua Nobilitas, quamvis perniciosa satis et
iuri contraria fuerint, per quinquennium observare curavit. . . . Volumus, teque
oneramus, ut non obstantibus promissionibus et iuramentis predictis, quibus te

In order to make money by Indulgences, Alexander
claimed jurisdiction over the other world.   When the
Jubilee of 1500 was celebrated, he was advised that it
would produce far more if it were made applicable to the
dead.   Divines reported that this power was included in
the Pope's prerogative.[1]   Sixtus IV. had attempted to
restrain this superstition, but Alexander allowed it to
prevail, and the idea that the release of a soul could be
insured by a mass at a particular altar became in his time
the recognised belief in Rome.[2]   It was supposed that
the two last kings of Portugal had died under sentence of
excommunication.   The Pope gave them posthumous absolution, on condition that their successor discharged their
debts to the Church.[3]   It was he who simplified and
cheapened the deliverance of souls in purgatory, and instituted the practices which Arcimboldus and Prierias, in
an evil hour, set themselves to defend.   The mass was
not held necessary ; to visit the churches did as well.[4]
Neither confession nor contrition was required, but only
money.[5]   It came to be the official doctrine that a soul

nullatenus teneri tenore presentium declaramus, denuo tentes, ac ea omnia agas,
que tibi necessaria videbuntur quo eadem uxor tua, relicta pessima Ruthenorum
secta, tandem resipiscat (to Alexander of Lithuania, June 8, 1501).   Per
censuras ecclesiasticas et alia iuris remedia, etiam cum invocacione, si opus fuerit,
brachii secularis, cogas et compellas . . ., Concedens licentiam eidem Alexandro
ipsam Helenam auctoritate nostra apostolica ex lecto, domo et omni maritali
consorcio penitus excludendi, illamque pro meritis errorum suorum, etiam dotem
et omnia alia bona eiusdem confiscata declarando, punias. . . . Non obstantibus
quibus vis promissionibus eciam iuramento firmatis (to Bishop of Wilna ;
Theiner, *Monumenta Poloniae*, ii. 288-90).

[1] Duke of Ferrara to Cardinal of Modena, Jan. 1, 1501.
[2] It was officially affirmed by the legate Raymundus at the Jubilee of
1500.
[3] Tibi per presentes committimus et mandamus ut Alfonsum et Joannem, si
in eorum obitu manifesta penitentie signa apparuerunt, ab excommunicationis
sentencia necnon aliis censuris et penis ecclesiasticis si quas propterea incurrerunt
. . . absolvas (to Bishop of Oporto, July 3, 1502 ; *Corpo Diplomatico
Portuguez*, i. 39).
[4] Quam Ecclesiam (St. Laurentii) si quis visitaverit in omnibus diebus Mercurii
per totum annum, habet a Deo et Sanctis Laurentio et Stephano istam gratiam
extrahendi unam animam de purgatorio (Raymundus, in Amort, *De Origine
Indulgentiarum*, ii. 283).
[5] Valde iniquum est quod pauper defunctus gravissimis peccatorum penis
tamdiu affligatur, qui liberari posset pro modica substantie parte, quam post se
reliquit. . . . Neque in hoc casu erit opus contribuentibus esse corde contritos
et ore confessos, cum talis gratia charitati, in qua defunctus decesserit, et contri-
butioni viventis duntaxat innitatur (Instructiones Arcimboldi, 1514 ; Kapp,
Urkunden, iii. 190, 191).

flew up to heaven as fast as the money chinked in the box.[1] Whoso questioned the rightfulness of the system was delared a heretic.[2]

By these measures in the spiritual order Alexander exercised vast influence over the future of the Catholic Church, whilst by his nepotism he caused the Papacy to become a political power in Italy. His nepotism is commonly explained by his desire to enrich his kindred. But there was more than this. There was the desire to put in the place of almost independent feudatories a prince who represented the person, and could be trusted to do the will, of the Pope, and to strengthen and sustain the Papacy by the introduction of an hereditary element. It is a wise saying of Guicciardini, that the Popes were badly served because their reigns were short, but that the Borgias proved what could be accomplished by a well-served Pope.[3] It was a substitute for the security derived from dynastic interests and influence. There was a vulgar nepotism in the solicitude of Alexander to heap wealth and titles on his obscurer sons and kinsmen. But Cæsar's career of conquest, the great reproach of the Borgias, was not a mere pursuit of mean and sordid objects ; it belonged to a system of policy founded on reason and design, and pregnant with consequences not yet extinct.

The secret of Cæsar's power over his father was not love but fear. Machiavelli saw that he really controlled the action of the pontiff, and advised the Florentines that they would obtain more by keeping an agent at Cesena than by their embassy at Rome ;[4] but he did not discover

[1] Praedicator, animam quae in Purgatorio detinetur, adstruens evolare in eo instanti, in quo plene factum est illud, gratia cujus plena venia datur, puta dejectus est aureus in pelvim, non hominem, sed meram et catholicam veritatem praedicat (Prierias, "Dialogus," in Luther, *Opera Latina*, i. 357).

[2] Qui circa indulgentias dicit, ecclesiam Romanam non posse facere id quod de facto facit, haereticus est (Prierias, *Ibid.*).

[3] Essendo communemente di brieve vita, non hanno molto tempo a fare uomini nuovi ; non concorrono le ragioni medesime di potersi fidare de quelli che sono stati appresso allo antecessore . . . in modo che è periculo non sano più infedeli e manco affezionati al servizio del padrone, che quelli che servono uno principe seculare. Dimostro quanto fussi grande la potenza di un pontefice, quando ha uno valente capitano e di chi si possa fidare (Guicciardini, *Opere Inedite*, i. 87 ; iii. 304).

[4] Se ne ha contentare costui, e non il Papa, e per questo le cose che si concludessino dal Papa possono bene essere ritrattate da costui, ma quelle che si

the nature of the relations that existed between the father and the son.   There was complicity, mutual dependence, even confidence, but not affection.   The immense value which Alexander set on the advancement of his son, the perils and sacrifices he incurred to promote it, were not caused by family feelings.   He justified his resignation of the Cardinal's hat, and his marriage, by saying that his presence among the clergy was enough to prevent their reformation.[1]   He spoke of Cæsar with the bitterness of aversion.   When the Spanish and Portuguese ambassadors boldly reproached him with his nepotism, he answered helplessly that Cæsar was terrible, and that he would give a quarter of his dominions to keep him from Rome.[2]   At other times he complained that he could not be made to reside there,[3] and that, when he did, he allowed ambassadors to wait an audience for months, and turned night into day, so that it was doubtful whether after his own death his son would be found capable of keeping what he had got.[4]   The year before his death he said to an envoy who was trusted with his secret plans, that he hoped Cæsar's character would change, and that he would learn to tolerate advice.[5]   Twelve months later, when he was at the height of his fortunes, Alexander was still lamenting that he would listen to nobody, that he made enemies everywhere, and all Italy cried out against him as a bastard and a traitor.[6]   At last, when nothing else would restrain him from attacking Siena, the Pope threatened him with excommunication.[7]

When Alexander was dead, Cæsar Borgia attempted

concludessino da costui non saranno gia ritrittate dal Papa (Desp. Cesena, Dec. 14, 1502 ; *Opere*, v. 354).

[1] Una de las mas principales causas que dava, para que el Cardenal de Valencia dexasse el capelo era, porque siendo aquel Cardenal, mientras en la Iglesia estuviesse, era bastante para impedir que no se hiziesse la reformacion (Zurita, 126).

[2] Que bien conocia que era muy terrible : y que èl daria la quarta parte del Pontificado, porque no bolviesse a Roma (*Ibid.* 160).

[3] Saraceni to Duke of Ferrara, Sept. 22, 1501.

[4] The same, Oct. 6.

[5] Dicendomi Sua Santità che epso Il^{mo} Sig^r Duca era uno bello Signore, et che sperava mutaria natura, et se lasaria parlare (the same, April 6, 1502).

[6] Constabili to Duke of Ferrara, Jan. 23, 1503.

[7] The same, March 1, 1503.

to excuse himself by attributing his own acts to his father's will. He wrote to Ferdinand that he had sought the French alliance against his own wishes, in obedience to the Pope. He tried to conciliate the Duke of Urbino, the most tame and patient vassal of the Church, whom he had twice driven into exile. Cæsar knelt before him, pleaded his own youth, and cursed his father's soul, whose baseness had led him astray.[1]

One point of contrast between the two, which the Pope was in the habit of urging, is curious, for it does not turn quite to Cæsar's disadvantage. The Pope used to represent him as implacably cruel in punishing his enemies, and loved to dwell on his own generosity towards those who had injured or insulted him. In Rome he said speech was free, and he cared not for the things which were published against himself.[2] This praise was not quite hollow. That he was not excessively sensitive, that he could bear with adversaries, appears from the fact that he sent Ludovico di Ferrara to offer a cardinal's hat to Savonarola.[3] He did not proceed to extremities against him until Savonarola had written to the monarchs of Europe bidding them make a new Pope. Cæsar was capable of equal self-restraint, less from temperament than his father, and more from calculation. When, by an act of consummate treachery, he made himself master of Urbino, he published a general amnesty, and observed it even against his worst enemies.[4] But he caused all those to be seized and punished who had betrayed their former master to him, showing, says the chronicler, that he hated the traitor though he loved the treason.[5]

It was said with truth that Alexander VI. succeeded

[1] Incolpando la giovintù sua, li mali consigli soi, le triste pratiche, la pessima natura del Pontifice, et qualche uno altro che 'l haveva spirito a tale impresa; dilatandosi sopra el Pontefice, et maledicendo l' anima sua (Letter from Rome in Ugolini, *Duchi d' Urbino*, ii. 524).
[2] Constabili to Duke of Ferrara, Feb. 1, 1502.
[3] Quétif et Echard, *Script. O. P.*, i. 883.
[4] Ugolini, ii. 111.
[5] Per dar ad intender a tutti, che 'l Signor over Signori hanno appiacer del tradimento, ma non del traditore (Priuli, July 6, 1502).

beyond his designs.[1]   When Cæsar stood at the head of
a victorious army, the only Italian army in existence, the
ambition of the Borgias soared to great heights.   They
were absolute in Central Italy, where no Pope had
exercised real direct authority for ages.[2]   The kingdom
of Naples was the Pope's to grant, to take away, or to
distribute.   Lucretia was married to the heir of Ferrara.
A marriage was proposed between an infant Borgia and
the Duke of Mantua.   Cæsar possessed Piombino ; he
threatened Florence, Siena, Bologna, Ravenna, even
Venice.   He received tribute as *condottiere* from the chief
independent States of Italy.   The King of France offered
Naples to the Pope.[3]   The King of Aragon proposed that
Cæsar should receive Tuscany with the title of king.[4]
Men spoke of him as the future emperor, and dreamed of
Italy united and independent, under the sceptre of a papal
dynasty.[5]   Public expectation went at least as far as the
secret hopes of Borgia.   And it is certain that Cæsar,
hateful as he was, and hated by the great families he had
overthrown, was not disliked by the masses of the people
whom he governed.[6]

It is not just to condemn the establishment of a
powerful dynasty in Romagna as an act of treason against
the rights of the Church.   Though not done for her sake,
it was not done at her expense.   Cæsar was more powerful than Malatesta or Varano, but not practically more
independent.   Rome had derived little benefit from her

[1] Furono i successi sua più volte maggiori che i disegni (Guicciardini, *Opere
Inedite*, iii. 304).

[2] Fu più assoluto Signore di Roma che mai fussi stato Papa alcuno (*Ibid.*).
Donde viene che la Chiesa nel temporale sia venuta a tanta grandezza, concios-
siachè da Alessandro indietro i potentati Italiani, e non solamente quelli che si
chiamono potentati, ma ogni Barone e Signore, benchè minimo, quanto al
temporale, la stimaba poco ; e ora un Rè di Francia ne trema (Machiavelli,
"Principe," *Opere*, i. 55).

[3] Constabili to Duke of Ferrara, Aug. 3, 1503.

[4] Zurita, 242.

[5] Nobody execrated the Borgias more than the Venetian chronicler Priuli.
After the destruction of the Condottieri at Sinigaglia, he writes : "Alcuni lo
volevano far Re dell' Italia, e coronarlo, altri lo volevano far Imperator, perche 'l
prosperava talmente, che non era alcuno li bastasse l' animo d' impedirlo in cosa
alcuna" (Jan. 11, 1503).

[6] Aveva il Duca gittati assai buoni fondamenti alla potenza sua, avendo tutta
la Romagna con il ducato di Urbino, e guadagnatosi tutti quei popoli, per avere
incominciato a gustare il ben essere loro (Machiavelli, "Principe," *Opere*, i. 35).

suzerainty over the petty tyrants whose dominions were merged in the new duchy of Romagna, and incurred no positive loss by the change. In reality there was closer connection with Cæsar than with the vassals he had deposed, and more reliance to be placed in him. His fidelity was secured, for he could not maintain himself in opposition to the Pope. He had no friends in the other Italian States. Supported by the inexhaustible wealth of the Church, he could keep up an army which no power in Italy could resist ; and the Papacy, assured of his fidelity, obtained for the first time a real material basis of independence. Before the French invasion of 1494, the Italians had so little habit of serious warfare that the various States enjoyed a sort of inert immunity from attack.[1] The expedition of Charles VIII. showed how little there was of real security in the general proneness to inaction. By the aid of Cæsar Borgia the Papacy became a military power. That aid was purchased at a great price, but it was sure to be efficient.

The danger was not that the provinces would be alienated, but that the Papacy would fall under the sway of its formidable vassal. Alexander not only foresaw this result, but anxiously contrived to make it certain. It meant that his family should not relax their hold on the Church, to which they owed their elevation. He did not wish to weaken the staff on which they were obliged to lean. His purpose was not to dismember the State, but to consolidate part of it in such a way that his descendants should be the servants and yet the masters of his successors, and that a dynasty of Borgias should protect and should control the Papacy. There was ruin in the scheme, but not the obvious ruin commonly supposed. It was not inspired by religion or restrained by morality, but it was full of intelligent policy of a worldly sort. Cæsar's principality fell to pieces, but the materials enabled Julius II. to build up the Roman State, which was destined to last so long. The Borgias had laid so

---

[1] Chi aveva uno Stato era quasi impossibile lo perdessi (Guicciardini, *Opere Inedite*, i. 109).

firmly the foundations of their power, that the death of
the Pope would not have shaken its stability if Cæsar
had not been disabled for action at the moment when he
was left to his own resources.[1]

Gregorovius, like Ranke, accepts the story that Alexander perished by poison which had been prepared for
others.	It was the common rumour.	Two other guests
at the fatal supper, Cæsar and Cardinal Adrian, were
seized with illness at the same time, and the latter assured
Giovio that he had been poisoned.	This statement,
recorded by Giovio, is the only evidence that positively
supports the suspicion.	The report arose before the Pope
was dead, as soon as the sudden illness of the others
became known.[2]	But it was founded entirely on con-
jecture.	Guicciardini, who did much to spread it, possessed
no proof.	He says that the story is confirmed by the
fact that the Pope died within twenty-four hours.[3]	In
reality he died on the seventh day after his attack.	The
witness who has been hitherto the principal authority
proves, therefore, to have no evidence.	There are almost
daily accounts of the Pope's state between the 12th and
the 18th August from Giustinian to Constabili.	They
suggest nothing more unusual than a violent Roman
fever.

[1] Se nella morte di Alessandro fusse stato sano, ogni cosa gli era facile
(Machiavelli, "Principe," *Opere*, i. 39).
[2] Per la qual infermità si giudicava fosse stato avoelenato, e questo perchè
etiam il giorno sequente il prefato Duca Valentino et il Card[l] s' erano buttati ai
letto con la febre (Priuli, Aug. 16, 1503).
[3] Guicciardini, *Istoria d' Italia*, iii. 162.	E che questa sia la verità, ne fà
fede che lui mori o la notte medesima o il dì seguente (*Opere Inedite*, iii. 302).

III

SECRET HISTORY OF CHARLES II.[1]

IN the register of the House of Novices of the Jesuits at Rome there is the following entry: *Jacobus de la Cloche ingressus* 11 *Aprilis* 1668. From another list, which is signed by the novice himself, we learn that he came from the island of Jersey, and was a subject of the King of England; that his age was about twenty-four; and that he presented himself for admission in the dress of an ecclesiastic, with scarcely any luggage but the clothes he wore. This youth, whose name occurs no more in the books of the Order, and has never yet been pronounced by history, was the eldest of the sons of Charles the Second, the elder brother of Monmouth, and destined to be for a moment his rival in the fanciful schemes of his father. So well was the secret of his birth preserved that throughout the long intrigue to save the Protestant succession, and to supplant the Duke of York by the son of Lucy Walters, no man ever discovered that there was another who, by his age and by his mother's rank, had a better claim than the popular favourite, and who had voluntarily renounced the dazzling fortunes which were once within his grasp. The obscurity which he preferred has endured for nearly two hundred years, and even now is not entirely dispelled; but the facts which I have to relate add a new and interesting episode to the chequered history of the Stuarts, and clear up whatever remained uncertain as to the attachment of Charles II. to the Catholic Church.

This attachment, which excited so keenly the curiosity of the world, and influenced so many of the actions of his

[1] *The Home and Foreign Review*, July 1862.

reign, has been admitted with greater unanimity by recent historians than by those who spoke from personal observation, and whom Charles succeeded in partially misleading. " It was not," says the ablest of the statesmen who approached him, " the least skilful part of his concealing himself to make the world think he leaned towards an indifference in religion." [1]   That belief was long since found to be untenable.   Mr. Fox, and the author of the *Annals of England*, believe that he had been actually reconciled to the Catholic Church ; and Mackintosh fixes the date of that event in the year 1658.   Hallam justly rejects this opinion, but is certain that the king had imbibed during the period of his banishment a persuasion that if any scheme of Christianity was true, it could only be found in the bosom of an infallible Church.   Dr. Vaughan believes that, so far as he could be said to have any religion, he was a Catholic ; and Macaulay exactly agrees with Dr. Vaughan.   Lingard, who declares his early professions of regard for Catholicism a pretence, supplies no psychological explanation of the discrepancy between the scene at his death and his previous insincerity ; while Dod more reasonably considers the reconciliation at the last moment a proof that he had inwardly espoused the Catholic doctrines before.

Many things contributed during the life of Charles to spread and to keep alive the report of his conversion. His mother's sincerity and zeal in religion were well known.   She had attempted to instil the sentiments of her faith into her eldest daughter Mary, afterwards Princess of Orange, and although this was prevented by the king, she obtained his consent in her exile that their youngest child Henrietta should be educated a Catholic.   At Paris Henrietta Maria exerted herself to induce the Duke of Gloucester to change his religion ; and when the exhortations of Charles, the influence of Ormond, and the memory of the last solemn parting with his father prevailed against her efforts, she drove him from her presence.   Charles I. had feared that the

---

[1] Halifax, *Character of Charles* II., p. 11.

religion of his queen would injure the cause of his son, and sent earnest warnings to both when the prince joined his mother in France. To the former he wrote from Oxford, 22nd March 1646: " I command you, upon my blessing, to be constant to your religion ; neither hearkening to Roman superstitions, nor the seditious and schismatical doctrines of the Presbyterians and Independents ; for know that a persecuted church is not thereby less pure, though less fortunate. For all other things I command you to be totally directed by your mother." [1] Shortly after, he wrote to the queen from Newcastle : " In God's name, let him stay with thee till it is seen what ply my business will take ; and, for my sake, let the world see that the queen seeks not to alter his conscience." [2] Clarendon entertained the same fears, and endeavoured to keep the prince at Jersey, away from his mother's influence. But he bears testimony that, for six years, down to 1652, when the fortunes of the Stuarts seemed desperate, and the motives for prudence had disappeared with the hope of success, Henrietta Maria was sensible of the impolicy of a step which, more than any other act, must have alienated the English people from their king. [3] That she recognised it at first we may conclude from the failure of the match between Charles and Mademoiselle de Montpensier, the cousin of Lewis XIV. That princess insisted that the difference of religion was an insurmountable obstacle ; and Jermyn, who was conducting the business, and must have spoken the thoughts of the queen-mother, thereupon replied that the king could not change his religion for her sake without forfeiting for ever the crown of his kingdom. [4]

When, at length, it appeared certain that no chance of recovering the throne remained, except through the support of the Catholic Powers, the exiled courtiers began to debate whether some sacrifice might not be made for the purpose of obtaining their assistance.   " The Protestant

[1] Clarendon, *History of the Rebellion*, x. 8.
[2] *Clarendon Papers*, ii. 239.
[3] *History*, xiii. 131.
[4] *Mémoires de Mademoiselle*, 57, ed. Michaud.

religion was found to be very unagreeable to their fortune, and very many exercised their thoughts most how to get handsomely from it. . . . Many made little doubt but that it would shortly be very manifest to the king that his restoration depended wholly upon a conjunction of Catholic princes, who could never be united but on the behalf of Catholic religion."[1] Digby, Clifford, and Bennet became Catholics, and proved their sincerity at their deaths ; but they all agreed that it would be dangerous for Charles to imitate them. Clarendon, whose purpose it was to divert from his master the suspicion of popery, wished it to be believed that no religious scruples, no doubts in the orthodoxy of the Anglican Church, had ever invaded the exiled court, and that the Catholic inclinations or professions of some of its members were the effects of political design. He had argued with great force that even though Charles should give no cause for suspicion, the fact of his residence in a Catholic country would be a pretext for his enemies to accuse him. It would not be hard, he wrote to Jermyn, to persuade them who believed the king a papist when he was seen every day at Church in England, to believe the prince a papist when he had no church in France to go to.[2] But the other advisers, who were less sturdy Protestants than the Chancellor, knew that nothing was to be expected for their cause from a change of religion. In the period of the administration of Mazarin and the peace of Westphalia, no reasonable man could believe that any State would incur the expense and the risk of war for the establishment of a Catholic dynasty in England ; and even those who believed that Charles leaned from conviction towards Rome, and whose sympathies were on the same side, were careful to conceal the fact.[3]

A rumour reached their friends in England, and caused an extreme alarm. " There is a report," wrote Mordaunt to Ormond, in November 1659, " so hot of your master's

[1] *Clarendon*, xvi. 74.
[2] Lister, *Life of Clarendon*, i. 284. He would not allow the prince to attend the service of the French Calvinists at Charenton (*History*, xiii. 133).
[3] The testimony of Ormond and Burnet, and the worthless reports to the same effect in Kennet and Echard, are collected in the *Biographia Britannica*, ii. 177D, 2nd ed.

being turned papist, that unless it be suddenly contradicted, and the world disabused by something coming
expressly from him, it is likely, in this extraordinary conjuncture, to do him very great injury amongst his friends
both in city and country, in both which his constancy all
this while hath rendered him many considerable pros-
elytes." [1]   This letter justly represents the position of
affairs, and the state of public feeling ; and Clarendon
took his measures to undeceive his party and to silence
their enemies.

Yet, although political interest forbade a public declaration, there was truth in the reports circulated in England,
and so stoutly contradicted by the royalists.   It is
certain that Charles had, during the last years of his
exile, secretly adopted the Catholic faith, although the
fear of detection prevented a formal abjuration of Protestantism.   Burnet says he was received before he left
Paris, and that Cardinal de Retz and Aubigny had a
hand in it.   This information he had obtained from two
sources, and indirectly, he affirms, from Retz himself.
When Charles was at Paris, after the flight from Wor-
cester, he received instruction in religion from Olier, the
celebrated founder of the seminary of St. Sulpice.   His
conferences were no secret, for Olier had informed his
friends of his hopes, and entreated their prayers.   They
probably gave occasion to the exaggerated report of
Burnet.   Charles, it is true, wrote from Paris to the Pope to
ask for assistance in recovering his dominions.   Innocent
would have been satisfied, under the circumstances, with
a private abjuration ; but this was refused, and the king
could not even obtain an answer to his application. [2]   But
although he was not received into the Church, he had
advanced so far in his opinions that he might, as Thurloe
affirmed, in his communications with the Spanish Government have declared himself in private to them to be a
Catholic. [3]   Neither France nor Spain had any inducement

[1] Carte's *Collection*, ii. 264.
[2] *Vie de M. Olier*, ii. 489, from the French Archives.
[3] Carte, ii. 102.

to publish what would diminish the chances of monarchy
in England, and strengthen a Government they feared and
hated.   The story that Ormond discovered Charles on
his knees hearing mass in a church at Brussels comes to
us through two independent channels, Carte and Echard.
The latter supposes the ceremony of abjuration to have
occurred when the king was at Fuentarabia, at the time
of the treaty of the Pyrenees.   There is much reason in a
remark which is made by Welwood : " The truth is, King
Charles was neither bigot enough to any religion, nor loved
his ease so little, as to embark in a business that must at
least have disturbed his quiet, if not hazarded his crown."[1]

Ludovick Stuart, Lord Aubigny, to whom Burnet attributes the conversion of Charles, appeared at Whitehall
immediately after the Restoration.   In France, where he
was educated and ordained, he had joined the party of
Cardinal de Retz and the Jansenists, and had been made
a canon of Notre Dame.   As a relative of the royal
family, and at one time an inmate of St. Sulpice, he was
probably aware of the conferences which Olier, and perhaps others,[2] held with Charles during his residence at
Paris.   In April 1661, he officiated at the private
marriage of Charles with Catherine of Braganza, and
became almoner to the queen.   His royal descent, and
the position he had already attained in the Church,
pointed him out as a suitable person to conduct the
projected intercourse between the English court and the
Holy See.   In order to obtain that office, he sought the
aid of a more powerful negotiator.

His friend Cardinal de Retz had taken the foremost
part in the troubles which distracted both Church and
State in France in the days of the Fronde, and after
balancing for a season the power of Mazarin, had been
deserted by fortune, and suffered in banishment the disgrace both of the French and of the Roman court.   Upon
the death of Cromwell Ormond had recourse to him in

[1] *Memoirs*, p. 131.
[2] Charles is reported to have said that though many persons had discoursed
with him on religion, none had affected him so much as Olier (*Vie de M. Olier*,
ii. 490).

the name of the king, who promised, if the Cardinal would obtain for him some assistance from the Pope, to protect the Catholics after his restoration.   Retz, hoping that the merit of having secured a promise of indulgence for the Catholic subjects of the King of England would power-fully assist his own cause, undertook the negotiation, and sent one of his adherents, the Abbé Charier, to Rome. The envoy could not, however, obtain an audience of the Pope ; and he was assured by one of the Cardinals that the promises of Charles had made no impression, and that the prospect of relief to the oppressed Catholics would never induce Alexander VII. to furnish him with money.[1] The Restoration soon altered the position of affairs, and improved the prospects of the Cardinal.   He came to London in 1660, and received not only promises of sup-port from the king, but large sums of money, on condition that he would promote the objects which Charles was pursuing in the court of Rome.   These objects were of such importance that the notion of a marriage with one of the nieces of Mazarin was entertained for a moment by Charles as a means of securing them,[2] and was eagerly adopted by Retz for the purpose of recovering his favour at Paris.   Mazarin despatched a special envoy to England charged with the mission of promoting the match.   He found an auxiliary in Aubigny, who represented to Charles the beauty of the Cardinal's nieces, but more particularly their virtue, of which, says the envoy, the king was much pleased to hear.   Together with this futile intrigue, Retz was pleading at Whitehall for the Catholics, and at Rome for the settlement of that important affair to which the alliance with Mazarin and the elevation of Aubigny were expected to contribute.   The first of these subsidiary negotiations was speedily abandoned ; the other was pur-sued with a strange pertinacity for several years.

[1] *Mémoires de Guy Joly*, p. 140, ed. Michaud.
[2] " Aujourd'hui la reine a reçu une lettre du roy son fils, où il parle positive-ment, et dit qu'après avoir considéré toutes les raisons de son mariage, il se conformoit à son sentiment pour vostre nièce, en vue du grand dessein à quoi il estoit porté de jour en jour avec plus de faveur" (Lionne to Mazarin, 7th July 1660, in Champollion, *Complément des Mémoires de Retz*, p. 589, ed. Michaud).

At first Charles desired a mitre for his kinsman,[1] but he soon raised his demands, and insisted on having him created a cardinal.   Clarendon, who was ignorant of the real design of which this was to be the prelude, entered into the idea, and drew up the instructions with which, in October 1662, the queen's secretary, Sir Richard Bellings, was sent to Rome.   In the following year the Chancellor's share in these transactions was made a part of the abortive charge preferred against him by Bristol ; and it appears from the articles that the great importance which was given to this negotiation, and the correspondence with the Roman cardinals, were generally known at the time. Retz advised Charles to secure the compliance of the Pope by sending a squadron to cruise off Civita Vecchia, and then proceeded to Hamburg to obtain the powerful intervention of the Queen of Sweden.   He was charged at the same time with the distribution of a sum of fifteen thousand pounds, which Charles had determined to devote to the interests of Aubigny.[2]   Letters were written by both the Queens of England to Cardinal Orsini, Protector of Portugal, urging him to press the suit, and assuring him that if the promotion should be refused, lamentable consequences might be apprehended from the disappointment of the king.   Orsini, after an interview with Bellings, warmly took up the cause, and declared in a letter to the famous Cardinal Pallavicini, that he might, by assisting him, render a great service to religion.   They also wrote to the two most influential men in Rome, Cardinals Chigi and Azzolini, the latter of whom was an active promoter of the design.   His letter to the king, of 8th April 1663, advising the continuation of his efforts, and that of Cardinal Chigi, written on the following day, are in the State Paper Office.[3]

The question was maturely debated at Rome, and an opinion was drawn up in favour of Aubigny, founded partly on the statements of Bellings, and partly on the

[1] Dod, *Church History of England*, iii. 239.
[2] *Mémoires de Guy Joly*, p. 149.
[3] Italian States, Bundle No. 24.

elaborate memorials of Retz, in which the services of the king were set forth.   This opinion was to the following effect : the Restoration had improved the condition of the Catholics, and whatever relief they enjoyed was due to the influence of Charles himself, and was disliked by the Parliament and the country.   The abolition of the penal laws could not be expected, for the royal authority was competent only to suspend them.   Indeed, it might be considered almost more advantageous, under the cir- cumstances, that the laws should be suspended than toleration proclaimed.   For the same disabilities from which the Catholics suffered extended in great part to the Presbyterians, and the other sects who were hostile to the monarchy.   They could not therefore be abrogated without depriving the king of the weapons the law gave him to defend the crown against the Nonconformists, while a partial abolition would excite fresh envy against the Catholics, and add to the number of their enemies. Legislative toleration, inasmuch as its benefits would be shared by the Dissenters, was not to be desired, even if it could be obtained.   It was necessary to rely solely on the power and the favour of the king.   For his authority might be trusted not only as a security against the heretics, but also against that portion of the Catholics who were in opposition to the Jesuits.   To his salutary influence was to be attributed the suppression of the measure for Catholic relief which had been brought forward in July 1662, in answer to the petition presented by that party, who had offered to swear that they did not hold the doctrine of the temporal authority of the Holy See, and that they would "oppose with their lives and fortunes the Pontiff himself, if he should ever attempt to execute that pretended power." [1]   Again, when the Irish protestation of allegiance, which many leading Catholics had signed, was found in like manner to be very far removed from the obedience due to the Apostolic See, Charles had refused to countenance it, and had exhibited an unvarying respect for the Pope.   Queen

[1] Lingard, ix. 35.

Henrietta Maria, who was now supporting the cause of Aubigny, had formerly obtained the same dignity for Conne, and only his death had prevented him from enjoying it. The state of the Catholics was more satisfactory and more hopeful than when the favour now asked for had been granted before, and the new king had in several ways shown that he was favourably disposed. Before leaving the Low Countries to ascend his throne, he had sent a rich present to the English nuns at Ghent. He had given audience to several Jesuits, and among others to two successive provincials, to whom he had promised his protection in case of need. He had been seen in a posture of adoration at high mass in the queen's chapel.

These were the views at that time entertained at Rome concerning the religious character of Charles II., and the arguments advanced in support of the promotion of Aubigny. Nevertheless the demand was rejected. The Pope's answer was conveyed in such terms that Charles was not offended, and accepted the explanation. The refusal, indeed, was only temporary. The solicitations of the English Court were soon after renewed, and they were at last successful. In November 1665, Aubigny, who was then at Paris, received his nomination, and died almost immediately after.[1] His name does not appear in the list of the cardinals created by Alexander VII., but his elevation, and the influence by which it had been obtained, were known, and had excited hopes for the Catholic Church in this country, which caused his death to be regarded as a serious calamity. The general of the Jesuits, on hearing of it, wrote to one of his correspondents : " The clouds which are gathering over Holland, Poland, and Constantinople are so dense, that every prudent man must see reason to apprehend enormous catastrophes, and storms that will not be ended without irreparable disasters. But in my mind all these coming evils are overshadowed by the death of the

[1] Moréri, *Dictionnaire Historique*, ix. 597 ; his epitaph in Douglas, *Peerage of Scotland*, ii. 101.

Abbé Aubigny, which deprives the Church, for a time at least, of the joy of beholding an English cardinal of such illustrious blood, created at the public instances of two queens, and at the secret request of a king : a prodigy which would without doubt have confounded heresy, and inaugurated bright fortunes to the unhappy Catholics."

The affair of the cardinal's hat was not the principal object of the mission of Sir Richard Bellings.   It was intended as a preliminary to that more important negotiation which the envoy was instructed to reserve if the first should fail, and inspired Queen Catherine with so much anxiety, and Cardinal Orsini with such sanguine hopes of the advancement of religion.   The two queens knew that Charles was at heart a Catholic, and they pressed him to declare himself.   He was now firmly seated on his throne ; the Established Church had recovered its supremacy, and was not only profoundly loyal, but still strongly impregnated with those Catholic tendencies which had hastened its fall ; the Puritans and Independents were yet prostrate beneath the ruins of their political system, and the great body that reverenced Baxter as their chief was comparatively tolerant.   Charles, believing that the step which would have prevented his return might now be taken without involving the risk of a new revolution, resolved to feel his way towards a reconciliation with the Holy See.   In addition to the instructions drawn up by Clarendon, Sir Richard Bellings carried to Rome proposals for the submission of the three kingdoms to the Church, and presented to Alexander VII. the king's profession of faith.[1]   Charles declared that he was willing to accept the creed of Pius IV., the decrees of the Council of Trent and of all general Councils on faith and morals, and the decisions of the two last Pontiffs in the affair of the Jansenists, saving the particular rights and customs of the nation, as is the practice in France

---

[1] Oblatio ex parte Caroli II. Magnae Brittanniae Regis pro optatissima trium suorum Regnorum Angliae, Scotiae et Hiberniae cum Sede Apostolica Romana reunione.

and in other countries, and provided always no new laws should be imposed upon his realm, and he should be free to complete in his own way the work of reconciliation. He declared that he renounced and detested all the heresies which had involved his country in ecclesiastical and civil troubles, and made England the most distracted State in the world. He undertook to restore the hierarchy as it was under Henry VIII.; and added that the Protestants should have toleration as long as they did not disturb the peace.

In this very remarkable document, Charles, who believed that many of his subjects would follow his example, gave one of the earliest instances of what has since been constantly witnessed,—that princes who, as head of the Protestant Church in their dominions, enjoy an almost unlimited authority, cannot view without jealousy the ecclesiastical liberty which is claimed by Catholicism. He carefully restricted the papal jurisdiction both of doctrine and discipline, and reserved to himself the rights which the Gallican system attributed to the secular power. He even proposed that the Church should abandon her essential function of judging and defining matters of faith as occasion should arise. Although this is a condition contrary to the nature of the Catholic Church, the document proposing it, which is followed by twenty-four articles on particular points, exhibits so much familiarity with ecclesiastical forms that it must have been drawn up by a Catholic hand. It is not probable that many persons were admitted on this occasion into the confidence of Charles. The whole scheme was not discussed beyond the door of the royal closet. It betrays the hand of a layman, for no priest could have expected the Church to discontinue her dogmatic progress; and Aubigny, the only priest likely to be consulted, was not likely to introduce the clause against Jansenism. Now we know that the secret was imparted to one lay Catholic, the agent who was charged with the negotiation. No man was more likely to be chosen for that important mission than he to whom the affair had been confided from the first,

or who could discuss the proposals better than he who
had helped to devise them.   Bellings was a man of note
and distinction among the Catholics in both islands, and
was often employed by the court in confidential missions.
His father had been one of the leaders in the opposition
to the nuncio Rinuccini, and was the author of that
protestation of allegiance which had been adopted by a
large party in Ireland, and which was so badly received
at Rome.   The son was, therefore, not unlikely to
suggest those limitations of ecclesiastical authority which
he undertook to defend, and which corresponded with the
views of his father and of those who, in the language
of Bristol, were Catholics of the Church of Rome, not
of the court of Rome.

The answer of Alexander was probably not very encouraging, for the negotiation was broken off.   A suspicion
was awakened that the king was in correspondence with the
Pope, and Charles, in his alarm, took measures to prove
his aversion of Catholicism.   He opened Parliament on
the 18th of February 1663 with a demand for new laws
to restrain the progress of popery, and gave his assent to
a proclamation ordering all priests to quit the kingdom
under pain of death.   He explained, five years later, in a
letter to which I shall presently return, the failure of his
negotiation, and the inconsistency of his subsequent conduct : " Quoy qu'elle nous fust présentée avec touttes les
circonstances necessaires, et par personne catholique, toutte-
fois ce ne peut estre avec tant de prudence que nous ne
fussions soupçonnés d'intelligence avec le pape par les
plus clairvoyants de nostre cour ; mais ayant trouvé le
moyen d'étouffer le soubçon que l'on començoit d'avoir
que nous fussions catholique, nous fusmes obligé, crainte
de ne le faire renaistre dans les esprits, de consentir aux
occasions a plusieurs choses tournant au desavantage de
plusieurs catholiques de nostre royaume d'Hybernie, ce
qui est cause encore que bien que nous eussions escry
assez secrettement à sa saincteté pour nostre rangement
à l'eglise catholique, au mesme temps que nous prions
sa saincteté de faire cardinal nostre très cher cousin le

H

Milord d'Aubigny, dont nous fumes refusés pour bonnes raisons, nous n'avons peu poursuyvre nostre pointe." The scheme was not resumed for several years. Times were not propitious. The Dutch war, the Plague, the Fire, the Triple Alliance, intervened. Public animosity was inflamed against the Catholics ; and Charles had no confidential agent whom he could employ without danger to propose, if not the reconciliation of the country, for which he was not disposed to make great efforts or great sacrifices, at least his own submission to the Catholic Church. During this interval, Jacques de la Cloche made his appearance for the first time in England.

In the spring 1646, during his first residence in Jersey, Charles fell in love with a young lady of high rank, who became the mother of a child, who enjoyed the prerogative, denied to all the other natural children of the king, of bearing his father's name. He was called James Stuart, and was brought up in the Protestant religion on the Continent. " Il nous est né lorsque nous n'avions guères plus de seize on 17 ans, d'une jeune dame des plus qualifiées de nos royaumes, plustost par fragilité de nostre première jeunesse que par malice." The last words appear to indicate Charles's respect for the mother and the care with which he protected her fame. Unlike the Clevelands and Portsmouths who afterwards disgraced his court, the lady who was the object of his earliest attachment obtained of her royal lover the concealment of her fault, and her name has never been divulged. She is nowhere mentioned in the correspondence relating to her son ; and if she died before his arrival in England, the reputation of her family may have induced the king to conceal his birth. After the Restoration he allowed him to remain abroad unnoticed, and under the disguise of an assumed name, until the year 1665. In that year he sent for him to England, supplied him with money, and gave him a certificate in which he recognised him as his son, but which he commanded him to show to nobody whilst his father lived. This document, written and signed by Charles's own hand, and sealed with his private seal, is dated Whitehall, 27th September 1665,—a time at which the plague was at its height, and the court was not in London. For greater security he obliged his son once more to change his name. That which he had borne till then is not known. He was now called James de la Cloche du Bourg. It is not easy to say whether the last of these names may afford some clue to the discovery of his mother's family among the three thousand royalists who took refuge in Jersey at the same time as the Prince of Wales.[1] The former name had been made popular in that island when Charles arrived there by the spirit with which Mr. de la Cloche, a clergyman, had resisted the authority of Government.[2] After lying nearly a year in prison, he was released upon the arrival of the Prince, and then left the island. Had his release anything to do with Charles's private affairs? Was the boy christened by him, or afterwards committed to his charge?

James was unwilling to remain in England. It was not his country; he did not speak the language; he had no career and no recognised station; and his position was not to his taste. He had made great proficiency in his studies abroad, and he desired to continue them in the Dutch universities. His father did not know what to do with him in England, and allowed him to go. Eighteen months later, on the 7th of February 1667, he sent him another document, recognising his birth, and directing his successor to give him £500 a year. A condition was attached to the grant of this pension, that it could be enjoyed only while the claimant resided in London, and remained faithful to the religion of his fathers and to the Anglican liturgy. Six months after receiving this letter, on the 29th of July 1667, James Stuart became a Catholic at Hamburg.

The Queen of Sweden, who filled Europe with the fame of her abdication, her abjuration, her talents, and her eccentricities, was for the second time residing at Hamburg, and appears again on the scene of the secret history

---

[1] R. Augier to the Speaker, in Cary, *Memorials of the Civil War*, i. 7.
[2] Le Quesne, *Constitutional History of Jersey*, p. 325.

of Charles. She signed a paper for his son, certifying that he had been received into the Church at that particular place and time, in order that he might be able, in case of need, to satisfy his confessor of the identity of the convert of Hamburg with the Protestant whom the King of Great Britain had privately recognised as his son. This was now necessary, because he had determined, immediately after his conversion, to enter the novitiate of the Jesuits. Christine knew who he was, probably because he had been compelled to apply to her chaplains, or at least for her protection, in order to be received. The Senate of Hamburg exercised with extreme severity the right which the Treaties of Westphalia gave to each Government of exacting religious conformity ; and the neighbouring town of Altona, peopled by the Catholics, Anabaptists, and Jews whom the Lutherans had expelled, grew up a monument of the intolerance of the Free City. The queen had attempted, some years before, to obtain freedom of conscience for her own religion through the intervention of the Catholic Powers ; but the Emperor, whose rights were derived from the same treaty by which the senate justified its rigour, and who was not disposed to surrender them, refused to disturb the settlement of Münster. At the very time when James was converted, the town had been thrown into confusion by the uproar caused by a fête which Christine gave, in the midst of a Protestant population, to celebrate the election of Clement IX. Charles was much annoyed to learn that she was in his son's confidence. " She is prudent and wise," he said ; " but she is a woman, and that is enough to make us doubt whether she is able to keep a secret."

James de la Cloche was hardly settled at Rome when his father determined to have him about his court. That vast intrigue had just commenced which was to raise France to the pinnacle of power, and which, by a timely subservience, promised to emancipate the princes of the House of Stuart from the control of Parliament, and from the terrors which had postponed the king's design of reconciliation with Rome. In that conspiracy the motives of religious belief and political ambition were strangely blended. Turenne, who was destined to be the foremost actor in the execution of the design, was a sincere Calvinist. He had shortly before refused the great dignity of Constable of France, when it was tendered as the reward of his conversion. On the 23rd of October 1668 Turenne became a Catholic. He was shortly after followed by his old lieutenant, a confederate in the new scheme, the Duke of York. James had applied to the Provincial of the Jesuits, and then to the Pope, for permission to conceal his religion, and had been told that it was impossible. With this answer he caught the conscience of the king. On the feast of the conversion of St. Paul, 1669, Charles summoned his Catholic counsellors, declared with tears how uneasy he was not to profess the faith which he believed, and consulted them as to the best mode of carrying out his resolutions. They concluded that the only way was to do it in conjunction with France.[1] A few months before this resolution was finally taken, in August 1668, Charles had written to the General of the Jesuits to send him his son, whose presence he needed for the good of his soul.

He had long sought in vain, the king said to Oliva, for a person with whom he could confer on spiritual matters without creating suspicion. The priests who lived in London were so well known that no disguise could conceal them ;[2] but the conversion of his son, and his entrance into Orders, at length gave him an opportunity of receiving the sacraments without alarming the Protestant zeal of his subjects. His son might remain unknown, as the queens alone were aware of his existence ; but before long he should be publicly acknowledged. " Plusieurs raisons considérables, et concernantes la paix de nos royaumes, nous ont empesché jusques à présent de le reconnestre publiquement pour notre fils ; mais ce sera pour peu de temps, parceque nous sommes

---

[1] Clarke, *Life of James II.*, i. 441.
[2] We know, from the account of his death, that none of the Portuguese chaplains of the queen could speak either English or French.

maintenant en dessein de faire en sorte de le reconnestre publiquement devant peu d'années." In case he was not a priest, and could not be ordained before starting, Charles directed that he should go to Paris, and address himself either to the king or to the Duchess of Orleans, who knew of his own design, and would have James ordained without betraying his rank ; or, if he preferred it, the two queens would find an opportunity for his ordination in England. As soon as he had received his father into the Church, he would be free either to return to Rome or to live in England, so as to be within call ; but not in London, lest people should suspect that the king's son was a Jesuit. This was written on the 3rd of August. On the 29th, Charles, having heard that the Queen of Sweden was on her way to Rome, wrote again to hasten the departure of his son ; for he feared that Christine, if she saw him, would discover the purpose of his intended journey. If that should become known in England, he said, it would infallibly cost him his life. He therefore desired that his son, instead of stopping at Paris, should come with all speed to London, and there make himself known to the queen-mother by delivering to her a sealed letter in the form of a petition. This letter was scarcely sealed, when he wrote a third time to the General. It had occurred to his mother and his wife that a novice is not allowed among the Jesuits to travel alone. Charles hoped that this regulation would be dispensed with, and that his son would be permitted to set out by himself in the dress of a layman. Secret warning had already been given at the southern ports that a foreign prince, whose appearance was described as near that of James as possible, was about to seek refuge in England, and would arrive without any companion. The presence of a Jesuit father would have spoilt this plan. The better to meet the arrangements which had been made, the novice was to call himself Henry de Rohan, a name well known as that of one of the great Huguenot families of France. Charles declared on his royal word, *en foy de roy*, that the sole object of his letters was the salvation of his soul, and the good of his son and of the Order, and that he would either induce the Pope to make him a cardinal, or allow him, if he should prefer it, to remain a simple religious.

In the middle of October 1668 the young ecclesiastic started for England, disguised as a French cavalier. Together with his letters to Oliva, Charles had written to him in terms of the warmest affection.   The temper of Parliament, he said, had hitherto made it necessary to defer the public acknowledgment of his birth, but the time was approaching when it would be possible for him to assume the rank which belonged to him.   It behoved him, therefore, to reflect maturely on his altered prospects before entering irrevocably into sacred orders.   His title was better than that of the Duke of Monmouth, and he had a right of precedence over him, " par touttes raisons, et à cause de la qualité de votre mère."   The queen was childless, and the children of the Duke of York were delicate ; and if the Catholic religion should be restored in England he would have a claim to the crown : " Nous pouvons vous asseurer que si Dieu permet que nous et notre très honoré frère le duc d'Yorck mourons sans enfans, les royaumes vous apartient, et le parlement ne peut pas legitimement s'y opposer ; si ce n'est qu'en matière d'estre catholique vous en soyez exclus. . . . Croyez que nous vous avons toujours eu une affection particulière non seulement à cause que vous nous este né dans nostre plus tendre ieunesse, lorsque nous n'avions guères plus de 16 ou 17 ans, que particulièrement à cause de l'excelent naturel que nous avons toujours remarqué en vous."

Prince James Stuart, as the king now calls him, remained scarcely a fortnight in England.   On the 18th of November he was sent back to Rome on a secret mission to the General of the Jesuits, with directions to return as soon as he had obtained what the king desired.   It does not appear what that was.   It is probable that Charles wished, like his brother, to be allowed to keep his change of religion a secret ; and the application which James says

that he made to the Pope at this time may have been
conveyed, on the part of both brothers, by the youth
whom Charles had already selected to be the medium of
communication with the Holy See.   The Duke of York's
letter to the Pope required secrecy, and we know that no
messenger was trusted by Charles but the young Stuart
himself.   This was not, however, the only condition he
desired to exact in making his submission to the Holy
See.   We have seen the tenor of his demands in 1662.
In his letters to his sister, published by Dalrymple, he
mentions other points, which on the former occasion were
probably included in the clause allowing him to carry out
the details of the restoration of Catholicism in his own
way.   " He talks," says Hallam, who has investigated the
history of this period more carefully than any other writer,
" of a negotiation with the court of Rome to obtain the
permission of having mass in the vulgar tongue, and
communion in both kinds, as terms that would render his
conversion agreeable to his subjects." [1]   Before departing
for Rome, James must have assured his father that his
resolution was fixed, and that he would live and die a
Jesuit.   Charles, who had promised not to interfere with
his vocation, gave him a large subsidy for the new novitiate
at St. Andrea on the Quirinal, which Oliva was then
erecting, in addition to the old building of St. Francis
Borgia.   He also desired that on this second journey his
son should be accompanied by a Jesuit; for, as he was
not a priest, he was unable to receive his father into the
Church, or to administer the sacraments to him.   With
these instructions James left England.   From that day
he disappears from history ; and after his arrival in Rome,
in November or December 1868, the name of De la
Cloche, by which he was known in the novitiate, figures
no more in the books of the society.

Towards the close of the year a young gentleman, who
passed for an Englishman, and travelled with a servant
and a well-stored purse, took up his abode at a very
humble inn at Naples.   The host had a daughter, Teresa

[1] *Constitutional History*, ii. 387.

Corona, whose extraordinary beauty won the heart of the
guest.   After he had satisfied the ecclesiastical authorities
that he was a Catholic, they were married on the 19th of
February 1669.   It was not long before the attention of
the neighbours was roused by their manner of life.   Gold
was observed to be suspiciously plentiful in the household of the poor innkeeper, and it began to be whispered
that his English son-in-law was related to the King of
Great Britain.   Rumours came to the ear of the Spanish
viceroy, who, in his solicitude for the honour of royalty,
caused the stranger to be arrested.   Letters were found
in his possession bearing the title of Highness, together
with many jewels and heaps of pistoles.   He declared
that he was Prince James Stuart, a son of the King of
England, born in Jersey ; and he sent for the English
consul in order to obtain his release.   But he could
neither speak English nor give any satisfactory evidence
in support of his statement.   The viceroy wrote to England to ascertain the truth of the story, and in the meantime treated his captive as a prisoner of State, and sent
him to the fortress of Gaeta, whilst he shut up his wife in
a convent.   Nobody knew what to believe.   " Which,"
writes the English agent, Kent. to Williamson, on the
30th of March, " whether will end in prince or cheat I
shall endeavour to inform you hereafter."   The bewildered
governor allowed his prisoner fifty crowns a month for his
maintenance, and permitted his wife's family to visit him.
Early in June came the answer of King Charles to the
viceroy, who thereupon proclaimed the mysterious personage an impostor, removed him from his honourable
confinement at Gaeta to the dungeons for common malefactors at Naples, and condemned him to be whipped
through the city.   Teresa Corona was taken from her
convent on the discovery of her husband's real character ;
and the story, which was believed at the time, goes on to
say that instead of being punished he was released at her
intercession, and allowed to go to France, on a visit, as
he affirmed, to his mother.   Two months later he was
again at Naples, asserting that his mother was dead.   He

called her the Lady Mary Stuart, of the house of the Barons of St. Mars, as it is in the contemporary English translation, or of San Marzo, as it stands in the Italian copy of his will; and said that it was in consequence of her relationship with the royal family that the king was unwilling to acknowledge him. The will is dated 24th August 1669, and two days later the testator died, reiterating his statements in the same breath in which he recommended his soul to the mercy of God and the intercession of Our Lady, in terms of the deepest piety and resignation. He appointed his cousin, Lewis XIV., his executor; demanded of Charles, for his unborn child, either the principality of Wales or Monmouth, or a royal dukedom, with an income of a hundred thousand crowns, besides his mother's fortune, amounting to £16,000 a year; and left enormous legacies to his wife's relations and to the Church. "And this," says Kent, "is the end of that princely cheat, or whatever he was." The cautious agent did not venture to determine the adventurer's quality; and in the manuscript letter of news sent weekly to the English Government, called the *Gazzetta di Roma*, from which most of his information was derived, the Englishman is constantly called the English prince.

Yet none of these contemporaries knew that there was actually at that time a son of King Charles born at Jersey of a lady of high rank, privately addressed as Highness, provided with money, and speaking French as his native tongue. Had they known it, and could they have discovered that the illegitimate prince was really called James Stuart; that though a novice he was not ordained; and that all authentic traces of him were at an end from the moment of his arrival in Italy, at the very time when the English traveller put up at the inn of Corona,—if, in short, their knowledge had extended generally as far as ours, and had stopped where ours stops, it is probable that they would not have hesitated to believe in the claims of the prisoner at Gaeta. The king's denial, and what followed, would not have shaken their conviction. Charles was always careful to conceal the existence of his son, and he was particularly tender of the mother's name. When informed that the young Jesuit who had refused his favour, and had gone forth to prepare the way for his father's conversion, was the husband of a publican's daughter at Naples, and had been thrown into prison after apprising the people of his rank and wealth, he would certainly not have responded to the appeal of the viceroy by a public acknowledgment. It was necessary, in order to shield the father, that the son should be proclaimed an impostor, and sentenced to condign punishment. But it was not necessary that he should be actually punished. Charles's interests were satisfied by his removal to the felons' prison, his sentence, and his immediate pardon. If the accusation had been true, the pardon could not have followed instantly on the discovery ; the culprit, after leaving the scene of his disgrace, would not voluntarily have returned so soon ; and he would not have mingled with his dying prayers the solemn repetition of a lie, which could serve no further purpose but to bring down disappointment and notoriety on his widow. The claims which he prefers for his child, though inconsistent with his own disinterested conduct, might have proceeded from a natural anxiety to provide for his posterity.

This is the case for the prisoner. It falls to the ground in cross-examination. The tenor of the will itself is fatal to it. The real James Stuart, who was sure of being able to obtain every just demand, would not have compromised the reasonable prospects of his family by the falsehoods and the extravagance of this document. He had, moreover, in his possession papers which proved his claim, and would have delivered him from the rigours of the Spanish governor. There was no reason for his sudden appearance at Naples at the very moment when he was charged with a negotiation of the greatest moment to his father, his Church, and himself. Nor would he have called his mother by a name and title which are unquestionably fictitious. And yet in that imaginary name and title there may perhaps be found a key to the mystery of the birth of the young James Stuart. For though the

Neapolitan adventurer was an impostor, he enjoyed good
sources of information, and possessed, though imperfectly,
the secrets of King Charles's son.   He knew that he was
born at Jersey, and that his birth had been recognised by
his father, and he had secured some of his papers and
some of his property.   All the wealth he showed at Naples
did not come from that source, for the young novice was
not so rich, and the impostor must have robbed other
people.   But he had certainly either accompanied, as his
servant, the man he represented, or stolen his letters.
Whatever be the secret of this strange adventure, it is so
certain that it was not the real James Stuart who died at
Naples in August 1669, that it is worth while to institute
a further inquiry as to the probable events of his subsequent
career.[1]

He must have returned almost immediately to his
father's court ; but here too he was compelled to lay
aside the name which he had borne on his former journey.
The same Henry de Rohan could not twice in two
months seek an asylum in England without awakening
the suspicions of that suspicious age.   The name which
he finally assumed is unknown, and we are unable with
certainty to trace him further.   But it can hardly be
doubted that among the French Jesuits of that period the
eldest son of Charles II. may yet be identified.   He was
by speech and education a Frenchman, and it is likely
that he again took a French name, and completed his
novitiate in France or in Flanders.   Had he quitted the
Order, he would have taken with him the grant of his
pension, which lies at Rome.   Had he returned to Rome,
he would have resumed his former name.   Had he
remained in England, it is hard to believe that he could
have escaped discovery at the time of the Popish Plot, or
among the clergy who frequented the palace.   He did
not succeed in effecting the actual reconciliation of his

---

[1] The papers from which this account is given are in the State Paper Office,
" Italian States," Bundle 32 ; *Letters of Kent*, March 30, 1669, June 16, August
31, and September 7 ; *News Letters*, or *Gazzette di Roma*, of March 23, April 6,
April 13, April 20, June 11, September 7.   The will is in the Domestic Papers,
Bundle for August 1669.

father with the Church, for it is certain that that event did not occur before the eve of Charles's death. When Charles feared that his brother would expose himself to danger by bringing a priest, and when James declared he would do it at the risk of his life, they could only allude to the law which made it penal to receive a convert. The mere administration of the Sacrament to one already Catholic could get no one into trouble. Huddlestone says that the king declared "that he was most heartily sorry for all the sins of his past life, and particularly for that he had defferred his ¬econciliation so long." This is implicitly confirmed by what he told Aprice, another priest, who wrote ten days later: "As Mr. Huddlestone himself has told me, by a particular instance of God's grace, the king was as ready and apt in making his confession, and all other things, as if he had been brought up a Catholic all his lifetime." [1] If we had not these proofs that Charles had not been received into the Church before his last illness, still there could be no doubt upon the subject, as the application of James for leave to conceal his religion was rejected, and the publication would also, in the case of the king, have been the necessary condition of his admission into the Church.

James Stuart's ministrations to his father must therefore have been confined to the discussion of the Catholic doctrines. It is possible that a memorial of these discussions and exhortations may still be extant. Manuscript copies of the two papers on religion, in the handwriting of Charles, which were found in his cabinet and published by his brother, were sent to Rome by Father Giudici, the confessor of Mary Beatrice. These copies, attested by King James's own signature, are in French. That which was printed in England was a translation. It would have been useless to publish a French text in England, where an immediate and general effect was required. There could be no object in sending a copy of the translation to Rome, where the original could be understood and interpreted. The title of the copies in

[1] Harris, *Life of Charles II.*, ii. 391.

Rome proves that the publication had already taken place.   If the originals were printed, it would have been enough to send a printed copy, which would have possessed greater authenticity than a manuscript translation.   It is impossible to compare the French and the English versions without perceiving that the latter is a translation of the former—inelegant, somewhat abridged, and not entirely faithful.   The word *apogrifes*, which occurs in the French for *apocryphes*, shows that the papers were in the writing of a person who did not know theology. Father Giudici would not have allowed it to stand in the copy if it were not in the original manuscript of the king; but in the English edition the word was altogether omitted, probably because it would not be understood by Protestants in the sense in which the writer used it.

These papers, though in the handwriting of Charles II., were not composed by him.   They are in the form of an argument, addressed by one person to another. For this he had no occasion, and he had no reason to write them in French.   On the same ground, they cannot have been written by Bristol or Aubigny, to whom Burnet is inclined to attribute them.   Bristol did not converse with the king in French.   Aubigny, it is true, had spent most of his life in France, but he had not forgotten his native language.   Little is known concerning him, but it is on record that his knowledge of English once saved his life.   He was attacked at night by two English bloodhounds, who were kept in the garden of the Jacobins, and he pacified them by speaking to them in English.[1]   Tallemant, who tells the tale, adds, that a thief who, being a Frenchman, had no means of making himself intelligible to the foreign dogs, was seized by them in getting over the wall, and soon despatched.

An ecclesiastic who conferred with Charles concerning his conversion after he had ascended the throne, and who knew French better than English, must have been the author of these compositions.   This would bring the evidence to bear on the French priests about the queen-

[1] *Historiettes de Tallemant des Reaux*, vii. 293.

mother or the Duke of York, such as Mansuète or La Colombière. But the tone of these writings is not that which would be adopted by a foreign priest addressing the king. They are written with confidence, frankness, and even familiarity, and they must have been written by one who, though he could not write in English, might consider himself an Englishman. England is more than once spoken of as "nostre Angleterre." There is reason, therefore, to suspect that we have in these letters a record of the religious earnestness and filial piety of the Stuart who preferred a cloister to the steps of his father's throne.

Two years after the day when we lose site of James Stuart, the question of the reconciliation of Charles II. with the Catholic Church had become a part of European politics, and an element in confederations and treaties. Lewis XIV. proposed that D'Estrées, then Bishop of Laon, and afterwards cardinal, the most successful negotiator in his kingdom, should be employed to bring the matter before the Holy See. Charles received the proposal coldly. He told the French ambassador that he had already made choice of an English priest to treat with the Pope for his conversion, and that instructions were being prepared for him.[1] Arlington undertook to hasten his departure; but he was then at St. Omers, and the illness of Clement IX. made the king anxious to wait, as he did not wish, he said, to confide his secret to a dying man. It is most probable that the English priest at St. Omers, whom Charles had already arranged to send to Rome, was the same through whom he had previously opened the business. On his return from Rome at the end of the year 1668, Prince James Stuart found that the king had resolved to discuss his design with the ministers, and that the great interests involved, and the choice of the mode, and the time of declaring himself, would necessarily postpone the event. The negotiation with France for the dissolution of the Triple Alliance, on which it depended, required time, both on account of the secrecy which had to be preserved, and of

[1] Mignet, *Négociations relatives à la Succession d'Espagne*, iii. 232.

the vast preparations which were made for the war, which was to be the signal for the change. James must have perceived that his time had not arrived, and he was doubtless anxious to finish his novitiate and to receive ordination. It is natural to conclude that he would retire to some house of the Society where he could satisfy this desire, and still be at hand whenever his father's plans were ripe, and he should be summoned to be the instrument for their accomplishment. The college of St. Omers, or the neighbouring English novitiate at Watten, would be the fittest and likeliest place for him to inhabit.

We have no other probable record of his life. Once more, in the midst of the excitement of the Popish Plot, the mysterious figure of a foreign priest crosses the life of Charles. A gentleman told Welwood that he was employed to bring over privately a Romish priest, then beyond sea, by whose means the king had some secret matters to manage. The king and the priest were a considerable time together alone in the closet. At last the priest came out, with all the marks of fright and astonishment in his face. Charles had been seized with a fit, and the priest would have called for help ; but the king, who feared that their interview should become known, had strength and resolution to hold him till he had recovered his speech.[1] Was this priest, with whom Charles was in correspondence, whom he caused to be fetched secretly from foreign parts, and the discovery of whose presence he so passionately dreaded, his own son?

Among the letters of Oliva there is one that bears no date, addressed to a king who is not named, respecting a certain Jesuit, whose name is also concealed. This father, it appears, had received from the king an important office, which he used for the purpose of interfering in affairs of State, and had not only made enemies by his imprudence, but had injured the interests of the king, and had alienated, by the acrimony and disrespect of his language, persons who belonged to the royal party. He was accused

[1] Welwood's *Memoirs*, p. 146.

of bearing himself more like a prince than a religious, and his superiors feared that when the king, who was the protector of the Society, should be no more, they would incur great dangers through the animosity he had provoked. The General, therefore, asked leave to summon the father to Rome, promising that he should be treated with kindness. Of the seven kings then living in Europe, two, those of Sweden and Denmark, could not have been in friendly communication with the Jesuits, and neither of them in any way deserved to be called their protector. In France, in Spain, and in Portugal, it is difficult to understand what could be meant by the royal party, or by the fear of great calamities on the death of the king. Poland and England alone remain. Now there are in the collection other letters of Oliva to the King of Poland, and no secret is made about his name. The position of this father must have been quite peculiar. It is clear that he was not the king's confessor, and that he was not, like Father Petre, officially employed in political affairs ; yet he had received from the king such a position that he could not be recalled like an ordinary Jesuit, and that the General was obliged to use elaborate precautions in order to obtain the king's consent, and to make the measure appear in his eyes as gentle as possible. This suggests a suspicion of some mystery. The general of the Jesuits writes to a sovereign, whose name he does not venture to publish, for permission to summon to Rome a father of the Society, who, though neither the confessor of the king nor a member of the Council, possesses considerable influence, and enjoys so much of the royal favour that, although his imprudence has injured the court, a pledge must be given in removing him that he will be treated well. If we imagine the Jesuit James Stuart established in England exercising some influence over his father and the men of his confidence, and led astray, partly by zeal, partly by the presumption engendered by his royal descent, to commit some acts of imprudence, such as those which were so soon after so greatly exaggerated by popular rumour, and so cruelly punished by the popular fanaticism,

I

it would exactly answer all the conditions of the case. These letters of Oliva were prepared for publication by himself. Everything that is omitted is therefore designedly omitted, and the same caution which obliged him to conceal the name of the sovereign whom he addressed would have prohibited any more distinct allusion by which the position of the offending Jesuit might be betrayed.

These grounds, however, are far from sufficient to justify us in believing that James Stuart, who began life with so much discretion and reserve, afterwards became an ambitious and intriguing politician, and put in jeopardy his father's crown and the fortunes of his Order. That Order occupied in Poland a position in which great influence at court was combined with great unpopularity with his party among the nobles. At the election of 1668, a cry was raised that the new king should be forbidden to have a Jesuit for his confessor ; and, at the same time, the grand Hetman, Sobieski, was taking a Jesuit confessor with him to bless his arms in the Turkish war. To him, in the year 1673, Oliva sent his congratulations on his election. He tells him that the Jesuits whom he may place over his conscience or his chapel must be faithful to their rule, and abstain from politics ; and in speaking of the new king's affection for the society he uses a word, *svisceratamente*, that occurs in the same connection in the letter which is not directed. It may therefore refer to a father to whom Sobieski had committed some important functions in his court, and the name of the patron may be omitted lest the name of the offender should be surmised. Long after the probable date of this letter, John sent a bitter complaint to Oliva of the faults of the brethren in Poland. " I feel bound," he said, " both by interest and affection, to advise you to seek a remedy for the growing evils, and to remove from the Jesuits in Poland the too visible contagion of ambition and cupidity."[1] Between his predecessor and Oliva there had also been a friendly correspondence. Michael Korybuth was afflicted with a fabulous voracity. The stories told of the classical

[1] Salvandy, *Histoire de Jean Sobieski*, ii. 97.

gluttons of antiquity are eclipsed by his horrible achievements. Once, it is related, the burghers of Dantzig presented him with a thousand China apples, and before night he had devoured them all. Oliva, like a prudent general, attacked this monarch at his weak point. A quantity of the finest chocolate has been sent to him from Mexico, and he straightway despatches one of his fathers to lay it at the feet of the King of Poland, " impelled," he says, " by a reverent solicitude to minister as well as I can to the weakness of your stomach, which has already been fortified by drugs of this kind." On the whole, then, it is most probable that James Stuart is not the subject of the General's letter to the nameless correspondent ; and comparing his letters written to the two kings it is more likely to have been sent to John Sobieski than to his respected but inglorious predecessor.

The manuscripts I have quoted, most of which I owe to the industry and kindness of Father Boero, librarian of the Gesù,[1] by whose care they have been brought to light

[1] I subjoin a list of the documents for which I am indebted to Father Boero. They are manifestly too long to be published *in extenso* in a Review.

1. Lettre de la Reine Mère (Henrietta) au Card. Orsini. De Londres, October 30, 1662.
2. Lettre de la Reine Catherine au même. De Londres, October 25, 1662.
3. Voto in favore della promozione al Cardinalato del Signor d'Aubigny.
4. Favori e benefizi fatti ai cattolici d' Inghilterra dal Re presente (in sixteen articles).
5. Bellings to Father Thomas Courtenay, October 22, 1662.
6. Lettera dal Card. Orsini al Card. Sforza Pallavicino. 24 gennaio 1663.
7. Oblatio ex parte Caroli II. Magnae Britanniae Regis pro optatissima trium suorum regnorum Angliae, Scotiae et Hiberniae cum Sede Apostolica Romana reunione.
8. Certificate of Charles II. in favour of Sieur James Stuart, his natural son.
9. Another certificate of the king to the same.
10. Certificate of Christine Queen of Sweden concerning the same, on his conversion at Hamburg.
11. Letter of Charles II. to the General of the Jesuits, Oliva, at Rome. Whitehall, August 3, 1668.
12. Letter of Charles II. to his son James Stuart at Rome. Whitehall, August 4, 1668.
13. Letter of Charles II. to Oliva, General of the Jesuits, at Rome. Whitehall, August 29, 1668.
14. Letter of the same to the same, without date.
15. Reply of Oliva to the king's three letters. Livorno, October 14, 1668.
16. Certificate of Charles that he will pay the expenses of his son's voyage. November 18, 1668.
17. Letter of Charles to Oliva. Whitehall, November 18, 1668.
18 and 19. Two Memoirs written by Charles II. on the Catholic religion.

and transcribed, reveal the influence actually exerted by religious sentiment in those transactions between Charles and Lewis XIV., which, as the occasion of the Popish Plot, and the commencement of that policy which terminated in the Revolution of 1688, occupy so important a place in our history. The intention of declaring himself a Catholic manifested by the king in the early part of his reign, and checked by the attitude of Parliament, was revived, as we have seen, in the summer of 1668. In the month of April Charles first expressed to the ambassador of Lewis the wish to form an alliance with his master.[1] As he had lately joined a league of Protestant Powers, whose purpose it was to arrest the ambition of that monarch, he desired that the understanding between them might be private. He said that he wished to treat as between gentlemen, and that he preferred the word of Lewis to all the parchments in the world. At first Lewis received these advances with reserve, and Charles and his brother were unwilling to trust to the ambassador the secret object of their overtures. But early in 1669 Lord Arundel was sent to Paris, accompanied by Sir Richard Bellings,[2] who was instructed to draw up the articles of the treaty by which England was to join France against the Dutch; while Lewis undertook to support Charles with money, that he might be able to declare himself a Catholic without having a parliament to fear. Of the two leading ministers of the Cabal, the Catholic Arlington was friendly to the Dutch alliance, whilst Buckingham, a Protestant, was a partisan of France. Though the latter encouraged the notion of a French alliance, he knew nothing of his master's design relative to the Catholic religion. It was confided to Arlington, and at length overcame his political scruples, but he was never reconciled to the war with Holland, and he endeavoured to postpone hostilities until the change of religion had been declared. The French envoy suspected that he wished to delude

---

[1] See the Despatches of the French ambassadors Colbert and Ruvigny, in Mignet, iii. 10 sq., and iv. 42 sq.
[2] Clarke, i. 442.

Lewis into supplying the means by which the king's conversion could be published without danger, and when that was done, to avoid quarrelling with the Dutch.   The confidential envoys of Charles at Paris evidently entertained the same idea,[1] and the scheme was near succeeding.

Charles opened his mind to the French ambassador, the brother of the great Colbert, on the 12th of November 1669.   It was, he said, the most important secret of his life, and he would probably be considered mad, and all those with him who were undertaking to restore Catholicism in England.   Nevertheless he hoped, with the help of Lewis, to succeed in that great work.   The sects hated the Established Church more than the Catholic religion, and would make no resistance if they obtained the freedom they desired.   The great fortresses were in the hands of trusty men, and the Irish army might be relied upon, for Lord Orrery, who was at heart a Catholic, wold take the lead if Ormond should refuse.   On this point Charles was mistaken, for Orrery was sent for, and had an interview with the king, in which he was informed of the design, and refused to take part in it.[2]   " He ended by saying that he was urged by his conscience, and by the confusion he saw increasing daily in his kingdom, to the diminution of his authority, to declare himself a Catholic ; and that, besides the spiritual advantage he would derive from it, he considered also that it was the only way of restoring the monarchy."   Lewis applauded the intention, but advised that it should be postponed until after the war ; for he feared that he might be deprived of the assistance of England by the internal dissensions which that measure would be sure to provoke.   These two influences contended for a while in the mind of Charles, but he had not strength of purpose to resist the pressure that came from France.

---

[1] " Il m'a paru que l'affaire de religion étant ce qui tient le premier lieu dans l'esprit de M. le Comte d'Arondel, il n'y a que le retardement de la déclaration qui le touche ; et comme il croit que la guerre contre les Hollandais produiroit cet effet-là, c'est la seule raison pour laquelle il s'y oppose " (Turenne to Ruvigny : *Mémoires de Turenne*, i. 669).

[2] Morrice, *Life of Orrery*, p. 86.

Arlington said of him, that he saw at once what was to be done in every affair that was submitted to him, and supported his opinion with good reasons, but that he did not take the trouble to go into the objections that were made, and, if he was spoken to again, often allowed himself to be carried away by the opinions of others.[1] This description was now verified.   Charles shrank from the incongruity of the life he was then leading with a conversion which would be an arduous political undertaking.   " The danger," says Colbert, " greatly alarms all who are in the secret, yet it has no effect on the mind of the king.   But his mode of life—un peu de libertinage, si j'ose parler ainsi—makes him put it off as long as he can."   The famous journey of Henrietta, Duchess of Orleans, to Dover, in May 1670, settled the question in favour of France.   The treaty which was then signed by the four Catholic counsellors of Charles was first published from the English copy by Lingard.   Mignet gives it from the French archives, and the texts do not entirely correspond.

Henrietta was in the secret of the whole scheme from the beginning, and we learn through her that Charles was at that time in direct communication with the Holy See. There was a French prelate whom she patronised, Daniel de Cosnac, Bishop of Valence and afterwards Archbishop of Aix, a clever, witty, and extravagant man, highly ambitious of a cardinal's hat.   A year before the treaty was signed she wrote to him that, among a variety of affairs which were being treated between France and England, this country would soon have one with Rome of such consequence, and on account of which the Pope would be so happy to oblige the king her brother, that she was persuaded he would refuse him nothing.   She had already taken her measures with him to make him ask for a cardinal's hat, without saying for whom ; Charles had promised, and it was to be for Cosnac.[2] After her return from Dover, but a few days before that

---

[1] *Mémoires de Gourville*, p. 566, ed. Michaud.
[2] *Mémoires de Cosnac*, i. 383.

tragic death scene which Bossuet has made memorable by
the most striking of his orations, she informed the
Bishop that she had succeeded in her mission, and that
her brother had given her his word once more. Cosnac
was not satisfied with these assurances. The influence of
a Protestant king appeared to him a poor security for
his elevation. But the Duchess told him that she not
only had her brother's promise, but that the Pope had
already granted his request, and she informed him, he
says, of all that had passed between Pope Clement IX.
and the Kings of France and England.[1] This statement
is not, however, supported by any of her letters that have
been preserved ; and we must bear in mind the judgment
of his biographer, the Abbé de Choisy, on the character
of Cosnac : " He is a man of surprising vivacity, and of
such eloquence that it is impossible to doubt his words,
although their number is so great that they cannot all be
true." The agent on this occasion appears to have been
the Lady Diana Digby, daughter of the Earl of Bristol,
who had been so eager, six years before, to bring home to
Clarendon a charge of corresponding with the Pope and
cardinals. In June 1669, she arrived at Rome, in the
coach of Cardinal Rospigliosi, the Pope's nephew, and
lived for a time in one of his palaces so privately that her
own cousin, James Russell, was not allowed to see her.
But she was in correspondence with the English priests,
and it was believed in Rome that the nomination of
Archbishop Plunket to the See of Armagh, which was
much opposed by Spain, had been obtained by her
influence.[2]

Before anything could be done, the design was again
betrayed, and once more, and for the last time, Parliament
intervened. It was generally believed that the object of
the war against Holland was the establishment of the

---

[1] *Ibid.* ii. 81. " Retardabant eum voluptates blandissimae dominae, et
quaedam iners et pene somniculosa natura, quam tamen plura animi ingeniique
bona comitabantur. Huic quidem stimulos admovisse suspicor Clementem per
occultos homines " (Fabroni, *Vitae Italorum*, ii. 107).

[2] State Paper Office, " Italian States," Letters of Kent, June 29, July 6,
August 10, 1669.

Catholic faith. It is said that Arlington divulged the secret, partly in order to ruin Clifford, and partly to dissolve the French alliance. Even Protestant statesmen, talking in private with the king, spoke of it as a thing about which there was neither doubt nor concealment. Temple, before returning to the Hague in 1674, had an interview with Charles. He went, as he expresses it, to the bottom of the matter, showing how difficult, if not impossible, it was to set up here the same religion and government that was in France, and assuring him that even those who were indifferent to religion would not consent to have it changed by force of an army.[1] Charles relinquished his design, and recalled the warning which his father on the scaffold had intended to impress on his son, as well as on Juxon, by the famous word "Remember," —that if ever he came to the crown, he should so govern his subjects as not to force them to extremities. He declared that he was too old to go abroad again, and that he left that to his brother, if he had a mind to try it. For the ten remaining years of that reign, James took the lead in all the schemes for the restoration of the Church. It was of him that Coleman wrote in his fatal letter to La Chaise: "If he could gain any considerable new addition of power, all would come over to him as the only centre of our government, and nobody could contend with him further. Then would Catholicks be at ease, and His Most Christian Majesty's interest secured with us in England, beyond all apprehensions whatsoever." But the most Christian king, as he had prevented the declaration of religion before the Dutch war, endeavoured afterwards to have the design abandoned. He found that the English Parliament was not averse to the French alliance provided it was not used for the promotion of Popery and arbitrary power in England ; and Lewis was quite willing that religion should be sacrificed in order to save his popularity with the English Protestants. Finding that the supposed connection of the king's conversion with the French alliance had brought suspicion on his ambassador,

[1] Courtenay, *Memoirs of Sir W. Temple*, i. 425.

he replaced him by Ruvigny, who was a Calvinist. The new laws which were made against the Catholics, for the purpose of diverting suspicion, received his approbation ; and he acted upon the hint given him by Bristol, that the House of Commons would be favourable to the French alliance if the belief in the existence of the secret treaty for the restoration of Catholicism could be removed. That unhappy scheme defiled all that it touched, and neither those who shared in it nor those who condemned it came out of the transaction with honour.

If in the seventeenth century, which achieved so much for civil liberty, freedom of conscience was not established in England, the fault lay with the oppressed communities as much as with the crown or the dominant church. The Catholics and the Protestant sects were alike intolerant. The latter deserved what they received, and justified by their theories and their acts the penal laws by which they suffered. They were ready to do to others what was done to them. No religious party in the country admitted the right of minorities to the protection of the law. Religious liberty grew up in England as the fruit of civil liberty, of which it is a part, and in conjunction with which it has yet much way to make. But if the Protestants were not sincere in arguing for toleration, the Catholics were not honest in the means by which they endeavoured to obtain it. They sought as a concession that which was a right ; they wished for privilege instead of liberty ; and they defended an exception and not a principle. The Catholics of that age had degenerated from the old mediæval spirit, which stood by the right and respected the law, but did not stoop to power. In the great constitutional struggle they disregarded the impending absolutism and the outraged laws, and gave to the royal cause, when it was most in fault, a support which, by prolonging the contest, drove the parliamentary opposition into lawless extremes, and postponed for half a century the establishment of freedom. After the Restoration they again trusted their interests to the favour of the court, and were willing to purchase advantages for their religion by political guilt, and to gain private ends at the price of a common servitude. That criminal and short-sighted policy brought quick retribution upon them, and explains how the party which saved the constitution in 1688 imposed disabilities on those who, by similar inconsistency, had been the declared adversaries of that freedom which their church had helped to institute.

IV

THE CIVIL WAR IN AMERICA

ITS PLACE IN HISTORY [1]

FOR many years before the outbreak of the Civil War the
United States had become an object of anxiety or of
envy to many, of wonder and curiosity to all mankind.
Their prosperity, attached by a thousand beneficent links
to the prosperity of England, seemed even more splendid
and more secure. The rapid growth of their population
united the marvels of Lancashire with the marvels of
Australia ; it created vast cities, and peopled an enormous
territory with their overflow. The accumulation of riches
was as great as in Europe, whilst they were diffused so
much more generally that poverty as well as idleness was
all but unknown. All the sources of agricultural and of
mineral wealth enjoyed by the old world were tenfold
multiplied in the new, and were exempt from the drain of
those political causes which restrain commercial enterprise,
and expend on objects that yield no adequate return the
resources of the people. The money thus rescued from
unproductive waste was reserved to extend and equalise
education.

In a society organised like our own it is desirable that
education should be fitted, in nature and degree, to the
special character and occupation of the several ranks in
life to which each man belongs, but in a country where
there is no distinction of class, a child is not born to the

---

[1] A lecture delivered at the Literary and Scientific Institution, Bridgnorth, on
18th January 1866.

station of its parents, but with an indefinite claim to all
the prizes that can be won by thought and labour.   It is
in conformity with the theory of equality to check the
causes which disturb it, and to give as near as possible to
every youth an equal start in life.   Every American is a
self-made man, and they are unwilling that any should
be deprived in childhood of the means of competition.
Therefore in several States a system of instruction was
introduced which enabled a pupil to advance from the
first rudiments of knowledge to the end of a university
course, and to prepare himself for the learned professions,
without payment of a single shilling.   Taxation was
scarcely felt ; there was no standing army ; a navy that
weighed lightly in the Budget, an inconsiderable public
debt.   No neighbouring Power threatened the safety of
the country.   No internal disaffection disturbed the peaceful reign of law.   And this material progress, though checked
by serious drawbacks, was not obtained at the expense
of the higher elements of civilisation.

In literature at least I entirely dissent from the
opinion which denies to Americans an honourable place
beside European nations.   It may be said that they have
had no first-rate poet or painter, and that they have
done little for scholarship and antiquities.   But it appears
to me impossible with justice to deny that they are our
equals in political eloquence and philosophy, or that they
surpass us as writers on the history of the continent and
on the art of government.   In practical politics they had
solved with astonishing and unexampled success two
problems which had hitherto baffled the capacity of the
most enlightened nations : they had contrived a system
of federal government which prodigiously increased the
national power and yet respected local liberties and
authorities ; and they had founded it on the principle of
equality, without surrendering the securities for property
and freedom.   I call their success unexampled, not because
it is a forcible term, but because it exactly indicates the
peculiar character of the history of the American Constitution, and its special significance for ourselves.

And this reminds me of the wise and salutary regulation which obliges me here to abstain from topics which may supply the occasion of discord. In order to estimate in its nature and its causes the subject which is before us, we must be guided by the light of that political science which resides in serene regions, remote from the conflicts of party opinion ; a science whose principles are clear, definite, and certain, and not more difficult to apply than the principles of the moral code. It is in this spirit I wish to speak of the exemplary value of events in America. Example is of the first importance in politics, because political calculations are so complex that we cannot trust theory, if we cannot support it by experience.

Now the experience of the Americans is necessarily an impressive lesson to England. Our institutions as well as our national character spring from the same roots, and the fortunes they encounter must serve as a beacon to guide us, or as a warning to repel. Now the world had never yet beheld a Democracy combining a very advanced civilisation with a very extensive territory. Democracies have coexisted with the highest social and intellectual refinement, but then they had not to overcome the difficulty of space. Those which extended their dominion perished between the cognate perils of anarchy and despotism. Above all, a Democracy has never even attempted to adopt the system of representative government which is the supreme and characteristic invention of the British monarchy. Therefore it had become almost an axiom in political science that that which ancient Rome and modern France attempted and failed to accomplish is really impossible ; that Democracy, to be consistent with liberty, must subsist in solution and combination with other qualifying principles, and that complete equality is the ruin of liberty, and very prejudicial to the most valued interests of society, civilisation, and religion. That was, until a generation ago, the verdict of history ; whose decision the Americans have undertaken to reverse. No more memorable attempt was ever made by men. If they succeeded in their momentous pleading—if they proved by experiment that a vast community, rich, intellectual, and civilised as those of Europe, guided by the accumulated experience of the older hemisphere and without its special difficulties, prejudices, and dangers, could be governed by the principles of pure Democracy, without any sacrifice of those more exalted objects which political forms exist to serve, they would inevitably exercise an overwhelming pressure on the ancient society of Europe. If they could demonstrate that to be possible which was deemed a chimera, because it is contradicted by the experience of ages,—if they showed us that the objects aimed at by our political and social system may be enjoyed still more amply without the penalty which Europe has always paid, in the shape of so much iniquity and so much suffering, by irresponsible authorities, sanguinary wars, and wanton injury, in the oppression of class by class, of race by race, and of religion by religion,—in the elaborate, deliberate, intentional degradation of the weaker party, for reasons of state, or religious zeal, or by the pride of blood, or by the blind and resistless action of superior wealth and force— if they could exhibit to the world the spectacle of a country as extensive as Russia, as secure from aggression as France, as intellectual as Germany, as free and as obedient to law as Great Britain, cursed with no restrictions on personal freedom, without fleets or armies, without pauperism or national debt,—if, in short, America could give the light without the shade of political life, then I believe that the venerable institutions of European polity would go down before that invincible argument.

Those institutions have grown old, and their old age is vigorous, because we are confident that they will stand the tests of expediency and right, because they are either necessary or conducive to the general advantage. But if America should destroy the validity of that defence, then the only inducement by which the masses of mankind will be made to tolerate the evils and injustice incident to our system of society, will be the short-lived argument of force. There were many who believed that the mighty problem was solved, and that America had accomplished the work;

and this conviction has already exerted a disturbing influence over the affairs of Europe. Historians affirm that the French Revolution was partly caused by the successful revolution which founded the United States. If that could be at a time when nothing had been achieved but independence, and their Constitution was only beginning the career it has so grandly run, it is easy to estimate how much their influence would be increased by the permanence of their success. Accordingly America exercised a power of attraction over Europe of which the great migration is only a subordinate sign. Beyond the millions who have crossed the ocean, who shall reckon the millions whose hearts and hopes are in the United States, to whom the rising sun is in the West, and whose movements are controlled by the distant magnet, though it has not drawn them away?

The time has come for all men to perceive that these judgments were premature. Five years have wrought so vast a change, that the picture which I have faithfully given of the United States as I found them under President Pierce could not be realised in the awful realities of the present day. Their debt now imposes a heavier charge than that which England contracted in the great war, and it has been incurred, not to repel invasion or defeat a national enemy, but to slaughter fellow-citizens, and carry fire and sword over the cornfields and the homesteads of a country which is their own. The armies they have raised and lost were larger in proportion to the population than those of the Emperor Napoleon or the Emperor Alexander. Their prisons have been peopled with disaffected citizens. Part of their territory has become desolate, because those who should have tilled the soil were taken by the war ; part because the armies laid it waste. The Union which was founded and sustained by the attachment of the people has been restored by force, and the Constitution which was the idol of Americans is obeyed by millions of humbled and indignant men, whose families it has decimated, whose property it has ravaged, and whose prospects it has ruined for ever.

Doubtless, in this crisis of its political existence the nation has displayed many noble qualities: patriotism, fortitude in adversity, respect for authority, and in some measure the difficult arts of subordination and discipline. The civil power has never been threatened or weakened by the resistance of a popular commander; differences of social station have not interfered with the organisation of the army; military rank has not disturbed the level surface of ordinary life, the officer and the soldier have been merged in the peaceful citizen. In the number of the leaders there have arisen men of high ability, and at least one who has built himself a name among names that will never die. Nevertheless the judgment which overtook the American Union was not undeserved. Convulsions such as this spring from causes of commensurate importance, and cannot be the work of a short time or of a few men. Americans themselves would acknowledge this, but their explanations contradict each other. Some would say that the fault was with slavery, others would accuse the tyranny of the North. On the solution of the question depends the place which is to be assigned to the American Civil War in the history of the world.

It is remarkable that the Constitution was little trusted or admired by the wisest and most illustrious of its founders, and that its severest and most desponding critics were those whom Americans revere as the fathers of their country. Washington explained, in a conversation which Jefferson has recorded, his fears for the permanence of the new form of government. He stated that at one period of the deliberations the Constitution promised to satisfy his ideas, but that the great principles for which he contended had been changed in the last days of the convention. He meant the law which required a majority of two-thirds in all those measures which affected differently the interests of the several States. This provision, which would have given protection to minorities, was repealed in consequence of a coalition between the Southern and Eastern States, for the benefit of the slave-owners in the South, and of

the commercial and manufacturing interests in the East.
He said "that he did not like throwing too much into
democratic hands ; that if they would not do what the
Constitution called on them to do, the government would
be at an end, and must then assume another form." He
stopped here, says Jefferson, "and I kept silence to see
if he would say anything more in the same line, or add
any qualifying expression to soften what he had said, but
he did neither." There was one superior to Washington
among the statesmen who surrounded him—Alexander
Hamilton ; and his prognostications were still more gloomy.
He said: "It is my own opinion that the present government is not that which will answer the ends of society,
by giving stability and protection to its rights, and it will
probably be found expedient to go into the British form."
"A dissolution of the Union after all seems to be the
most likely result." Later in his life he called the Constitution a frail and worthless fabric, and a temporary
bond. The first President after Washington, John Adams,
said "he saw no possibility of continuing the Union of
the States ; that their dissolution must necessarily take
place." On another occasion he pointed out the quarter
from which he anticipated danger. "No Republic," he
said, "could ever last that had not a Senate deeply and
strongly rooted, strong enough to bear up against all
popular storms and passions. That as to trusting to a
popular assembly for the preservation of our liberties, it
was the merest chimera imaginable ; they never had any
rule of decision but their own will."

If I were to continue my extracts I could still more
clearly show that the authors of the most celebrated
Democracy in history esteemed that the most formidable
dangers which menaced the stability of their work were
the very principles of Democracy itself. With them the
establishment of a Republican government was not the
result of theory, but of necessity. They possessed no
aristocracy, and no king, but otherwise they inherited our
English laws, and strove to adapt them as faithfully as
possible to a society constituted so differently from that

K

in which they had their origin.   The earliest interpreters of the Constitution and the laws strove to be guided by English precedents, and to approach as nearly as they could to the English model.   Hamilton is the chief expounder of these ideas: " It has been observed that a pure Democracy, if it were practicable, would be the most perfect government.   Experience has proved that no position in politics is more false than this.   The ancient Democracies, in which the people themselves deliberated, never possessed one feature of good government.   Their very character was tyranny, their figure deformity.   If we incline too much to Democracy, we shall soon shoot into a monarchy.   Those who mean to form a solid Republican government ought to proceed to the confines of another government.   There are certain conjunctures when it may be necessary and proper to disregard the opinions which the majority of the people have formed.   There ought to be a principle in government capable of resisting the popular current.   The principle chiefly intended to be established is this, that there must be a permanent will."

These are not individual opinions.   They were shared by a powerful party, that watched the cradle and guided the first steps of the American Republic, and they display the moderate, wise, and English spirit which presided over its early councils.   In this combination there was an inconsistency, which time necessarily developed.   The laws of England do not flow from a single principle, they are the result of many influences, they acknowledge authority and tradition, balance one set of interests by another, and aim at serving very various rights, and are determined by many considerations of expediency.   Of all conceivable things that which is most alien to their spirit is to sacrifice any distinct interest or particular right to the requirements of some vague abstraction.   But it was difficult for Norman kings and feudal parliaments to legislate in a manner that would satisfy the wants of American society. Modifications were needed, and they were naturally directed by that new element which called for them, a purely Democratic principle.

The most eminent advocate of this principle, whom
Tocqueville has called the most powerful apostle that
Democracy ever had, was Jefferson.   One or two sentences
taken from his writings will furnish the most forcible
illustration of the contrasts which then existed together,
and whose struggles for supremacy were to occupy the
history and decide the fate of the American Constitution.
Jefferson says that "his object was to restrain the
administration to Republican forms and principles, and
not permit the Constitution to be construed into a
monarchy, and to be warped, in practice, into all the
principles and pollutions of their favourite English model.
Every people may establish what form of government
they please ; the will of the nation being the only thing
essential.   I subscribe to the principle that the will of
the majority, honestly expressed, should give law.   I
suppose it to be self-evident that the earth belongs to the
living ; that the dead have neither powers nor rights in it.
No society can make a perpetual Constitution or even a
perpetual law.   The earth belongs always to the living
generation.   Every Constitution then, and every law,
naturally expires at the end of thirty-four years."   Between
this revolutionary doctrine and the ideas derived from
England, there was an irreconcilable antagonism.   It was
intolerable to Jefferson that the engagements of one
generation should bind another, that any rights should be
deemed too sacred to be confiscated by the vote of a
majority.   He desired law to be in a constant state of
fluctuation, and every change to realise more and more
the momentary wishes of the people.   No man, therefore,
and no interest would enjoy any security against popular
feeling, and men would be compelled to struggle permanently not only for influence, but for safety.

Yet Jefferson himself was one of those who despaired
of the Union.   When the great controversy of the
extension of slavery first arose, he wrote to a private
friend : "I consider it at once the knell of the Union.   It
is hushed indeed for the moment, but this is a reprieve
only, not a final sentence.   A geographical line coinciding

with a marked principle, moral and political, and conceived and held up by the angry passions of men, will never be obliterated, and every new irritation will make it deeper and deeper."

But it seems clear to me that if slavery had never existed, a community divided by principles so opposite as those of Jefferson and Hamilton will be distracted by their antagonism until one of them shall prevail ; and that a theory that identifies liberty with a single right, the right of doing all that you have the actual power to do, and a theory which secures liberty by certain unalterable rights, and founds it on truths which men did not invent and may not abjure, cannot both be formative principles in the same Constitution. Absolute power and restrictions on its exercise cannot exist together. It is but a new form of the old contest between the spirit of true freedom and despotism in its most dexterous disguise. One scene I often look back upon, for it appears to me to contain the key of that which followed. I was sometimes present at the debates of a Convention which met at Boston after an interval of thirty years to revise the Constitution of the most enlightened State of the Union. There were treated some of the first principles of politics, and one of the questions was as to the appointment of the judiciary. It is quite an elementary truth that a judge should be independent, and saved from the danger of being influenced by the favour of either the court or the people. But an eminent and highly cultivated orator, now one of the first of American statesmen, now perhaps quite the first in European fame, spoke in favour of short, I believe annual, terms of office, and for the election of the judges by the people. He did not dispute that the laws would be more honourably and faithfully administered by independent judges. But he maintained that consistency is better than justice, that the people, as the source of all authority, ought to control those to whom they delegate it, and that no argument from expediency ought to be allowed to disturb the application of the Democratic principle. I could not help remembering that there is also a principle of absolute monarchy in the world, which makes the Crown the only source of authority, and makes the judiciary agents of the court. It is the boast of modern civilisation to have undone this system and to have substituted for it that which experience proves to be most favourable to justice. But the absolutists of Democracy and monarchy rank their principles of government at a higher value than the purposes of society and civilisation, and create an idol to which they are ready to sacrifice the safeguards of property, the protection of virtue, and the sanctity of private life. All governments in which one principle dominates, degenerate by its exaggeration. The unity of monarchy gravitates towards the despotism of a single will. Aristocracy which is governed by a minority, inclines to restrict that minority into an oligarchy. In pure Democracies the same course is followed, and the dominion of majority asserts itself more and more extensively and irresistibly. We understand liberty to consist in exemption from control. In America it has come to mean the right to exercise control.

In order to describe the encroachment of this illiberal and tyrannical principle, it would be necessary to pass in review the entire history of the last seventy years. I can only illustrate my meaning by the language which eminent Americans themselves have used. The President Madison wrote: "When a majority is included in a faction, the form of popular government enables it to sacrifice to its ruling passion or interest both the public good and the rights of other citizens. If a majority be united by common interests, the rights of the minority will be insecure." Justice Story says that the people must be reminded of the fundamental truth in a republican government, "that the minority have indisputable and inalienable rights; that the majority are not everything and the minority nothing; that the people may not do what they please." Channing says: "The doctrine that the majority ought to govern passes with the multitude as an intuition, and they have never thought how far it is to be modified in practice, and how far the application of it ought to be controlled by other principles." Finally, let me quote the words of a very recent publication, which is from the pen of the chief of Sherman's staff, of a man therefore who cannot be supposed insane. "How can there be justification for revolution under a government where there is universal suffrage? For my part, I would rather say, how is it possible that thoughtful men should so long have tolerated a system which is at the same time so oppressive and so extremely stupid?"

We must bear in mind the one decisive contrast between Europe and America, that there society is cut adrift from the traditions and influence of an ancient civilisation. The nations of Western Europe are so bound to each other by their origin, by their close intercourse, and the similarity of social interests and character, that a comprehensive public opinion extends over their boundaries, and sustains in each the habits, ideas, and constitutions which are common to all. The protest of European opinion would react powerfully in favour of those habits and ideas against any European State that should reject them. But Americans enjoy no such protecting influences, and nothing is safe that is not supported by popular favour. The ideas of past generations and of civilised contemporaries are not permitted to share or to limit the absolute authority of the present moment. The revolutionary principle which Jefferson introduced cuts them off from one as completely as the Atlantic separates them from the other. The voice of European civilisation, and the voice of the past alike, come to them from another world. History is filled with records of resistance provoked by the abuse of power. But whereas in the old world the people produce the remedy, in America they produce the cause of the disease. There is no appeal from the people to itself. After having been taught for years that its will ought to be law, it cannot learn the lesson of self-denial and renounce the exercise of the power it has enjoyed. Therefore it has been laid down by political writers as a universal rule that a degenerate republicanism terminates in the total loss of freedom. Many have prophesied that this would be the end of the American Republic.

But a confederacy possesses one resource against such a catastrophe which is denied to a single State. Centralisation finds a natural barrier in the several State governments. "This balance," says Hamilton, "between the national and State governments is of the utmost importance ; it forms a double security to the people. If one encroaches on their rights they will find a powerful protection in the other." That is indeed the peculiar merit of American institutions ; it alters but does not settle the question. It gives to liberty in its struggle against centralisation a valuable auxiliary in the feudal system, but it does not decide the issue. That aggressive, absolute spirit which is the bane of pure Democracies prevailed much sooner and more completely in some States than in others, and the States which it animated strove to give it the supreme direction of the central government of the Union. They did not choose that other portions of the nation should be exempt from a kind of power to which they themselves submitted. But as soon as the different States made themselves the champions of opposite principles of government, the Union was in jeopardy.

Now there was one broad line of demarcation between the States, which divided them both in political principles and financial interests, and coincided moreover with the difference of climate and of modes of cultivation, as well as with certain early diversities of race. I mean, of course, that which was the immediate cause of the late revolution, that which, you will say, I have kept out of sight too long, the division between the slave States and the North.

If my present theme were the institution of slavery in general, I should endeavour to show that it has been a mighty instrument not for evil only, but for good in the providential order of the world. Almighty God, in His mysterious ways, has poured down blessings even through servitude itself, by awakening the spirit of sacrifice on the one hand, and the spirit of charity on the other. But negro slavery in America had features of its own too strongly marked to admit of general observations. Arguments have been advanced in mitigation, stories have been published to prove the greatness of the actual suffering. The judgment which I shall ask you to accept, for our present purpose, shall be founded neither on the existence of great abuses nor of kind and Christian masters, but on the provisions of the servile law. The most suggestive enactment I could adduce to illustrate the idea of personality in the negro, is, that if the life of a slave was taken by the law, his owner received his value in money from the State treasury. No slave could make a valid contract ; therefore he could not contract a legal marriage, even with the consent of the master. All the safeguards of virtue, all penalties on the breach of the marriage law, or of those laws which are anterior to all human legislation, were held inapplicable to the negro family. I am sure that the voice of nature and of humanity constantly mitigated the law of the land, but it is certain that the Southern jurisprudence denied that the negro is bound by the same moral code as ourselves, and that this belief was shared by the leaders of secession.

In a great speech at the beginning of the movement, Mr. Stephens, the Vice-President of the Confederacy, spoke these words : " The corner stone of our new government rests upon the great truth that the negro is not equal to the white man ; that slavery, subordination to the superior race, is his natural and normal condition. Our new government is the first in the history of the world based upon this great physical, philosophical, and moral truth." Here, then, was a society adopting inequality, not as the natural product of property, descent and merit, but as its very foundation,—a society, therefore, more aristocratically constituted than those of feudal times. The Southern slave-owner was in contradiction to the two principles which animated the Democracy of the Northern States. He denied the absolute essential

equality of all men in civil rights ; and he denied the
justice of the doctrine that the minority possesses nothing
which is exempt from the control of the majority, because
he knew that it was incompatible with the domestic
institution which was as sacred to him as the rights of
property.   Therefore the very defect of their social system
preserved them from those political errors which were
transforming the original characters of the Northern
Republics.   The decomposition of Democracy was arrested
in the South by the indirect influence of slavery.

Thus it came to pass that the South, to protect themselves, sought to restrain the central power, while the
North wished to make it superior to all restraint.   To
one party it was a sword, to the other a shield.   And so
it happened that the long reign of Southern politics at
Washington, down to the year 1860, provoked no rupture,
because they desired self-government, and not empire ;
whereas the victory of the North in the election of Mr.
Lincoln gave at once the signal for dissolving the Union.
The Constitution failed to provide against the consequences which were to be expected whenever considerable diversities of character, of material interests, and of
political spirit should estrange the several States.   For
this reason certain States accepted it with reluctance, and
joined the Union with conditions which betrayed the
apprehension that perhaps the bargain might turn out ill.
Virginia, in the act of ratification, declared " that Powers
granted under the Constitution, being derived from the
people of the United States, may be resumed by them
whensoever the same shall be perverted to their injury or
oppression."   New York and Rhode Island said the same.
From time to time these fears revived, and single States
meditated revoking the Act of Union.   At length certain
measures for the protection of manufactures in the East
aroused a united opposition in the agricultural States, who
were to pay for the benefit of the others.   That was the
first threatening of the storm that did not burst for thirty
years.

Two great men stood forth as the champions of two

great causes, and the contest derived from the eminent
ability of the combatants all the interest of a personal
struggle.   The philosopher of the South, Mr. Calhoun, of
whom it was said, to describe his influence, that as often
as he took a pinch of snuff all South Carolina sneezed,
put forward what was called the theory of nullification.
He maintained that if an interested majority passed a
law injurious to the settled interests of any State, that
State had a right to interpose a veto.   He was answered
by Daniel Webster, the most eloquent of Americans, who
asserted the absolute right of a legislature where all were
fairly represented, to make laws for all.   Then Calhoun
insisted that if a State could not prevent the execution of
a law which it deemed unconstitutional and injurious, it
had the right to withdraw from the Union which it had
conditionally joined.

The North shrunk from provoking this extremity, and
made concessions which pacified the people of the South.
But at the same time Webster laid down, in immortal
speeches, that the Union is not a compact between the
States, but a fundamental law no longer subject to their
choice, and that each State is bound up with the rest
by cords that cannot be legally severed.   Thenceforward
the opinion of Webster prevailed among American jurists.
The right of redress was taken away from the South, and
the Northern Republicans, taking advantage of this constitutional victory, entered upon those violent courses
which ended in making the Union intolerable to those
who were opposed to them.   At that time the abolitionists commenced their crusade, which was directed as much
against the Union, which they denounced as an " agreement with hell and a covenant with death," as against
slavery itself.   It became a settled doctrine among them
that the North and the South could not continue together,
and they made the public familiar with the idea of dissolution.   " The Union," said Mr. Horace Greeley, the
editor of *The Tribune*, " is not worth supporting in connection with the South."   But the stronger part of the
Republicans resolved to make themselves masters of the

central government, for the purpose of coercing the South to submit to their political opinions. The Lieutenant-Governor of Massachusetts confessed that " the object to be accomplished was this, for the free States to take possession of the government."

The spirit in which they meant to exercise it is expressed with the characteristic force and candour of American language by the representative of the same State in Congress : " When we shall have elected a President, as we will, who will not be the President of a party, nor of a section, but the tribune of the people, and after we have exterminated a few more dough faces from the North, then if the slave Senate will not give way, we will grind it between the upper and nether millstones of our power." A pamphlet, which was widely circulated and was read in Congress, contains the following sentence : " Teach the slaves to burn their masters' buildings, to kill their cattle and hogs, to conceal and destroy farming utensils, to abandon labour in seed time and harvest, and let the crops perish." Mr. Chase said, in 1859: " I do not wish to have the slave emancipated because I love him, but because I hate his master." A Senator from Ohio said very truly : " There is really no union now between the North and the South, no two nations on earth entertain feelings of more bitter rancour towards each other than these two nations of the Republic."

In this state of public feeling and political division, the candidate of Abolitionists and Republicans was elected President. Four years before, a former President, Mr. Fillmore, prophesied the catastrophe that would ensue. " We see a political party presenting candidates for the Presidency and the Vice-Presidency, selected for the first time from the Free States alone, with the avowed purpose of electing these candidates by suffrages from one part of the Union only, to rule over the whole United States. Can it be possible that those who are engaged in such a measure can have seriously reflected on the consequences which must inevitably follow in case of success ? Can they have the madness or the folly to believe that our

Southern brethren would submit to be governed by such a Chief Magistrate?"

The opinion we must form on the revolution that followed ought to be guided by the events which led to it, not by the motives of the leaders. In point of fact they were divided, like the Union, by the question of slavery. To one party it was the real object of the war; they believed it could not be safe against the assaults of Northern politicians, whatever might be the pledges of the federal government. Another party desired secession in order to establish a new Union on the old principles which the North had disavowed. The great issue between them was the arming of the slaves. Those who deemed it too dear a price to pay for independence succeeded in preventing it by narrow majorities until the eve of the fall of Richmond. When the Act was passed by which the negroes would have acquired the benefits without the dangers of emancipation, it was too late, and the end was at hand.

Slavery was not the cause of secession, but the reason of its failure. In almost every nation and every clime the time has come for the extinction of servitude. The same problem has sooner or later been forced on many governments, and all have bestowed on it their greatest legislative skill, lest in healing the evils of forced but certain labour, they should produce incurable evils of another kind. They attempted at least to moderate the effects of sudden unconditional change, to save those whom they despoiled from ruin, and those whom they liberated from destitution. But in the United States no such design seems to have presided over the work of emancipation. It has been an act of war, not of statesmanship or humanity. They have treated the slave-owner as an enemy, and have used the slave as an instrument for his destruction. They have not protected the white man from the vengeance of barbarians, nor the black from the piti-less cruelty of a selfish civilisation.

If, then, slavery is to be the criterion which shall determine the significance of the civil war, our verdict ought, I think, to be, that by one part of the nation it was wickedly defended, and by the other as wickedly removed.   Different indeed must our judgment be if we examine the value of secession as a phase in the history of political doctrine.   When the Confederacy was established on the right of secession, the recognition of that right implied that there should never be occasion for its exercise.   To say that particular contingencies shall justify separation is the same thing as to say that the Confederate government is bound within certain limits, under certain conditions, and by certain laws.   It is a distinct repudiation of the doctrine that the minority can enforce no rights, and the majority can commit no wrong. It is like passing from the dominion of an able despot into a constitutional kingdom.

Further, definite safeguards were provided against the abuses which had sapped liberty in the Union.   One of these was the imposition of taxes for the advantage of interests which were confined to certain States, and at the expense of the others.   Therefore it was enacted that "no bounties shall be granted from the treasury, nor shall any duties or taxes on importations be levied to promote or foster any branch of industry."   One great means of throwing influence into the hands of the central government had been internal improvements.   It was enacted that they should never be carried out by the Confederate government.   Finally, the abuse of patronage had furnished the President with such opportunities for corruption that I have heard as many as 60,000 offices changed hands as often as a term expired.   It was enacted that none but Cabinet Ministers should be removed from office without the cause of the removal being submitted to the Senate.   These were the political ideas of the Confederacy, and they justify me, I think, in saying that history can show no instance of so great an effort made by Republicans to remedy the faults of that form of government.   Had they adopted the means which would have ensured and justified success, had they called on the negroes to be partners with them in the perils of war and in the fruits of victory, I believe that generous resolution would have conferred in all future ages incalculable blessings on the human race.

They would have supplied the advocates of freedom hereafter with a peerless model. They would have realised the ideals of its friends, and disarmed the resistance of its foes. The cause that was to triumph comes forth from the conflict with renovated strength, and confirmed in the principles which must react dangerously on the other countries of the world. The spurious liberty of the United States is twice cursed, for it deceives those whom it attracts and those whom it repels. By exhibiting the spectacle of a people claiming to be free, but whose love of freedom means hatred of inequality, jealousy of limitations to power, and reliance on the State as an instrument to mould as well as to control society, it calls on its admirers to hate aristocracy and teaches its adversaries to fear the people. The North has used the doctrines of Democracy to destroy self-government. The South applied the principle of conditional federation to cure the evils and to correct the errors of a false interpretation of Democracy.

After paying a tribute to the genius of General Lee, the lecturer concluded as follows : It is a noble sight to see this mighty soldier, the greatest of the countrymen of Washington, exhorting his people to obey their conquerors, and giving the example of peaceful retirement and submission. But it is also a noble sight to see the chief of a mighty and victorious nation, who was not trained to greatness, but was taken from the tailor's board and raised to his high place when passions were inflamed by an intoxicating triumph and an awful crime, staying the hand of vengeance, remitting punishment and disbanding armies, and treating as an equal the man who had been so lately and so long the most terrible of enemies, and whose splendid talents had inflicted on the people of the Union a gigantic loss in treasure, blood, and fame. It is too soon to despair of a community that has among its leading citizens such men as these.

V

THE RISE AND FALL OF THE MEXICAN EMPIRE[1]

THE scene of the tragedy which I will attempt to describe is a country on which Nature's fairest gifts have been lavished with an unsparing hand, but where man has done his utmost to thwart the designs of Providence. Its social condition is so far removed from our experience that I must ask you to forget this evening the maxims and even the political terms we use nearer home.

Mexico possesses a territory more than thrice as large as France, with the fertility of the tropics, and the climate of the temperate zone, seated between two oceans, in the future centre of the commerce of the world. Its wealth in precious metals is so enormous that the time will come when the market will be flooded with silver, and its price will not allow the mines to be worked with profit. The only drawbacks on its prosperity are the badness of the harbours, the excessive dryness of the plains, and the disappearance of the forest timber, a curse which almost always follows the footstep of the Spaniard.

When England recognised the independence of the Spanish colonies, Mr. Canning declared that he had called a new world into existence to redress the balance of the old. But it was long before the new States justified the boast, and it is still generally believed that in point of political and material success they contrast much to their disadvantage with the North American Republic. In the

---

[1] A lecture delivered at the Bridgnorth Literary and Scientific Institution on 10th March 1868.

143

greater part of South America this is no longer true, for in several of those vast communities population and trade are growing at a rate that exceeds that of the Union.

Mexico is the saddest and most conspicuous exception in the midst of the general improvement. It is the pride of the colonial system of Spain, and the one merit in which it was superior to our own, that it succeeded in preserving and partially civilising the native race. The English settled in a region where the natives were hunters and wanderers, unskilled in the cultivation of the soil, who roamed into the West to elude the grasp of civilisation, or perished by its contact. The colonists retained their own congenial laws, the purity of European blood was maintained, and the portentous problem of race was happily averted. But in Mexico Cortez found a numerous and settled population, dwelling in cities, tilling the land, and brilliantly though superficially civilised. It was part of the Spanish system to protect, to preserve, and to convert the conquered heathens, whose number vastly exceeded that of their masters ; a people of mixed blood sprang up between them, and thus there were three races separated by a very broad line, and isolated by the pride and the jealousy of colour. The Indian nobles were mostly exterminated, and the land was distributed among the families of a small group of conquerors. This arrangement of property remains unchanged. The natives are still without any interest in the land, and the immense estates have not been subdivided. In one of the richest districts on the Atlantic, the coast, for one hundred and fifty miles, is owned by one proprietor.

A society so constituted could not make a nation. There was no middle class, no impulse to industry, no common civilisation, no public spirit, no sense of patriotism. The Indians were not suffered to acquire wealth or knowledge, and every class was kept in ignorance and in rigorous seclusion ; when, therefore, the Mexicans made themselves independent, the difficulty was to throw off, not the bondage, but the nonage in which they had been held, and to overcome the mental incapacity, the want of enterprise, the want of combination among themselves, and the want of the enlightenment which comes from intercourse with other nations. They formed a republic after the model of their more fortunate neighbours, and accepted those principles which are so inflexible in their consequences, and so unrelenting in their consistency. It soon appeared that there was not propelling power in the State equal to the heavy burden of a half-barbarous population. The intelligent minority was too undisciplined and too demoralised to elevate and to sway the degraded millions of the Indian race. The habits of authority and subordination departed with the Spaniards, and the faculty of organisation could not exist in a people that had never learned to help themselves. No man of very superior character and understanding arose. The leading men in the various provinces sought to maintain their own power by the continuance of anarchy; they combined against the central authority as fast as it changed hands, and overthrew thirty Presidents in thirty years. The requisite conditions of a Republican government did not exist. There was the greatest social inequality that can be conceived between the wealthy landowners and the Indian masses, who possessed neither the mental independence conferred by education nor the material independence which belongs to property. There was Democracy in the State, while society was intensely aristocratic.

The largest landowner in Mexico was the Church; and as there was no religious toleration, it was the Church of the whole nation, the only teacher of the moral law to the natives, the sole channel through which the majority of the people had access to the civilisation of Christendom. Therefore the clergy enjoyed an influence of which there has been no example in Europe for the last five hundred years, and formed a strong basis of aristocracy and the most serious barrier to the realisation of the Democratic principle that nominally prevailed. To establish a real Democracy the first thing to be done was to reduce this immense and artificial influence. For the

L

last twelve years this has been the one constant object of the Democratic party. It was a war of principles, a struggle for existence, on either side, in which conciliation was impossible, and which could only terminate by the ruin of one of the contending forces.

Now, as long as the conflict was confined to America, the Republicans could not be utterly defeated, for they could fall back on the unfailing sympathy and resources of the United States. Sooner or later the end would be the confiscation of the lands in mortmain, and the downfall of the Conservatives. Their only hope was in the assistance of Europe, and the establishment of a monarchy under foreign protection. Long before the antagonism became so definite and so extreme, the idea had begun to gain ground that a monarchy was the only form of government adapted to the character of Mexican society, and capable of arresting its decay ; and the monarch, if he was not to be a party chief, must be a European prince. Negotiations for this object were opened as early as 1846 ; Mexican emissaries, acting in concert with the then President, addressed themselves to Prince Metternich, who received them coldly, to Bavaria, and then to France, where the plan was favourably entertained, when it was interrupted by the revolution of 1848. It was revived twelve years later by the progress of events in Mexico. In 1857 the Democratic party carried a new Constitution, abridging the privileges of the clergy, and including a law of mortmain which obliged them to convert their estates into money.

This was the signal for civil war. The Conservatives, led by a young man who, at the age of twenty-seven, had shown a remarkable capacity for war, Miguel Miramon, gained possession of the capital, and their President was recognised by Europe. The Constitutional President held the important seaport of Vera Cruz, and was recognised by the United States. His name, destined like that of his rival to a wide and melancholy celebrity, was Benito Juarez. He was an Indian of pure blood, nearly sixty years old. He had ascended to power by means of his eminence as a lawyer, and because, in the midst of almost universal corruption, he was deemed incorruptible. Unlike the intriguers and the soldiers of fortune who were his rivals, he had risen slowly, without perfidy and without violence, —a patient, steadfast man, and, as we should say, a man of extreme opinions. It would seem that in this educated, ambitious, successful Indian, the pent-up hatred of the oppressed race for the oppressor had broken forth, and formed his strongest political motive; and that he was striving for the social and political emancipation of his people when he tore down the privileges and annihilated the power of the class that lorded over them. He professed the principles of 1789, principles which had triumphed in France by a civil war, a reign of terror, ten years of military despotism, and sixty years of intermittent revolution. There was no reason to think they would succeed more easily in a country so backward as Mexico, but Juarez was ready to abide the issue. As there was no system of regular taxation, and all manufactured articles were imported by sea, the customs were the chief source of revenue. It was an advantage to Juarez to possess the chief seaport of the country, and as he dwelt under the cannon of European men-of-war, he was careful not to make enemies by plundering the foreigners.

Miramon, up in the interior, had neither the same resources nor the same restraint. There was no money to be had but that of foreign residents, or of the Church. He could not rob his own party, so he determined to turn to the other source of supply. He had so used his power, and his lieutenant, Marquez, had acted so ferociously, that the English Minister had left Mexico, when Miramon seized a sum of £130,000 belonging to British landholders, which was deposited at the Legation. He also contracted a loan with the Swiss banker, Jecker, on terms so exorbitant that it seems to have been a stratagem to embarrass those who were to come after him. These two measures were eventually fatal to Miramon, for they were the cause of the European intervention.

Juarez immediately obtained his recognition by England by promising to restore the stolen money, and to satisfy other British claims. He made the same promise to France. With this moral support, and by undertaking to grant away to his partisans the property of the Church, he obtained the means of expelling Miramon from Mexico, and in 1861 he was elected President for a term of four years. He at once dismissed the Spanish and the Papal envoys, decreed the absolute confiscation of the Church lands, and carried out with ruthless energy the triumph of his opinions. But he proved incapable as a ruler, and utterly unequal to the desperate task of restoring order in a country distracted by passion and ruined by anarchy.

The condition of affairs in the summer of 1861 is described by the English Minister in the following passages, which are important because they determined the policy of England : " As long as the present dishonest and incapable administration remains in power, things will go from bad to worse ; but with a government formed of respectable men, could such be found, the resources of the country are so great that it might easily fulfil its engagements, and increase threefold the amount of its exportations, not only of the precious metals, but of those productions for which they receive British manufactured goods in exchange. Mexico furnishes two-thirds of the silver now in circulation, and might be made one of the richest and most prosperous countries of the world ; so that it becomes the interest of Great Britain to put a stop by force, if necessary, to its present state of anarchy, and insist on its government paying what it owes to British subjects. All the respectable classes look forward with hope to a foreign intervention as the sole means of saving them from ruin, and preventing a dissolution of the Confederation, as well as a general rising of the Indians against the white population. Every day's experience duly tends to prove the utter absurdity of attempting to govern the country with the limited powers granted to the Executive by the present ultra-liberal Constitution, and I see no hope of improvement unless it comes from a foreign intervention, or the formation of a rational government, composed of the leading men of the moderate party, who, at present, are void of moral courage and afraid to move, unless with some material support from abroad. If the question was, what form of government would most conduce to the welfare of Mexico, by the establishment of order and a permanent state of things, there can be no doubt that a Constitutional monarchy is the one most likely to have central power sufficient to enable it to consolidate the nation, perhaps the only form of government that would give much hope of such a result ; but as the question is not what is best for Mexico, but what are the wishes of the Mexican people, I fear that the answer must be that the great mass of the intelligent population are in favour of Republican institutions. Many well-educated and intelligent individuals who stand well in society form a well-grounded desire for a strong government, but these people are unfortunately timid, and passive in action, ready to accept what is done for them, but incapable of doing anything to bring about what they desire."

As it turned out, these were prophetic words. The sale of the Church property was carried on in a very disorderly way, and the money was squandered. A scheme to satisfy the urgent European claims with money lent by the United States, though entertained by the American Government, was rejected by the Senate, and in July 1861 the Mexican Congress resolved that all payments on European agreements should be suspended for two years.

The Powers most concerned in this act of repudiation— France, Spain, and Great Britain—now determined to intervene jointly, and to obtain by force of arms some real security for the property of their subjects, and for the establishment, if necessary, of a more trustworthy government. The conjuncture was favourable, for the Civil War had just broken out in the United States, and from that quarter there was no immediate danger of interruption. Spain took the lead, her military establishment at Cuba enabling her to act promptly, with some suspicion of a desire to recover her ancient dominion.   England followed warily, with an eye only to mercantile interests.   France did not yet reveal her intentions, and probably had not yet matured them.

The allied forces, amounting to about 6000 men, without means of transport or materials for a campaign in the interior, were placed under the command of the Spanish general Prim, a clever, showy, and ambitious officer, but a capricious and unstable politician.   On their arrival, the town and fort of Vera Cruz were evacuated by the Mexican troops.   In this extremity Juarez strengthened himself by putting at the head of the Ministry General Doblado, the leader of the moderate party, a man whose reputation for caution and ability stood high, and whose acts in office prove that it was well-deserved.   In January 1862, he issued a decree directing all those who should be taken in arms against the Republic to be tried by court-martial and put to death as traitors.   This is the law by which the Emperor was to die, and which gave a legal character to his execution.   Doblado had an interview with Prim, expatiated on the deplorable condition of the country, and undertook that the legitimate demands of the allies should be faithfully complied with, provided only they would recognise the existing government.   These terms seemed acceptable to the allies, who were not equipped for a campaign, and they took Doblado at his word.   But the agreement had to be sent to Europe for approval, and in the meantime it was arranged that the allies should move up from the pestilential swamp of Vera Cruz to healthier quarters on the first range of hills.   This placed them within the outer line of the Mexican defences, and it was stipulated that if the preliminaries were not ratified, before commencing hostilities they should first withdraw to the plain below.

The claims of the three Powers had now to be specified. Those of Spain and England were clear, and easily ascertained.   The French commissioners demanded, in addition to other large sums, three millions sterling for the banker Jecker.   Their colleagues protested against this excessive demand. They affirmed that the sum advanced by the banker to Miramon was only £160,000, and they pointed out that he was not a Frenchman but a Swiss, and that the guardianship of Swiss interests in Mexico pertained to the American Legation. Jecker was immediately naturalised a Frenchman, and the French Government bought up his bonds. Agents were sent for this purpose with sealed instructions to America, two of whom, when they discovered the errand upon which they were employed, indignantly threw up the commission. Whilst this transaction was sowing discord in the allied camp, several Mexican exiles of the Conservative party made their appearance at Vera Cruz. One of these was Miramon. He was arrested and sent away by the British Commodore, on the ground that the expedition could not connect itself with one party while acknowledging the government of the other.

Miramon was speedily followed by General Almonte, for many years the chief agent of the Conservative party in Europe, and the secret councillor of the French Government, a man of high character and great influence. He stated that he came with a mission from France to establish a provisional government, to introduce a monarchy, and to procure the election of the Archduke Maximilian. The English and Spanish Commissioners demanded his expulsion, when General Lorencez arrived with French reinforcements, and announced that Napoleon had rejected the convention with Doblado, that he had sent Almonte to Mexico, and meant war. The alliance of the three Powers was at once dissolved; the Spaniards sailed for Cuba in English ships, and France was left alone, to accomplish the avowed design of erecting a throne beyond the Atlantic.

In the intention of the Emperor Napoleon, the Mexican expedition was the first step towards the execution of a bold and magnificent scheme, to which he gave the name of the regeneration of the Latin world. The ancient rivalry between France and England was expanded into the rivalry of the Latin with the Anglo-Saxon race. If we carry back our thoughts for a century, it will not be difficult to find in the history of the two nations the motives which suggested the idea. Scarcely one hundred years ago vast territories in Canada, on the Mississippi, and in the West Indies belonged to the Crown of France, and French adventurers of great daring and ability were laying the foundation of an Empire in Hindostan. One by one these possessions have gone, and France, watched by jealous neighbours, has nearly lost the power of expansion in Europe.

What has been, in the meantime, the progress of England? The colonies which France has lost have almost all been won by her. England, not France, wields the sceptre of the Great Mogul. Her people have encircled the globe with a girdle of British settlements. New continents, I may almost say, have arisen out of the Southern ocean to receive the incessant overflow of her population. Her colonial empire is a nursery of mighty nations, that carries to the distant places of the earth the language and the laws of home. George III. inherited dominions peopled perhaps by ten million human beings. His grand-daughter reigns over two hundred millions. In America the children of our race are waiting the time when the whole continent shall be theirs.

But on that continent there are thirty millions of men, not of French descent, but of a stock allied with the French, who derive their literary culture and intellectual impulse from Paris, whose traffic is carried on with French ports, who look up to France as their head, and turn to her to protect them from being absorbed by an alien race. The trade of France with South America is nearly equal to her trade with the United States, and is more profitable because it is carried in French ships. In the ten years before the expedition, it had grown from £6,000,000 to £20,000,000 a year. South America is the largest and safest opening that remains for the development of French commerce, the most increasing market for French industry. It was manifestly the interest of France to prevent it from falling under the control of the narrow mercantile policy of the United States, and to secure her own influence over nations with such a future. In the words of the Emperor: "It is not our interest that the United States should grasp the whole Gulf of Mexico, the Antilles, and South America, and become the sole dispensers of the produce of the New World. We have seen by sad experience how precarious is the fate of an industry which is forced to seek its raw material in a single market, under all the vicissitudes to which that market is liable." The establishment of a French dependency in Mexico would have checked the southward progress of the Union, and have cut the continent in two.

When Juarez repudiated his engagements with European creditors the Confederates had won their first victories, and the North was not able to repel the intervention upon its frontier. Shortly after, the Southern Commissioners were seized on board the *Trent*, and England began to arm. The French Emperor calculated that he would be able to do his work without interruption, and that England, in case of need, would help him to support the South. Therefore, from the end of 1861 he lent a willing ear to the Mexican exiles, who displayed the sufferings and the capabilities of their country, and allured him with the splendid vision of a nation to be regenerated by France. They persuaded him that the presence of his troops would be welcomed, that there would be no serious resistance, and that a powerful party would rally to his standard. In this belief, and with Almonte in their camp, the French advanced against Mexico, 6000 strong. On the 5th of May 1862, they appeared before Puebla, the second city in the land, on the road from Vera Cruz to the capital. They were received with so vigorous a cannonade that they were forced to retire to a position where they could await reinforcements without danger of being dislodged. After this military repulse, public opinion in France supported the Emperor in despatching an army of 30,000 men, provided with all the appliances of war.

They landed in the autumn, and the winter was spent in preparations.

A whole year had been lost before Puebla fell, after an obstinate defence, and in June 1863 the French entered the city of Mexico. The early reverses and the long delays of the French greatly strengthened the position of Juarez. The invasion exalted the Indian leader of an extreme party into a champion of the dignity and the independence of the country, and his tenacity in upholding the cause did not allow this halo to depart from him even in the worst times. The capital was not fortified, and when the French appeared, Juarez carried the seat of his government to one of the Northern towns.

A new provisional government was instituted, in which Almonte was associated with the Archbishop of Mexico, and an assembly of notables, selected and convened by the French, met to decide on the future of the country. Many of the principal men in the capital who had been invited, refused to attend, and the assembly was composed of Conservatives who took their orders from Almonte and the French. The orders were to proclaim a monarchy, and to offer the Crown to the Archduke. They were obeyed on the 8th July 1863. The long-deferred hopes of the Mexican royalists seemed to be fulfilled, when a deputation proceeded to Europe to invite the Archduke to ascend the throne of Montezuma. Ferdinand Maximilian, the next brother of the Emperor of Austria, had long occupied a peculiar and exceptional position in his native country. There were circumstances which made him appear a possible rival to his brother, and the many errors of Francis Joseph, the waning confidence in his fortune and his judgment, kept alive the habit of looking to the Archduke, who was altogether excluded from the conduct of affairs, as a refuge in extremity. He possessed some of the best qualities of a ruler, honesty and firmness of purpose, a kind and true heart, and a mind fixed on high designs. In spite of much and various experience of mankind, he retained an unpractical imaginativeness, which is often connected with extreme cultivation, and a certain impetuous generosity frequently marred the effect of his sagacity. Though undoubtedly very intelligent, he was so often deceived that he must have lacked the faculty of judging men and choosing friends, without which there is no success in government. His ardent, lofty spirit, perpetually curbed and chafed by the prevailing dulness, selfishness, and incapacity in Austria, imparted something that was cold and sarcastic to his manner. His outspoken censure of his brother's unstable policy caused an estrangement between them, which was increased by his marriage with the daughter of the wise Leopold, a clever and accomplished woman, whose family has grown great by renouncing those principles of strict legitimacy which Austria specially represents. The Archduke was the last Austrian Governor of Lombardy. In that thankless office it was impossible to conciliate the Italians, and he could not permanently serve the interests of his country. But he made many friends, and men believed that he would willingly have been the Minister of a less unpopular system. It was even whispered that he had wished to set up a throne for himself in Lombardy and Venice, separate from the Austrian monarchy. At least he had so far deserted the ancient ways of his family as to fall under the ban of distrust and suspicion at Vienna. About the time of the marriage of the Princess Royal he visited the British Court, and made so favourable an impression that there were some who regretted that he could not have been a candidate for her hand. For who could then have dreamed that the reserved and unpretending Prussian was to be the spoilt darling of victory, while the genial, frank, and brilliant Austrian was destined to a traitor's death? He devoted his care to the navy, a department always neglected in Austria, and the virtue of his administration became apparent when the fleet which he had created won the greatest sea-fight of our time. The war of 1859 deprived him of his high position, and reproaches and recriminations followed, which separated him yet more from the Emperor. He dwelt in his castle of Miramar at the head of the Adriatic, mourning over wasted talents, a ruined career, and an unsatisfied ambition.

Very soon the prospect of a new adventure opened before him. By a strange fatality his wife, the daughter of a Princess of the House of Orleans, was an enthusiastic Bonapartist, and not only admired, but trusted the Emperor Napoleon. When, therefore, he proposed to hand over his conquest to the Archduke, hoping thereby to conciliate Austria, the Archduchess Charlotte urged her husband to accept it. Their unsettled position must have become very irksome to her, for when they left their home Maximilian wept bitterly, and she showed no emotions but hope and joy. His brother's government employed strong measures to dissuade him from accepting, and it was decided that he must renounce his place in the succession, and be counted last after all the princes of the line.

When the vote of the Assembly of Notables was made known to him, he replied that he could not accept the crown unless he was assured of the support of the great Powers, or until it was offered to him by the free choice of the whole Mexican people. The French are skilled in managing the machinery of a spontaneous election ; and in April 1864, a second deputation carried to Miramar a sceptre of Mexican gold, with the assurance that the whole nation had elected Maximilian Emperor. In reality the French were masters of a very small portion of the country, and the vast majority were not polled at all. Where the French were present there was no serious difficulty, though in some places the chief inhabitants were thrown into prison before they gave in their adhesion. Maximilian was fully informed that the pretended election was nothing but a ceremonious farce. A Mexican Republican made his way to Miramar, and warned him that the real feeling of the country was adverse to the invaders, and that the expedition would end in disaster.

But the promises of France were excessively enticing. The French army was to complete the pacification of the

country, and a powerful corps was to be left for several
years in the service of Maximilian. France negotiated a
loan in his behalf, and seventeen chests filled with gold
pieces found their way to Miramar. The Archduke was
not in a position to disregard such inducements, for his
private fortune was in disorder, and the first £300,000
of the Mexican loan went to clear his debts. Other
points were raised which have been kept secret, and the
friends of Maximilian still look for important revelations.

At his trial he instructed his counsel to say that
Napoleon had required the cession of a portion of
Mexican territory as large as Great Britain, and that he
had indignantly refused to dismember the country which
had given him a crown. He accepted it at a time when
the tide of success had turned in the American War, and
the prospects of the Confederacy were no longer hopeful.
The Archduke demanded a pledge that he should be
supported by a French alliance in case of war with the
United States ; and it is positively asserted that Napoleon
gave the required pledge. He gave it believing that
England would join him in recognising the South, if it
was found that its resistance would be crushed without
aid from Europe, and the time came when he made the
proposal of a joint recognition to Lord Palmerston. It
happened that the two foremost statesmen in the Ministry
had made speeches in the provinces which appeared
to show a disposition favourable to the Confederates ;
and the Emperor believed that they would carry their
colleagues with them. This was the gravest miscalcula-
tion he made in the whole Mexican affair. The Cabinet,
taking one of the most momentous resolutions ever
adopted by a Ministry, rejected the proposal, and the
Emperor shrank from a war single-handed with the
United States.

Maximilian, on his part, undertook to pay a million a
year while the French remained, and to liquidate all those
accumulated claims which Juarez had rejected. In fact,
he submitted to conditions impossible to meet, and commenced an undertaking predestined to financial ruin. He

reached Mexico in June 1864, and was favourably if not warmly received. The French had ruled the country through the provisional government for a whole year, with almost uninterrupted military success. But they had encountered a difficulty of a formidable and unexpected kind. Juarez had had more than two years to accomplish the overthrow of the clergy, and their property had passed into the hands of speculators, chiefly foreigners, who, it was thought, would not easily be compelled to restore it. The Church party had called for intervention in the hope of recovering these losses, and when the French placed the leaders of the party at the head of the State, they preferred their claims with a sure expectation of success.

The Church in France is supported by the State, and owns no independent property. The French supposed that the practice of their own country could not be unsuitable to Mexico, where a revolution would be required to restore the ancient order, and where the clergy would not bear a comparison with the salaried priesthood of France. The demand was summarily refused. The Episcopate united to denounce the sacrilegious invaders, and the Archbishop ceased to be a member of the provisional government. The breach, for the moment, was complete ; and the only hope of the clergy was in Maximilian. He knew that, for a Sovereign to be strong, he must be identified with no party. It was his mission to conciliate and blend together interests severed by years of antagonism. In declining the crown for the first time, he had signified that he would consent to receive it only as the gift of the entire nation. In accepting it afterwards, he made known that he looked upon himself as the elect of the nation, not as the nominee of a powerful interest. From the moment of his arrival he held out the olive branch to the Republicans, and sought their confidence by offering them place and power. Many accepted his offers, and he was surrounded by men who were hateful to those who had seated him on the throne. In adopting this policy it was impossible to draw a line, to examine antecedents, or to reject utterly any candidate for favour. The Emperor was often deceived, and lost on one side without gaining on the other.

After a long delay, which exasperated the trembling holders of Church property, as well as those whom they had despoiled, he decided that all legal purchases should be confirmed, and those which were fraudulent revised, but that nothing should be restored to the clergy, who were to be paid by the State. The Nuncio quarrelled with him upon this, and left the country. Maximilian, irritated by the hostile attitude of the clergy, went further, and restored what was called the *Exequatur*, a law forbidding any document to be published in ecclesiastical affairs without the consent of the civil power. This right has been abandoned by his brother, in Austria ; by the Italian Government, last year ; and even in Mexico, by Juarez, who adopted the voluntary principle. It could not be defended as a liberal law, and its revival seemed to be simply a blow at the independence of religion. The clergy protested that they had not borne the burden of civil war and brought foreign armies into the country, in order that a prince of their choosing should confirm decrees which had made their property the spoil of their enemies.

They declared that their position was worse under their friend then it had been under their persecutor Juarez. Thenceforth they withdrew their support, and observed a hostile neutrality, watching the time when the Emperor, driven to extremities, would be ready to purchase their assistance at any sacrifice they might demand. In some instances they even fomented the Republican opposition.

This was the first great and visible disaster that the Empire incurred. Another was soon known to be imminent. Financial capacity, rare in every country, was not to be found in Mexico ; and Napoleon, who wished his creation to succeed, sent out a Chancellor of the Exchequer from France, with a staff of clerks. But the imported Minister died, and could not be replaced. The finances broke down so completely that Maximilian was obliged to ask for money from the military chest of the French army, and thus fell into the power of its com-

mander.   As he could not fulfil his engagements with
the Emperor Napoleon, he was guilty of a breach of the
treaty signed between them, and gave France an excuse,
when her turn came, to justify her own breach of faith.

The year 1865 passed prosperously, on the whole.
Maximilian visited many of the towns, saw what he could
with his own eyes, and devoted his time to the fabrica-
tion of decrees by which he hoped to regenerate the
country.   These decrees are generally sensible and just ;
they incline in a good direction, but not always by the right
road, and ornamental superfluities sometimes usurp the
place of more difficult but more essential things.   Maximilian was an anxious and determined educator, and his
zeal was praiseworthy, for ninety per cent of the people
could neither read or write.   But it shows a want of
practical capacity when in a community wanting the first
necessaries of popular instruction the Sovereign founds
an Academy of Sciences, and gravely inculcates on his
Ministers the importance of encouraging the study of
metaphysics.   He found himself in the rare position of a
lawgiver called to legislate in a country for which everything remained to be done, and he enjoyed the luxury of
carrying out, at least on paper, systems nurtured in days
of visionary retirement.   He had not time or vigour to
execute much of what he had projected.

There was one question that called for an act of high
and generous statesmanship.   The Indians had been
reduced by their poverty and want of energy to the position of serfs.   They were in debt to their landlords, and
the whole hopeless labour of their lives, without the
chance of profit or release, was due to their creditors.
They had greeted the coming of Maximilian as the dawn
of their deliverance, and he might have made them the
willing prop of the imperial throne.   In the 800,000
square miles of Mexico, peopled by 8,000,000 of men,
but capable of sustaining 100,000,000, it would have
been easy, without any spoliation, to distribute land among
the countrymen of its ancient owners.   Maximilian
adopted a half measure.   He abolished the debts of the

Indians, and thus made them free ; but he did no more, and left them to relapse, under pressure of the old causes, into the old degradation. The Indians were not satisfied, and the landowners were alienated.

Something, but not enough, was done for the creation of a native army to defend the crown and country when the French should depart. An Austrian and a Belgian corps were formed, but did not answer expectation. Next to the French, the most efficient body was the division of the Indian general Mejia, a man of a very pure fame. But the French were successful in all they undertook during the whole of 1865. The Republican bands were scattered, many of their generals made their submission, and Juarez, driven from place to place, disappeared at last at a point in the extreme north of Mexico, on the American frontier, more than a thousand miles from the capital. It was reported that he had escaped into the United States. At this time also the four years for which he had been elected expired, and it was impossible to convene a Congress for a new election. Many of his followers now held that he had ceased to govern, and the Vice-President Ortega, the defender of Puebla, claimed the vacant post. The strict legality which had been the strength of the position of Juarez was seriously impaired, and his authority was unquestionably shaken. The country was in a wretched state of insecurity and misery. Plunderers and assassins plied their trade under pretence of being real combatants. Mexican warfare is often scarcely distinguishable from armed robbery, and, as it was the plan of the Republicans to fight in small guerilla bands, the line separating the soldier from the brigand was often indistinct. The Government thought the time had come to exterminate these bands, and to protect the inhabitants against their incursions. The victory over the regular army was complete, and it seemed that men who infested the roads, when organised resistance was over, did not deserve the treatment of prisoners of war.

On the 2nd of October Maximilian drew up a decree ordering all who should be taken with arms in their

M

hands to be shot, and when he signed it he signed his own death-warrant. Immediately after its publication a Republican force, commanded by Arteaga, was defeated, and the leaders were captured. In obedience to the new order the Imperial General Mendez put them to death. But the Republicans, though dispersed and dispirited, were not destroyed. A report made to the Emperor in November 1865 estimates their force at 24,000 men, and Juarez had not abandoned the struggle. He remained on Mexican territory, in a town on the Rio del Norte, from which a boat could take him in a few minutes to the American bank, and he remained in communication with the generals of his party. There he waited for the deliverance which he knew was coming. For at that moment, near the close of 1865, his cause was taken up by an ally so powerful and so much feared as to be able, without firing a shot or wasting a single life, to expel the French from Mexico, and to lay the Empire in the dust.

The United States had watched the intervention and the erection of the Empire with anger and alarm. They knew that it had sprung from a desire to cripple their influence, and they could not be indifferent to the presence of an European army on their frontier while they were embarrassed by a civil war. They denied that the Empire was the free choice of the Mexicans, and they highly disapproved of an Emperor that was absolute, for he retained in his own hands all the powers of the State. They refused to recognise him, but they remained neutral, determined not to act until they could act decisively. They rejected various schemes for assisting Juarez with money in return for land, and they declined not only the overtures of Napoleon and of Juarez, but one which was still more tempting. During the siege of Richmond the Confederates proposed that they should unite their armies for the conquest of Mexico and of Canada, but the North refused.

When the war of Secession was over, the Government of Washington had to apply a little diplomatic pressure to the Emperor Napoleon to hasten the recall of his troops.

The pressure quickly took the form of threats, and Napoleon very speedily gave way. Events were passing in Europe which made him impatient that Maximilian should restore his legions. In June 1866 war broke out in Italy and in Germany, and in the first week of July Prussia had struck a blow that made half Europe tremble, and menaced the military supremacy and the pride of France. In these circumstances it was certain that the offensive language of America could not be resented, and Mr. Seward used his advantage with cruel complacency. Napoleon informed Maximilian that he must provide for himself, and he informed the American Government that he would retire from Mexico in March 1867.

Rumours of this strange correspondence, and of its probable result, reached Mexico and gave new spirit to the Republicans. Maximilian had refused permission to 25,000 confederates to settle in his dominions ; but stragglers found their way to the armies of Juarez, and in June 1866 the important town of Matamoros was surrendered to Escobedo by Mejia. From the moment of that reverse fortune began rapidly to change ; and as the French retired from more distant posts, swarms of Republicans appeared in every direction.

When Maximilian learnt the altered intention of Napoleon, he foresaw the end, and spoke of abdication. The Empress persuaded him to remain, while she undertook a journey to Europe. She would compel the French Emperor to fulfil his promises. She would induce the Pope to reconcile the clergy with the Empire. She failed utterly in both endeavours, and in her last interview with Pius IX., perceiving that all hope was ended, she went out of her mind. Early in October the news reached her husband, and then his courage gave way. He had lately exchanged what was called a Liberal for a Conservative Ministry, and had offered the principal departments to two French generals. But they were forbidden by Napoleon to accept, and still no substantial help came from the clergy. Worn out with illness and sorrow, deserted on all sides, and knowing that his Empire was

crumbling, Maximilian started for the coast with an
undefined intention of sailing for Europe. His most
trusted adviser, a Belgian, who had accompanied the
Empress, attempted at this conjuncture to draw him
away by an appeal to his ambition. He described the
discontent of the humbled Austrians and assured him
that they wished his brother to abdicate, while sympathy
for himself was increasing throughout the country.

Francis Joseph was aware of this intrigue, but he
made a last effort to save his brother by restoring to him,
if he would return, his position at the head of the princes
of the blood. An aide-de-camp of Napoleon arrived in
Mexico to hasten the departure of the troops, and
instructed to use everything but force to induce Maximilian to abdicate. The French did not like the
dishonour of leaving him to his fate, and they hoped, if
he ceased to reign, to make their own terms with the
Mexicans, and to leave behind them a government not
utterly hostile to themselves. That the expedition was
a gigantic failure, injurious to the reputation of the army
and the stability of the throne, could not be disguised.
But the blow would be more keenly felt if the man on
whom they had made war for four years, and with whom
they had refused to treat, remained unshaken in his office,
victorious over the arms and arts of Napoleon III. So
great was their urgency that Maximilian felt insulted,
and at last believed himself betrayed.

Whilst he was wavering and lingering near the coast,
an American frigate appeared at Vera Cruz, conveying
General Sherman and Mr. Campbell, accredited as envoys
to Juarez. They had sailed from New York on the 11th
of November, when it was supposed that Maximilian had
abdicated, leaving the French in the country. The
Government at Washington were determined that in that
case their candidate, and not that of Napoleon, should
prevail. Mr. Campbell was charged to offer support and
aid to the Republic, and the presence of the ablest soldier
of the Union indicated ostentatiously of what nature that
aid was to be. When these envoys found that Maximilian

had not departed, they understood that their mission was a blunder and withdrew. The Emperor did not believe that an American Minister, escorted by such a personage as Sherman, had come all the way to Vera Cruz and had gone away without doing anything. He persuaded himself that France and America had come to an understanding, and had made a bargain of which his crown was to be the price. The pressing invitations to depart with the French appeared to him perfidious, and he thought it would be disgraceful that his life should be rescued by those who had bartered his throne.

Meantime the Church party, which had so long coldly stood aloof, thought that the moment had arrived when it could impose its own conditions. It was represented to the Emperor that the disappearance of the invaders would remove the cause of his unpopularity, and that good patriots would support him now, who had refused to acknowledge the nominee of a foreign Power. Miramon arrived from Europe at the critical moment and offered his sword to Maximilian. The Prussian Minister also advised him to remain. The clergy promised their powerful aid, and he yielded. There was nothing for him to look forward to in Europe. No public career was open to the man who had failed so signally in an enterprise of his own seeking. His position in Austria, which was distressing before, would be intolerable now. He had quarrelled with his family, with his church, with the protector to whose temptations he had hearkened. And for him there was to be no more the happiness of the domestic hearth.

In Mexico there were no hopes to live for, but there was still a cause in which it would be glorious to die. There were friends whom he could not leave to perish in expiation of measures which had been his work. He knew what the vengeance of the victors would be. He knew that those who had been most faithful to him would be most surely slaughtered ; and he deemed that he, who had never yet been seen on a field of battle, had no right to fly without fighting. Probably he felt that when a monarch cannot preserve his throne, nothing becomes him better than to make his grave beneath its ruins. He yielded, and returned, sullenly and slowly, to the capital. What concessions had been wrung from the party in whose hands he was, I do not know. But he addressed a letter to the Pope, expressing regret for the policy which had failed, and at Rome, where he was once re-garded as a persecutor and almost an apostate, the letter was hailed as a solemn and complete retraction.

From that moment Maximilian was no longer the chief of a national government, but a partisan leader, who had not even the control of his party. He laid aside the pomp of Majesty, and lived in private houses, especially as the guest of the clergy. He declared that he was only provisionally the chief of the State, and held office only until a national assembly had decided what should be the future of Mexico. He invited Juarez to submit his claim to the same peaceful arbitration, and proposed that there should be a general amnesty, to stop the shedding of blood. The Republicans saw nothing in all this but the signs of weakness, and of their own approaching triumph. They opposed no obstacles in the way of the departing French, but they closed in overwhelming numbers upon the feeble army of the Empire.

The defeat of Miramon on the great North road in February compelled Maximilian to take the field. He put himself for the first time at the head of his troops, and joined Miramon at Queretaro. On this day last year he was surrounded and besieged by Escobedo with an army which rose speedily to more than 40,000 men. Marquez was sent to Mexico for reinforcements, but he never returned, and spent the short time that remained in wringing money from the inhabitants. The siege pro-ceeded slowly, and on the 24th of April Miramon made a successful sally, and opened for a moment the road to the capital. But the men were worn out with fighting, and the Emperor refused to leave them. He declared he had not come to Queretaro to fly from danger. To those who saw him during those anxious days, haggard and aged, with a long beard flowing over his breast, and the fever of despair in his eyes, conducting the defence and constantly under fire, it seemed that he was longing for the glory of a soldier's death. At length the supplies were nearly exhausted, the certainty of the treason of Marquez removed all hope of relief, and it was resolved that the garrison should make an attempt to cut its way through the enemy on the 15th of May. It was too late. For four days Lopez, the second in command, had been in communication with Escobedo, and had accepted a bribe of £1400. Late in the night of the 14th he saw the Emperor; and then, at two in the morning, he introduced a Republican general into the fort. This general was disguised, and carried concealed arms. He remained two hours, and examined the interior of the works. Then Lopez withdrew the Imperial sentries, and their posts were silently occupied by the soldiers of Riva Palacio, the only officer who had been excepted, by name, from the decree of October.

At daybreak the bells of the churches of Queretaro announced to the Republican camp that the place was won. The traitor went up to the Emperor's room, and told him that the enemy was in the town. Maximilian rushed forth, and was stopped by Republican soldiers, who did not recognise him. Lopez whispered to the officer who it was. Then the generous Mexican allowed the Emperor to pass, pretending to take him for a civilian; and he escaped to a fortified position at some distance. Here he was joined by the faithful Mejia, and as many officers and men as could hew their way through the columns of Republicans that were now pouring into the town. Miramon alone attempted a forlorn resistance. A shot struck him in the face, and he fell, blinded with blood, into the hands of his enemies.

The position occupied by the Imperialists was swept by artillery and could not be defended, and at eight o'clock they surrendered. Among the prisoners was Mendez, who had caused the decree of October to be executed on Arteaga and his companions. He was shot

the same day.   The Emperor was shut up, with Miramon
and Mejia, in a cell of the Capuchin convent, and it was
announced to them that they would be tried by court-
martial, under the decree of January.   From that moment
Maximilian retained no hope of life.   He presented his
war-horse to Riva Palacio, the most chivalrous of his
enemies, and telegraphed to Mexico for the Prussian
Minister, and for legal advice in preparing his defence.

Mexico was already besieged by a Republican army,
and hollow shells were thrown into the town, stuffed
with telegrams proclaiming the fall of Queretaro.   But
Marquez, the most detested of the Imperial generals,
wished to gain time, and he suppressed the news.
Maximilian had deposited his abdication in the hands of
the President of Council, to be produced if he died or fell
a prisoner ; but Marquez compelled him to keep it secret,
and prevented for several days the departure of the
defenders who had been summoned.   The most eminent
of these was the advocate Riva Palacio, the father of the
general, a leading Republican, who had refused all solicitations to serve the Emperor in the days of his power.
The others seem to have been less distinguished, but they
were all chosen among the Republicans.   The Prussian
Minister, Baron Magnus, had lived on intimate terms with
the Emperor, and had been one of the advisers of the
expedition which had ended so fatally.   No European
Power was less compromised in Mexican affairs, or less
obnoxious to the dominant party than Prussia, and it was
thought that Baron Magnus would be the best mediator.

The seat of Government was at San Luis, 200 miles
beyond Queretaro, but connected with it by telegraph.
Two lawyers remained with the Emperor, while Riva
Palacio and the Prussian Minister repaired to San Luis to
intercede with Juarez.   The court-martial which was to
try the prisoners met on the stage of the theatre of
Queretaro on the morning of Friday, the 14th of June.
The house was lighted up and full of spectators.
Maximilian had been ill in bed for several days, and self-
respect forbad him to appear on such a scene.   The two

generals were present. Their case was manifestly desperate ; yet the defender of Mejia caused a deep impression when he claimed for his client the same mercy, which, in spite of stern decrees, he had always shown to his captives, and appealed to Escobedo to say how he had fared when he was Mejia's prisoner. The defence of Miramon was less dignified and less loyal. He pleaded that he had had no command while the French were in the country, that he had been hostile to the Empire which had sent him on an idle mission to Europe, and that he had offered his services to the chief of the Republic. These facts were true ; and at Paris Miramon had said openly that the end of the intervention would be to make him President again. Maximilian knew all this, and he knew the manner of his defence. This must not be forgotten when we come to the last scene of all, and see how the Emperor bore himself towards the brave but ambitious soldier, who had been ready to desert the cause in which he was to die.

The strongest points of the indictment against Maximilian were, that he had known the decree of January, which had been published long before he came ; that the necessity of foreign support must have proved to him that he was not the legitimate, national Sovereign, and that he could not therefore justify the October decree, by which it was pretended, with great exaggeration, that 40,000 Mexicans had suffered death ; that he was responsible for the continuance of civil war after the departure of the French, and for the introduction of Belgian and Austrian soldiers, whose Governments were not at war with the Republic, and who came therefore in the character of filibusters and assassins. The reply to these charges was narrow and technical, and not worthy of the occasion. It amounted in substance to that which the Emperor had said himself: " You may dispute the original probability of my success, but not the sincerity of my motives." As to the decree of October, his advocates defied the prosecution to name a single instance in which he had refused a pardon.

A little before midnight on the 15th the prisoners

were found guilty, and their sentence having been confirmed by Escobedo on the Sunday morning, they were informed that they would be shot at three o'clock on the same day. Meanwhile the issue of the trial had been foreseen, and the friends of the Emperor were pleading with Juarez for his pardon. On the ground of political expediency their position was undoubtedly more favourable than that of men restricted to legal arguments. During the war in Mexico a yet deadlier struggle had raged beyond the American border. The author of Secession was not a foreigner, like Maximilian, but a citizen of the country in which he had conspired. He too had been defeated and captured, and then, while European monarchies suppressed revolution with atrocious cruelty, Jefferson Davies had been released by the great Republic. Therefore, they said, the honour of Republican institutions was in the keeping of Juarez, and required that Mexico should follow that example of triumphant clemency, and should betray neither hatred for the past nor alarm for the future.

The President and his minister, Lerdo, listened patiently but coldly. They said that Europe could give no guarantee that it would not renew the same attempt, that Maximilian would continue, even in spite of himself, to be a pretext and a rallying cry for faction, and an instrument by which foreign Powers, when complications arose, might gain a party in the country. The decree of October cried for expiation, and the death of its author would enable them to spare the rest. Many Mexicans had been put to death under the decree of January, and the punishment of inferiors could not be justified if that of the leader was remitted. They seem to have believed that if the door-posts of the Republic were marked with the blood of a prince, the angel of destruction would pass them by. They showed no inclination to cast on others the responsibility of their act, but it is difficult to believe that it was determined by reason of state dispassionately weighed.

Juarez possessed but a precarious authority over the army; and the army was infuriated by strife, and thirsted to avenge the comrades who had been executed like murderers. We can imagine what their feelings would be towards the foreigner whose title was a vote extracted by the bayonets of invaders, who had ordered their country-men and themselves to be slaughtered, and who was now convicted of having been a pretender and a usurper, as he was the champion of the weaker party. It is probable that the real author of the Emperor's execution is Escobedo, and that Juarez was powerless to save him. When the news that he was to die in three hours reached San Luis at noon on the Sunday, the Prussian Minister prayed for a short delay. He knew that Maximilian had matters to settle before death, and there was some hope that foreign intercession would be in time to save his life. But the American Government, at the request of the Emperor of Austria, had already interceded for his brother, and had interceded in vain. A delay of three days was granted, but the order did not reach Queretaro till the last moment, when the prisoners had made themselves ready for immediate death. For himself, indeed, Maxi-milian had no hope, and was perfectly resigned. A report that his wife was dead made him meet his fate with joy. On the eve of his execution he telegraphed to Juarez requesting that he might be the only victim.

At six in the morning of Wednesday, the 19th of last June, he was led forth to the doom he had not deserved. His last act before going to the place of execution had been to write the following letter to his implacable conqueror : " I give up my life willingly, if the sacrifice can promote the welfare of my new country. But nothing healthy can grow upon a soil saturated with blood, and therefore, I entreat you, let mine be the last you shed. The fortitude with which you upheld the cause that triumphs now won my admiration in happier days, and I pray that it may not fail you in the peaceful work of conciliation that is to come." When they came to the appointed place, he gave money to the soldiers by whose hands he was to fall, asking them to aim at his heart, for he wished that his mother might look upon his face again.

The officer who was to give the word assured him that he detested the duty, and implored him not to die with a feeling of resentment against him.   Maximilian thanked him, and said that he must obey orders.   Mejia was in great trouble and dejection.   His wife had just borne him a son, and as he left his prison he had seen her rushing through the streets, raving mad, with the child in her arms. The Emperor bade him farewell affectionately, saying: "There is a reward in the next world for that which is not requited here."   He was standing between the Mexicans, but out of humility, or magnanimity, or because a solemn and sacred memory was present to his mind at that last awful moment, he turned to Miramon and said that out of esteem for his courage he would yield to him the place of honour.   His last words were: "I die for a just cause—the independence and the liberty of Mexico.   May my death close the era of the misfortunes of my adopted country: God save Mexico!"   Then he crossed his hands upon his breast and fell, pierced by nine balls.

He fell, and carried with him in his fall the independence of the people he had come to save.   Nothing henceforth remains that can permanently arrest the United States in the annexation of Spanish America.   If they have prudence to avoid European war, and wisdom to compose their own dissensions, they may grasp the most glorious inheritance the earth affords.   The conquest of Spanish America would be easy and certain, but beset with dangers.   A confederacy loses its true character when it rules over dependencies; and a Democracy lives a threatened life that admits millions of a strange and inferior race which it can neither assimilate nor absorb. It is more likely that the Americans will bind their neighbours by treaties, which will throw open the whole continent to their own influence and enterprise, without destroying their separate existence.

The memory of the fair-haired stranger, who devoted his life to the good of Mexico, and died for guilt which was not his own, will live in sorrow rather than in anger among the people for whom he strove in vain.   Already we may pronounce the verdict of history upon his sad career—his worst crime was in accepting the treacherous gift of Empire, but his misfortune was greater than his fault. I think he was well-nigh the noblest of his race, and fulfilled the promise of his words : " The fame of my ancestors will not degenerate in me."

VI

CAVOUR [1]

CAVOUR was the most thoroughly practical of the Italian statesmen. It is the special character of his career that his success was due to his own ability, not to the idea or the party he represented ; not to his principles, but to his skill. He was not borne to power on the wave of public enthusiasm, nor by the energy of an opinion incorporated in him, nor by the personal attachment of a mass of followers. He was not a representative man in the domain of thought, not a great partisan in the domain of action, not a popular favourite trained in agitation, or sustained by the prestige of great achievements. Yet he acquired and kept a position in which men who were his superiors in genius, in character, and in eloquence—Balbo, Gioberti, Azeglio—successively failed ; in which men who were identified with the chief memories and hopes of Italian patriotism—Manin, Mamiani, Farini, La Farina—were content to be his subordinates and assistants ; and where all his rivals sacrificed or suspended their own principles, animosities, and aspirations, in order to increase his power and his fame. The statesman who could blend such materials, and make of them the instrument of his greatness ; who could withstand at the same time the animosity of Austria and the ambition of France ; who could at once restrain the Catholics whom he injured and insulted, and the republicans whom he condemned ; and who, standing between such powerful enemies and such formidable allies, almost accomplished

[1] *The Rambler*, July 1861.

the unity of Italy to the Mincio, and increased fourfold
the dominions of his king—must always remain one of
the most conspicuous figures, as he is one of the most
distinct characters in the history of his country.

He was connected by descent with the family of St.
Francis of Sales. His mother, who belonged to a patrician
family of Geneva, was originally a Protestant, and the old-
fashioned political Calvinism of Geneva, which moulded the
character of Guizot, exercised from a very early age a profound influence upon Cavour. Events connected with his
family position inspired him with a precocious dislike for
the priesthood; and whilst his brother, the Marquis Gustave
de Cavour, grew up into an ardent defender of religion,
Camillo was looked on unkindly by his father, a politician
of the old school, whilst the authorities regarded him with
a suspicion proportioned to his cleverness and his petulance.
The position was intolerable to a man of his disposition,
and he left his country almost as soon as he was his own
master, carrying with him two sentiments already deeply
rooted in his soul,—animosity towards the Catholic hierarchy and towards the political system which was combined
with it in the reverence of the people, and in the hatred
of the Liberals. Time and experience appear to have
wrought no change for good or evil in these opinions. He
satisfied his vengeance on the Church without ever exhibiting unbelief, and he consummated a great revolution
without ever accepting the revolutionary doctrines. But
he confessed in the days of his greatness, consistently with
his whole career, that the impulse of his policy was derived
from personal motives rather than from public principles.

Yet undoubtedly his opinions grew into maturity and
harmony during the period which preceded his entrance
into public life. He spent several years in France and
England, attentive to things of practical material interest,
and adding to the cosmopolitan temper of his order a
warm appreciation and sympathy for the society of both
countries. He returned to Turin in 1842, where the spirit
of the Government kept him away from public affairs, and
where he devoted himself to the development of the pros-

perity of the country through the Agricultural Society, which he helped to establish and to conduct. Like similar associations in other countries, where the absence of freedom, obliging Government to seek a substitute for public opinion in espionage, and the people to seek it in secret societies, gives to every recognised society a political character, the *Associazione Agraria* became, from its organisation, an important channel and instrument of political influence. When the Italian movement began it became a centre of political action; "and," says Brofferio, in his autobiography, "in more than one discussion on the felling of timber, the germs of an imperfectly understood democracy revealed themselves."

Besides articles on agricultural and economical questions in the journal of the society, Cavour published during these years several essays on political subjects, not brilliantly written, but remarkable for grasp of thought, and because they are authentic memorials of the views by which he was guided in his after-career. In the paper on the Communistic theories, there is a character of Pitt closely resembling that given by Macaulay, some touches of which have been applied to Cavour himself. "He was not one of those who seek to reconstruct society from its foundations with the aid of general, philanthropic theories. A cold, deep intellect, free from prejudice, he was animated solely by the love of glory and of his country." And at the conclusion of this essay occurs a passage which distinguishes him favourably from those modern economists whose inflexible abstractions give an easy victory to the Communists :—

To every one his own work. The philosopher and the economist, in the seclusion of their studies, will confute the errors of Communism ; but their labour will bear no fruit unless men practise the great principle of universal benevolence, and act upon the hearts, while science acts upon the intellects.

It is no small merit to have understood that political economy is as much an ethical as a material science in an age when philanthropists and economists agree in condemning each other's efforts, and when both seem to

have forgotten that the same holy doctrine which teaches
the precept of charity supplies the basis of economical
science, by inculcating alike the duties of benevolence to
the rich and of industrious independence to the poor ;
for " the poor we have always with us," but " if any man
will not work, neither let him eat."

In 1847 the reforms of Pius IX. produced a reaction
against absolutism throughout Italy, which was soon felt
in Piedmont ; and in September Charles Albert began to
follow the footsteps of the Pope in the path of concession.
At the end of the year Cavour, in conjunction with
Balbo and others, took advantage of the new liberty of
the press to found the paper *Il Risorgimento*, which he
conducted with great ability.   Whilst others were
demanding reforms, he was the first to insist on a constitution, and in January 1848 he petitioned the king
" to remove the controversy from the dangerous arena of
irregular agitation to a scene of legal, peaceful, and regular
discussion."   On the 5th of February, his friend Santa
Rosa carried a similar vote in the Municipal Council of
Turin ; and on the 7th a Constitution, based on the
French Charter of 1814, was granted by the king.
Cavour was not elected at first ; when he obtained a seat
in the Chamber his friends Balbo and Boncompagni
were Ministers, and he joined the Right.   The war against
Austria was undertaken by the Ministry, with the condition
that Italy should owe her deliverance to herself.   France
was at that time a Republic, and her aid, it was apprehended by the monarchical advisers of Charles Albert,
would cause the triumph of the Republicans at Milan
and elsewhere, and would deprive the Sardinian monarchy
of every advantage.   The Ambassador at Paris, the Marquis Brignole, declared in words which later events have
made still more remarkable :—

The essential character of the movement which agitates Italy,
that distinguishes it from all that went before, is that it aims at
being above all Italian.   Each party deems itself called upon to
direct it, and to concentrate in one last attempt all the scattered
efforts which would be fruitless separately ; but there is no one that

N

desires to substitute France for Austria. It is necessary that it
should be well understood in France, that if the army of the
Republic crosses the Alps without being summoned by events, by
interests, and by desires, the influence of France and of French ideas
would be lost in Italy for a long time.   Throughout Northern Italy,
as at Florence, at Rome, and at Naples, everywhere except among
the Republicans of Milan, they will not have the military aid of
France until the day when a tremendous defeat has proved that
Italy is unable alone to drive the Austrians over the Alps.

Cavour was opposed to the Republican party which
sympathised with France, but he condemned the policy
of the maxim, *L' Italia farà da sè.*   "Republics," he said,
"have always pursued a policy of selfishness, and were
never promoters of civilisation."   His hopes were directed
towards England.   "My confidence in England rests
partly on the honourable character of the statesmen to
whose hands the reins of power are committed—on
Lord John Russell and on Lord Palmerston.   Lord
John Russell, I will say it openly, at the risk of being
considered more and more an Anglo-maniac, is the most
liberal Minister in Europe."   As the war went on, the
democratic party gained power, and Cavour was thrown
out at the elections in January 1849.   In December he
recovered his seat.   Azeglio was Minister, and Cavour
supported him, separating himself farther from his old
leader Balbo.   That great man was opposed to the laws
proposed by Siccardi on the civil condition of the clergy,
which Cavour supported in a speech by which he gained
great popularity, and which placed him in closer connection with the Left Centre, the party of Ratazzi, than
with his original friends.

Hitherto he had not stood in the front rank.   The
revolutionary period afforded no opening for a man of his
stamp.   He was too far from the Conservatives to join in
their resistance, and from the Democrats to join in their
movement.   In revolutions the extremes prevail, and
Cavour detested both extremes.   But the new reign
opened a new career for men of the Centre, after Balbo
had been thrust aside by the Revolution and Gioberti by
the reaction, and the candidates for the leadership of the

new party were Azeglio and Cavour. Less scrupulous both as regards political and ecclesiastical rights than the real Conservatives, but decidedly hostile to democracy and disorder, they nearly agreed in opinions, whilst they differed widely in character. The energy, boldness, and ambition of Cavour inevitably placed him in a victorious opposition to his dignified, careless, and somewhat indolent rival. He became Minister of Commerce in October 1850, and Minister of Finance in April 1851. His first administration was devoted chiefly to reforms in the fiscal system, which always bore with him a political character. " The political regeneration of a nation," he said, " is never separate from its economic regeneration. The conditions of the two sorts of progress are identical."

The commercial reforms of Sir Robert Peel had filled him with interest and admiration, and he had written an essay upon the consequences they would involve for Italy. The lesson he learnt was the same as that which has been since put in practice in England by the ablest of Peel's disciples—to make the laws of economic science subservient to considerations of policy. Accordingly he concluded a series of commercial treaties, both for financial reasons and for the purpose of making friends for Sardinia in other States. In one respect his position differed remarkably from that of Mr. Gladstone. The chief opponents of his commercial reforms were the democratic party. In Piedmont, finance is an instrument for democratic purposes ; in England, questions of finance have reared democracy.

The Government was opposed, therefore, by the extreme Left, and also by the extreme Right, in consequence of its ecclesiastical legislation. Azeglio relied on the support of the Right Centre, and sought to conciliate the Left by reforms in Church matters. The Left Centre, headed by Ratazzi, cared less for internal reform than for external aggrandisement ; they were the aggressive party in the Parliament. During the war of 1848 Ratazzi, then in office, demanded the suspension of all securities of liberty, saying that there would be no greater danger of abuse of

power in the absence of those laws than with them.   At
that time Cavour had declared that the Left wished to
rule in Piedmont, as the Emperor Nicholas ruled at
Petersburg.   But when he had attained a leading position,
the principles of these men suited his bold and active
mind.   A party who, in the desire for power, were ready
to make a sacrifice of freedom, was the natural ally of
a statesman who was ambitious of acquiring power by
heroic means.   Azeglio had nothing but the canon law
to sacrifice to them ; Cavour offered them the destruction
of international law, and they took the higher bribe.
Hence, under Azeglio, the religious reforms were the
question of the day ; under Cavour they became secondary
and subsidiary to the question of national aggrandisement.
The alliance was concluded on the occasion of the *coup
d'état.*   The new despotism seemed to menace its feeble
neighbours, and a law on the licence of the press was
proposed by the Government at Turin.

"Sardinia," said the Prime Minister, "has gained great renown ;
now it must be our object to obtain obscurity. . . . We are passing
by a sleeping lion, and must tread softly.   If one amongst us refuses
to take the necessary precaution, we must compel him to be quiet ;
if the lion attacks us, we must defend ourselves."

The Right wished to go farther than the Ministers—to
introduce into Piedmont the system of the 2nd of December,
to curtail liberties, to alter the electoral law, and to abolish
the National Guard.   These events determined the breach
between Cavour and the reaction and his alliance with
Ratazzi,—an alliance similar to that by which, ever since
the Reform Bill, the Whigs have obtained their majorities.
On the 5th of February, without consulting his colleagues,
Cavour, in a speech in defence of their proposal, publicly
invited Ratazzi to combine with him, promising a national
policy as the prize.   The excitement was extreme ; but no
breach ensued until, on the 11th of May, Cavour proposed
and carried the election of Ratazzi as President of the
Chamber.

He became by this manœuvre the leader of the most
powerful party in Parliament, but he lost his place in the

Government, and Azeglio formed a new administration
without him.   There was no event of his public life, he
said afterwards, of which he was prouder than this.

So long as the Republic continued in France, so long as the
fate of that nation seemed uncertain and the phantom of the Revolution was not put down, I could be sure that the reaction at home
would undertake nothing for the destruction of our constitutional
freedom.   But when the 2nd of December removed the danger of
disorder in France, when the red phantom had vanished, I thought
that from that time forward the Constitution was more seriously
menaced by that party than it had formerly been by the revolutionary
faction.   For this reason I deemed the formation of a great Liberal
party not only right, but necessary and essential; and I invoked for
that purpose the patriotism of all who agree in the great principles
of progress and of freedom, and who differ from each other only on
subordinate questions.

He had already gained the good will of the Emperor
Napoleon by his conduct in the debates on the freedom
of the press.   During his retirement he visited Paris, and
appeared with Ratazzi at the Tuileries.   That was the
beginning of the league between the two friends who
projected a national policy, and the ally who was to
profit by their enterprise.   Cavour's dread of an alliance
with Republican France did not apply to the alliance of
Imperial France.   The difference of principle had disappeared.   Meantime Azeglio attempted to prolong his
tenure of power by new ecclesiastical changes, and by
introducing a law on civil marriage; but the dismissal of
Cavour had deprived him of the energetic support of the
Radicals, and he could not prevail against the resistance
of the Holy See and of the Catholic party.   He persisted,
even after the Sardinian envoy in Rome had come to Turin
without leave, to press on the Ministers the necessity of
modifying their policy.   At length, on the 26th of October,
he resigned.   The condition of the accession of the new
Ministry was an altered tone towards Rome.   Charvaz,
Archbishop of Genoa, who had full instructions from the
Pope, was at this critical moment the chief counsellor of
the king.   He wished that Balbo should succeed Azeglio,
and when that hope failed, a fruitless attempt was made

by Alfieri di Sostegno. Cavour's turn then came. First of all an attempt was made to bring about an understanding between him and the Archbishop. It failed, and the difficulty of the crisis seemed insuperable. But Cavour was master of the situation, and on the 4th of November he formed an administration untrammelled by any condition, which was joined twelve months later by Ratazzi. The programme of this famous Ministry was to use the Italian movement and the friendship of Napoleon III. for the advantage of Sardinia. The ecclesiastical policy of Azeglio and Siccardi would be pursued or suspended, according to the exigencies which might arise in the pursuit of that more ambitious design. In reality there was a close internal connection between aggression abroad and the oppression of the Church ; and in Cavour's mind, as in that of many Italians, there was a strict union between Rome and Austria. From the speeches and writings of the Ministers we can discern how both were connected in his policy.

One of his biographers and admirers affirms that Cavour's notions of government and of freedom were English, not French ; but he adds that he never displayed them in his policy, because circumstances hindered him from carrying them out beyond the department of finance —*quantunque le quistioni ora di finanze, ora di politica, gli abbiano preoccupato l' animo, ed impedito di attuarlo in altro che nelle sue consequenze economiche.* In truth his policy was directed to the greatness of the State, not to the liberty of the people ; he sought the greatest amount of power consistent with the maintenance of the monarchical constitution, not the greatest amount of freedom compatible with national independence. To this question of State, this *ragion di stato*, everything else but the forms of the government was to be sacrificed.

Tocqueville has shown that the French Revolution, far from reversing the political spirit of the old State, only carried out the same principles with intenser energy. The State, which was absolute before, became still more absolute, and the organs of the popular will became more efficient agents for the exercise of arbitrary power. This was the work, not of the Reign of Terror and the period of convulsion, which was barren of political results, but of the ideas of 1789, incorporated in that Constitution of 1791 which continued for seventy years the model of all foreign Constitutions, until Austria returned to the mediæval originals which England alone had preserved. The purpose of all the Continental governments, framed on that pattern, is not that the people should obtain security for freedom, but participation of power. The increase in the number of those who share the authority renders the authority still more irresistible ; and as power is associated with wealth, those who are interested in the augmentation of power cannot be interested in the diminution of expenditure : and thus parliamentary government generally results in an improved administration and increased resources, but also in addition to the pressure and the expenses of the State. All this was singularly verified in Cavour's administration in Piedmont.

Like most of the continental Liberals, and like most men who are not religious, he considered the State as endowed with indefinite power, and individual rights as subject to its supreme authority ; whilst, like the revolutionists in France, he accepted the legacy of absolutism left by the old *régime*, and sought to preserve its force under contrary forms. Societies are really divided not into monarchies and republics, but into democracies and aristocracies ; whatever the form of Government, there are in fact only two types, organised and atomic society, and the commonest and most visible sign of the two is equality or inequality. The real basis of inequality is the privilege of a part as contrasted with the rights of the whole, and its simplest essential form is the privilege not of class, but of age—that is, inheritance by primogeniture. Nothing else is required for an aristocracy ; nothing else can create an aristocracy. Cavour, though a noble, and an enemy of democracy, was a decided assertor of its fundamental principle. "Civil equality," he wrote in *Il Risorgimento*, "is the great principle of modern society." The statute

gave the nomination of senators to the king ; he wished
to make them elective. " Often accused of blind admiration for England, and of secretly entertaining the guilty
design of introducing amongst us the aristocratic portion
of their institutions," he loudly declared—

> that to imitate Great Britain in this respect would be a fatal error,
> and would introduce into the Constitution the sure germs of future
> resolution. To attempt to institute a peerage similar to that of
> England would be the height of folly.

On the other hand, he was opposed to the seques-
tration of Church property ; for he had learnt from the
theories of Lamennais, perhaps from the experience of
the countries he had studied, that a clergy dependent
for support on the people is emancipated from the
influence of the State, and directly subject to the
authority of the Holy See. He desired that religious
liberty should be one of the foundations of the Constitution ; and in this he approached the French more than
the English type, for he understood by it not that one
religion should be favoured and the others tolerated, but
that the State should be indifferent to religious diversities.
The Constitution, by altering the position and distribution of authority, rendered it necessary that the
relations between the State and the Church should
undergo a revision, and should obtain the guarantee of
the nation's consent. The passage of a State from absolutism to constitutionalism involves a great alteration in its
position towards the Church, and the manner in which
her rights are respected is the test by which we may
determine whether the Constitution is a step towards
liberty, or a new and popular form of absolutism. For
the Church is affected not by the form of government, but
by its principle. She is interested not in monarchy
or republicanism, but in liberty and security against
absolutism. The rights and duties which she upholds
are sacred and inviolable, and can no more be subject to
the vote of a majority than to the decree of a despot. In
many cases constitutions have been her protection against

tyranny; but in many cases also constitutions have imposed on her a new tyranny. The period which immediately succeeded the Revolution of 1848 has been rich in conflicts between the Church and the States, for the Liberty which it sought to obtain was understood in two different ways. The Catholics saw in it the triumph of religious freedom and of independence for the Church; the Liberals, in most cases, used it as a transfer of power to their hands; between these contrary interpretations of the movement and of its institutions, frequent conflicts were inevitable. In Austria, in Holland, and in Wirtemberg the Catholic opinion prevailed. In Baden and in Piedmont the Revolution only added to the power of the State. The theory of liberty insists on the independence of the Church; the theory of liberalism insists on the omnipotence of the State as the organ of the popular will. It was accordingly affirmed by Azeglio that there was no necessity to treat with Rome, and that the ecclesiastical reforms which had become necessary through the civil reforms belonged exclusively to the jurisdiction of the civil power. He reversed the ancient theory that the Church alone decides on all things that trench on the domain of conscience and religious life, and declared that the State alone might determine all questions affecting civil society. The quarrel that ensued was not so much on account of the reforms themselves as of the principle on which they were made. The Church resisted not so much the changes that were introduced, as the principle of arbitrary authority. But among the laws proposed by the Ministry under Azeglio was a law introducing civil marriage, and it was under discussion when the change of Government occurred. Cavour had never insisted on this measure, and when the Senate resolved to modify the Bill, he consented to withdraw it. The spirit of the ecclesiastical legislation remained unchanged at Turin, but it was not pressed forward at first by the new Ministers, for they had a more popular bait to throw out to the Liberal party.

To the Conservative patriots of 1848 the war with

Austria was a war of deliverance, not a war of principles. Balbo wished the Austrians to be expelled, not out of hatred against them, but for the sake of Italy; and he wished that Austria should obtain on the Lower Danube and in the Turkish dominions an equivalent for the loss of her Italian provinces. With Cavour, the patriotic cause became an antagonism of political principles. The Austrian system was diametrically opposed to his ideas, not only when it was oppressive under Metternich, but when the great internal changes were commenced by the Concordat which have been carried out by Schmerling in the Constitution of the Empire. The Austrian notions of liberty were as hateful to him, in their way, as the Austrian absolutism had been; and the strength of his hatred increased as the emperor proceeded with his reforms. "Thanks to our political system," he said in the Parliament, 6th May 1856, "which King Victor Emmanuel has introduced and maintained, and which you have supported, we are farther removed from Austria than ever." In opposition to the policy of Balbo, he wrote in favour of the union of the Danubian Principalities :—

Austria has long had her eye fixed on the banks of the Danube. . . . Can it be believed that two small States, weakened by separation, will be able to resist her ambitious and aggressive policy? The influence of the Cabinet of Vienna will produce in the Principalities, especially at Bucharest, effects similar to those which are exhibited in the secondary States of Italy.

The relations between Austria and Piedmont grew more and more unfriendly and bitter, when the Crimean war broke out, and the Western Powers became most anxious for the support of the Austrian arms. In the course of negotiations it was made a condition of the Austrian alliance that the safety of her Italian dominions should be guaranteed whilst her armies marched against the Russians. Sardinia would thus have been over-reached; and the proposal of Lord Clarendon, that she should join the Western Powers, was extremely welcome. The arrangement with Austria was concluded on 22nd

December 1854; that with Sardinia on 26th January 1855. The Western alliance, said Lord Palmerston, thus became a league against tyranny. The first proposal having come from the Great Powers, Piedmont, having no prospect of immediate advantage, was able to make tacit stipulations for a later reward. The same condition which had been granted to Austria was also conceded to Sardinia, and there a defensive alliance was formed.

In immediate connection with the strain which this ambitious policy laid on the finances, came the secularisation of the religious Orders. The debate began on 9th January 1855, in the midst of the negotiations with the Western Powers. "The Budget," said Cavour, "could no longer provide for the support of religion." Financial reasons made an extreme measure necessary, in order that the expenditure of the State might be diminished and its resources increased, whilst the large number of poor and active priests would be enriched out of the property of the useless Orders, and out of the superfluity of the wealthier clergy. The moment was also perilous, from the combination of the democrats with the Conservatives against the Crimean war. Brofferio declared that they ought rather to have allied themselves with Russia, which was the only Power in Europe representing national independence. The act of spoliation was an instrument against this alliance.

"If we did not present," said the Minister, "a measure demanded by the majority of public opinion, we might have lost at a critical moment the support of the Liberals as well as that of the Reactionists. The postponement of this measure would alienate the first without conciliating the second. By presenting the law we secure the support of the Liberals, and the country will be united and powerful against every trial."

It is obvious that, whenever similar conjunctures should recur, the same policy would be pursued against all Church property. The Bill became law on 25th May 1855; and on 26th July the Pope declared that all who had proposed, approved, or sanctioned it had incurred excommunication.

The ideal of Cavour was the French system of dependence
of the clergy on the Government as their paymaster.   He
was with the king on his journey through Savoy when
the Archbishop of Chambéry concluded an address in
these words :—

> Your Majesty has seen in France a noble example of intimate
> union between the authorities and the clergy, and we trust that you
> will bestow this great benefit on your country by putting an end to
> the persecution of the Church by the Government.

Victor Emmanuel, in his reply, took advantage of the
opportunity afforded by this imprudent speech :—

> You are right in quoting the relations between Church and State
> in France as a good example.   I am so thoroughly convinced of it
> that I am resolved to place the clergy of my kingdom on the same
> footing as that of France.

The union between the ecclesiastical and the Austrian
question was made closer by the conclusion of the
Austrian Concordat.   The oppressed clergy of Piedmont
looked to Austria as the ally of the Church, and doubly
therefore the enemy of Piedmont.   On the other hand,
the Government believed that the Holy See, strengthened
by its recent triumph, would be little disposed to give
way to Piedmont, and would be more uncompromising
than before.   Whilst, therefore, the abandonment of the
Josephine system at Vienna widened the breach with a
Government which was walking in the footsteps of Joseph
II., it heightened at the same time the antagonism
between Turin and Rome.   Boncompagni went to
Florence with the mission to prevent the conclusion of
a Tuscan Concordat, and to support the revival of the
Leopoldine laws.   Cavour said :—

> We must wait till an improvement in the Roman Government
> reconciles people's minds with the Sovereign of those States, con-
> founded in popular opinion with the Head of the Church.   This
> opinion is shared by the eminent men of France and other countries,
> who formerly blamed, but who now approve, our conduct on these
> questions.   This result we owe to the Austrian Concordat, and for
> this reason we must rejoice at that act.

The discontent of Romagna afforded a convenient

diversion in the contest with Rome, which was ingeniously used at the Congress of Paris. The Sardinian Plenipotentiary took no share in the negotiations on the peace ; he was waiting for an opportunity to obtain the reward for which he had joined in the war. When that opportunity arrived, he used it solely to discuss the state of Romagna. That was where the Papal and the Austrian interests were combined, and where he could strike both his adversaries with the same blow. Minghetti sent him from Bologna the materials for his memorandum, in which be recommended things grateful to French ears—secular administration, conscription, and the Code Napoleon. It must be remembered that at that time the belief was gaining ground in Romagna, and was shared by the informants of Cavour, that it would soon be annexed to the Austrian dominions. On his return to Turin he said of his mission to Paris :—

We may rejoice at one great result. The Italian question has become for the future a European question. The cause of Italy has not been defended by demagogues, revolutionists, and party men, but has been discussed before the Congress by the plenipotentiaries of the Great Powers.

Mamiani declared that the Holy Alliance was at an end and Italian nationality recognised, as the Minister of an Italian State had been heard in the Congress pleading for Italy.

Whilst the reforms in Austria increased the bitterness with which she was regarded by the Liberal Ministers in Piedmont, their position towards Russia became extremely friendly. No incompatibility of political ideas was felt at that time between them. The intensity with which Austria was hated by Prince Gortschakoff made him recognise an ally in the Cabinet of Turin ; and a marked difference was made at Moscow, after the peace, in the consideration shown to the Sardinians, compared to their former position, as well as to their English and Austrian colleagues. Hatred of Austria was not, however, the only recommendation of Piedmont in the eyes of Russia.

The period which followed the Congress of Paris was

marked by a great increase in the Catholic party at Turin. They threw out, in May 1856, a Bill placing all education under the control of the State ; and, in order to diminish their opposition, Ratazzi retired from office. In 1858 the crime of Orsini obliged Cavour to introduce a conspiracy Bill, like our own, in which he encountered the resistance of the Left, but by which he strengthened the bonds of union with Napoleon.

This measure called forth a letter from Mazzini to Cavour, dated June 1858, in which the writer exhibits his own character and system as truly as he describes that of his antagonist, and which is one of the most expressive documents of the Italian movement.

" I have long known you," he begins, "more solicitous for the Piedmontese monarchy than for our common country, a materialist worshipper of the event more than of any sacred and eternal principle, a man of an ingenious rather than a powerful mind. . . . To that party whose extraordinary vitality is now admitted even by yourself, in the teeth of your friends who declared it at every moment dead and buried, Piedmont owes the liberty she enjoys, and you owe the opportunity of making yourself the useless and deceitful defender of Italy."

This is so far true, that the notion of Italian unity belonged originally to Mazzini, not to the Italian Liberals ; and that the success of the Roman movement, which the sect encouraged and then diverted, gave the impulse to the reforms of Charles Albert. The tone of Cavour, in speaking of the sanguinary practices of the sect, provoked a passionate but elaborate vindication of their theory :—

I loved you not before, but now I scorn you. Hitherto you were only an enemy ; now you are shamefully, infamously my enemy. . . . I believe that in principle every sentence of death—no matter whether applied by an individual or by society—is a crime, and if it were in my power I should deem it my duty to abolish it. . . . The abolition of capital punishment is an absolute duty in a free country. . . . But so long as war for the deliverance of one's country shall be a holy thing, or the armed protection of the weak against the powerful tyrant that tramples on him, or the defence by every means of the brother against whom the assassin's knife is raised, the absolute inviolability of life is a lie. . . . I see among your supporters, among those who cry out against the newly invented theory of the dagger, men who, before 1848, were active leaders of the Carboneria. But Young Italy banished the dagger, and condemned even the perjurer only to the horror of his brethren. . . . There must be law or war, and let him conquer who can. Where every bond is broken between the law and the people of the State, force is sacred wherever it undertakes, by whatever means they may be, to reconnect the one with the other. Where the equipoise is lost between the power of one and the power of all, every individual has the right and the mission to cancel, if he is able, the occasion of the mortal defect, and to restore the equipoise. Before the collective sovereignty the citizen reverently pleads his own cause; before the tyrant rises the tyrannicide—*divanti al tiranno sorge il tirannicida*. . . . Is there not between the tyrant and the victim of his oppression a natural and continual war? . . . To despatch the tyrant, if on his death depends the emancipation of a people, the welfare of millions, is an act of war, and if the slayer is free from every other thought and gives his life in exchange, an act of virtue. . . . If the malediction of a tortured people, miraculously concentrated into poison, could, instantly and without time for resistance, destroy all those who contaminate with their stupid tyranny, with the tears of mothers, with the blood of honest men, the soil that God has given us, the malediction would be sanctified before God and man.

This theory, that a tyrant is an outlaw, is an ingenious adaptation of the old doctrine of tyrannicide, which was borrowed from pagan and Jewish antiquity, and maintained of old in the schools from John of Salisbury to Mariana. The distinction between the two theories is, that whilst the divines held the tyrant condemned by actual law and implicitly sentenced by a visible tribunal, Mazzini, by means of his doctrine of popular sovereignty, invokes no higher decision than the individual subjective will. Unfortunately, guilty acts may be very easily justified by an obscure theory; and the crimes of Clément, Ravaillac, Guy Fawkes, were as horrible as those of Milano, Pianori, or Orsini, and it is not easy for the vulgar mind to distinguish between killing and murder, between the assassination of William the Silent or of Wallenstein, and that of Henry IV. or of Rossi. The doctrine is pernicious and perilous at best; as Mazzini defines it, it is untenable, because it is founded on the democratic principle. An outlaw may be slain; and it may be said that a sovereign who unites the guilt of usurpation with the guilt of tyranny is an outlaw at war with society; but he must be tried by public law, not by private judgment, and the act must be in acknowledged obedience to the laws by which society is bound, not to an arbitrary code. Private vengeance in a savage community is the commencement of civil law; in a civilised society it is the inauguration of barbarism. The crime of Mazzini lies not so much in the theory of the dagger as in the principle by which that theory is applied, and he sacrifices even the speculative basis of his view by denying, with Robespierre, that society has any jurisdiction over life and death.

" Victor Emmanuel," he declares, " is protected, first by the statute, then by his insignificance—*prima dallo statuto poi dalla nessuna importanza.* Even mutilated and often betrayed by you, the liberty of Piedmont is protection enough for the days of the king. Where truth can make its way in speech, where even, though by sacrifices, the exercise of one's duties is possible, regicide is a crime and a folly."

He defines the difference between himself and the party of Cavour, of the monarchical revolutionists, in a manner extremely remarkable.

If life is sacred, how as to war? . . . Did you not send forth two thousand of our soldiers' lives to be lost on the fields of the Crimea in battles not your own, solely because you discerned in that sacrifice a probability of increasing in Europe the lustre of the Sardinian Crown? . . . So long as I behold your laws constructed to protect the life of the man who was at war with his country and with the liberty of Europe, and who reached the throne over thousands of dead, and not for the good of the slaughtered people,—so long as I see you silent and inert before every crime crowned with success, and without daring for nine years once to say to the invader of Rome, " In the name of the rights of Italy, quit this land that is not yours,"—I shall deem you hypocrites, and nothing more. . . . Did they not conspire with me for ten years in the name of a regenerating faith—the men who in your Chamber quote Machiavelli to prove that politics know no principles, but only calculations of expediency and opportunity? Do not the journalists of your party recite the daily praises of Bonaparte, the tyrant in possession, whom they contemned when he was merely a pretender? Are not you ready to betray your country, and to cede Southern Italy to Murat, in order that the Empire may secure to you a compensation in land which is beyond your frontier? Partisans of opportunity, you have no right to invoke principles—*partito d' opportunisti, voi non avete diritto d' invocare principii*; worshippers of the *fait accompli*, you may not assume the garb of priest of morality.   Your science lives in the phenomenal world, in the event of the day—you have no ideal.   *La vostra scienza vive sul fenomeno, sull' incidente dell' oggi; non avete ideale.*   Your alliances are not with the free, but with the strong ; they rest not on notions of right and wrong, but on notions of immediate material utility.   Materialists, with the name of God on your lips, enemies in your hearts, but ostensible venerators of the words of the Pope, seeking by desire of aggrandisement to break those treaties of 1815 on which you rely to deprive the people of the right of insurrection, —between you and me there is no difference but this one : I say, holy is every war against the foreigner, and I reverence him that tries it, even though he succumb ; you say, holy is every war that succeeds, and you insult the fallen.   You heaped insults on the bold people of Milan on the 6th of February ; you would have proclaimed them magnanimous saviours of their country if they had prevailed.   Surely you do not deem that a people subject to foreigners, and capable of delivering itself, may not do it, simply because the arms that are left in its hands have not a given length. . . . If the people of Italy brandished their knives to the cry, *Viva il rè Sardo!* and conquered, you would embrace them as your brethren.   And if they conquered even without that cry you would embrace them the next day, in order to take advantage of their success.

And then, in that tone of prophecy which he often affects but has seldom assumed so successfully, he says :—

Piedmont is not a definite, limited State, living of its own vitality. It is Italy in the germ.   It is the life of Italy, concentrated for a time at the foot of the Alps. . . . Italy, whatever happens, cannot become Piedmont.   The centre of the national organism cannot be transferred to the extremity.   The heart of Italy is in Rome, not in Turin. No Piedmontese monarch will ever conquer Naples ; Naples will give herself to the nation, never to the prince of another Italian province.   The monarchical principle cannot destroy the papacy, and annex to its own dominions the States of the Pope.

In all this declamation there is not a little truth.   It is hard to show the error of the conclusions drawn by Mazzini from premises which he holds in common with Cavour.   There is a vast difference between the amount of misery inflicted by the French Revolution and by the absolutism of the old monarchy ; but there is an intense similarity of features and character between the crimes of the Revolutionists and the crimes of the Legitimists.   The

O

ancient monarchy does not stand higher in political ethics than the republic, and it is only from the habits and sympathies of a society accustomed to monarchy that we judge more leniently the partition of Poland, the suppression of the Jesuits, the *lettres de cachet*, and the royal police—which enforced, like the master in the fable, a perpetual tribute of the daughters of the defenceless class of Frenchmen—than we judge the horrors of the period of vengeance.   There is not much to rejoice at that the same wrong should be committed by a constitutional Minister instead of a republican, for the sake of monarchy instead of democracy.   Monarchy is not essentially connected with order, nor democracy with disorder, nor constitutionalism with liberty.   Blinded by our superstitious belief in forms, we forget that the destruction of the faith of treaties, the obliteration of the landmarks of States, the spoliation and oppression of the Church, the corruption of religion, the proclamation of unjust wars, the seizure of foreign possessions, the subversion of foreign rights,—all these are greater crimes and greater calamities than the establishment of republican institutions,—and all this has been done by a constitutional Minister ; and Mazzini, who has seen the best part of his purpose accomplished for him by those who denounce him as a criminal and a fanatic, has no instrument of agitation remaining to him but the Republic. Cavour made him powerless, simply by making him superfluous, and allowed him to do nothing, by doing his work for him.   He triumphed while he lived, because the governments are as corrupt as the demagogues, and because the revolution was his weapon instead of his foe. But he saved Italy from no evil except the Republic, and the highest praise that men can give him is, that he died like Mirabeau, when he alone could yet preserve the monarchy.   He had destroyed things more precious than monarchy, and he had trampled on rights more sacred than the crowns of kings.

The crime of Orsini was skilfully turned to account by the Italian refugees, who surrounded the Emperor.

On his return from the opera he saw the prefect of police, Pietri, who has since been so instrumental in advancing the designs of his master in Italy. Pietri was received with a storm of frantic rage ; and the calmness which the Emperor had exhibited in the moment of peril, and during the time that he remained in public, gave way to a passion of anger such as terror alone can inspire. Pietri, an old conspirator, perceived in this unwonted humour an occasion for the realisation of those schemes for which he and Prince Louis Napoleon had formerly intrigued, and for which Orsini had just exposed his life. There was no security for the Emperor, he said, until he had achieved something for Italy. Thus the instinct of self-preservation and of ambition coalesced with the projects of Cavour, and Napoleon resolved to promise the aid which had been so long and so earnestly demanded. The Piedmontese Minister had succeeded in preparing his country for war by erecting new fortifications, and in persuading the more politic of his friends that the danger of bringing French armies into Italy would be balanced by the resistance of England and of the other Powers. In July he accepted the Emperor's invitation to Plombières, and on his return he gave to his countrymen the signal for action. Then began that vast intrigue of the party of national union in Central Italy by which the popular insurrections were organised which broke out simultaneously with the war, and by which one part of the French designs was effectually baffled. Service in the National Guard was made compulsory on all men under thirty-five, and a severe system of discipline was introduced. On the occasion of the marriage of the Princess Clotilda, the Deputy Sineo made a declaration of political principles, which were those of his leader :—

In accepting this union the ancient dynasty of Savoy pays a new homage to the principles consecrated in France in 1789, which constitute to this day the basis of the public law of that nation. . . . Let us endeavour to seal anew the solemn and indelible compacts by which Charles Albert united his dynasty with the cause of the liberty and independence of nations.

Mamiani spoke quite as suggestively :—

> If there is provocation, it exists on both sides ; it is not in the
> facts only, but in the moral order.   On this side of the Ticino there
> is liberty ; beyond it slavery.   Here everything is done to secure
> the dignity of our country ; there, to oppress it.   That is the real
> provocation, which cannot be prevented.

In order to identify himself entirely with the event,
Cavour took everything into his own hands ; at the
opening of hostilities he was President of the Council,
Minister of the Interior, of Foreign Affairs, and of War.
His resignation after the Peace of Villafranca added vastly
to his popularity, and he returned to office afterwards with
redoubled power, but at a time of still greater difficulty.
It was now his part to finish the work which France had
left undone ; to accomplish alone, and in defiance of his
ally, what Napoleon had pronounced impossible ; to
conclude the revolution without permitting the triumph
of the revolutionary party, which had been deemed so
formidable on the morrow of Solferino ; to prepare for
the treaty of Zürich the fate which had overtaken the
treaties of Vienna.

A paper was circulated among the Great Powers,
bearing no signature, and appealing to their interest in
the independence of Italy from France, in order to justify
the annexation of the Duchies.   It was the last attempt
to save Savoy and Nice, which the principles of annexation by popular suffrage, and of national unity, required
as a penalty for the Italian Revolution.   By a just
retribution, it happened that the conduct of the Ministry
in the course of the negotiations in which this sacrifice
was made, was as ignominious and dishonourable as that
by which they had gained their ambitious ends in Italy.
Circumstances rendered their position hopeless ; they
themselves made it infamous.   On the 10th of January
1860, the new governor of Savoy received the Municipality of Chambéry, with the assurance that "in Turin
there had never been a question of surrendering Savoy
to France."   On the 18th the organ of the annexionists,
the *Avenir de Nice*, declared :—

We repeat with still greater confidence that the annexation of Nice to France is certain : the time of its accomplishment is a question not of months, but of days.

The editor was told to leave the country, and then forgiven. On the 29th the Governor of Savoy said :—

The policy of the Government is sufficiently known : it has never entertained the design of surrendering Savoy. As to the party which has started the question of separation, it is useless to give it an answer.

On the 3rd of February Sir James Hudson writes that he had seen Count Cavour, who expressed his astonishment at the report about the annexation of Savoy, and declared that he did not know how it could have arisen. He wondered, he said, at the change of opinion among many people in Savoy, who wished to join France before the war and were now against it. Sardinia, he averred, had never had the remotest intention of surrendering, selling, or exchanging Savoy. On the 24th, the French Government wrote to Turin, that if Sardinia incorporated in her dominions part of Central Italy, the possession of Savoy became a geographical necessity for the protection of the French frontier. Sardinia lost no time in replying :—

March 2nd : We feel too deeply what Italy owes to the Emperor, not to consider most earnestly a demand which is founded on the principle of respect for the wishes of the people. At the moment when we are loudly insisting on the right of the inhabitants of Central Italy to decide on their own fate, we cannot refuse to the subjects of the king beyond the Alps the right of freely expressing their will, and we could not refuse to recognise the importance of their demonstration, expressed in a legal way and consistently with the directions of Parliament.

The last words were omitted in the *Moniteur*, as France did not wish the transaction to be left to the Chambers, to which Cavour looked as the last resource, to prevent the loss or to share the blame.

These matters were hardly settled when a prospect of compensation opened out in Southern Italy. Early in the year Mazzini had offered to Victor Emmanuel to create a rising in the Neapolitan dominions, on condition of receiving indirect assistance.   The Government of Turin was not ready to incur the chances of a new war; time was needed to consolidate the State and to reorganise the army.   But it suited the policy of France that the delivery of the South should not be the work of Sardinia, and that she should not enjoy the fruit of it.   Cavour could not resist the pressure of the Republicans supported by the connivance of France, and he determined so to conduct himself as to turn the enterprise to his own advantage.   This he accomplished in a way which was a triumph of unscrupulous statesmanship.   Garibaldi went forth as the instrument of a party that desired a Republican Italy and of a power that desired a Federal Italy, and he did the work of monarchy and unity. When Palermo had fallen, the Piedmontese party insisted on annexation.   Garibaldi refused to surrender the dictatorship, which he required in order to complete the conquest of the mainland.   "Garibaldi," said La Farina, "wished the annexation to follow only after the deliverance of all Italy, including Rome and Venice." He thought that by retaining the power in his own hands he would be able ultimately to compel the Turin Government to follow him against the Pope and the Quadrilateral; and his Mazzinist allies supported him, in order that the deliverance might be achieved by the revolution alone, and that the revolution might then be master of Italy.   La Farina, Cavour's agent with Garibaldi, and the head of the national party organised by Manin, which aimed at unity without democracy, was forced to give way.

"I openly and quietly informed the General," he says, "of the reasons of my discontent.   He treated me kindly at first; but he reproached me with my friendship for Cavour, my approbation of the treaty of cession, and my opposition to his design on Central Italy."

Garibaldi sent him to Genoa, and declared that he would retire rather than annex Sicily to Sardinia before his work was done.   "I came to fight for the

cause of Italy, not for Sicily alone." If the annexation
of Sicily had been obtained Cavour could have postponed
the attack on Naples, and the imminent quarrel with the
Power that held Rome. At Naples Garibaldi was entirely
in the hands of the Republicans, and in open hostility
to the Turin Ministry, and he declared that he was resolved to go on to Rome, and to deliver Italy in spite of
them,—*piaccia ò non piaccia ai potenti della terra.*

In this extremity, with the Mazzinists masters of the
situation by their influence over Garibaldi, with the
prospect of a breach with France, of an attack on Rome,—
which would make peace with the Catholics impossible
for ever,—of a great democratic movement and an untimely
war, Cavour took that desperate resolution which, next to
the introduction of the French into Italy, is the most
important of his whole career. In defiance of the angry
protests of all the great Powers, and of the traditions
and forms of the law of nations in time of war, he decreed
the invasion of the Roman and Neapolitan dominions.

"If we are not in La Cattolica before Garibaldi," he wrote,
11th September, "we are lost; the revolution would spread all
over Italy. We are compelled to act."

On the same day Cialdini entered the Marches, and
Cavour found himself at last master of Italy, reaping
where Mazzini and Napoleon had sown. His triumph
was completed when Garibaldi carried his opposition into
the Chamber.

Our purpose has been, not to give a biographical
account of the life of Cavour, but to point out the words
and deeds most illustrative of his character. He conducted the Italian revolution with consummate skill, and
his means were, on the whole, better than his end. The
one great reproach against his foreign policy is, that he
was the author of the Italian war; that he sought to
deliver Italy from foreign oppression. And yet great
part of Italy was atrociously misgoverned, and the misgovernment was due to the presence of the Austrians.
A vast pressure weighed down religion and literature;

society was penetrated with corruption; self-government was almost unknown. Down to 1848 this was due to the Austrians. Their policy has to answer for the degradation of Italy, and for the perils which have befallen the Church. Nor has the change that has passed over the Empire in the reign of Francis Joseph brought any serious improvement in the condition of Italy. For this the Italians alone are responsible; for they have rejected every advance, and have feared nothing so much as Austrian concessions. The war of 1859 had not the moral excuse of the war of 1848. The justification of a rising against the old *régime* did not apply to the new. In the recent war Austria was attacked, not because of misgovernment, but because of national antagonism. The first plea was fiercely repudiated by the Italian patriots, and that which they substituted is absolutely revolutionary and criminal. The fall of the other thrones followed, by the law of gravitation, when the Austrian supremacy was removed; and the reason urged against the government of the Pope and of the King of Naples, whether rightly or wrongly applied, was sound in principle; whilst Tuscany and Lombardy were taken from the Austrians on grounds which are in all cases false. The real charge against Austria was, that she prevented reforms in the States which she influenced; the misgovernment of these States was the chief weapon by which she was expelled. That Austria alone should be expelled, whilst the other sovereigns remained, would have been an inversion of the order both of ideas and of things. The events of the last two years are secondary to the Italian war, and possess neither the same importance in principle nor the same proportion of guilt which give to that event its foul pre-eminence in modern history.

But the policy of Cavour was revolutionary at home as well as abroad; and it is his notion of government and of the position of the State, more than his ambitious policy, that brought him into collision with the Church. He was not intentionally a persecutor, or consciously

an enemy of religion.   Nothing in his whole life could
justify a suspicion of the sincerity of his Christian end,
or lead us to imagine that he would make any retractation.
The writings of Gioberti show how bitter a hatred of
the clergy may, in Catholic countries, coexist with
an earnest faith.   Such sentiments, in the years that
preceded the Reformation, were common among men
who recoiled with horror from the heresy of Luther.   In
the mind of an ambitious and keen-sighted statesman,
inspired with the ideas and with the knowledge of his
own age only, and aware of its aspirations and feelings ;
who finds that in all great questions of secular interest
which he knows that he understands he is opposed by
almost all the priesthood, and supported by the ablest
men out of the Church ; who has been accustomed from
his youth to connect the clergy with a system of government which excites his just and honest indignation,—is
not necessarily an unbeliever if he cannot distinguish
between the party and the cause, and fails to discover the
true solution of the great problem in which better men
have gone astray.   He thought he could reconcile religion
and modern society without injury to either, and he was
mistaken ; but not more grievously and fatally mistaken
than the mass of those by whom he was denounced.
His ignorance of religion has been a great calamity,
but not a greater calamity than his ignorance of the true
nature of liberty.   The Church has more to fear from
political errors than from religious hatred.   In a State
really free, passion is impotent against her.   In a State
without freedom, she is almost as much in danger from
her friends as from her enemies.   The annexation of all
Italy under the Sardinian Crown would not have been,
perhaps, so much an evil as a blessing to religion, if the
political system of Sardinia had been sound.   The incompatibility of the Piedmontese laws and government
with the freedom of the Church is the real danger in the
loss of the temporal power.   If Cavour had been what he
believed himself to be, a liberal statesman, the Roman
question would have lost much of its complication.   A

State in which rights are sacred, in which the independence of the two orders is a fundamental and essential principle, in which property is secured, and in which government usurps no social functions ; where, in short, the Episcopate is safe in the discharge of its duties and in the enjoyment of its rights, from the encroachments of a hostile or patronising sovereign and from the changes and caprices of popular will ; and where the sphere of religion is removed from the interference of the legislative as well as of the executive power, in that State, if such there be, it would be possible for the Holy See to enjoy perfect independence and immunity from even the suspicion of influence, supported by a system of domains and guaranteed by the public faith of Europe.

But Piedmont was more remote than many foreign countries from the character of freedom.   The spirit of her institutions was profoundly hostile to the Church, and she did great injury more by her laws than by her policy : of these Cavour was not the author ; Azeglio and others are as deeply responsible as he.   It is the common policy of foreign Liberals, founded on those ideas of 1789, which are in irreconcilable opposition with liberty and with religion.   Unfortunately those among the Italian clergy who, considering religious interests, ardently desire an extensive change, seem hardly aware of the real nature of that constitutional government which promises so much but commonly fulfils so imperfectly its promise ; and there is as much to deplore in the partiality of one party of Catholics for the internal policy of Cavour as in the injustice of others towards his feelings of religion.

Cavour had seen the clergy in alliance with a tyrannical government, and he dreaded their influence in the State. He deemed that the Austrian supremacy and the temporal power must stand and fall together, and he united them in the same attack.   He was a stranger to that fierce animosity which inflames so many of his countrymen, and especially that party whom he most resolutely opposed.   But he did much of their work for them, impelled by very different motives, and aiming at a widely

different end.   At any time he would have been ready
to sacrifice ecclesiastical as well as any other rights, if
they were obstacles to the accomplishment of his purpose.
He had been Minister for several years when Gallenga
wrote of his administration :—

Since the legislative power was taken from the hands of the
Crown, gaming, theft, robbery, and all other crimes have increased
greatly ; the Government plays and sports with public morality.
Whilst whole bands of robbers steal with impunity, the Ministry says
that the police are not yet organised.   One Minister coolly proposes
to sacrifice the fat monks, and to spare the lean ones for a time,
and makes of every sacred principle a mere question of finance. . . .
Our Constitution was dictated by haste and uncertainty, not to say
by confusion, despondency, and disorder.   Never before was there
a real tyranny in the land.

His enthusiastic biographer, writing in the last year of
his life, says :—

Certainly the internal administration does not proceed with order
and expedition in any of the Italian provinces.   Assuredly in every
part of it there are many errors, old and new, to be repaired. . . .
Assuredly the decay of the finances is appalling, and makes it necessary
to require the people to make sacrifices for liberty before they have
felt and discovered from her benefits that she is a goddess.

The political ideas which have led to so much evil are
common to the majority of Liberals with Cavour.   But
whilst few possessed his ability and courage, he was more
free than many others from passion and from ill-will
towards those whom he thrust aside from his path ; and
whilst he was resolute in the pursuit of certain practical
ends to which he was enthusiastically devoted, he disliked
extremes, and was never carried away by the wish of
realising a theory and completing a consistent system.
In all this he was far superior to the men who are to
carry on his work, and he is justly regretted by all parties.
While the Revolutionists have to fear that the cause of
national unity will fail in less powerful hands, the Catholics
have to fear that many fierce passions will be let loose
which he restrained, and that principles will be carried to
their worst results which had no power over the practical
mind of Cavour.

VII

THE CAUSES OF THE FRANCO-PRUSSIAN WAR [1]

THE Bismarck revelations are studiously calculated to confuse the central problem of his career, the responsibility for the war of 1870. All the voluminous literature regarding Moltke and Roon ignores the question ; and the significant suppression of the memoirs of Bernhardi, Bismarck's agent in Spain, shows that there is a secret still to be concealed.

Let me illustrate by a curious instance the difficulties that beset the path of a historian. Bismarck relates that Count H——, the Bavarian Master of the Horse, was sent from Versailles to negotiate with the King of Bavaria for the proclamation of the German Empire, and that the emissary travelled to Munich and back without loss of time. The story which these bald words are meant to hide is as follows : After the fall of Bismarck his successor found a deficit of a couple of hundred thousand pounds in the sequestrated Guelphic Fund, which the Chancellor administers beyond the control of Parliament, and he found that the money had gone to Munich. He requested the Bavarian Minister at Berlin to go home at once and find out what it meant. It meant that the King of Bavaria had agreed to propose the erection of the German Empire in return for £15,000 a year, to be paid to him secretly out of the Guelphic Fund, and that his Master of the Horse was handsomely rewarded out of the same

[1] A paper read at the "Eranus," the Trinity College Historical Society, and the S. Catharine's College Historical Society.

purse. When this was detected it was kept quiet, but H——, who had done the work, was superseded on the plea of ill-health. This transaction, splendidly illustrating the devious dexterity of the Chancellor, is still shrouded in utter darkness.

In investigating the true cause of the war, we are confronted by the interesting fact that Sybel, writing with the sanction and support of Bismarck, exonerates the Emperor, and also the Empress, while Thiers vehemently denied the guilt of the Prussian Chancellor. The explanation of this generosity on the part of Thiers is that he desired at that moment to conciliate Bismarck. He was negotiating with Germany to prepare for the election of the next Pope, and he wished to propitiate him in favour of his own candidate, who was Cardinal Ginoulhiac, Archbishop of Lyons, a dull man, but reputed the most learned prelate in France. It was in the midst of these communications with Arnim that the wrath of the royalists overtook him.

The evidence I have collected makes it difficult to approve these verdicts of absolution. The question goes back to 1865. In that year the Emperor's illness became known, and men began to doubt whether he would live to consolidate the dynasty and to secure the succession for his son. In that year also the surrender of Lee altered the conditions of European politics. The victorious Americans, combining the forces of North and South, resolved to expel the French from Mexico, where they had set up an offending European monarch under cover of the Civil War. They appointed a general to command the army of Mexico, which was to be recruited largely among the Confederates, and to relieve the Union of a disturbing element, and they sent him to Paris to show his patent to the Emperor. Napoleon saw and understood. Without a struggle, without a protest, he recalled his army and left Maximilian to his fate.

The moment when he underwent this terrible humiliation was the moment when Prussia was preparing to fall upon Austria. It was necessary for his existence on the throne to do something for his prestige.   He would be ruined with the army if, after bringing them back from one disastrous failure in America, his policy exposed them to another in Europe.   The French Empire was imperilled as much as the Austrian by the war of 1866.   Napoleon made his choice, laid his plans, and did what other men have done before and since—he put his money on the wrong horse.   All his generals excepting two, Bourbaki and Berckheim, believed that the Austrians would win ; and he accordingly came to an agreement with Austria for the dismemberment of Prussia and the division of the spoil.   He neglected to hedge.   He made no similar arrangement beforehand with the other side.   When his schemes were shattered at Königgrätz, he sought to make terms with the victor.   He urged that their victory was due to his neutrality and forbearance. The balance of power was overthrown, and he claimed compensation.

Austria was not yet subdued.   Archduke Albrecht, crowned with the glory of Custoza, was on the march with the army which had defeated the Italians.   Cholera was in the camp.   Bismarck asked Moltke whether in those circumstances he was willing to fight the French. In a paper, which is wonderful for its matter-of-fact simplicity, Moltke explained that he was quite willing. It would not be possible, he said, to defend the frontier. But he undertook to meet the French army on equal terms after it had crossed the Rhine.

Fortified by this memorable statement, Bismarck determined to make peace at once with Austria, but to stand his ground as regarded France.   The determination was quickly followed by the most dramatic incident in his life. The French demands came.   When Pfordten, the Bavarian Minister, saw what they were, saw that Napoleon claimed the Palatinate, which is Bavarian territory, he threw himself into the arms of the hated Chancellor, and at once concluded the treaty of peace and the secret treaty of military alliance in time of war.   With the French telegram in his hand, with the resolution to fight for the integrity of Germany, he created the force that conquered France and made the Empire.

Beust hurried to Paris, but found the Emperor so much weakened by disease and pain that he could not be roused to action. The American surrender had been followed by a European surrender. The Government was profoundly discredited, for, after miscalculating the issue of war, they had mismanaged the issue of diplomacy. Drouyn de l'Huys, the Minister who had insisted on the policy of compensation, resigned office. He was followed by the Minister of War. It was believed, rightly or not, that the want of a military demonstration to back the menacing demands was due to him. He was succeeded by Niel, who reorganised the army on a scheme of 400,000 men in line, 400,000 reserve, and 400,000 National Guards. It would take five years to complete the reserve and nine years for the *Garde Nationale mobile*.

Looking upon History as an affair of Reason, I do not assign these preparations for a war with Germany to national pride, or ambition, or the like irrational causes. The superiority of the German army was apparent, and it was due not only to an established organisation but to excess of numbers. The population of France had almost ceased to increase. The population of Germany increased rapidly. Four German children were born for one French. Berthelot pointed out that France possessed not only fewer children, but more old men. There were fifty-eight Prussians unfit for service to a hundred French. A leading newspaper computed that Germany already had 58,000 valid recruits annually more than France. A deputy argued that the German army, in a few years, would exceed the French by 800,000. The power that was already formidable would soon be overwhelming, and France would be at its mercy. So far as politics can be reduced to figures the thing was clear.

If it followed from this that France must increase her armaments, it followed still more certainly that France must seek alliances. Marshal Niel understood the situation. He admitted to General Jarras that they could

never cope with Germany single-handed. He relied on a
system of alliances either to make war impossible or to
make it profitable. In April 1869 he said to the
Empress, who constantly urged him to make the army
ready for a conflict with their neighbour, " I have obeyed
your orders, Madame. I am ready, and you are not." On
the 5th January 1868, Benedetti wrote that things were
growing urgent, that the effective unity of Germany would
soon be accomplished, and could only be prevented with
Austrian aid. Prince Napoleon was sent to Berlin, and
when he had failed to obtain an amicable understanding,
secret negotiations with other powers were begun and were
carried on by the sovereigns themselves, behind the back
of Ministers.

Austria, governed by Beust, who personified the defeat
of 1866, was the first and necessary ally. Austria would
not move without Italy, would not move, that is, with
Italy hostile in its rear. France and Italy were divided
by Rome. Napoleon attempted to avoid the difficulty by
allowing the Spaniards to occupy Rome instead of the
French ; but while this arrangement was in progress the
friendly government of Queen Isabella was overthrown.
Then the negotiations were resumed with Francis Joseph
and Victor Emmanuel, and were suspended in June 1869.
By that time the Emperor knew that the warlike support
of both would be his, if he would pay the price. Italy
had no ground of quarrel with Prussia ; to run the risk it
required compensation. There were two things the Italians
desired—one was Rome, the other was the debatable land
on the Austrian frontier. It was the policy of Beust that
the price should be paid, not in Austrian territory, but at
Rome ; and he insisted that the Roman thorn should be
taken out of the Italian foot. In other words, he required
that France, not Austria, should be the loser, as France,
not Austria, had the initiative in the warlike combination.

The project which Napoleon left in abeyance in the
summer of 1869 was taken up again early in 1870, not
by France but by Austria, and not by the Austrian
Government but by the Court. The Archduke Albrecht,

the most illustrious personage in the Empire, not only the head of the army, but the head of the war party, the man who, in 1866, had not been granted the opportunity of measuring swords with Moltke, made a tour in the south of France, and it was announced that he would go home by way of Paris, as the convenient route to Vienna. He conferred with the Emperor, assured him that a war without Austrian help would be hopeless, which was true, and proposed his strategic conditions. Nothing was settled at the time. A new Ministry had come into office on 2nd January, which was not only constitutional, but liberal and pacific, pledged not to tolerate personal government and not to oppose the union of Germany if it was desired by Germans. The visit of the Archduke was a defiance of both pledges. Some months before, when the correspondence between the monarchs had been interrupted, Napoleon had sent his confidential aide-de-camp, Fleury, to see what could be obtained from Russia. This was the man who carried through the *coup d'état* when Louis Napoleon wavered. He was well received at St. Petersburg, and was making way when the new Minister, Daru, required that there should be no negotiation that was not official, and none that was not pacific. This declaration condemned the mission of the Archduke to failure, and it condemned France to isolation. The Emperor got rid of his visitor with good words, promising that he would send a trusted officer to confer with him when he obtained a free hand. This he did by means of the *plébiscite*.

In April Daru resigned. On the 8th May the *plébiscite* affirmed the Emperor's policy. On the 15th May the Duke de Gramont, his ambassador at Vienna, who had already arrived at Paris, became Minister of Foreign Affairs. Four days later, 19th May, the chiefs of the staff were summoned to discuss the Austrian plan for a joint campaign in Germany. When they had made up their minds, one of them, General Lebrun, started for Vienna, to carry the result of their secret deliberations to the Archduke. On a previous mission he had visited the camp of Beverloo, where he saw a breech-loading steel gun from Prussia,

P

which was so true that the Belgian officers stood exposed, four feet from the target, at 1200 metres. He reported his alarming discovery, and was not one of the generals satisfied with their own country and its resources. In order to dispel suspicion he passed through Berlin, and I have been assured that the object of his journey remained unsuspected. I have some hesitation in believing it. Bismarck was liberal in paying for information, and Schuwaloff said that it was a weakness of his to believe too easily reports he had paid for. Bunsen once heard him quote a French official document to a group of astonished deputies, when he added that they might trust him for he possessed not a mere copy but the original. On the other hand, Émile Ollivier, the French Prime Minister, never heard of the mission until some years later.

Lebrun came to an understanding with the Archduke for an attack on Germany to be made in common, Austria coming into action three weeks later than France. During that interval the French would have to fight single-handed. To redress their inferiority, the fleet, after giving succour and encouragement to Denmark, would threaten the Baltic coast, and occupy a large Prussian force for the defence of Lübeck, Stettin, Danzig, and Königsberg. An Austrian army of 80,000 men collected on the Bohemian frontier, within striking distance of Berlin and of the lines connecting Silesia with the centre, would hold fast a larger number on the other side for the protection of vital parts. Meanwhile, the French were to seize Kehl, make for the heart of Bavaria, and reduce the South to inaction. Deducting the southern contingent and the two armies watching Bohemia and the sea, the Germans would lose the advantage of numbers, and France ought to maintain the struggle until Austria and Italy came to her support.

Lebrun had no political mission. He was not instructed to discuss the means of bringing on the war ; and he did not see Beust. But, on 14th June, he had secret audience of the Emperor at Schönbrunn, and received a communication of weightier import than the somewhat loose and visionary reasoning of the Archduke. Francis Joseph said that if France went to war for the declared purpose of delivering the South from the grasp of Prussia, the feeling of his people would compel him to take part in it. This was a statesmanlike idea; for they would have the South on their side, and there were materials in the Southern States for dexterous manipulation. In 1868 the Grand Duke of Hesse offered his possessions on the left bank of the Rhine to the Emperor. His Minister, Dalwigk, promised to find a pretext for French intervention in Germany. He entreated the Emperor to cross the Rhine, and to take the offensive vigorously. At the first success all the South would march with him.

What might have been done to detach the South by the arts of peace became apparent when the Bavarians debated the *casus foederis*. The Committee of the House of Deputies voted by 7 to 2 against the war credits, and by 6 to 3 in favour of armed neutrality. The Court, the aristocracy, the clergy, the mass of the country people dreaded to be ground in the mills of Prussia. The army and the manufacturers, scenting increase of trade, were on the other side. It was only by a tumult in the streets, by the overbearing vehemence of the President, by the production of a false telegram, that the Chamber was induced to reject the report of its Committee by 89 to 58, and to carry the war credit by 101 to 47. The archives of the Prussian legation were packed so that they could be despatched in a moment. At the Austrian legation a list of new Ministers was in readiness, who were pledged to resist the Prussian demand for co-operation. The Prime Minister himself, who was in office at the time, proposed neutrality at Paris. He eagerly adopted the English proposal for a general agreement excluding the members of the reigning houses from other thrones. The Prussians did not oppose the idea, for they denied that Leopold of Hohenzollern was a prince of the reigning house; but the French refused it for they had helped to seat his brother on the throne of

Roumania. This minister, Count Bray, has spoken to me with bitter regret of his success on that occasion. He complained that neither France nor Austria gave him the means of proclaiming neutrality—Austria, because it desired to overthrow him and his colleague at the War Office ; France, because Gramont was confident of gaining the first victory, and with it the support of the Southern States.

Lebrun returned to Paris and made his report to the Emperor on the 21st June. Napoleon was disappointed. He said that the letters of Francis Joseph had justified him in expecting more than this. He must have known already the inevitable slowness of the Austrian mobilisation from his conversations with the Archduke. It would appear that the Austrian Emperor had promised more in their earlier correspondence. The limitation of the quarrel to a single issue selected by Austria compelled him to follow a policy which was not his own, and which Ollivier had emphatically repudiated. Besides, if the ally would only fight for one cause, what if the vigilant enemy should raise a conflict on another? It became his evident interest to do it at once, and to excite and inflame any topic of dispute that would provoke resentment in France, before the scheme of a challenge on the ground of the Treaty of Prague could be matured. If Bismarck knew his business, that is, if he suspected what was brewing, he had the strongest inducement to precipitate matters without waiting until the enfeebled Emperor had constructed all his batteries. That was the result of the secret correspondence between crowned heads, of the conference with Archduke Albrecht, of the *plébiscite*, of the substitution of Gramont for Daru, of the mission of Lebrun. The long intrigue passed suddenly into an acute crisis. It was necessary to be prepared for an immediate outbreak.

The next move of the great conspirator is most mysterious. A few days after the interview with Lebrun, the specialists were called in for a consultation. They met on 1st July, and drew up a report which was signed by only one name. Their conclusions were unfavourable, indicating that an operation would be desirable. But Nélaton, the Sir Henry Thompson of France, did not wish to operate. Marshal Niel had died in his hands, and he was apprehensive of what happened, three years later, at Chislehurst. On the second day after the consultation the report was handed to the Emperor's physician. It contained these remarkable words: "The moment would be favourable for a more thorough examination, as the malady is not just now particularly acute." But then, why were they summoned? Apparently not because the suffering was worse than usual. Therefore for some reason that was not pathological, but political. Did the Emperor consult his experts because he wished to know whether he was fit to take the field in a certain impending event? That event was very near, for on the 3rd of July, the day when Conneau received the medical report, it became known that Leopold had accepted the crown of Spain. The report was not produced, for it was too late. It was shown to the Empress only, and the Empress replied: *Le vin est tiré, il faut le boire.*

That is the contribution of France to our problem. For two years Napoleon had laboured in secret to raise up enemies to Germany, and to prepare a war for 1871. It was a question of security for France, since so much power had been concentrated in the hands of the most audacious and aggressive of men. That was a powerful and an honourable motive. There was also the just motive of discontent in the states of Southern Germany.

There was the same question of existence on the other side. In 1867 Bismarck averted war by concessions with regard to Luxemburg which somewhat damaged his popular renown. In the following year the Spanish throne was vacant, and among possible candidates the name of Leopold of Hohenzollern was discussed. He was not the choice of any party; but many names were put forward by royalists who did not accept Montpensier. Early in 1869 Bismarck learned from Florence that Napoleon was preparing a triple alliance against him. He sent Bernhardi to Spain to join the Prussian legation. Theodor von Bernhardi had been sent on a similar mission to Italy in 1866, and was certified by Moltke as the best military writer in Europe. He was eminent also as an economist, a historian, and a politician, and it would have been hard to discover his equal in any European Cabinet. What he did in Spain has been committed to oblivion. Seven volumes of his diary have been published : the family assures me that the Spanish portion will never appear. The *Moniteur* of 7th June 1870 described him as the man who arranged the affair with Prim. The Austrian First Secretary said that he betrayed his secret one day at dinner. Somebody spoke indiscreetly on the subject, and Bernhardi aimed a kick at him under the table, which caught the shin of the Austrian instead. He was considered to have mismanaged things, and it was whispered that he had gone too far. I infer that he offered a heavy bribe to secure a majority in the Cortes. Fifty thousand pounds of Prussian bonds were sent to Spain at midsummer 1870. During the siege of Paris they came over here to be negotiated, and I know the banker through whose hands they passed. The money was thrown away, as the question never came to a vote. I associate this significant fact with the disgrace of the successful emissary.

But if Bernhardi was neglected by Bismarck, he received a distinction from Moltke in the presence of the army of which he might well be proud. One of the war correspondents, Sala, I believe, has related what he saw on the day when the Germans entered Paris. A group of four horsemen came out from the mass at the Bois de Boulogne, rode full speed up the rise, and were the first of their countrymen to pass under the *Arc de Triomphe* and gaze on the conquered city. The *Telegraph* goes on : " In front, ten paces before the others, rode a young officer of about twenty, sword in hand. The young fellow in the van looked so plucky, as he galloped with head well up and sabre in air, that I could not help admiring him. If that youngster's mother could have seen him, she would have been proud of her son that day. I asked the young hussar his name and regiment. He answered, ' Lieutenant Bernhardi of the 14th Hussars.'" That was the reward of the man who obtained the offer of the Spanish crown, which brought the Germans to Paris.

On 2nd January 1869 Bismarck wrote that war was inevitable, but the later the better. In April Napoleon instructed Benedetti to say that the acceptance of the crown would be taken as a hostile act. Benedetti had already spoken to Thill, the Prussian Minister of Foreign Affairs, and in May he spoke to Bismarck. They both said as little as possible, and put him off with measured words. He warned his Government that he found grave cause for suspicion. Both Thill and Bismarck afterwards denied that these conversations had taken place, Thill adding, later on, that he only meant to say that he had forgotten. Stranger still, they were forgotten at Paris, as I was told by M. de Courcel, who was at the Foreign Office at the time; and Benedetti was obliged to call attention to the despatches in which he had warned his Government. But he did not warn Bismarck, as explicitly as he was intended to do, that the consequences would be very serious.

At that time, however, no offer had been made, and no decision required to be taken. The offer came in the autumn of 1869. Count Werthern, Prussian Minister at Munich, had been at the legation at Madrid, and knew Prim. In September the Spanish deputy Salazar came to him with letters from Prim, and on the 17th Werthern took him to Weinburg, on the Lake of Constance, and introduced him, after nightfall and with every precaution, to the Prince of Hohenzollern. His mission was to feel his way, and find out what hope there was of his son if the crown was formally offered to him. Father and sons were against it, but the refusal was not a positive one. Leopold stipulated that Spain should be tranquil, and that he should not be opposed by other claims. Then, he might reconsider his reply. In October Werthern came to Baden and urged the family not to reject such a future.

The father had previously stated that he never would consent, and that France could never allow it. Besides, they were not sure of the Cortes. We are assured by Sybel, who had it from Werthern, that he did all this on his own responsibility, and that his Government did not hear of it till much later. On the return of Salazar Prim tried several other candidates. He applied at Florence for the King's younger son and at Harrow for the Duke of Genoa, who is said to have incurred animadversion from the headmaster for the distractions the prospect gave him.

When the Italian princes had refused, and when order had been restored in the disturbed provinces, Salazar returned to Germany, this time with an official proposition addressed to the King of Prussia. The prize had gained in value. The Government making the offer had suppressed the revolts both of Carlists and Republicans, and were masters of the country. No complications were to be feared from rivals belonging to reigning families. In these circumstances Bismarck resolved to push the matter through. On 15th March a special consultation was held, and the royal family, with the public men who had taken part, dined with the Hohenzollern. The Ministers all favoured acceptance. No question arose of French opposition ; but at table Moltke's neighbour, Delbrück, asked him how it would be if Napoleon took it ill. Moltke replied that it would be all right. Bismarck insisted that it was a duty to the Fatherland, that a friendly power on the Pyrenees would be a great advantage. The King was undecided. The Crown Prince warned his cousin that there was no intention of keeping him on the throne ; that the whole thing was no more than a move in a game. Leopold refused. But it was resolved to send an intelligent observer to ascertain the state of feeling in Spain, and for this service Bismarck selected his own man, Lothar Bucher. He had become extremely eager. The Archduke was prolonging his stay at Paris ; on the other hand, it might be well to come to blows while Daru and Ollivier were in office, for they would make alliances difficult.

At the end of May Bucher reported all well, and early
in June the resistance of Prince Leopold was overcome.
Thereupon Bismarck requested Prim to renew his offer,
and obtained the assent of King William. It was the
time when Lebrun was at Schönbrunn. The King was
annoyed at the obstinate recurrence of the question, having
hoped that it was disposed of. The Crown Princess wrote
to our Queen: "I fear it is a sad mistake on the part of
the Hohenzollerns." This is what we know from authentic
documents on the German side. It is clear that Bismarck
took up the Hohenzollern candidature when he knew of
the grand alliance that was preparing, and when the
enmity of France became dangerous. But we cannot tell
whether the idea occurred to him earlier. That he employed it to hasten the crisis before the hostile alliance
was concluded, is certain.

Both parties laboured to bring about war—the one
after the conclusion of alliances, the other before. The
Berlin Government played its cards best because it was
united. At Paris the warlike members of the Government
were intriguing to get rid of the Prime Minister and the
constitutional system which weakened the executive. The
King was at Ems; the Chancellor at Varzin. Moltke
was at his country-house driving his family about in a
brake. One day a messenger met him on the road with
a despatch, which he read and pocketed without a word.
But as he presently knocked the wheel against a kerb-
stone the people inside began to suspect what the despatch
contained. At tea-time they knew. For the Marshal
struck the table, exclaiming: "With the South or without
the South, we are a match for them!" and then rose and
walked away.

The breaking out of hostilities at that moment upset
all the Emperor's policy. He had not concluded a single
treaty. Nevertheless there was no hesitation in resolving
that there must be no Prussian King of Spain, even if it
could only be prevented by a deadly struggle without
allies. It was true that Prince Leopold was descended
from Murat; that he was more nearly connected with the

French Emperor than with the King of Prussia ; that his ancestor, after Jena, had asked Napoleon to set him in the place of the reigning Hohenzollern, over what remained of the territory of Brandenburg. But there was an unforgotten feud. The Empress had promoted a match between one of them and her cousin, the daughter of the Duke of Hamilton, and he had broken off the engagement at the last moment. The Emperor made an attempt to bring European opinion to bear, and solicited influence in every quarter. He sent for Rothschild and asked him to obtain the friendly offices of the English Government. A long telegram was sent over, which was deciphered by the present Lord Rothschild, who took it, after breakfast, on Wednesday, 6th July, to Carlton House Terrace. Gladstone was on the point of leaving his house to present Lord Granville as Foreign Secretary at Windsor, and his visitor drove him to the station in his brougham. After a long silence he told Rothschild that he did not like to interfere with the choice of the Spaniards, but that he would probably be overruled in the Cabinet. The Ministry were divided. Bright would do nothing for Belgium ; Lowe did not care what happened to Germany ; Lord Granville asked himself what would be the position of England with the French at Berlin. Cardwell, at the War Office, estimated that they would get there in about six weeks. All agreed that the Germans had no chance, and that it would be doing them a service to get them out of the scrape. They were taken by surprise. Lord Clarendon had known about the Hohenzollern project, and had spoken of it to the Queen, and the Queen informed the Ministers. For Lord Clarendon died at the end of June. He had conferred with Moltke at Wiesbaden the year before, and learned from him that they expected to be at war shortly and to reach Paris in the way they afterwards did.

So far as I know, Dean Church was nearly the first man in England who saw that the quarrel had been brought on by Bismarck ; and what the Dean wrote in private was published in the *Times*, with much acuteness and some errors, by another divine, who took the name of

"Scrutator," and carried on a skirmish with Max Müller. Sanderson, then a junior at the Foreign Office, drew the same inference. For they had information that iron girders were ready in Germany, of the proper length to bridge the rivers on the road to Paris ; and it is on a bridge of this sort, made with the proper measurements, that they crossed the Moselle above Metz, as was reported by Hozier. The Government had no such suspicion ; and the *Edinburgh Review* had an article in October, the authorship of which could not be doubtful for a moment, containing these words : "The whole proceedings of the French Government in the conduct of its controversy constituted one series of unrelieved and lamentable errors." By that time, however, a well-informed diplomatist, in the confidence of German headquarters, had written as follows, 30th September : "From statements made to me confidentially, I have obtained the certainty that the Hohenzollern candidature was deliberately arranged by Bismarck with a view of bringing on the collision with France in such a way as to make Germany appear to be acting on the defensive." Treitschke and Bernhardi at the time, and Bismarck in 1874, regarded the French aggression as the effect of an Ultramontane plot, part of the same design as the Vatican Council; and in the same connection it was often represented as the act of the Spanish Empress, prompted by the prelates and chaplains of the Tuileries. Bismarck affirmed it in the midst of the *Culturkampf*, to rouse a feeling against Rome. The same view made an impression on Ministers in London. Our agents in Alsace found the Protestants in a state of alarm, expecting a new St. Bartholomew, prodigal of stories of Catholic exultation and menace.

The part played by the Empress is difficult to determine. Lord Granville wrote, 16th September, to Ponsonby : "I am glad the Queen thinks of writing to the Empress. Her misfortune is great, although it is much owing to herself—Mexico, Rome, war with Prussia." General Du Barail, one of the first men in France, says in his Memoirs : " I am forced to acknowledge that she was the principal author of the war of 1870, if not the only one." She is reported to have said to Moceni, at Florence : " As to the war they accuse me of having provoked, I can only say that it might have saved, that it ought to have saved, the Empire and the Papacy." When Thureau Dangin, the historian and academician, was here, he told me this : " Lebœuf, the Minister of War, inquired whether the Emperor was in a condition to go through a campaign. Ollivier thereupon demanded to see the report of the physicians. The Empress replied that the Emperor suffered from rheumatism, and might be unable to take the field in winter ; but that was all. She did not produce the document." Lord Malmesbury writes : " Gramont told me that the Empress, a high-spirited and impressionable woman, made a strong and most excited address, declaring that war was inevitable if the honour of France was to be sustained. She confessed to the Queen, with tears, that she was responsible for the declaration of war." Grant Duff questioned Émile Ollivier on the subject in 1874, but there is nothing about it in his published Diaries. He sent me the suppressed passage, which says that when he asked whether she had been for war, Ollivier answered, *Passionnément.* Lord Frederick Cavendish saw her at Chislehurst, and the same day he related to a friend of my own at Brooks's that she had admitted it was her war. As my informant did not know that Lord Richard Cavendish lived at Chislehurst, which explains the visit, I attach weight to his testimony, although Lady Frederick declares that her husband never spoke to the Empress. Lastly, Parieu, the President of the Council of State, who was present at the Council referred to by Lord Malmesbury, says that when they were leaving she asked him what he thought of it. He replied that he wished England would do them the service of finding some way out of it. " M. Parieu," said the Empress, " I am much of the same opinion." This is in a published book. But in a private letter he wrote to a person whom I know that her words were, *C'est ma guerre à moi.*

The action of our Government was this: They discouraged the candidature, and remonstrated against it, advising that it should be withdrawn. When that was done, they thought the German position a good one. Lord Granville wrote, 10th July: "Under the menaces of the French it is difficult for North Germany to make a concession, or to discourage the Prince in his candidature." Nevertheless the Cabinet came to a decision which they communicated to the Queen which was taken very ill by the Germans. It proposed that they should do for a consideration what they had already done unconditionally. For the Germans had withdrawn their candidature, and the King had expressed to Benedetti his approval of the measure. But the French refused to withdraw their new demands. And when Gramont persisted, regardless of our advice, Lord Lyons assured him that it made no difference in our sentiments. His other despatches, during the crisis, were received with approbation, and an approving despatch always followed from the Foreign Office. No such reply was given to this outrageous blunder. For by that time the French Government was bent on war. At first the moderation shown by the King of Prussia in receding from his position, and accepting in patience so grave a repulse, made a bad impression at Paris, and was attributed to fear. The Imperialists were elate. If Prussia was willing to accept one humiliation, why not another? If one leek went down, why not two? They had gained, with the moral support of Europe, a great diplomatic victory. They began to think it possible to extract something more from the situation. The Emperor said to Ingra: "Public opinion in France would have preferred another solution—that is, war. But I recognise that this is a sufficient, a satisfactory solution, and removes every pretext for war—for the present." Rothschild received this telegram: "The Prince has given up his candidature. The French are satisfied." The Prime Minister announced peace, with effusion, and was positively triumphant. This was not the purpose of the majority. They wished to upset him ; they found that he was consolidated. They declared that the withdrawal was no satisfaction, and announced an interpellation. Gramont proposed to retain office, sacrificing Ollivier and other colleagues. He put himself on the side of those who wished for further concessions, even at the risk of war. It had been a deliberately hostile act, a meditated offence, long and carefully prepared, insolently denied. It demanded reparation. The malefactor could not be allowed quietly to withdraw, and to say that it was all right.

The King was not really committed. He had sanctioned the withdrawal, but he had also sanctioned the candidature, leaving the initiative of deciding in both cases to Prince Leopold. He was quite free to do the same thing, and to sanction a second acceptance as he had done the first. He held in his hands a convenient *casus belli*, to be used or dropped at pleasure. The argument was rather subtle ; but it would be used with effect in the Chamber against the Ministry. It was better that it should be used by the Ministry against Prussia ; used to strengthen Gramont, not to destroy him. Therefore he demanded a guarantee for the future, and as the ambassador assured him that there had been no idea of offending France, he told him that the same assurance coming from the King himself would be very favourably received. Ollivier was present, and agreed. But when he heard late at night, and accidentally, of the demand for a guarantee, he was indignant, and obliged Gramont to alternate his despatch by another, stating that this was not a *sine qua non*. He spent a sleepless night, reflecting whether he ought not to resign. He did not perceive, he hardly acknowledges now, that his colleague was intriguing against him with the undiluted Imperialists, and with the Empress. Therefore, on the following morning, 13th July, while all men were applauding the diplomatic skill of the French, or the superb temper of King William, the unhappy Benedetti had an audience on the promenade of Ems. It was less friendly than the ambassador ever afterwards maintained, excepting once in private, but it was not actually hostile. The

King rejected the new demand, and when the Frenchman asked for another audience, he was told that the King's answer was final, and that he desired to hold no further parley on that subject. This is the famous insult of which so much was made in France, and which was the delight of Treitschke and of every Teutonic schoolboy. There was a very popular picture of the French ambassador, in gold lace and bareheaded, with the Prussian lackey shutting the door in his face. In reality the refusal was conveyed in courteous terms by Prince Radzivill, as who should say, the Duke of Northumberland. The schoolboy of to-day knows pretty well who invented the imaginary insult, and knows the extraordinary scene.

The withdrawal of Leopold, which had been suggested by the King himself, struck at the policy and prestige of Bismarck. He had carried the candidature through with all his energy, in spite of indifference in Spain, of reluctance in the house of Hohenzollern, of the universal disapproval of Europe. What he had prepared with such an expenditure of force and skill was now abandoned without a word, and without his assent. He had already forwarded Eulenburg to Ems to stiffen the back of the King; he now followed, intending to resign, or to try resignation. When he got to Berlin he had some friends to dinner; and although they were the two strongest men on earth, when they heard of the surrender of Ems they hung their heads, like Heine's grenadiers. Then came the second despatch, with the audience refused, and the situation was saved. The journey to Ems became unnecessary. He drew his long pencil and altered the text, showing only that Benedetti had presented an offensive demand, and the King had refused to see him. That there might be no mistake, he made this official by sending it to all the embassies and legations. Moltke exclaimed: "You have converted surrender into defiance." All three knew that war must follow. Bismarck asked how it would be. The Marshal answered, "Only let me command in France, and the devil may fetch this old carcase as soon as he likes." Roon was equally confident. Two days later, when the King arrived at the Potsdam terminus, he held the deciding council on the platform, surrounded by a throng of expectant officers.   They saw the Chancellor put the telegram into his hands, saw him turn to his War Minister, and heard a grave voice say, "There is no difficulty.   Everything is ready."   So much so that he had only to sign an order lying on his desk before he went to bed, and he says in his Memoirs, that the ensuing fortnight, when the incessant battalions were springing into line, was the idlest of his life.

When the King at Ems read the despatch in the morning, he gave it to Eulenburg, saying, with emotion, "This is war," and he hurried to Berlin.   At Paris it produced the same impression.   Nevertheless, the peace party continued to prevail in the Government.   They met at ten o'clock at night on the 14th, and still resolved not to call out the reserves.   But at eleven a message was brought in which at once determined the declaration of war.   They had borne the recall of Werther, the scene at Ems, the despatch recounting it, the communication to the Powers. Lebœuf could not remember what the decisive paper contained.   Gramont declined to compromise the persons who sent it from Berlin to Vienna, or from Vienna to Paris.   But he says that it proved Bismarck's resolution to fight, and so made a peace policy untenable.

On the 13th Loftus congratulated the Chancellor on the preservation of peace by the retirement of Prince Leopold.   Bismarck replied that he was mistaken, that he meant to demand satisfaction for the language of Gramont—implying that it must be made clear that they yielded to the unanimous feeling of Europe, not to the threats of France.   He said: "We must require some guarantee that we may not be subjected to a sudden attack, like a flash of lightning in perfect darkness, which suddenly reveals to sight a band of robbers."   The despatch was printed in the Blue Book without these words.   Gramont tells us that his text was fuller than that which Lord Granville published.   Consequently he knew that Bismarck intended to provoke a conflict, and called the Emperor and his Ministers a band of robbers. Discussion after that was silenced. Beust, who declared that he regarded French interests as his own, and would help as far as possible, transmitted this report from Vienna, and he sent his confidant, Count Vitzthum, from Brussels to Paris, to establish an understanding for purposes of war. Gramont stated afterwards that the visit of Vitzthum, which coincided with the calling out of the reserves, restored the friendly feeling towards Austria which her protest against the *casus belli* in the Hohenzollern affair had disturbed. Hohenzollern was out of the way, and Bismarck's action on the 13th constituted a challenge. It was a war against the union of Germany, and on that basis Austria stood by France. So that the responsibility rests not only with Bismarck, with Napoleon, the Empress, and Gramont, but with Count Beust and Francis Joseph. But whereas Napoleon depended on alliances, and satisfied questioning Ministers by opening a drawer and producing the letters from the Emperor of Austria and the King of Italy, the Duke de Gramont felt quite secure without them.

Q

VIII

THE WAR OF 1870 [1]

Opus adgredior opimum casibus, atrox proeliis, discors seditioni-
bus, ipsa etiam pace saevum.—TACITUS, *Hist.* i. 2.

To exhibit a coherent chain of causes in the revolution of
the last nine months, which has shifted the landmarks of
European politics, and has given new leaders to the world,
is still an impossible task.   Many links remain concealed;
and the very questions which most excite curiosity are
those which cannot yet be solved.   The communications
that passed through private or official channels between
Marshal Prim and the Governments of France and
Prussia; the nature of the understanding between the
Russian Emperor and King William; the consultations
in which Prince Leopold of Hohenzollern spent six days
before refusing to be the cause of war; the motives that
paralysed the splendid army of Bazaine; the real object
of the Germans in bombarding Paris, and the immediate
reason of its capitulation,—these are the things on which
it is not safe to pronounce with certainty, and I must be
content to leave them unexplained.   Whenever these
gaps are filled up, and the secrets of recent history come
to be declared, it is probable that the events I am going
to relate will appeal in a different connection and an
altered light.

The storm that burst last summer had hung for four
years over Europe.   The war of 1866, which destroyed

---

[1] A lecture delivered at the Bridgnorth Literary and Scientific Institution on
the 25th of April 1871.

the Germanic Confederation, had enlarged Prussia, but had diminished Germany ; Austria was cast out, and the Southern States retained their connection with the North only by military and commercial treaties. The vital problem of policy for Prussia was to reconstruct Germany by bringing the eight millions of Southerners into the compact Confederation of the North. It was a fixed maxim with the Emperor Napoleon and the majority of French politicians, that the progress of Germany towards unity and strength must be interrupted by war unless France could obtain some territorial equivalent as the price of her consent. The Emperor tempted Prussia during more than a year with subtle schemes for compensation. Count Bismarck continued to put him off with vague words and indefinite suggestions, tending to divert his ambition from German territory to Switzerland and Belgium, where he would have to deal with England ; and the Emperor, deluded with false hopes of a profitable bargain, resisted the pressure of his friends and enemies at home, to avenge the defeat of Austria and restore the preponderance of France. Finding that he lost credit with the nation, and that nothing was to be wrung from Prussia by peaceful arts, he began gradually and methodically to prepare for war. His health was declining, and his prestige, impaired by the Mexican expedition and the formidable development of Prussian power, was insufficient to maintain his family on the throne. If he died without the glory of new victories, his dynasty would perish with him. As his influence sank, and his grasp on France relaxed, he turned for support to the Constitutional party, and formed a Liberal Ministry. Its chief, M. Ollivier, had frankly said that France had no right to interfere with the internal changes of Germany, that she had no just reason to be jealous of German unity, and could not hope to prevent its accomplishment. In entering on his office, the new Minister of Foreign Affairs, Count Daru, became aware that schemes were set on foot for a Russian alliance against Germany, and he required that they should be broken off. But in the spring of 1870 the Emperor submitted the new institutions to a vote by the whole people, thereby stultifying the principle of government by representation, and Daru resigned.   He was succeeded by the Duke de Gramont, a man of less temperate judgment, and less inaccessible to the solicitations of the war party at Court.

No part of the German people desired war with France, except the Prussian officers, who had advised it as early as 1867, not only from professional zeal, but as the one infallible means of completing the national unity. Count Bismarck was firm in resisting their counsels, and he even incurred some loss of reputation by his moderation, and, as many thought, his want of spirit, in the Luxemburg compromise.   He believed that, if he could remain at peace during the life of Napoleon, he would not have to fight at all.   And he was in no hurry to admit the Southern States.   He feared the large increase of the democratic and of the Catholic element ; and he rebuked, with some ostentation, the eagerness of Baden to be absorbed.   He knew that he was safe as long as he did not provoke war by meddling with the independence of the South, and raising a quarrel in which France could ally herself with the offended patriotism of Bavaria and Wirtemberg.   If Prussia was attacked on any other ground, the military alliance ensured the co-operation of the Southern forces—ensured, in other words, the establishment of German unity by brotherhood of arms on the field of battle.   Count Bismarck waited, scrupulous to avoid every demonstration of hostility, but quite ready to accept a challenge, and disturbed by no doubts as to the result of any conflict with France alone.

The extraordinary vigour of the Prussian State and the efficiency of its armies are due not to any innate superiority of the race, but to the perfection of a system which aims at subduing the common impediments of tradition, locality, and custom, in order to bring all the moral and physical resources of the nation under the dominion of mind.   The Government is so enlightened, the clearness of intellect is so apparent in its operations, that

the people, educated and thoughtful as they are, consent
to barter away some of the political privileges which the
inhabitants of more free but less well governed countries
cherish more than life. Other commonwealths have submitted sometimes to the fascination of eloquence. The
spell that holds Prussia captive is the charm of a good
administration. The re-modelled military system has
been fatal to the Constitution. In its new developed
form it is a creation of the present reign. During the
generation that succeeded the great wars, Prussia neglected
her army and allowed her political influence to decline,
while she obtained the supremacy in literature. The
maxim that knowledge is better than power prevailed for
many years before it yielded to the discovery that knowledge is power. The intellect of the country did not
control its affairs, until the accession of the remarkable
triumvirate whose union has raised it to such a height
of greatness. In 1858 Moltke was appointed chief of
the staff. And it is a signal instance of the power of
scientific thought that this mighty soldier was almost
entirely without practical experience of warfare until he
was sixty-three years old. The reorganisation of the
army was carried out by General Roon, the Minister of
War ; and Count Bismarck made it law, in defiance of
Parliament and with a contempt for Constitutional
obstacles that Strafford could not have surpassed. The
new army was tested in 1864 and 1866 ; and since
then it had been almost doubled. General Roon was
able, in three weeks, to place 500,000 men in France ;
and when that was done, 500,000 more were waiting
orders to march. Officers in all kinds of disguises had
taken plans and measurements and photographs in France.
The width of the rivers at the points where they had to
be crossed on the march to Paris had been accurately
measured, and iron bridges of the necessary length were
ready to follow the army. The French had batteries of
mitrailleuses, their rifles were better than the needle gun,
and their infantry, when under fire, could hardly be
excelled. But in numbers, in artillery, in organisation,

foresight, and military capacity, the Germans were so far superior that little was left to chance. The appointment of the Liberal Ministry in January 1870 was hailed in Prussia as an assurance of peace. But the *plébiscite* in May, and the appearance of Gramont at the Foreign Office, were a warning to make ready, and Bismarck, hushed in grim repose, waited till the Emperor made the mistake of attacking him.

On 5th July it became known that the young Prince of Hohenzollern had consented to be put in nomination for the crown of Spain. On the same day the French Government informed the North German Ambassador, Baron Werther, that they would prevent the election, if necessary, by war: and on the 6th, amid general applause, they repeated the same declaration in Parliament. The project had once before been put forward, opposed by France, and withdrawn. Various circumstances combined to make it unwelcome, especially at that moment. The settlement of the Spanish throne was the point at which the interests of France and those of the Emperor went furthest asunder. For there was a French Pretender, the Duke de Montpensier, in whose behalf, partly, the revolution of Cadiz had been accomplished, and who might already have occupied the throne, had not the Emperor peremptorily refused to tolerate the elevation of a prince of the House of Orleans. The dynastic interests of Napoleon had prolonged the vacancy, and it was for the sake of the Empire, and not of France, that the question which was about to drag her into war was kept open. The exclusion of the only French candidate was a trial for French patriotism. But if the Emperor, having excluded the Frenchman for dynastic reasons, now sanctioned the German, it would have appeared that the safety of the Empire was purchased by the humiliation of France. He himself had just brought forward another claimant. He had induced the deposed Queen of Spain to make over her rights to her son, and he hoped to make him king. Almost immediately after, he learnt that a rival had been preferred,

a rival manifestly favoured by Prussia, and that the
Prussian party had foiled the plans of his friends in
Spain.   The fact that Prince Leopold was only distantly
connected with the royal family of Hohenzollern, and was
much more nearly related to the Emperor of the French,
did not make his nomination less mortifying.   It was not
the Prussian prince so much as the Prussian subject, and
the representative of Prussian influence, whose success
was so bitterly resented.   The actual disadvantage to
France would have been slight.   Indeed, there had been
thoughts at one time of adopting one of the young
Hohenzollerns as the avowed candidate of France.   As
things were, the repulse to the Emperor's influence was
serious.

The European Governments, startled by the sudden
vehemence of the French Ministers, exerted themselves to
remove the cause of anger.   They thought that France
would not be justified in opposing the election by force,
but they also thought that Spain ought not to insist on
having a king who would cost so much blood.   The
Spaniards maintained a strict reserve, waiting for the
course things would take in Germany.   The Ministry in
Berlin ignored the whole affair ; they said that it did not
concern the North German States, and that it was not
their business to permit or to prevent the accession of
any prince the Spaniards might choose.   The Prussian
press, well trained in the native discipline of the country,
took the hint, and met the fury of the Paris journalists
with uncommon prudence.   As there was nothing to be
got at Berlin, the French Ambassador, Count Benedetti,
travelled to the baths of Ems, and addressed himself to
the King, who informed him that he had approved the
acceptance of the Prince, and would not withdraw the
approval he had given.   Meantime, however, the Duke
de Gramont had stated that a voluntary renunciation by
Prince Leopold would be a satisfactory solution of the
question.   The Prince was out of the way, and several
anxious days were spent in secret negotiation.   It
appeared that Spain was not going to fight for the

monarch of her choice, and that South Germany felt no deeper interest in so remote a question than Spain herself. On 12th July Prince Leopold revoked his acceptance. M. Ollivier immediately proclaimed that France had got what she wanted, that she had gained a brilliant and bloodless victory, and that the dispute was at an end. The success, indeed, was great, for it had been gained by threats, and Prussia seemed to have quailed before the danger. Her ascendency in Germany was imperilled. Her enemies in the South raised a storm of derision at the retirement of Hohenzollern. For twenty-four hours her friends were in a distressing perplexity.

At Paris opinion was at first divided. Many rejoiced with the ingenuous Ollivier, and several of his colleagues believed that the war clouds were dispersed. But the position had not been made quite clear. The retirement of the Prince had been first announced by an anonymous telegram, stating that he retired in order to leave to Spain the right of a free initiative. There was a suspicion of hidden meaning in these ambiguous words. They did not imply unconditional renunciation, and did not shut the door against a renewal of the offer. Another despatch of the same date said that the Prince made his candidature depend on the consent of Spain to join Prussia in case of war. This might mean that he would resume it whenever Prussia and Spain had come to an understanding. It may be that these telegrams, however unauthorised, confirmed the French Government in the belief that the Prince's renunciation might be a profound manœuvre, and not a final settlement. The warlike portion of the Ministry was encouraged not to rest content with this solution by the motion of Duvernois, a deputy and journalist, thought to be more trusted by the Emperor than Ollivier himself, who demanded that Prussia should be made to give security that nothing of the kind should occur again. On the 13th Gramont felt the pulse of the Chamber by saying that he had no positive information to give, but that the dispute was not yet over. His speech was received in a way which showed that he would be strenuously supported if he carried matters with a high hand and strove to inflict humiliation on Prussia.

The Prussian ambassador at Paris, having visited the King at Ems, returned to his post on the 12th, and was closeted with Gramont when the telegram of the Prince of Hohenzollern was put into his hands. The Duke intimated that the withdrawal was perhaps due to the influence of the King. Baron Werther denied it, and assured him that the Prince had judged and acted for himself. Then the Duke de Gramont perceived that Prussia was eluding his pressure altogether, and that he had won only a shadowy and impalpable triumph. It was not yet clear that the King, who had approved the act which France resented, now approved the concession which had been made to her demand. Irritated by the dexterity of Prussia, and encouraged by her seeming moderation, and by the violence of the French Imperial press, which designated the Government a Ministry of shame, Gramont proceeded to ask for further satisfaction. He said that the Prince would never have been allowed to ascend the throne, so that his retirement was a matter of course, and could not allay the excitement in the country. Baron Werther had informed him that the King had not imagined that the affair of the Spanish crown would be taken as an insult to France. The Duke proposed that King William should repeat this declaration in a letter to the Emperor. He said that if the King explained his good intentions, and expressed a hope that all ground of future quarrel would be removed by his assent to the Prince's retirement, the publication of such a letter would have an excellent effect in France. He also required that the King should forbid the Prince to retract his renunciation at any future time.

If the French Ministers had contented themselves with the concession of their original demand, it is probable that their moderation would have come too late to avert the war. But it was this fatal determination to make the King acknowledge his error that brought overwhelming calamities on France, by depriving her of all sympathy among the nations, and by uniting the whole of Germany under the standard of the discreet and wary Prussians.

Although the Duke de Gramont's new demands were insulting, there was yet one thing which Prussia might concede, not for the sake of peace only, but to make her own position unassailable. England advised that the King, having sanctioned the Hohenzollern candidature, should now declare that he also approved its withdrawal. Count Bismarck indignantly rejected the proposal, and refused to submit it to the King. Meanwhile the King, acting at a distance from his Minister, had already done what the English Government recommended. On the 13th he met Count Benedetti on the promenade at Ems, and pulling out a newspaper with the Hohenzollern telegram, declared that he approved it, and rejoiced that the question was at an end. The Ambassador replied that he was instructed to ask for a promise that should secure France against the danger of its revival. The Duke de Gramont avowed to Lord Lyons that they did not want the King to prevent, but only to prohibit the renewal of the candidature. In fact he was trying to bind not Prince Leopold, but King William, and seeking not so much a practical security for the future as the exaction of a penalty for the past. But Count Benedetti went further and demanded, if the Prince was hereafter tempted to resume the project, that the King should compel him to forsake it. King William having unreservedly adopted and confirmed the renunciation, and deeming that it was honestly made, refused to entertain the proposal of a more explicit pledge. The conversation ended on friendly terms. In the afternoon the King sent word to the Ambassador that he had just received a letter from the father of Prince Leopold confirming the report, and that he looked upon it as settling the question. Count Benedetti had also received despatches from Paris containing further considerations to be submitted to the King, with a view to modify the determination he had expressed in the morning. He formally requested an

audience for the purpose. The King sent his aide-de-
camp to tell him that he had given his final answer, that
he declined to reopen the question, and left it for the
future in the hands of his Ministers. On the following
day the Ambassador paid his respects to the King at the
station. There had been no breach of the forms of diplomatic courtesy. King William travelled to Berlin through
towns tumultuous with the enthusiasm of war; and a
paper which a man waved in his hand, trying vainly to
stop the train, near Potsdam, contained a message from
Paris which was the death-warrant of 100,000 men. A
great change had happened on the night of the 13th.

Whilst Benedetti was arguing at Ems, the Prussian
Ministers had strictly maintained their attitude of indifference to the Spanish question, and were unmoved by the
threats and taunts of France. On the 11th a council,
presided over by the Minister of War, decided that there
was no occasion for measures of defence, as the system
was perfect enough to do its work after war was declared.
On the following day Count Bismarck arrived at Berlin
from the country. The Hohenzollern question was out
of the way, and the time for the waiting game was over.
Prussia was delivered from the imputation of making a
dynastic war. If she was now involved in a struggle for
the safety and dignity of the country, she could expect
the moral support of Europe and the armed assistance of
the South—that is, the coveted union of all Germany.
What had seemed to many an excess of caution and conciliation, and had for a moment threatened the popularity
of the Government, had rectified their position and
indefinitely strengthened their hands. On the 13th
Count Bismarck informed the British Ambassador that
he did not mean to let matters rest where they stood,
and that even if France professed herself satisfied he
should not be satisfied. He allowed Lord Augustus
Loftus to perceive that he regretted the conciliatory disposition shown at Ems to Benedetti, and declared that
he would never speak to him until Gramont had revoked
his insulting words. He was determined to ask for an

explanation of the French armaments, and for some security against the recurrence of similar quarrels.   He wished for an opportunity of turning the tables and assuming the diplomatic offensive.   If the French, faithful to their declarations, had been content with their first success, they would have received a counter-challenge, and being no longer the immediate aggressors, they would not have brought upon themselves the unanimous repro- bation of Europe.   But their persistency in demanding apologetic pledges from the King supplied Count Bismarck with the desired opportunity of soothing the disturbed and angry spirit of his countrymen.   A few hours after he had betrayed to Lord Augustus Loftus that Prussia was about to abandon her patient and pacific attitude, and after the same thing had been said in his official organ, news came of the scenes that had just occurred at Ems.   At nine that night the newsboys filled the streets of Berlin, crying a special edition of the *North German Gazette*.   It contained a telegram stating that the King had refused to receive the French Ambassador, and had sent an aide-de-camp to say that he had nothing more to communicate to him.   The statement was literally true, but the absence of particulars made it appear that the King had broken off intercourse with Benedetti, and that the dignity of France had been wounded in the person of her representative.   The report was immediately sent by Bismarck to the diplomatic agents of Prussia, to show, as he said, that his tone was firmer than had been supposed. At Berlin it was received with a passionate outburst of applause.   Many people learnt for the first time that France, by raising her demands, had placed herself so irretrievably in the wrong that no sophistry could now avail to prevent the union of the Germans.   The whole country was persuaded that Benedetti, by his personal importunity, had affronted the King, and had been justly punished for his insolence.   And the story continues to be told in pictures and in print how the Prussian aide-de- camp showed the door to the Ambassador of France. Germany, on the whole, had borne the trial with fortitude ;

the sudden explosion of national resentment and pride showed that the trial had been severe.   Baron Werther, who had transmitted the invitation of Gramont that the King should make a public profession of regret, was compelled to quit the service.   When King William reached Berlin on the night of the 15th nothing remained to be done but to put the army in the field.

Up to the morning of the 14th the peace party at Paris had not relinquished hope, and the most influential journals held that the quarrel ended with the Hohenzollern affair.   But the Ems telegram, interpreted in France as it had been interpreted in Germany, roused an irritation that threatened to sweep away the Ministry.   Even then, opinions were so nearly balanced in the final council that the choice of war was made by a majority of a single vote. Marshal Lebœuf answered that in case of peace he could not answer for the army.   The Empress too had thrown her influence into the scale, and Ollivier himself voted at last for war.   One of the Ministers drew his watch.   It was four o'clock.   A solemn hour, he exclaimed, in the history of the world.   On the 15th the Ministers announced their decision to the Chambers, and asked for supplies. They stated that their demand of a guarantee from the King of Prussia against his enterprising kinsman had never been made as an ultimatum, and that they continued negotiating after its rejection.   Even the refusal of an audience had not been received as an irreparable breach.   But Prussia had informed foreign Powers of the repulse of Benedetti, and had recalled her Ambassador. So much stress was laid on a communication from Count Bismarck to other Powers touching the scene at Ems that the opposition asked to see the note in which it was made.   Ollivier refused to produce it.   There was a question of honour, he said, not a question of texts.   It was afterwards discovered that he had nothing to produce except the telegram from Ems.   France declared war not because the King refused the required guarantee ; not because of his treatment of Benedetti ; not even because a misleading account of it had been published, but because a substantially correct report had been sent to the North German envoys at several Courts. The declaration of war reached Berlin on the 19th.

The faults of the triumphant war party had isolated France. She was without allies; but it was confidently expected that South Germany could be detached from the Northern Confederation. The French agents held out no such prospect. They wrote black, but their Government would read nothing but white. France had done nothing involving offence to the South Germans, and would not believe that they would spend their blood and treasure in a quarrel which was not their own. The opposition to Prussia was strong in the South. But the Bavarian Government declared that to shrink from their engagement at a time when Prussia was attacked would be a shameful breach of faith. The Prime Minister, Count Bray, had signed the treaty of alliance himself in 1866. He told the Chamber that they might turn him out of office, but that he would never consent to betray his conviction or to deny his signature. After a close struggle the proposal of neutrality was defeated; and the day after the declaration of war was delivered at Berlin, 38,000,000 of Germans were united to meet it. The adherence of the South added 150,000 men, brave but not highly disciplined, to the armies of Prussia. It added infinitely more to her moral force, for it closed the door against French influence beyond the Rhine. Among the greater Powers England alone wished to favour neither of the combatants. Austria was the natural ally of France, for she wished her defeat in 1866 to be avenged, and Prussia at first set an army to watch the Bohemian frontier. But Russia calculated on deriving relief for her Eastern policy from the defeat of the French, and made it known from the first that she would ensure the neutrality of Austria. The Emperor Napoleon invited succour from Italy, by recalling his troops from Rome; and he drew encouragement from the warlike tone of Victor Emmanuel. There was a French party at Florence, who thought that the interference of South

Germany for a recent enemy justified Italy in redressing the balance in favour of an old ally. Count Bismarck thought the danger so serious that he offered a great price for the neutrality of the Italians.   He was ready to pledge himself, if Italy abstained from war, to sign no peace that did not make her mistress of Nice, Savoy, and Rome.   The Italians declined to enter into an ungrateful conspiracy against France.   In August, Prince Napoleon came to Florence.   The King was eager for the fray. The sword of Savoy, he said, used not to rust in its sheath when there was fighting to be done.   But the Ministers, supported by the leading statesmen of the country, restrained him.

War had been declared a week when Count Bismarck isolated France more completely by publishing the draft of a treaty which he had extracted from Count Benedetti in 1867, in which France was to have the aid of Prussia for the conquest of Belgium.   The immediate effect of the publication was to show that Europe had much to dread from a French victory, and to make the Emperor Napoleon a sort of international outlaw.   England invited Germany and France to enter into new engagements for the inde- pendence of Belgium.   As the proposal was suggestive of the suspicion of perfidy which the secret treaty had aroused, the French signed it with a bad grace.   This startling revelation did not increase the sympathy for Prussia as much as it damaged France.   If the draft had been communicated to England early in the Hohenzollern controversy, the language of this country might have been more cogent in striving to restrain the impetuosity of France.   Lord Lyons had assured the Duke de Gramont that his course of action in forcing on the war was not of a kind that could diminish the friendly feeling of England.   The tone of his remonstrances might have been less comforting if we had had proof of the plot against Belgium.   By keeping back the document until war had broken out, Count Bismarck had been suppressing one of the chances of peace.

Having made himself safe against the armed interference of Europe, he endeavoured to fortify himself against the interposition of diplomacy to rob Germany of the full profit and enjoyment of victory. He affirmed that he had reason to believe that Napoleon, after the first collision, would be willing to treat for peace at the expense of Belgium. The object was to make the neutrals suspicious of premature negotiations after the butchery had begun. The Power whose pacific intervention was most generally expected was Great Britain. By at once raising a dispute about the exportation of arms, which led to much excitement in Germany, Count Bismarck endeavoured to create the belief that our mediation would not be welcomed as that of a friendly Power.

The latter part of July was spent in bringing up the armies to the frontier. The Germans proceeded methodically, waiting until each army corps was ready in its appointed province before they sent any portion to the front. Napoleon intended to invade Germany from Strasburg, in the direction of Frankfort, so as to separate the North and South, and break up their alliance. He was not ready in time. But for a week the German frontier was almost unprotected, and it was expected that the struggle would begin on German soil. On 28th July the Prussian Staff made known that the interval of danger was over, and that they were ready to carry the war into the enemy's country. Three roads lie before a German army invading France. Near the Swiss frontier the gap that separates the Jura from the Vosges is guarded by the fortress of Belfort, which ultimately became the scene of the least brilliant operations of the Germans. North of Belfort the Vosges mountains bound the valley of the Rhine and separate the nations. They are crossed by the great road from Strasburg to Nancy, Châlons, and Paris. At the northern end of the Vosges, wide valleys, running east and west, lead from the German stronghold of Mentz on the Rhine, to Metz, the bulwark of France, on the Moselle. The armies of Southern Germany, led by the Crown Prince of Prussia and General Blumenthal, were gathered near the lines of

Weissenburg, the advanced point of French territory, where it receded from the Rhine. They were to make for the Strasburg route. To the right, the two armies of Prince Frederick Charles and Steinmetz approached the frontier on the roads that lead to Metz. Moltke himself has pointed out the vice of this arrangement, and attributes to the division of command the Austrian reverses in 1859. In the Prussian army the waste of time and power was counteracted by the diligent use of the wires, which followed every corps as fast as it marched, and kept every separate command in daily communication with Moltke, who never left the King, and controlled the movements of all the armies. This is the reason why the strategy of the Germans was so superior to their tactics, and, while some of their actions were fought clumsily, and won by hideous slaughter, all the larger combinations were executed with a precision and ability never surpassed in war. Napoleon stood at the head of 300,000 men, on a line 100 miles long, from Metz to Strasburg. Three men principally excited expectation in the French army. Marshal MacMahon, the conqueror of the Malakoff and the victor of Magenta, stood highest in public esteem. When the idea of invading Central Germany was abandoned, he was left with 50,000 men in the neighbourhood of Strasburg. Marshal Bazaine, who commanded on the left, near Metz, was said to have greater experience of war than any living Frenchman, but the stupendous failure of Mexico overshadowed his reputation, and his authority was not equal to his ability. A general who has kept in the background, and almost in disgrace, was commonly reputed the most accomplished officer in France. Trochu had made himself illustrious in the Crimea and in Lombardy, but he had written a singularly candid and clever book on the defects of the army, and he was odious to the Court. He was popular with the Opposition, and when it became necessary to conciliate the malcontents, the Emperor reluctantly appointed him Governor of Paris.

Hostilities began on the 2nd of August. Napoleon

R

came to the front and shelled Saarbrücken, a frontier town at the junction of the Prussian railways. The Prussians, who were not in force, evacuated the place. It was at once reported that the French had burnt a defenceless town, and the indignation caused by the rumour did its work in Germany before it was ascertained that Saarbrücken had suffered little. The French, finding that the Germans, who were concealed in the forests, declined their challenge, did not pursue their success, but established themselves on the heights overlooking the valley of the Saar. They were not prepared to take a real initiative, and the Germans at once returned the blow and invaded France. On the 4th the Crown Prince surprised the French under Douay at the exposed position of Weissenburg. MacMahon hurried up from Strasburg with 40,000 men to defend the passage of the Vosges. The Crown Prince, with a vastly superior force, defeated him, on the 6th, between Wörth and Reichshofen, where the famous regiment of Zouaves, and the Cuirassiers, charging for the first time since Waterloo, were cut to pieces. Some of the troops fled in disorder to Strasburg, which was soon after besieged by the Germans. The rest of the French right wing, including Failly, who had not been in the battle, and Felix Douay, who was called up in haste from Belfort, fell back 150 miles ; and the Crown Prince was able to advance half-way to Paris without encountering an enemy. The results of this battle, out of all proportion with its apparent importance, suddenly revealed the weakness and the peril of France. It relieved Prussia from the apprehension of a landing on the coast, and set many thousand men free for the invasion, and it chilled the warlike dispositions of those neutrals whose wishes were for France. The Emperor, announcing the disaster in desponding telegrams, declared that all might yet be retrieved. This language threw Paris into a ferment. The Ministry that had begun the war was overthrown by the news of the first battle, with the Emperor's full connivance. The Empire was in imminent danger, and resorted to the thorough-going

Imperialists for protection. The head of the new Ministry, General Montauban, named Count of Palikao for his victories in China, was a soldier of undoubted capacity. His mission was to call out the resources of the country, and to keep down the enemy most feared and hated by the Bonapartes,—the democracy of Paris. The Empire crumbled to pieces in his hands, and largely through his fault.

Whilst the Crown Prince was engaged with MacMahon on the left of the German line, Steinmetz, on the right, stormed the heights of Spicheren above Saarbrücken. The French fell back on Metz, where the Emperor stood with 190,000 men. But in France the Sovereign, not his Ministers, was responsible, and public opinion was not content with the change of Ministry ; for it was the Emperor who had mismanaged the opening of the campaign and brought the enemy into the country. Ollivier fell on the 9th, and on the 11th Napoleon made over the supreme command to Bazaine. The new commander-in-chief objected to the presence of the Emperor in his camp ; and from the moment of his departure from Metz until the surrender at Sedan, he ceased to influence the destinies of France.

The Germans advanced slowly. The Crown Prince had the mountains to cross. Steinmetz was held back on the right, to lull the French in Metz, whilst Prince Frederick Charles, in the centre, preceded by that immense force of cavalry which has become so characteristic of all the German movements, pushed forward to prevent the junction of MacMahon and Bazaine. The French generals were very reluctant to retire from Metz, and to bring the unbroken army of the Rhine back into the heart of France ; and the notion that their right place was at Metz, where they could hold fast great part of the invading armies while a stubborn resistance was organised with the inexhaustible resources of the country, was so strong among them that it interfered with the execution of the opposite plan, which was preferred. On the 13th Bazaine gave orders to retreat

by Verdun on Châlons, where MacMahon was to form a
new army with reinforcements sent from Paris. The
Germans were out of sight when the retreat began on the
morning of the 14th, but they detected the movement,
and the same day Steinmetz threw himself on the French
rearguard outside the forts of Metz. The French held
their own that evening, but the retreat was interrupted,
half a day was lost, and Prince Frederick Charles had
time to get across the Moselle with part of his army.
Bazaine marched by two roads, which part a few miles
west of Metz, at Gravelotte, and unite at Verdun. On
the 16th the Germans overtook him on the southern
road, near Mars-la-Tour. They were greatly outnumbered,
for the bulk of their force was many miles to the rear,
and the French divisions that were following the northern
road came up in time. They gained their object with a
loss which, in proportion to the numbers they brought
into action, is almost unexampled in European warfare,
—a loss of 17,000 men. That night an Englishman
seeking a drink of water for the wounded in a stream
that crossed the battlefield, found it so dark with blood
that he was obliged to walk three miles to fill his bucket.
Bazaine had been stopped, but not actually defeated, and
the northern road was still open to him. But the shock
of the great battle made him lose a day. He feared to
be cut off from Metz, and resolved to give battle under
cover of the fortress, in a position which would force the
Germans to fight with their backs to Paris, and their line
of retreat interrupted by the Moselle. His movements
after the battle converted what was no more than a
repulse into a gigantic disaster. The Germans on the
following day did not know the extent of their good
fortune. They brought together more than 200,000
men, and early on the 18th they set out to look for
Bazaine on the northern road to Verdun. They found
him in a strong position near Gravelotte, immovable,
leaning on the outworks of Metz, with a force less
by 60,000 men than their own. Wheeling round to
their right they began the attack about the middle of

the day, and at nightfall Bazaine retired behind the forts.
The Prussians had again suffered terribly and had won
scarcely any trophies.   But the object for which they had
sacrificed 35,000 men in five days was completely
gained, and Bazaine, with an army equal to the largest
the great Napoleon ever handled in action, was finally
locked up in Metz.   Prince Frederick Charles, with the
victors of Gravelotte, sat down to wait his surrender, the
Saxons were detached to watch for any offensive movements on the part of MacMahon, and the Crown Prince
advanced towards Châlons.   MacMahon, with an ill-
appointed army of more than 100,000 men, proposed to
fall back on Paris and to prevent the siege.   Trochu
believed that without the help of a large regular army
the defence would be impossible.   But the news from
Bazaine frightened the Government.   The state of Paris
was such that they dared not confess the truth, and they
believed that the reappearance of the Emperor would be
followed by his deposition.   After the battles round
Metz the Empire was only preserved by a system of
fiction and concealment that could not last long, and the
Emperor himself seemed to be forgotten by the advisers
of the Regent.   They required that an attempt should be
made to pass the Crown Prince and deliver Metz.   Mac-
Mahon and the Emperor fell back from the camp of
Châlons as the Crown Prince approached.   Instead of
retreating on Paris they went north to Rheims, leaving
the Germans to continue their march.   For three whole
days the Germans were ignorant of MacMahon's movements, and by dint of great rapidity he might have
reached Metz before the Crown Prince could come up
with him, but the audacious plan which Palikao had
imposed on the obedient Marshal was spoilt by delay.
On the 26th the Crown Prince and the Saxons faced
north, and MacMahon informed the Government that
they were intercepting his march, and that he must
give up the attempt to reach Metz, and return towards
Paris.   Palikao replied that a revolution would break
out if they abandoned Bazaine.   MacMahon felt that the

enterprise was desperate, but attempted it, as the last chance for the Empire. Late on 31st August, after three days' fighting, he was driven back to Sedan.

Prince Frederick Charles had drawn off part of his force from the investment of Metz, in order to meet MacMahon if he should force his way through the two armies that had been sent against him, and the Germans were listening to the cannonade sixty miles off when the French, led by Canrobert and the old Orleanist Changarnier, burst out of Metz. The German positions were taken, and Bazaine had only to pursue his success with real vigour to be free once more. But Manteuffel brought up fresh troops in the night, and early on 1st September the French were driven back into their lines. This was the battle of Noisseville, one of the most hard-fought actions of the war. It proved that it was the fault of the French if they did not escape. Either Bazaine did not know how to handle large masses of men, or he hesitated to face the difficulties that would begin when he got out into the open. That day Mac-Mahon gave battle at Sedan to forces double his own. He was disabled by a frightful wound early in the morning. By two o'clock the French were completely surrounded. Every road was occupied by the Germans, every crest was crowned with their batteries, and the French infantry, when their generals appealed to them for one more effort, refused to move. Then, in spite of protests from the unfortunate general who had succeeded the wounded marshal, Napoleon displayed the white flag on the ramparts, and sent an officer to the King of Prussia announcing his surrender. He went into captivity with 84,000 men.

After the decisive victory of Sedan, France had no longer an army in the field, and the Germans believed that their toils were over. The Regency must needs make peace; or, if the Regency fell, no other Government would be willing to take up the game where the Emperor left it. Orders were sent to Berlin to countermand the multiplying of the maps of France; and it was proposed that the Germans should abandon the offensive, and take up impregnable positions in the territory already conquered.   But although the Regency instantly resolved to conclude peace, it no longer had the power. It had expelled the German residents in Paris, and had filled the prisons as fast as news came from the seat of war, and the discontent became troublesome.   Before treating for peace it would have become necessary to arrest the leaders of the Opposition ; and this could not be done, for the Opposition was supported by General Trochu.   All the available soldiers had been sent to MacMahon ; the National Guards were masters of Paris, and Trochu was master of the National Guard.   The regular army is the State in arms ; the National Guard is the people in arms.   It is the force that obeys, not authority, but opinion.   Its function is to preserve order against anarchy, and freedom against oppression.   A Government may be constitutional in its forms, and may be founded on popular election, but if it has the control of a large standing army it is virtually absolute.   The National Guard is the check upon this absolutism.   It supplies aid to a popular Government, and a hostile control to an unpopular Government.   Therefore the sceptre passed away from the Empire when it was forced to commit the defence of the capital to the National Guard.   During the twenty-four hours after the news came from Sedan, Trochu held in his hands the destinies of his country.   At the morning sitting of the Legislative Assembly, on Saturday, 3rd September, the facts were but imperfectly known, and Jules Favre's proposal that Trochu should be Dictator was repelled with indignation.   In the course of the evening the intelligence spread through the city.   Trochu and Gambetta addressed large crowds, promising decisive action for the morrow ; late at night the Chamber was again summoned.   Palikao had been fetched out of bed, and he was not prepared for action. In the midst of a significant silence on the benches, from which interruptions used to pour on his grave stern eloquence, Favre asked the Chamber to declare that the

Bonapartes had ceased to reign, and to put Trochu at the head of the State. The discussion of this motion, which meant the Republic, was adjourned to the next afternoon. The Imperialists were by this time conscious that there was no longer an Empire. Its existence was not in debate on that fatal Sunday. The option was between a Republic and a provisional Government, compatible with the future advent of monarchy; the question was whether the Liberal party throughout France or the Revolutionists of Paris should inherit the power and the misfortunes of the fallen Empire. The Liberals of the left centre, led by Thiers, Daru, and Buffet, wished to institute by a parliamentary vote a new executive that should possess the sanction of law and the requisite authority to keep down insurrection and to conclude peace. They pressed the Empress-Regent to abdicate, in order that the validity of the new Government might be undisputed by the masses that had sustained the old. "Ah!" she exclaimed, "in France it will not do to be unfortunate." But although she was unable to resist by force, she refused to damage by abdication the prospects of her son. She was ready to give up the reality of power, provided the nominal sovereignty of her family was preserved. The Ministry accordingly proposed that the Chamber should commit the defence of the country to a Directory of Five, to be controlled by Palikao. Favre repeated his motion of the night before; and Thiers, supported by the moderate party, proposed a provisional Government, which, without prejudging the final question, would have given to him and his friends the supreme conduct of affairs. The supremacy of the moderate Liberals was the thing most feared by the Republicans, who form the mass of the people of Paris. They saw in the proposal of Thiers a plot for the perpetuation of monarchy and the restoration of the House of Orleans. They were resolved not to miss the opportunity of re-covering what they had lost by the *coup d'état* of 1851. Early on the Sunday morning emissaries went round summoning the Republicans to assemble before the

Legislative body at noon, for the purpose of supporting
their deputies. They came in tens of thousands, headed
by National Guards, who claimed that it was their
privilege to guard the Assembly. The Assembly was
guarded by all the troops Palikao could muster. They
were but few, and when the sitting commenced things
looked so threatening that people hurried to the Governor
of Paris, and besought him to come and prevent bloodshed. Trochu refused. He could not act, he said, with
such a man as Palikao; he would not interfere unless the
Chamber sent for him. The absence of Trochu decided
the defeat of the Liberals and the triumph of the
Republic. The Commission appointed to report on the
three schemes adopted the scheme of Thiers, and it was
about to be voted by the majority of deputies when the
people and National Guards forced their way in. The
Assembly dispersed without act or vote, and at three
o'clock Jules Favre and his friends proclaimed the
Republic at the Hôtel de Ville. When the people were
pulling down the eagles, and were about to break into
the Chamber, the Prefect of Police appeared at the
Tuileries, and informed the Empress that all was over.
She quietly bade farewell to her attendants, changed her
dress, and fled, almost alone. This was the fall of the
second Empire, ruined by the overthrow of its armies.
It fell between the enervation of its friends and the contemptuous moderation of its enemies. In eighteen years
it had failed to plant in the hearts of the Parisians the
strength for one hour of resistance. Not a shot was
fired, not a drop of blood was spilt, to save it. No act
of vengeance stained the hands of the liberated people.

In the evening the remnant of the Assembly, chiefly
Liberals of the Left Centre, met to deliberate. Jules
Favre appeared, and, without pretending to care much
about it, exhorted them to ratify what had been done.
Several members expressed their indignation at the viola-
tion of the Legislative Assembly, and wished to record
a protest. Thiers, who presided, induced them to hold
themselves neutral. They could not recognise a Govern-

ment founded on the destruction of the only popular authority in France, nor resist men who were about to conduct the defence of the country. Thus the Liberal party, representing the wealthier classes, separated itself definitely from the new Government, and left the Republic to administer with its own resources the disastrous legacy of the Empire.

The Government of National Defence was formed of the deputies of the capital. It was evident that the next and vital stage of the war would be the siege of Paris, and there was propriety in committing its defence to the men whom it had trusted. There was no time to obtain a legal title by consulting the nation. Paris, which had always opposed the Empire, and had been kept down by means of the country voters, resumed its lost supremacy. It was only theoretically a government by Parisian deputies. Thiers, the most eminent of their number, preferred to wait for the restoration of peace, and Trochu, the commander-in-chief, was neither a Parisian nor a deputy. Except Picard, their financier, they appear to have been without administrators ; and much of the real work was done, subsequently, by two outsiders, Dorian, the Minister of Commerce, and Laurier, Secretary-General of the Interior. By the defect of its origin the new Government had not authority to govern France, to keep down the mobs of Paris that had created it, or to give the enemy guarantes for peace. It had sprung, not from revolution, or even insurrection, but from a street riot, and was liable to end as it began. There was nothing to inspire the invaders with confidence in its power or in its stability. The only remedy was the immediate convocation of a National Assembly. The foreign Republics and the States of Latin Europe recognised the Government of National Defence, but the great European Powers, Russia, Austria, and Great Britain, waited until the French people at large should pronounce. One great advantage belonged to the new Government. Most of its leading members had been among the ten courageous deputies who, on the 15th of

July, had voted against war. Jules Favre especially was one of the very few men, almost the only public man in France, who had consistently condemned, not only this, but all wars of ambition, even that of 1859. While the Liberals, by their sarcasms and declamations, were goading the Emperor to grasp the Rhine, Favre had risked his popularity by resisting them. He seized, with great effect, the advantage which belonged to his position. In a circular, written with a rare eloquence, dignity, and grace, and impressive from the honourable consistency of the writer, he proclaimed the guilt of France, and the justice of the ordeal which had crowned the Germans with the glory of stupendous victories. He was ready to sue for peace, and to pay as indemnity all the money that could be raised in France. The funds, which had fallen seven per cent, immediately rose more than two per cent. And yet this grand State paper has cost more lives than the wrath of Achilles, for it contained the memorable words—" We mean to surrender not one stone of our fortresses, not one inch of our soil."

M. Favre immediately requested England to intervene in favour of peace, and by the mediation of our Government, Favre and Bismarck met on the day when the investment of Paris was completed. Count Bismarck had made known before the end of August the terms he meant to offer to the defeated Empire. He wanted no territory, but he would take the fortresses of Strasburg and Metz, as a sort of twin Gibraltar for the protection of Germany. In the middle of September, after the ruin of the Empire, and when he was preparing for his interview with Favre, he raised his terms, and claimed the whole of Alsace and part of Lorraine, or a strip of territory about thirty miles in width along the whole line that separates France and Germany. These were the same terms to which the French submitted four months later. The Germans could scarcely bring themselves to treat with the Government of National Defence. They distrusted it, both for its revolutionary origin and for its democratic character. Monarchy, as understood in Germany, is not, as we understand it, the condition under which a nation secures self-government ; it is not government by law, but government by authority.   It is antagonistic to Republicanism, not in form only, but in its essential spirit.   The establishment of a French Republic was not only an offence to the aristocratic feudalism of Prussia, but an actual danger, by encouraging the elements of popular resistance in Germany.   Therefore the Germans were tempted to underrate its vitality, and to look for signs of hope for the Empire.   Political sympathies helped to betray them into a grievous error.   They persuaded themselves that the new Government would be speedily overthrown, and they were ignorant of the impulse which a Republic defending the integrity of France would give to the slumbering forces of the land.   They drew their lines round Paris in the belief that popular tumult would come to their aid.   But, apart from this mistake, they had full reason to doubt the use of negotiations with a Power too recent to give good security for indemnity, and too dependent on momentary favour to yield up territory. When the two statesmen met it was at once apparent that the terms of peace would be such as only a National Assembly was competent to entertain.   The only practical question between them was the armistice necessary for elections throughout France.   At their final meeting Count Bismarck was not punctual to his appointment. He had been detained by a conference with a Bonapartist agent.   The appearance of this voluntary, unaccredited negotiator was welcomed as a sign that the Imperialists were stirring.   For the Empire still possessed a great army under three marshals at Metz, whereas it was not certain that the Republic had the command of any efficient force.   Whatever terms the Empire accepted might be enforced by Bazaine.   It was the beginning of a mysterious intrigue whose object was to employ the army of Metz to restore the Regency, and to impose on France the conditions to be dictated by the Germans. The prospect thus opened of wringing a mighty ransom out of an exiled Empress and an imprisoned army made

Count Bismarck rigid in his tone to M. Favre. The armistice would be so injurious to the military position of the Germans that it could not be granted without an equivalent ; and the equivalent he wished to obtain was the surrender of the fortresses that interfered with the communications, which were Strasburg, Toul, and one other place. As Toul and Strasburg were then on the point of falling, and were taken, the one in three days, the other in eight days after the interview, this stipulation was hardly exorbitant. But when Favre was asked to give up the garrison that had been defending Strasburg for a month, and had already become the legendary idol of the populace of Paris, he lost his self-control and broke off the conference. He was oppressed by the knowledge of the ulterior conditions which were to be demanded for making peace. Beyond the loss of Strasburg he saw the annexation of Alsace, and the darker terrors in the background disturbed his vision. M. Favre had gone out secretly, without even the sanction of his colleagues. When it was discovered that he was in the enemy's camp suing for peace Paris was furious, and the leaders of the Red Republic became instantaneously formidable. But when it was known that he had indignantly rejected the proffered terms, and had proclaimed war to the end, he became the hero of the hour. It was pretended that Bismarck had demanded not only Toul, Verdun, and Strasburg, but the fort that commands Paris, and Metz, with the army of Bazaine. When Favre reported to his colleagues the failure of his mission, there were some who listened with a secret joy, for they were willing that the Republic should have a chance of retrieving the disasters which had crushed the Empire. " We may have to submit to the abuse of force," said Favre, " but not to a voluntary degradation." They were not very sanguine of success. But the deeper resources of the country and the vitality of the Republic were still untried. It behoved them to show what could be done by the enthusiasm of an armed people where the professional soldiers had failed. The Empire had fought for preponderance, and had been justly punished.   France had now to defend her territory, the citizenship of her people, and her newly recovered freedom.   An heroic struggle ending in a disastrous peace would be less surely fatal to the Republic than the immediate acceptance of the best terms that could be got.   The majority of the Government did not wish for peace, and no Government at that time could have ventured to admit the surrender of the Eastern Departments.

The moral position of France before the world was much improved when she continued the war on the ground that a State owes a duty to its citizens not to forsake them while it has a million of men to call into the field.   On the other hand, the position of Germany was unchanged.   Count Bismarck, adopting the inflexible requirements of the Staff, insisted on acquiring a frontier that should protect Germany against attack ; and having stated these conditions in September, he did not raise them after all the fortresses had fallen and all the armies had been dispersed.   Conquest is a precarious foundation for rights ; but Europe had never held that conquest is in itself a wrong.   Whole States were violently incorporated by Prussia in 1866, and the world looked on unmoved. Of all civilised communities France was the one least able to contend with decency that compulsory annexation is a crime.   For the most intense desire of almost all French-men has been for the acquisition of territory not their own.   Liberals and Republicans shared with Imperialists this diseased and guilty longing, and urged the Government to enlarge the Eastern boundary.   " Let Napoleon take the Rhine," said Montalembert, "and I shall not quarrel with him again."   It is only in the last few years that popular and able writers, like the novelists Erckmann-Chatrian, and the historian Lanfrey, have created a reaction against this, the besetting sin of their country-men.   Both the English and the American Governments expressed the opinion that it is becoming to bear with manful courage the common penalties of defeat.

At the time when the second period of the war began,

although the ultimate issue was hardly doubted by any
soldier, the position of France was not so desperate as to
require that she should submit to degradation. M. Thiers
started on a journey to the neutral capitals, asking for
intervention in behalf of the balance of power, and of a
Government which had injured nobody, had not sought
war, and was now fervent in its desire for peace. His
diplomatic mission was not auspicious ; but there was
reasonable hope of some military success, as long as
200,000 Germans were made unavailable by the tenacity
of Bazaine. The Germans had surrounded Paris without
attempting to force an entrance. On the day when their
lines closed round the city the garrison went out to meet
them, and the Zouaves were routed and came back in
such disorder that Paris expected to see the Germans
already within the gates. Trochu had said to a friend—
" The Prussians will enter Paris when they like, and as
they like ; there is not an educated officer that is not
aware of it." Thiers himself, the originator of the fortifications, talked of the possibility of resisting for a week.
When it was seen that Moltke, like the allies at Sebastopol,
thought the defences more formidable than the defenders
knew them to be, the chances of the Republic rose. If
Prince Frederick Charles could be kept inactive until an
army was formed strong enough to fall upon the rear of
the besiegers, Paris would be delivered. A branch of the
Government was fixed at Tours, beyond the Loire, to
draw new armies from the untouched districts of the
South and West. Early in October the Minister of the
Interior, Gambetta, escaped from Paris in a balloon, and
set about raising the Provinces. He was a young
advocate, recently made conspicuous by the violence of
his language in opposition. He had voted for war. He
had great energy both of work and speech, but little
political instruction, and his impetuous arbitrary temper
made him a dangerous defender of liberty. He prevented
the convocation of a National Assembly, dissolved the
centres of local self-government, and, surrounded by a
club of coffee-house politicians, obtained an undisputed

dictatorship.   The nation rose at his call.   The generals whom he appointed and dismissed at will obeyed him. He gave a command to Garibaldi in the East, and to the Colonel of Papal Zouaves, Charette, in the West.   Arms and ammunition were brought over from England and America, and enormous armies were set on foot.   The German officers doubted whether their own country, after such defeats, would have been capable of such an effort. But the new levies were badly officered, and, compared with the Imperial legions, they were of so poor a quality that Moltke, who had been careful to have numbers on his side against MacMahon and Bazaine, provided for their defeat with very inferior forces.   The later victories of Prince Frederick Charles, Göben, and Werder were gained when the French were two, and sometimes even three, to one, and were gained at comparatively small cost.   The whole loss of the Germans in the battles of January, against Chanzy, Bourbaki, and Faidherbe, amounted to less than their loss on a single day at Gravelotte, to less by 7000 men than their loss at Mars-la-Tour.

But the character of these later struggles brought on a loss of another kind—a decline of the chivalry of war. The success of the Germans was not more due to valour than to the assiduity of the officers, the hearty respect for the principle of authority.   For the Prussian ranks are filled, like those of our Volunteers, from all classes of society.   They entered France with the order and discipline of troops on parade.   The ripe grapes were being gathered as they passed the vineyards of Champagne, and not a soldier trespassed.   No French women were insulted by the invaders.   A hungry English gentleman having picked an onion in a garden was very much surprised to find himself marched off under arrest. Another well-known Englishman took charge of a church which was filled with wounded from Metz, and immediately ordered the woodwork of the seats to be used for beds. The Prussian officers were horrified at this interference with the rights of property.   My friend replied that Church property was fitly employed for the comfort of dying men ;

but the Prussians would not hear of it. In the country houses they occupied round Metz they hung up at the door of each room an inventory of the objects within. But most of the facts which English and American observers have recorded in testimony of the splendid discipline of the Germans come to us from the army of Prince Frederick Charles. The presence of men not belonging to the North German Confederation, unaccustomed to the rigour of the Prussian system, or drawn from populations less highly cultivated, made the task of the Crown Prince more delicate. That proud perfection of discipline which brought the Germans so much true fame at first, did not pass unscathed through the trials and temptations of the winter campaign. Their temper was sorely tried by the conduct of the peasantry in some of the battles. At Wörth a wounded German was found with his eyes put out. Near Metz an officer lying unconscious on the field was brought to himself by a new sharp pain, and found a woman hacking his fingers to get at his rings. It was found that she had a bag full of rings got in the same way. At Bazeilles the inhabitants picked up wounded Bavarians in the street and burned them alive; and the Bavarians in consequence set fire to the town. The Germans were soon driven to an awful severity in retaliation. The country people went out with rifles and fired at small detachments, so that it became hard to tell a peaceful citizen from a disguised soldier, and a peaceful village from a military position. Death was decreed against every civilian taken in the act of fighting, and against the free-shooters. An officer who in the course of the war had ordered more than sixty of these for execution, said that very many of these were men of position. At last the number of free-shooters taken was so great that the rigour was relaxed, and they were sent to Germany. It came to be assumed that the owner of an empty house was out with a rifle in his hand, and the house was liable to pillage. Many country houses were devastated in this way, sometimes in the presence of their owners. At times the railway system broke down, and as

S

supplies failed, the requisitions degenerated into plunder. Unfortunately, the Germans had been led by the early events of the war to lose respect for their opponents. They knew that many thousands of their countrymen gaining their livelihood at Paris had been brutally expelled, and that prisoners were sometimes treated by the French with ferocious insolence. The citadel of Laon, having surrendered, was blown up at the moment when the Germans entered it, and the generality of the French press celebrated this as a glorious and heroic act. And there was a pitiful boastfulness in the midst of defeat which a generous warrior would despise. A popular French writer, after describing the retreat from Wörth, exclaimed, "And now, who will say that the French army has been conquered, or does anybody suppose that it can be, with such soldiers, commanded by a man like MacMahon?" and Victor Hugo, the first of imaginative writers living, published a letter to the Germans after Sedan, in which he says, "You have had the victory, and we have had the glory!" Contempt for the character of an enemy is always demoralising, and acts were committed by several corps—acts not only of ruthless severity, but of lawless violence—which will long rankle in the memories of the best and most thoughtful men in France.

During the whole of September Prince Frederick Charles was patiently starving out the French at Metz. Steinmetz was gone. That gloomy veteran had learnt too much of the ancient ways of war under Blucher in his youth to adapt himself, when past seventy, to the calculating science of Moltke. The intelligent officers of the new school who served under him were often startled by his orders, for he tried to do by brute force what could be better done by brains. After the wasteful slaughter at Gravelotte he disappeared from the army. Bazaine was not molested with cannon, but whenever he attempted to break out, he found the Prussians too strong for him. After his defeat at Naisseville and the capitulation of Sedan, he remained quiet during some valuable weeks, and then, learning from Prince Frederick Charles that the Republic was not accepted by the whole country, he involved himself in the Bonapartist intrigue. He was surrounded by men personally attached to the dynasty— Lebœuf, who knew that the Republic would ask him to account for so much ruin ; Frossard, the governor of the Prince Imperial, the Imperial Staff, and the Imperial Guard. He knew that the Germans distrusted the new Government and preferred the old, and he believed that Paris could not long prevent the discussion of peace. They would then be glad to treat with the commander of the only remaining army in France, and to place the new Government, whether a Regency or a National Assembly, under the protection of his sword. He could not hope to be delivered ; and after his troops began to eat the horses he could not escape. He tried to profit by the political position to rescue himself from the military position. He sent first Bourbaki and then Boyer to sound the Empress. Count Bismarck sent her word that she might return to the Tuileries if she would consent to his conditions ; and the Empire might have been restored in October on better terms, at least in respect of the indemnity, than those which the Republic accepted in March. Among the exiled Bonapartists in England there was much impatience at the coldness with which the Empress received the overtures from Versailles and Metz. But neither Bismarck nor Bazaine bound himself with pledges definite enough for security, and the Empress refused the terms. Bazaine, whose men for a whole week had declined to fight, and whose provisions were running short, so that two leeches were sold for £7, capitulated on the 27th of October with 173,000 men. It was not easy to prove why so large and so brave an army should have been unable to pierce the lines of an enemy scarcely superior in numbers, and divided by a river. It was supposed that Bazaine had been dazzled by the hope of serving the Empire, that the Germans had made skilful use of his delusion, and that political motives had barred his defence. Gambetta, whose plans were ruined by the fall of Metz, proclaimed him a traitor.

When it became known that he was in communication with the Germans the alarm was great at Tours, and the Government became very urgent for neutral intervention. Just then M. Thiers returned from his mission, and announced that all hope of armed assistance must be abandoned.   Russia had maintained her resolution to prevent Austria from joining the war, and Austria still submitted, not very reluctantly, to the restraint.   In Italy the position had been altered since the Empire fell, and Thiers was able to bring severe pressure to bear on the Italian Ministers.   On 20th September, with the consent of the French, they had taken Rome, and overthrown the Papal Power.   M. Thiers warned them to make friends with France in her need, lest they should hereafter have another Roman expedition, and a French army besieging their new capital.   He asked for 100,000 men.   The sword of Victor Emmanuel again rattled in its scabbard ; but Thiers obtained only Garibaldi and a handful of volunteers.   He came back convinced that resistance was useless, and that an armistice for the election of a National Assembly ought to be obtained at once.   He got permission to cross the German lines and to bring his dismal news to Paris.   Then he repaired to Versailles, hoping that Count Bismarck would prove more propitious than he had been to Favre.   The German Chancellor was desirous that a legal Government should be created by the suffrages of the people, with undisputed authority to conclude peace.   The Bonapartist combination was at an end, and the surrender of Bazaine was sure to influence the negotiations favourably.   Thiers further stipulated that supplies of food should be permitted to enter Paris, in proportion to the number of days that the armistice was to last, so that when it ended the inhabitants should be no worse off than when it began. Count Bismarck would have been inclined to yield this point.   The siege train was far from being ready, and the bombardment was still so remote that the armistice could cause no delay.   But the demand was peremptorily rejected by Moltke.   The King and his staff were averse to bombarding Paris, and wished to reduce it, like Metz, by famine. They already computed that it would have exhausted its provisions by the end of January. To admit food for a month, as was proposed, would carry the siege on to the end of February, and keep the army for four winter months in the dreary lines. On the other hand, Paris was so well supplied that it risked nothing by giving up the proposed condition. If the provinces could not raise the siege in three months, they could not raise it at all. But the Government of National Defence refused to entertain the notion of an armistice without revictualling Paris, and thus ended the last attempt to terminate the war before the extreme of misery had befallen the people of France.

The failure was not felt at first to be so disastrous, either at Paris or at Tours. During the conferences at Versailles there had been an abortive revolution against Trochu and Favre. The siege had lasted six weeks with an exasperating tranquillity. The Germans made no attempt to get in, nor the French to get out. Although the garrison was twice as numerous as the besiegers, Trochu did not esteem it capable of raising the siege by winning a pitched battle ; and he waited the moment for a combined attack when an army should come up from the provinces. His troops, seeing that he would not face the enemy, began to share his despondency. The inaction of Trochu, and the departure of Gambetta, who was popular in the streets, caused the Government to lose ground with the advanced democracy. The municipal elections had been promised and then postponed. The Government, which had not the sanction of the popular vote, dreaded the presence of a body sprung from universal suffrage, and the Red Republicans knew that the election of the Municipality would give the supreme power to them. The Emperor had taken the power out of the hands of the people, and exercised it for his own independent purposes, and not in the interest of any section of society. His merit in the eyes of France had been that he suspended the conflict between property and

labour, between class and class, which had raged so
furiously after the fall of Louis Philippe.   An absolute
democracy where the theory of political equality is contrasted with the fact of an extreme social inequality is
either a government by property or a government by
poverty ; labour will expect to be sacrificed to wealth
unless it can make wealth subject to the interests of
labour.   In France the balance could only be maintained
by an authority indifferent to their antagonism.   When
the power which was above the parties and restrained
them was removed, their strife was renewed.   And thus
it happened that Socialism, which had slumbered under
absolute monarchy, rose up in arms against the Republic.
One of the traditions of the great French Revolution was
the institution of a permanent and irresponsible body
holding the power of insurrection, and using it for the
purpose of controlling the organised authorities.   Analogous
instances of a secret despotism, veiled by constitutional
forms, have occurred many times in history.   At Paris
this office was discharged by the Commune, or Corporation, a body that had no defined department in the
Government, but was able to bind or loose the turbulence
of the masses.   It was by the restoration of this institution, and by allying themselves with the Jacobins, who
upheld it as an essential principle of Government, that
the Socialists hoped to make themselves masters of Paris
and of France.   And we have seen the prodigious power
they acquired when, in addition to their own especial
motives, Paris was infuriated at the peace, at the triumph
of the reaction at Bordeaux, and at the transfer of the
Parliamentary capital to Versailles.   At the end of
October the news that Bazaine and all his forces were
prisoners of war filled Paris with consternation.   Just at
this moment the garrison had obtained a first success
at Le Bourget, which had been followed by a smart
defeat.   At the same time Thiers appeared at Paris, and
it was known that negotiations were on foot, negotiations
apparently prompted by despair at the loss of Metz.   On
31st October an armed mob burst into the room where

the Government of National Defence was sitting, and took them prisoners. Somebody told Trochu to escape, or he would be shot. " Sir," he replied, " I am a soldier, and mean to die at my post." For many hours Trochu, Favre, and several of their colleagues were as helpless as Louis XVI. in the hands of the populace. The list of a new Government was handed about, which was to call the Municipality into existence, and in which Dorian, the Minister who had become known to the people, because he was active in setting in motion great factories of war-like munitions, was to have been Dictator. In the middle of the night a few faithful battalions rescued the captive Government. There had been no bloodshed. It was but the prelude to the terrible explosions that were to come. The Government immediately appealed to the people, and was confirmed in office by an overwhelming majority of votes. The consequence of their deep humiliation was to confer upon them a moral authority they had never before enjoyed.

But while Favre and Trochu were suffering the vicissitudes of popular favour at Paris, Gambetta ruled France with unresisted sway. He had sent carrier pigeons to warn Favre against the armistice, for he knew that a National Assembly would speedily depose him, and would bring to power those Moderate Liberals who had been betrayed on 4th September and had never been reconciled to the Government of National Defence. He had nearly succeeded in equipping an army fit to take the field when the fall of Metz released the victorious forces of Prince Frederick Charles. His preparations were so secret, and the exaggerations of his language were received with so little credulity, that the Germans did not take alarm at the really formidable army that was being welded together by strict disciplinarians behind the curtain of the Loire. They divided the army that had captured Metz. Part overran the north of France, while Prince Frederick Charles advanced towards the centre and the south. The Bavarians, who occupied the post of danger at Orleans, received no supports.   Although the army of the Loire was not yet fully organised, there was time to deliver a blow before the Germans could provide for their defence.   On 10th November the French, under Aurelle de Paladines, entered Orleans after a battle in which they had forced the Bavarians to retreat.   They were not only numerous and brave, but they were commanded with real ability, and France hoped for a moment that the Germans were not only outnumbered but out-generalled.   The week that followed the recapture of Orleans was their hour of peril.   Aurelle was slow and cautious in pursuing his success.   But on the 15th it was believed that he had got past the covering armies, and was about to take the besiegers in the rear.   The baggage was packed at headquarters, and everything was held in readiness to raise the siege in a moment.   Prince Frederick Charles was called up to combat the army of the Loire.   But Aurelle fell back on the following day to a fortified position before Orleans, and the gleam of hope was quenched.   During the elation caused by his first success-ful advance, an event happened in the political world which might have afforded France a chance of forcing Europe into war.   When Metz had fallen, and things were looking at their worst, Russia announced that she held herself no longer bound to observe the neutrality of the Black Sea, which she had been made to consent to by the Crimean war.   Prussia, though she had signed the Treaty of Paris, had been always indifferent to its objects ; and connivance at the repudiation of one of its clauses was a moderate price to pay for the support of Russia in the present war.   But for England and Austria the Russian declaration was a hostile and un-warranted act, and the feelings of the old Western alliance for the protection of Turkey began to stir again. If French diplomacy had not been at a standstill by the exclusion of all the most experienced statesmen from public affairs, there would have been good materials for embroiling the neutrals.   It was a conjuncture which brought home to them forcibly the value of France in

the European system, and the danger which would come
from her eclipse.   But the French failed to derive any
present benefit from the threatening revival of the Eastern
Question.   At the end of November, Aurelle, having
made his arrangements with Trochu, advanced from the
Loire with the flower of the Republican armies, whilst
Ducrot and Vinoy went out to meet him.   They carried
several villages on the Marne, and inflicted great loss on
the Saxons and Wirtembergers.   For two days it seemed
that they were going to break through.   But Moltke gave
orders that the lost positions should be retaken at any
cost, and the French were stopped ; but they kept part
of the conquered ground, and built an advanced fort
on Mont Avron that seriously vexed the besiegers.
While Ducrot was repulsed on the Marne, the army of
the Loire came upon Prince Frederick Charles and met
with a series of reverses, ending in a decisive defeat at
Orleans on 4th December.

   After the defeat of the army of the Loire, the failure
of the great sortie, and the arrival of Prince Frederick
Charles upon the scene, the deliverance of Paris became
a military impossibility, and the continuation of the war
was prompted by illusions.   There was only the dreadful
choice between fire and famine.   It was simply a question
of more or less suffering to be borne by women and
children.   Therefore on the day after the fall of Orleans
the Germans summoned Paris.   Moltke informed Trochu
that his last hope, the army of the Loire, was defeated,
and invited him to send out an officer to verify the fact.
Trochu declined the offer.   The capital was in no humour
to capitulate.   The classes whose turbulence is its standing
danger were taken into the pay of the State as its National
Guards, and easily resigned themselves to a condition of
things in which idleness was as remunerative as toil.   The
inhabitants had not yet suffered severe privations ; but
they were prepared for them.   They were calm and
patient.   The disorders which are the disgrace of the
city in happier times were banished, and crime had
almost disappeared.   A system of charity admirably

organised relieved the poor. The dignity of sacrifice had transformed the city. Even in the worst extremity, when an appalling death-rate proclaimed the approaching agony, and the wailing of mothers was in every house, there were no serious bread riots. The Red Republicans, fed on extravagant fictions and willing to be deceived, were on the watch for signs of weakness in the Government. Long after a courageous journalist had announced that Paris was virtually lost already, and that the Government knew it well, Trochu was obliged to promise that he would never surrender. Every soldier knew that the promise was nothing but a melancholy boast; but the hand of the Red Republicans was heavy on their rulers, and none had the courage to give way, while the people waited for the end with an heroic sadness.

When Trochu's reply to Moltke made known that the resistance was to be prolonged beyond the limits of reasonable hope, a great dispute broke out at the head-quarters of the Germans. Count Bismarck declared that the moment had arrived to bring the population of Paris under the influence of terror. He thought that much purposeless and wanton havoc might be averted, and many lives of soldiers and non-combatants preserved, if the Government of Paris could be emancipated from the tyranny of an excited populace; and he could urge with justice that to bombard a city is less cruel than to starve it. Moltke opposed the bombardment. There had been a feud between these men ever since they conquered the Austrians together in 1866, and it is possible that the Crown Prince, looking to the future and disliking Bismarck, might think that he would be a too powerful and unmanageable subject if, in addition to his immense prestige, he had the cordial support of the army and its glorious chiefs. Count Bismarck had opposed the march to Paris, and believed that the siege was a blunder, and that the defences might have been forced at once. But he was not admitted to the military councils, and he shut himself up in disgust, and gave out that he was ill. He set the obedient press to work to agitate opinion at home

in favour of the bombardment until the impatience
caught the army.   The whole of December was spent in
bringing up heavy artillery, and it was Christmas before
the guns were ready to pour their fire on the forts.

At that time a new enemy was giving trouble in the
north.   An army had been formed under Faidherbe,
drawing its supplies from the sea, resting on the stronghold of Lille, and provided with a powerful artillery.
Faidherbe understood the art of war, and the force
opposed to him was small ; but it was led by Göben,
reputed in the German camp one of the most consummate
officers in Europe, and Faidherbe could not make his
way to Paris.   The army of the Loire had been cut in
two at Orleans ; and one half retired by the left bank of
the river towards Bourges, where it spent some weeks in
inaction ; while the stronger half, under Chanzy, closely
pursued by the Duke of Mecklenburg, turned towards
the west.   Chanzy proved the hardest hitter among the
generals of the Republic.   His troops fought day by
day, losing ground but not losing courage, until the
Bavarians, who had seen so much of the roughest work
of the campaign, had almost melted away.   Defeated at
Beaugency, Chanzy retreated slowly towards Brittany,
and established himself at Le Mans, to the west of Paris ;
while the Tours Government, having no army to protect
it, retired to Bordeaux.   The defeat of Aurelle and
Chanzy on the Loire made it clear that the armies
charged with the duty of covering the siege of Paris
were equal to their task, and the French turned their
thoughts in another direction.   In the east of France
Garibaldi had not answered the expectations of Gambetta,
and his Italian soldiers had sometimes fought better
than their French brothers in arms.   His campaign in
Burgundy had not served the prestige either of France
or of the Republic, while the loyal and religious men of
La Vendée had shared the laurels of Chanzy.   Gambetta
raised the army of Bourges to 130,000 men, gave the
command to Bourbaki, the General of the Imperial Guard,
and leaving the western army of the Loire to its fate, sent

him to raise the siege of Belfort and threaten Germany. Prince Frederick Charles, who had kept watch at Orleans, seeing no enemy in his front, marched against Chanzy, defeated him at Le Mans on 12th January, and drove him into the west. Meantime Bourbaki fell upon Werder near Belfort, and was compelled to retreat after three days' fighting. Werder, with only 40,000 men, was too weak for a vigorous pursuit. · But as soon as the nature of Bourbaki's expedition was ascertained, Moltke had sent Manteuffel and Fransecky across France to intercept him, and quietly announced at Versailles that the Germans had got too many prisoners, and that Bourbaki would be driven over the frontier and disarmed by the Swiss. Every movement was so well planned and conducted that Bourbaki, seeing that all was lost, attempted suicide, and 80,000 of his troops laid down their arms in Switzerland.

While these things were passing amid the snows of the Jura, Paris had already fallen. The Germans, having detached all the men they could spare to put an end to the resistance in the provinces, proceeded to batter the defences. The southern forts proved too strong for their siege artillery; but it was ascertained that their guns carried right into the heart of Paris, and the bombardment commenced in earnest. It did little damage, for Paris, rebuilt by the Emperor of stone and iron, is the least combustible of cities, and the loss of life was small. The inhabitants bore this trial well, but they could not bear the inaction of their defenders. At last, on 19th January, when the bombardment had lasted a fortnight, and the mortality among non-combatants from disease and want of nourishment exceeded the usual rate by 500 deaths a day, when the remnants of the relieving armies under Bourbaki and Chanzy were in full retreat, and while Göben, at St. Quentin, was gaining the last pitched battle of the war, Trochu led 100,000 men against the Germans in the direction of Versailles. It was the last effort of the besieged, and when it failed, Trochu took no pains to disguise the magnitude of the disaster. On the

next day the irretrievable defeat of Chanzy was made
public.   Riots broke out, bread ran short, and Trochu
resigned his command, while the Germans opened an
overwhelming fire to the north, on the weakest point of
the fortifications.   The Government appealed to all the
officers successively down to the rank of Captain.   Not
one was willing to take on himself the task of prolonging the defence.   The fort of St. Denis was about to
fall, and then the populous regions of Paris would be
commanded by the Prussian guns.   On 24th January
Favre went out to Versailles, and after four days' discussion an armistice was concluded.   The defence had
long ceased to be justified by the rules and purposes of
military science.   But the Parisians were persuaded that
they were yielding only to famine, and had persevered
up to the verge of starvation.   It was reported that the
Government had miscalculated the duration of the supplies
by a week, and that there was imminent danger.   The
Germans, on the contrary, believed that Paris yielded to
force, that the bombardment had hastened the end by
a month, and that provisions would have lasted, with the
cruel economy practised in many famous sieges, far into
February.   They offered six millions of rations, but they
were not sent for.   They brought large supplies of flour,
but it was left untouched for many days.   The omnibuses
were still running in Paris, and of the horses that were
private property very few had been killed.

Favre had no real authority over the rest of France,
and there was doubt whether the armistice he had signed
would be accepted at Bordeaux in the name of the
provinces.   Favre, acting under false impressions, and
hoping to save Bourbaki, had excluded him from the
range of the armistice ; and as the rout of his army
speedily followed, Gambetta reviled the Paris Government and denounced their act.   He submitted, however,
and prepared for the inevitable election of a National
Assembly in such a way as to make it serve his purpose
of renewing the war, which Chanzy alone among the
leading generals was ready to conduct.   The elections

occurring at the moment when the efforts of the Republic
had brought the country lower than the Empire had left
it, were sure to be reactionary.   The restoration of
Monarchy under the House of Orleans, through the instrumentality of Thiers, seemed near at hand.   Gambetta
decreed that all men should be ineligible who had held
any office under the Empire.   Under the appearance of
excluding the Imperialists, who were no longer feared,
this was a blow aimed at the friends of Constitutional
Monarchy, and it was immediately annulled by Jules
Favre as an audacious infraction of the principles of
liberty.   Gambetta resigned, and the triumph of the
Moderate and Peace party was secured.

    Paris elected a long list of illustrious writers, together
with the chief revolutionary leaders.   The long seclusion
of the capital had estranged it from the rest of France.
Its influence had been too long suspended to be easily
recovered.   There was no sympathy between the city
that had cost such sacrifices and the provinces that had
made them in vain.   The temper of the Assembly was
so hostile and intolerant to the war party, that Victor
Hugo and some other Paris deputies quitted it.   Garibaldi also resigned, but attempted afterwards to speak.
The majority marked their abhorrence of the party he
represented by refusing to hear him.   Thiers, who
was elected in more than twenty constituencies, and had
received a million and a half of votes, was put at the head
of the State, that he might quickly come to terms with
the conquerors, and then curb the revolutionary movement.   He is a considerable writer, an admirable speaker,
and the cleverest talker in France.   As a statesman he
had shown boldness and fertility of expedients, but he
was growing old, and his action since the beginning of
the war had not sustained his fame.   He has exulted so
much over French conquests, and so often flattered with
ingenious sophistry the vainer and more selfish patriotism
of his country, that he could not adopt the lofty though
fatal declarations of Jules Favre about the integrity of
the national soil.   He courageously accepted the conse-

quences of such tremendous reverses. He had left Versailles in November, believing that the Germans would have restored Metz, on condition of levelling the works, and would have been content with taking £120,000,000. Three months of war had doubled the indemnity, and the generals would not hear of losing Metz. It is remarkable that M. Thiers appealed to England for aid in reducing not the demand for territory, but the demand for money. A telegram from Count Bernstorff arrived at the critical moment, and £40,000,000 sterling were struck off the indemnity.

The end of war is peace; but in France the proclamation of the peace was the signal for civil war. The conspirators who control the fierce democracy of Paris repudiated a Government which was imposed on the artisans of cities by the peasant proprietors of France. Two months after the last Prussian gun had been discharged, Thiers was battering down the walls which he himself had built, and Favre was throwing shells into the city in which he had so lately learnt the terrors of bombardment. The provinces, which had failed to deliver the capital from the German armies, were striving to reconquer it from the Revolution. But the victory of the lawful Government over the dreaded enemy who must always remain within the walls and cannot be got rid of, cannot end in a settlement compatible with freedom. No absolute republic can reconcile the conflict between wealth and labour in arms, for it must lead to the domination of one class of society and the economic subjugation of the other. The Revolution is destroying the Republic, and France is once more drifting on a resistless current towards Monarchy. The House of Orleans has not stood above the parties, but was identified with that dominion of the middle class which is the main cause of Socialism. This has produced the unexpected influence of the Legitimists, of that party whose monarch claims the crown on abstract principle, and not by virtue of any positive interests, and causes thousands who are not Legitimists to wish for the restoration of the head of the House of Bourbon, guarded by the able and politic princes of the younger branch.

The events which have dissolved society in France have consolidated Germany. For the first time since Frederick Barbarossa was drowned in the Crusade, it has become a powerful Empire, under a National Emperor. While the centrifugal forces make France their prey, the danger of the Germans lies in the immense preponderance of the Prussian Crown. But a Federation between Sovereign States is perhaps of all forms of government the one that promises to provide, in the long-run, the strongest and safest securities for the liberty and progress of the world.

IX

GEORGE ELIOT'S LIFE [1]

IF it is true that the most interesting of George Eliot's characters is her own, it may be said also that the most interesting of her books is her Life. Mr. Cross has made known what is in fact the last work of the great English-woman. He possesses that art of concealing the artist which is still the rarest quality of biographers, and, apart from a few necessary pages, gives nothing but letters, journals, and fragmentary memoirs, written partly with a dim vision of publicity. The volumes will be read less for the notes of travel, the emphatic tenderness of the letters to friends, often on a lower plane, and the tonic aphorisms devised for their encouragement, than for the light they shed on the history of a wonderful intellect. The usual attractions of biography are wanting here. We see the heroine, not reflected from other minds, but nearly as she saw herself and cared to be known. Her own skilled hand has drawn her likeness. In books variously attributable to a High Church curate and to a disciple of Comte, the underlying unity of purpose was not apparent. For valid reasons they invite interpretation as much as *Faust* or the *Paradiso*. The drift and sequence of ideas, no longer obscured by irony, no longer veiled under literary precautions or overlaid with the dense drapery of style, is revealed beyond the risk of error now that the author has become her own interpreter.

[1] "George Eliot's Life as related in her Letters and Journals, arranged and edited by her husband, J. W. Cross. In three volumes, London and Edinburgh, William Blackwood & Sons, 1885." *The Nineteenth Century*, March, 1885.

The Life, while it illustrates the novels, explains what they do not indicate,—the influences which produced the novelist.   George Eliot was no spontaneous genius, singing unbidden with unpremeditated art.   Her talents ripened successively and slowly.   No literary reputation of this century has risen so high after having begun so late. The even maturity of her powers, original and acquired, lasted only thirteen years, and the native imagination was fading when observation and reflection were in the fulness of their prime.   Mr. Cross's first volume describes the severe discipline of life and thought, the trials and efforts by which her greatness was laboriously achieved.

Marian Evans spent the first thirty years of her life in a rural shire, and received her earliest and most enduring impressions in a region of social stability, among inert forces, away from the changing scenes that attend the making of history.   Isolation, the recurring note of her existence, set in early, for her urgent craving for love and praise was repelled by the relations around her, and her childhood was unhappy.   We are assured that she was affectionate, proud, and sensitive in the highest degree ; and the words are significant, because they bear the concurrent testimony of her brother and her husband. The early letters, written with the ceremonious propriety of Miss Seward, give no sign of more than common understanding.   She was just out of her teens when she wrote the following words :—

Men and women are but children of a larger growth ; they are still imitative beings.   We cannot (at least those who ever read to any purpose at all)—we cannot, I say, help being modified by the ideas that pass through our minds.   We hardly wish to lay claim to such elasticity as retains no impress.   How deplorably and unaccountably evanescent are our frames of mind, as various as the forms and lines of the summer clouds !   A single word is sometimes enough to give an entirely new mould to our thoughts ; at least I find myself so constituted, and therefore to me it is pre-eminently important to be anchored within the veil, so that outward things may be unable to send me adrift.   Society is a wide nursery of plants, where the hundreds decompose to nourish the future ten, after giving collateral benefits to their contemporaries destined for a fairer garden.   The prevalence of misery and want in this boasted nation of prosperity and glory is appalling, and really seems to call us away from mental luxury. Oh, to be doing some little towards the re-generation of this growing travailing creation!

Beneath the pale surface of these sentences, and of one touching "that joyous birdlike enjoyment of things which, though perishable as to their actual existence, will be embalmed to eternity in the precious spices of gratitude," there are germs of sentiments to which the writer clung through the coming years. But the contrast with her developed character is stronger than the resemblance. She is struck at this time with compassion at the spectacle presented by people who go on marrying and giving in marriage. Music seems to her an unholy rite. On a visit to London she buys a Josephus, but refuses to go to the play with her brother. Even Shakespeare is dangerous. She lamented that novels had been supplied to her early, teaching her to live by herself in the midst of an imaginary world; and she had been disturbed at reading in *Devereux* that religion is not a requisite to moral excellence. She concluded that history is better than fiction; and her growing energy, her accuracy, her power of mastering hard books, seemed to promise a rival to Clinton or Long. The first literary enterprise in which she was engaged was a chart of ecclesiastical history, intended to include an application of the Apocalyptic prophecies, "which would merely require a few figures,"—the sense of humour was still dormant. The taste for material erudition was soon lost, and turned to bitterness. In her books George Eliot has twice exhibited the vanity of pointless learning, and she looked back gratefully upon the agencies which rescued her from the devious and rugged ways by which history approaches truth.

Evangelical and Baptist teachers had imbued her with practical religion, and she enjoyed the writings proper to the school. In after-years Sydney Smith's account of his occupations about this time must have seemed to her a burlesque of her own: "I console myself with Doddridge's *Exposition* and *The Scholar Armed*, to say nothing of a very popular book, *The Dissenter Tripped*

Up." She was intent on Doddridge, Wilberforce, and Milner, admired Hannah More, and commended *The Infidel Reclaimed*. Respect for the logic of Calvinism survived most of her theology, and it was attended originally by a corresponding aversion for what pertains to Rome. She reads the Oxford tracts, and unconsciously applying a noted saying of St. Thomas, detects the Satanic canker amidst so much learning and devotion.

This seriousness is the most constant element which early education supplied to her after career. She knew, not from hearsay or habit, but from the impress of inward experience, what is meant by conversion, grace, and prayer. Her change was not from external conformity to avowed indifference, but from earnest piety to explicit negation, and the knowledge of many secrets of a devout life accompanied her through all vicissitudes. Writers of equal celebrity and partly analogous career, such as Strauss and Renan, have made the same claim, somewhat confounding theological training with religious insight, and deliberate conviction or devotional feeling with faith. But George Eliot continued to draw the best of her knowledge from her own spiritual memories, not from a library of local divinity, and she treated religion neither with learned analysis nor with a gracious and flexible curiosity, but with a certain grave sympathy and gratitude. Her acquaintance with books had been restricted by the taste or scruples of teachers who could not estimate the true proportions or needs of her mind, and the defect was not remedied by contact with any intelligent divine. Such instruction as she obtained has supported thousands faithfully in the trials of life, but for an inquisitive and ambitious spirit, gifted with exceptional capacity for acquiring knowledge, it was no adequate protection under the wear and tear of study.

In the summer of 1841 the thought quickens, the style improves, and a new interest is awakened in disputed questions. She already aspired after that reconciliation of Locke with Kant which was to be the special boast of one of her most distinguished friends, and she was impressed by Isaac Taylor's *Ancient Christianity*, allowing some drawback for his treatment of the Fathers. At this point, while still a trusted member of the Church, Miss Evans was introduced at Coventry to a family of busy and strenuous freethinkers.

The first visit to their house was early in November 1841, after which she speaks of being absorbed in momentous studies, and on the 13th of the same month she writes to her most intimate friend : "Think! is there any conceivable alteration in me that could prevent your coming to me at Christmas?" The obstacle announced in these words was a vital alteration in her religious principles. The revolution was sudden, but it was complete. For a time she continued to speak of eternal hope and a beneficent Creator ; in deference to her father she even consented, uneasily, to go to church. But from that momentous November until her death it would appear that no misgiving favourable to Christianity ever penetrated her mind or shook for an instant its settled unbelief. There was no wavering and no regret. And when George Eliot had become a consummate expert in the pathology of conscience, she abstained from displaying the tortures of doubt and the struggles of expiring faith.

The history of a soul is never fully told, even for edification. We learn that Miss Evans was initiated in the mysteries of scepticism at her first encounter with cultivated society ; and her early convictions, artlessly propped upon Young and Hannah More, yielded to the combined influence. Her new friend was the wife of Mr. Bray, who had written *The Philosophy of Necessity*, and sister to Mr. Hennell, the author of *An Enquiry concerning the Origin of Christianity*. The formal country schoolgirl, whose wondering companions called her " Little Mamma," who gathered them for prayer, who knew how to organise and to invigorate district work, and had dismissed her own brother for his High Church propensity, was fascinated and transformed by these surroundings. She pronounced Mrs. Bray the most religious person she knew, and Mr.

Hennell a perfect model of manly excellence. She read his *Enquiry* twice through, and found it more interesting than any book she had seen. It represented in its day the antepenultimate stage of Biblical study; and Strauss, swathing his German criticism in politer Latin, said that it was written *Britannis, Britannice*. Mr. Hennell's reading of Gospel history was not the outcome of untried method or hypothesis, and those whom he convinced were tempted to conclude that arguments so specious and acceptable to themselves ought in fairness to satisfy others. They impressed Miss Evans, and at the critical moment she met with some unfavourable specimen of the Christian advocate. "These dear orthodox people talk so simply sometimes, that one cannot help fancying them satirists of their own doctrines and fears." Endowed with many virtues which go to constitute the ideal of the Christian character, with self-knowledge, unflinching sincerity, and an ardent devotion to the good of others, she became impatient of minds that could not keep pace with her own, and learnt during a portion of her life to reckon prejudice, fallacious reasoning, and wilful blindness among the properties of orthodoxy.

Strauss himself never made so important a proselyte. He provoked a reaction which nearly balanced his direct influence, and the *Leben Jesu* had already become, like the *Génie du Christianisme* and the *Sermon on National Apostasy*, the signal of a religious revival. Between Hennell's *Enquiry* and George Eliot's answer there is no proportion. His views need not have implied condemnation of all foreign and American Churches. She was more thorough in her rejection of the Gospels, and she at once rejected far more than the Gospels. For some years her mind travelled in search of rest, and, like most students of German thought before the middle of the century, she paid a passing tribute to pantheism. But from Jonathan Edwards to Spinoza she went over at one step. The abrupt transition may be accounted for by the probable action of Kant, who had not then become a buttress of Christianity. Out of ten Englishmen, if there were ten, who read him in 1841, nine got no further than the *Critique of Pure Reason*, and knew him as the dreaded assailant of popular evidences. When George Eliot stood before his statue at Berlin she was seized with a burst of gratitude, but she hardly became familiar with his later works.

Mr. Bray was a phrenologist who remained faithful to the cause after it had been blighted by Dr. Carpenter; and he soon found out that, if there is truth in phrenology, Miss Evans must be a portent. Mrs. Bray and her sister, the Cara and Sara of the biography, relieved the sadness and the solitude of her life at home, and comforted her in fits of nervous depression, in her fretful introspection, in her despair of ever winning affection or doing work worth living for. She associated with their friends, used their library, and surveyed the world through their windows. Greek and German, and the depths of unconscious energy within, carried her presently beyond their sphere, and she followed her own path in literature. A time came when the correspondence between them fell under constraint. But for ten eventful years, in which her mind was forming and settling upon fixed lines, this family group was able to encourage and to limit her progress, and the letters to Miss Hennell, written under the stress of transition, described her first attempts to steer without the accustomed stars :—

Of course I must desire the ultimate downfall of error, for no error is innocuous ; but this assuredly will occur' without my proselytising aid. I cannot rank among my principles of action a fear of vengeance eternal, gratitude for predestined salvation, or a revelation of future glories as a reward. The mind that feels its value will get large draughts from some source if denied it in the most commonly chosen way. Where is not this same ego ? The martyr at the stake seeks its gratification as much as the court sycophant, the difference lying in the comparative dignity and beauty of the two egos. People absurdly talk of self-denial. Why, there is none in virtue to a being of moral excellence. There can be few who more truly feel than I that this is a world of bliss and beauty ; that is, that bliss and beauty are the end, the tendency of creation, and evils are its shadows. When the soul is just liberated from the wretched giant's bed of dogmas on which it has been racked and stretched ever since it began to think, there is a feeling of exultation and strong hope. We think we shall run well when we have the full use of our limbs and the bracing air of independence, and we believe that we shall soon obtain something positive which will not only more than compensate us for what we have renounced, but will be so well worth offering to others that we may venture to proselytise as fast as our zeal for truth may prompt us. But a year or two of reflection, and the experience of our own miserable weakness, which will ill afford to part even with the crutch of superstition, must, I think, effect a change. Speculative truth begins to appear but a shadow of individual minds ; agreement between intellects seems unattainable, and we turn to the truth of feeling as the only universal bond of union.

We find that the intellectual errors which we once fancied were a mere incrustation have grown into the living body, and that we cannot, in the majority of cases, wrench them away without destroying vitality. We begin to find that, with individuals as with nations, the only safe revolution is one arising out of the wants which their own progress has generated. It is the quackery of infidelity to suppose that it has a nostrum for all mankind.

So much of George Eliot's permanent characteristics had taken root independently of Rousseau, Spinoza, Feuerbach, Goethe, Comte, or Spencer, and before the dynasty of thinkers began to reign in her mind. Mrs. Cross would have recognised herself in these confessions of 1843. The acute crisis was over : a long period of gradual and consistent growth ensued.

Miss Evans translated the *Leben Jesu* from the fourth edition, in which Strauss betrayed the feeling roused by the violence of the conflict, and withdrew the concessions which his ablest opponents had wrung from him. It was not a labour of love to the translator. In her judgment the problem was exhausted. She had her own more radical solution, which the author did not reach for twenty years, and she shared neither his contentious fervour, his asperity, nor his irresolution. The task was accomplished under a sense of growing repulsion. One of her friends even says that she gathered strength to write on the Crucifixion by gazing on the crucifix, and we may infer from this remark that some confusion of thought prevailed at Coventry.

When she visited Germany in 1854, the first person

she met, at Cologne, was Strauss.   A miniature revolution
had driven him from the career for which he was bred,
and he was leading an indeterminate existence, without
an occupation fitted for his powers, and without a home.
Cologne irritated him by want of literature, and by the
cathedral which a Protestant government was proceeding
to complete, while those to whom it belonged had been
content that it should stand for centuries a monument
of profuse and miscalculating zeal.   Theology made him
sick, and fame did not console him, for he was tired of
being called the author of his book, and was not yet
reconciled to popularity among classes that could neither
substitute precept for dogma nor ideas for facts.   The
meeting left no agreeable impression.   In the life of
George Eliot Strauss is an episode, not an epoch.   She
did not take him up to satisfy doubts or to complete an
appointed course.   These studies were carried no further,
and she was not curious regarding the future of the
famous school whose influence extended from Newman
and Ritschl to Renan and Keim.   But there is no writer
on whom she bestowed so large a share of the incessant
labour of her life.   Two years spent in uncongenial
contact with such a mind were an effectual lesson to a
woman of twenty-six, unused to strict prosaic method,
and averse from the material drudgery of research.   She
could learn from Strauss to distrust the royal road of
cleverness and wit, to neglect no tedious detail, to write
so that what is written shall withstand hostile scrutiny.

Five studious years followed, which strengthened the
solid qualities of her mind.   There had been much docility
in complying with the nearest teaching and taking the
line of least resistance.   There was some risk of falling
into worn channels, as men do who keep the colours of
school and college, who read for agreement, and privately
believe in some sage of Highgate or Westminster, Chelsea
or Concord, as chance determines.   George Eliot set herself earnestly to get out of the current, to be emancipated
from the forces about her, and to secure the largest area
of choice for guidance and instruction.

I say it now, and I say it once for all, that I am influenced in my own conduct at the present time by far higher considerations, and by a nobler idea of duty, than I ever was while I held the evangelical beliefs.   It seems as if my affections were quietly sinking down to temperate, and I every day seem more and more to value thought rather than feeling.   I do not think this is man's best estate.   Now I am set free from the irritating worn-out integument.   I am entering on a new period of my life, which makes me look back on the past as something incredibly poor and contemptible.   I am beginning to lose respect for the petty acumen that sees difficulties.

I love the souls that rush along to their goal with a full stream of sentiment, that have too much of the positive to be harassed by the perpetual negatives, which after all are but the disease of the soul, to be expelled by fortifying the principle of vitality.   The only ardent hope I have for my future life is to have given to me some woman's duty, some possibility of devoting myself where I may see a daily result of pure calm blessedness in the life of another.

After losing her father and spending several months at Geneva she settled down to a literary career in London. At Geneva she is still remembered with affection.   Her days were spent obscurely, in the hard work which was her refuge from loneliness, from despondency, from the absence of a woman's joys and cares.   She kept the secret of her authorship, and avoided aggressive speech ; but those whom she trusted knew her as a pantheist and a stubborn disputant.   She is described as talking well but showily, like one overfed on the French of the days when Quinet and Mickiewicz were eminent.   France and the emotional philosophers had their time.   She became, and to some extent remained, a devoted advocate of Jean Jacques and George Sand, and she startled Emerson by her taste for the *Confessions*.

Half of the books mentioned at this period are in verse.   She knew how to distil working ideas from the obscurest poems ; and her decorated prose, artificial with the strain to avoid commonplace, charged with excessive meaning, and resembling the style of no other writer, was formed on the English poets.   She preferred Milton, Shelley, Wordsworth, and the early dramatists, specially excluding Marlowe.   No one was fitter by intellectual affinity to penetrate the secret of Shakespeare ; but the influence of Goethe was deeper, and perhaps near the end the influence of Dante. Goethe's preponderance is explicable by Strauss's reason, that Sirius may be larger than the sun, but ripens no grapes for us. It is recorded that George Eliot thought Shakespeare unjust to women ; and we may believe that a mind so carefully poised was repelled by his flagrant insularity, his leaning for obvious characters, his insensibility to the glories of Greece and the mystery of the Renaissance, his indifference to the deeper objects for which his generation contended. The preference for Dante, with all his passion, fanaticism, and poverty of logic, is a symptom of that swerving towards religious sentiments which, in spite of Comte, if not by virtue of Comte, marked the later years.

Beyond the pleasures of literature arose the sterner demand for a certain rule of life in place of the rejected creeds. The sleepless sense that a new code of duty and motive needed to be restored in the midst of the void left by lost sanctions and banished hopes never ceased to stimulate her faculties and to oppress her spirits. After the interrupted development and the breach with the entire past, only her own energy could avail in the pursuit that imparted unity to her remaining life. It was the problem of her age to reconcile the practical ethics of unbelief and of belief, to save virtue and happiness when dogmas and authorities decay. To solve it she swept the realm of knowledge and stored up that large and serious erudition which sustains all her work, and in reality far exceeded what appears on the surface of the novels or in the record of daily reading. For an attentive observer there are many surprises, like that of the mathematician who came to give her lessons and found that she was already in the differential calculus. It is her supreme characteristic in literature that her original genius rested on so broad a foundation of other people's thoughts ; and it would be hard to find in her maturer life any parallel to Mr. Spencer's historic inacquaintance with Comte, or to the stranger ignorance of Mr. Spencer's own existence avowed in 1881 by Michelet, the legendary mantle-bearer of Hegel.

George Eliot always read with a purpose before her, and there was no waste and little raw material in her learning. But her acquirements were mainly those of a person who had taught herself, and might not have satisfied University tests. The Latin is dubious in *Romola* and the Italian in *Mr. Gilfil's Love Story*. The Princess of Eboli, who is supposed in the Life to have been a beauty, wore a patch over her eye. A questionable date is assigned to the Platonic anniversary in *Romola*, and the affair of the Appeal is misunderstood. There is a persistent error regarding the age of Pico ; and Savonarola, instead of proclaiming that he went straight to heaven, gave his evidence the other way. These and all other mistakes which the patience of readers has detected are immeasurably trivial compared to those which occur in the most famous historical novels, such as *Ivanhoe* and *John Inglesant*.

Caution and vigilance in guarding even the vestige of inaccuracy are apparent in other ways than the trip to Gainsborough and the consultation with Mr. Harrison on the legal obscurities of *Felix Holt*. Ladislaw's fatal allusion to German scholarship, which shattered Dorothea's belief in her husband, was an audacious hyperbole. Comparative mythology was as backward in Germany as elsewhere, besides which the *Aglaophamus* was written in Latin and the *Symbolik* was already appearing in French. But George Eliot takes care to warn us that Ladislaw did not know what he was talking about, and that Casaubon scorned to learn from a German even writing in Latin. Macchiavelli, in *Romola*, blows hot and cold on the Frate, but the inconsistency is faithfully taken from his writings. While the enthusiasts prevailed he went easily with the tide ; but after he had been ruined and tortured for the Republic, and had become the officious expounder of Borgian theory to Medicean experts, he spoke as became him of the man who had the blood-feud with Borgias and Medicis. The discovery of a single epithet, of a single letter (*versuto* for *versato*), has determined his real opinion since George Eliot wrote. The supreme test of the solidity of her work is the character of Savonarola. She possibly under-estimates the infusion of artifice in the prophecies, but no historian has held more firmly the not very evident answer to the question how a man who denounced the Pope as fiercely as Luther, who was ex-communicated and consigned to death by Rome, should nevertheless have left such a reputation behind him that, within eleven years of his execution, Julius the Second declared him a true martyr, and was willing to canonise him ; that Paul the Third suspected any man who should venture to accuse him ; that he was honoured among the saints in the liturgy of his Order. The answer is that Savonarola assailed the intruder, not the institution. He was no reformer of the prerogative, and would have committed full powers to a pontiff of his choice. He upheld the Papal authority against the usurper of the Papacy. Three false Popes were once upon a time removed to make way for Clement the Third, for the same reason for which Savonarola deemed Alexander an illegitimate pretender, who ought to be made to yield his place to a better man.

The essential articles of George Eliot's creed were the fruit of so much preceding study that she impresses us less than some other writers by originality in the common sense of invention. She was anxious to make it known that her abiding opinions were formed before she settled in London. Mr. Spencer confirms the claim, and it is proved by her first paper in the *Westminster Review.* The doctrine that neither contrition nor sacrifice can appease Nemesis, or avert the consequences of our wrong-doing from ourselves and others, filled a very large space indeed in her scheme of life and literature. From the bare diagram of *Brother Jacob* to the profound and finished picture of *Middlemarch*, retribution is the constant theme and motive for her art. It helped to determine her religious attitude, for it is only partly true that want of evidence was her only objection to Christianity. She was firmly persuaded that the postponement of the reckoning blunts the edge of remorse, and that repentance,

which ought to be submission to just punishment, proved
by the test of confession, means more commonly the
endeavour to elude it. She thought that the world would
be indefinitely better and happier if men could be made
to feel that there is no escape from the inexorable law
that we reap what we have sown. When she began
to write, this doctrine was of importance as a neutral
space, as an altar of the Unknown God, from which she
was able to preach her own beliefs without controversy
or exposure. For whilst it is the basis of morals under
the scientific reign, it is a stimulant and a consolation to
many Christians, for whom the line, "The mills of God
grind slowly, but they grind exceeding small," expresses
an ancient observation sanctioned by religion, whereas the
words once spoken at Salerno, "Dilexi justitiam et odi
iniquitatem, propterea morior in exilio," are the last cry
of a baffled and despairing fanatic.

This fundamental principle, that the wages of sin are
paid in ready money, was borne in upon her by all her
early environment. Bray had written a book in its
defence, and the strength of Dawson's moral teaching was
largely ascribed to the firmness with which he held it.
Comte had said that obedience to each natural law has
its peculiar reward, and disobedience its appropriate
punishment; and Emerson stated his theory of compensation in these terms: "The specific stripes may follow late
upon the offence, but they follow, because they accompany
it. Crime and punishment grow out of one stem. We
cannot do wrong without suffering wrong." The same
law, that evil ensues of necessity from evil deeds, is the
pivot of Spinoza's ethics, and it was the belief of Strauss.
George Eliot accepted it, and made it bright with the
splendour of genius. Other portions of her system, such
as altruism and the reign of the dead, exhibit her power
of anticipating and of keeping abreast with the quicker
movements of the age. In this she plainly followed, and
she followed the lead of those who happened to be near.

She belongs to that family of illustrious thinkers whose
progress has been made by the ingenious use of existing

materials and respect for those who have gone before.
Mr. Herbert Spencer owes seminal ideas to Baer, Professor
Bain to Johannes Müller, Helmholtz to Young, Darwin to
Malthus, Malthus to Euler, Milne Edwards to Adam Smith,
Bentham to Hutcheson.   Newton has the demerit of
having been preceded in his greatest discovery by three
contemporaries, and Helmholtz by five.   One of Laplace's
theories was in s' Gravesande before him and the other in
Kant.   Comte, if Mill had not given him a release from
the study of German, might have found his law of the
three stages anticipated by Fries in 1819.   The *Westminster Review* adopted a new and characteristic motto
when she joined it.   There is another maxim of the same
writer, which she would have been willing to make her
own : "Alles Gescheidte ist schon gedacht worden ; man
muss nur versuchen es noch einmal zu denken."   Goethe's
new commentators track the derivation of his sentences,
as we in England know how much Latin and Italian
poetry was boiled down in Gray's "Elegy," and from
which lines of Coleridge Byron got the "Address to the
Ocean."   George Eliot's laborious preparation and vast
reading have filled her books with reminiscences more or
less definite.   The suggestion that she borrowed the
material of plots from George Sand, Freytag, Heyse,
Kraszewski, Disraeli, or Mrs. Gaskell, amounts to nothing ;
but the quack medicine which is employed to make the
Treby congregation ridiculous is inherited from Faust.
The resemblance of ideas is often no more than agreement.
The politics of Felix Holt may be found in Guizot—
"C'est de l'état intérieur de l'homme que dépend l'état
visible de la société."   A Belgian statesman has said,
"Plus on apporte d'éléments personnels, spontanés, humains,
dans les institutions, moins elles sont appelées à régler la
marche de la société."   Probably George Eliot had read
neither the one nor the other, though she may have met
with the same thoughts constantly.   But she had read
Delphine, and the conclusion of *Delphine* is the conclusion
of the story of *Gwendolen* : "On peut encore faire servir
au bonheur des autres une vie qui ne nous promet à nous-

mêmes que des chagrins, et cette espérance, vous la ferait
supporter." The passage on the roadside crucifix in
Adam Bede ends thus : " No wonder man's religion has
sorrow in it : no wonder he needs a suffering God ! "
The sentence reads like a quotation from Chateaubriand,
but it is the quintessence of Feuerbach. In the same
chapter of *Deronda* the lament of Francesca is quoted with
repeated emphasis, and the moon is entangled among trees
and houses. The figure occurs in the poem which Musset
wrote against those very verses of Dante. A motto before
the fifty-seventh chapter of *Daniel Deronda* comes very near
the preface to *Fiesco*. Several candidates have felt that
Mr. Brooke has purloined their speeches at the hustings.
One of his good sayings points to France. " I want that
sort of thing—not ideas, you know, but a way of putting
them." The speechless deputy in the comedy says, " Ce
n'est jamais les idées qui me manquent, c'est le style."

When she left Warwickshire, where Mr. Froude and
Miss Martineau had been her friends and Emerson had
shone for a moment, she was not dazzled by what she
found in London. The discriminating judgment, the
sense of proportion were undisturbed by reverence or
enthusiasm for the celebrities of the day. The tone
towards Macaulay and Mill is generally cold, and she
shrinks from avowing the extent of her dislike for Carlyle.
Dickens behaved well towards his lofty rival, but she feels
his defects as keenly as his merits ; and she is barely just
to Darwin and Lecky. A long ground-swell followed her
breach with Miss Martineau. The admiration expressed
for Mr. Ruskin—the Ruskin of 1858—is flavoured with
the opposite feeling ; and the opposite feeling towards
Buckle is not flavoured with admiration ; for her artistic
temper revolts against the abstraction of the average man
and the yoke of statistics, with its attendant reliance on
the efficacy of laws. George Eliot highly esteemed both
the Newmans. She wished to be within hearing of the
pulpit at Edgbaston. The *Apologia* breathed much life
into her, and she points out the beauty of one passage ;
but it is the writer's farewell to friends and no part of his

argument.   The early vituperation of Disraeli, of his
Judaism and the doctrine of race, is a landmark to measure
the long procession of her views.   In *Deronda* days she
judged Lord Beaconsfield more benignly, relishing his
disdain for the popular voice and his literary finish beyond
the effective qualities of his rival.

Promptness in opening her mind to new influence, and
ardour of gratitude and respect had changed into a quiet
resolve to keep cool and resist ascendency.   There was
nobody among her acquaintances to whom she owed such
obligations as she acknowledges to Mr. Herbert Spencer.
Although she underrated his constructive talent, and did
not overrate his emotional gifts, she foresaw very early
the position he afterwards attained.   He made the sunshine
of her desolate life in London ; they met every day, and
the two minds, strangely unlike each other, worked in a
like direction.   The friendship with Lewes made slower
progress.

George Eliot retired from the management of the
Review without having found her vocation or struck a
vein of ore.   She employed herself in translating Spinoza
and Feuerbach.   The *Essence of Christianity* had been
published more than twelve years, and expressed neither
a prevailing phase of philosophy nor the last views of the
author.   More than any other work it had contributed to
the downfall of metaphysics, and it contained an ingenious
theory of the rise and growth of religion, and of the
relation of the soul to God, while denying the existence
of either.   Feuerbach repudiated Christianity so decisively
that Strauss was distanced and stranded for thirty years ;
and it would have been difficult to introduce to the
British public any work of the same kind written with as
much ability.   It met no demand and was received with
cold reserve.   A letter of December 1874 shows that
Feuerbach's theogony survived in her system longer than
his scoffing and destructive spirit.   He learnt towards the
end of his life that a prominent American politician had
been converted from Christianity by his book in the
translation of Marian Evans.   The news would not have

U

gratified the translator. The book appeared in July 1854, and immediately after she accepted Lewes, who was completing the *Life of Goethe*, and they started for Weimar and Berlin.

Mr. Cross has judged it unnecessary to explain a step which is sufficiently intelligible from the whole tenor of George Eliot's life. The sanctions of religion were indifferent to her after rejecting its doctrines, and she meant to disregard not the moral obligation of marriage, but the social law of England. Neither the law which assigns the conditions of valid marriage, nor that which denied the remedy of divorce, was of absolute and universal authority. Both were unknown in some countries and inapplicable to certain cases, and she deemed that they were no more inwardly binding upon everybody than the royal edicts upon a Huguenot or the penal laws upon a Catholic.

George Eliot can neither be defended on the plea that every man must be tried by canons he assents to, nor censured on the plea that virtue consists in constant submission to variable opinion. The first would absolve fanatics and the other would supersede conscience. It is equally certain that she acted in conformity with that which in 1854 she esteemed right, and in contradiction to that which was the dominant and enduring spirit of her own work. She did not feel that she was detracting from her authority by an act which gave countenance to the thesis that associates rigid ethics with rigid dogma, for she claimed no authority and did not dream of setting an example. The idea of her genius had not dawned. That she possessed boundless possibilities of doing good to men, and of touching hearts that no divine and no philosopher could reach, was still, at thirty-five, a secret to herself. At first she was astonished that anybody who was not superstitious could find fault with her. To deny herself to old friends, to earn with her pen an income for her whose place she took, to pass among strangers by a name which was not her due, all this did not seem too high a price for the happiness of a home. She urged with pathetic gravity that she knew what she was losing. She did not know it. Ostensibly she was resigning a small group of friends and an obscure position in literature. What she really sacrificed was liberty of speech, the foremost rank among the women of her time, and a tomb in Westminster Abbey.

Mr. Cross is loyal to the memory of Lewes, and affords no support to the conjecture that she longed to be extricated from a position which had become intolerable, or ever awoke to the discovery that she had sacrificed herself to an illusion. With a history open to unfriendly telling there were topics difficult to touch upon and views to which she could not well do justice. She endeavoured, when she became an author, to avert celebrity, to conceal her identity, even to disguise her purpose, and to assume an attitude which was not her own. So essential did secrecy seem to success that the revelation compelled by the report that George Eliot was some one else was felt as a serious injury. There was some cause for diffidence, for toleration, and for a veil of irony. But so far was the difficulty of her position from depressing the moral standard that it served in one respect to raise it. Feuerbach thought it affectation to turn away from immodest scenes, and asserted that enjoyment is a duty. Strauss sneered at the text which laid down the law of Christian chastity. The *Westminster Review* praised a wife who had procured a mistress for her husband. Rousseau thought Sophie all the better for her sin. With these writers George Eliot had been associated. Her admiration for Rousseau, for Shelley, for Jacques, the most ignominious of George Sand's stories, her description of the indissolubility of marriage as a diabolical law, indicate that her opinions did not always keep the elevated level of her early religion and her later philosophy. But in her novels the tone is extremely high. It is true that the pure mind of Romola had been fed on *The Decamerone* ; but it is also true that Boccaccio, and not Dante, was the favourite classic of the Florentines of the Renaissance. Gwendolen, having been degraded by marriage without love, is rescued and purified by love without marriage ; but we are not suffered to forget for a moment that the marriage was criminal and the love was pure. George Eliot determined to write nothing from which it might be inferred that she was pleading for herself. She was scrupulous that no private motive should affect the fidelity of art. To write books, as *Corinne* and *Delphine* were written, in the interest of the writer, would have seemed to her degradation, and she never puts forward her own ideal of character.

Marriage was not the only chapter of social ethics touched by the Feuerbach phase, and it was not the gravest. Mazzini belonged to Lewes's circle, and Mazzini was currently suspected of complicity in practices which were distinctly criminal, practices for which the law prescribes its last and simplest penalty. George Eliot wavered a good deal between her interest in his cause and her distrust of his methods, but she would never have felt it a stigma to be on amicable terms with him. Elizabeth and Mary, James and William, lie under the same ban of imputed murder, and the friends of the republican conspirator had no reason to apprehend the censure of those who admired the heroes of Catholic and Protestant monarchy.

Those who remember George Henry Lewes in his prosperity, when he was the most amusing talker in the town, so well content with his labours as to regret nothing he had written, and running over with mirth and good-humour until he could bear contradiction, excuse folly, and even tolerate religion, saw what George Eliot had made him. She knew him first under less genial aspects. Disaster had settled on his domestic life ; he had set his hand to too many things to excel in any, and the mark of failure and frustrated effort was upon him. Varnhagen said in 1850 that Lewes's restless endeavours were repulsive, and that he would end badly if he did not mend his ways. His first books did not recommend him ; but there were signs in *Ranthorpe* of large undiscriminating knowledge, and he was, with Mill, the earliest propounder of Positivism in England.   He was introduced to George Eliot when his fortunes were almost desperate, and two years passed before she discerned that he was not the flippant man he seemed.   She helped him to attain a prominent if not quite an important place among men of letters.   For twenty years his *Life of Goethe* held its position even in Germany ; and the vacant record of incoherent error which he called a *History of Philosophy* is still read with pleasure.   Passing with the drift from the discarded illusions of metaphysics to physiology, and in intelligent pursuance of Comte's leading idea, he conceived the noble design of a *History of Science*, which, by displaying the discovery and application of scientific methods, would have fitly crowned the *Positive Philosophy*.

Lewes helped to dispel the gloom and despondency of George Eliot's spirits, and stood manfully between her and all the cares he did not cause.   His literary skill must have done her untold service, although the recorded instances of his intervention are contestable, and although his practice of keeping her aloof from all criticism but his own must have profited her comfort more than her art. She deferred to his judgment, but she knew that she could rely on his praise.   He admired her essays, her novels, and at last her poetry.   He was not quick in detecting her sovereign ability, and must bear the reproach that he under-valued his prize, and never knew until it was too late that she was worthy of better things than the position to which he consigned her.   During the years in which she rose to fame she lived in seclusion, with no society but that of Lewes, preferring the country to London, the Continent to England, and Germany to France.   In this perfect isolation the man through whose ministry almost alone she kept touch with the wider world exerted much influence.   He encouraged her in contempt for metaphysics, in the study of biology, in her taste for French and especially German writers, and in her panoramic largeness of view.   The point at which their ways parted and his action ceased most decidedly was religion.   She had kept up her early love of the Scriptures,

and she contracted a great liking for the solemn services
of the Catholic churches. Lewes saw no harm in these
tastes, and he even bought her a Bible. But he did not
like to hear of it. He was a boisterous iconoclast, with
little confidence in disinterested belief and a positive
aversion for Christianity. Even Bach, he said, was too
Protestant for him. George Eliot's interest in the
religious life was therefore kept up under resistance to
adverse pressure.

If Lewes did not debase her standard of rectitude, he
enlarged her tolerance of error. Having elected to be
subject for life to a man still encumbered with his youth,
she became indulgent towards sentiments she disapproved,
and appreciated the reason and the strength of opinions
repugnant to her. Lewes had detached her from the
former associations, and she did not accept his views.
Step by step, for good or evil, the process of her life had
brought her to a supreme point of solitude and neutrality
that would have been chilling and fatal to a feebler mind,
but gave her the privilege of almost unexampled independence and mental integrity. Her secluded life had
important literary consequences. It estranged her from
general society and from religious people.

The breach with zealous Churchmen was not new, but
it was now irreparable. She knew their ways from the
old books and early recollections ; but in the active
religious work and movement of her time she shows no
more concern than in Plato or Leibnitz. There is no trace
of solicitude about Christian Socialism, although Parson
Lot's letter furnished forth a speech for Felix Holt.
Neither Lamennais nor Gioberti is mentioned, although
three volumes are occupied with the protomartyr of
Liberal Catholicism. The literature of ethics and psychology, so far as it touched religion, dropped out of her
sight, and she renounced intercourse with half the talent
in the world. The most eminent of the men who pursued
like problems in her lifetime, among the most eminent
who have thought about them at any time, were Vinet
and Rothe. Both were admirable in their lives, and still

more in the presence of death; and neither of them could be taxed with thraldom to the formulas of preceding divines. George Eliot disregards their existence. At Heidelberg she passes before Rothe's house without alluding to his name. Although she knew and highly valued M. Scherer, she did not remember that he was the friend of Vinet, or that the history of his opinions is as remarkable as anything to be found in the *Apologia* or told in her own biography.

There are marks of a wound inflicted by Warwickshire pride, which would not heal. She knew how to construct an unseen creature from scanty materials, but the divination is more true, the touch more sure in dealing with classes that subsist for profit than with the class that subsists for pleasure. Having met some friends of Cavour on the Lake of Geneva, she declares that there is nothing but their language and their geniality and politeness to distinguish them from the best English families. The lawyer who on the opening day of the Rugeley trial pronounced Palmer a dead man, "John Campbell was so infernally polite," used an argument of which the author of *Romola* would have admitted the force. Long retirement prepared her to suspect a snare in conventional gentility, as if company manners concealed a defect of genuine humanity and served to keep classes apart. She would not have assented to the definition of a gentleman that he is one who will bear pain rather than inflict it. This is the angle at which a faint echo of Carlyle strikes the ear. She pursues with implacable vengeance the easy and agreeable Tito. Her chosen hero goes bare-necked and treads on corns. She will not see that Harold Transome is a brute, and salves over his inconsiderate rudeness by asserting, in parabasis, his generosity and goodness of heart. Garth, who might have sent in his resignation by post, prefers an interview which compels a cruel explanation. No rumours preserved in a family of land agents could justify the picture of Grandcourt; but his odiousness is requisite in order to contrast the wife's momentary flash of guilty delectation when he goes overboard with the ensuing expiation. The same discordant note appears in Gwendolen's impatience under the burden of gratitude. One of Charles Reade's characters exclaims, "Vulgar people are ashamed to be grateful, but you are a born lady," and an Academician, expounding the same text, has written, "Avant d'obliger un homme, assurez-vous bien d'abord que cet homme n'est pas un imbécile." The point is almost too subtle for argument, but it is one of the few marks of limitation in George Eliot's field of vision.

Between *Felix Holt* and *Middlemarch* her range expanded and she judged less austerely.

> We have made some new friendships that cheer us with the sense of new admiration of actual living beings whom we know in the flesh, and who are kindly disposed towards us.—Every one of my best blessings, my one perfect love and the sympathy shown towards me for the sake of my works, and the personal regard of a few friends, have become much intensified in these latter days.—I have entirely lost my personal melancholy. I often, of course, have melancholy thoughts about the destinies of my fellow-creatures, but I am never in that mood of sadness which used to be my frequent visitant even in the midst of external happiness.

Reverence for her genius, for the rare elevation of her teaching, bore down the inevitable reluctance to adjust the rule to an exception. Among the first of her new friends were the ladies of Mr. Cross's family, and they were welcomed with fervent gratitude. When George Eliot came to live near Regent's Park her house was crowded with the most remarkable society in London. Poets and philosophers united to honour her who had been great both in poetry and philosophy, and the aristocracy of letters gathered round the gentle lady who, without being memorable by what she said, was justly esteemed the most illustrious figure that has arisen in literature since Goethe died. There might be seen a famous scholar sitting for Casaubon, and two younger men—one with good features, solid white hands, and a cambric pocket-handkerchief, the second with wavy bright hair and a habit of shaking his head backwards, who evoked other memories of the same Midland microcosm while Tennyson read his own last poem, or Liebreich sang Schumann's " Two Grenadiers," and Lewes himself, with eloquent fingers and catching laugh, described Mazzini's amazement at his first dinner in London, or the lament of the Berlin professor over the sunset of England since Mr. Gladstone had put an Essay-and-Reviewer on the throne of Phillpotts.

The visit to Germany opened out wider horizons. To chat with Varnhagen von Ense, to explore his archives and admire the miniature of Rahel was a function awaiting literary visitors at Berlin, and Lewes, who had reached Weimar in time to see the Teutonic Boswell, Eckermann, had much to say to the man whom the profane Heine called the vicar of Goethe on earth. The chief interpreter of German thought to the travellers was Gruppe, a scholar of many accomplishments, who has since ended extravagantly, but who had vast knowledge of poetry, a keen sense of the exhausted vitality of speculation, and who in the history of cosmology had measured swords with Böckh. George Eliot spent her time in study, seeing little of the intellectual society of the place, and disliking what she saw. She continued to know Germany mainly as it was at the date of initiation in 1855. Even Feuerbach and Strauss remained embalmed in the attitudes of 1841. The æsthetic age, whose veterans still lingered about Dresden and Berlin, was always more present to her mind than the predominant generation between the parliament of Frankfort and the proclamation of Versailles, the Germany of Helmholtz and Mommsen, Jhering and Fischer, Virchow and Rümelin, Roscher and Treitschke. The only master of this stronger and less artistic school who fixed her attention is Riehl, an author worthy of such a commentator, but not faithful to the methods by which his people succeed.

She saw *Nathan der Weise*, not in vain. " Our hearts swelled and the tears came into our eyes as we listened to the noble words of dear Lessing, whose great spirit lives immortally in this crowning work of his." Twenty years later she explained the design of *Deronda* by the reasons given in the preface to the *Juden*. The altered attitude towards the Jews, which gradually prepared her last novel, began at this time, and she must have heard Humboldt's saying that Judaism is more easily reconcilable with science than other religions. The *Hamburgische Briefe* lay open before her at the *table d'hôte*; she pronounces the *Laokoon* the most un-German of German books, and notices nothing between Berlin and Cologne but "the immortal old town of Wolfenbüttel." If Lessing was the favourite, Goethe was the master. Life at Weimar, with the sublime tradition, closed for George Eliot the season of storm and strain. Although she never practised art for its own sake, or submitted to the canon that poetry is aimless song, Goethe's gospel of inviolate serenity was soothing to a spirit disabled by excess of sensibility, and taught her to be less passionately affected either by sympathy or sorrow. The contrast is great between the agonising tones of the earlier life and the self-restraint and composure that succeeded. The conversion was not immediate. A scene is recorded at Berlin which recalls the time when Miss Evans was too clever to succeed at Coventry, and the crude smartness of the Westminster articles (toned in the reprint),[1] the resentment and even misery caused by the impostor Liggins, were below the dignity of so noble a mind. But the change in the later years is unmistakable. Even the genial warmth of affection for persons was tempered by an impartial estimate of their characters and a disinterested neutrality towards their undertakings. A system that denies the hopes and memories which make pain and sadness shrink cannot be rich in consolation; yet she

---

[1] Some secrets of style reveal themselves to anybody who compares the articles in the *Review* with the text which she afterwards prepared, and there are many touches and omissions significant of the vast change her mind had undergone. The last essay, which supposes that Young came into the world without a wig, and calls George the First "that royal hog," was composed at the same time as the first novel; and the contrast shows with what effort and constraint the scenes were written. The perfection of language was not reached at once. A single paragraph of the *Mill on the Floss* contains the terms "phiz," "masculinity," "that same Nature." There is a slight mannerism in the formula "which has been observed"; and the perilous word "mutual" is sometimes misapplied. One of her favourite expressions is usual with Comte, and we used to hear another at school in "that central plain, watered at one extremity by the Avon, at the other by the Trent."

strove not to overdo the tragedy of human life. The
pathos of Mrs. Browning is less profound, the pathos of
the *Misérables* is less genuine, but they excite more
intense emotion. Happiness and success contributed to
that majestic calm which is the proper prize of intelligent
immersion in Goethe.

George Eliot came back conscious of much affinity
with the Germans, and impressed by their methodical
energy and massive power. The lack of literary
point and grace provoked her ; she yawned even over
Schiller and Goethe, and the relief she derived from
Heine accentuated the favourable estimate of his character in the essay on German wit. She was nowhere so
well and so happy ; but she described the North as a
region of unmannerly pedants, and preferred the cheerful
ease and cogent hospitality of the South. International
culture had disengaged her patriotism from prejudice,
and she felt less for the country between the four seas
than for the scenery, the character, and the dialect of the
Trent valley.

The Italian journey reveals that weakness of the
historic faculty which is a pervading element in her life.
Her psychology was extracted from fortuitous experience,
from observations made on common people in private life,
under the sway of thoughtless habit and inherited stupidity,
not from the heroic subjects, the large questions and
proportions of history. Italy was little more to her than
a vast museum, and Rome, with all the monuments and
institutions which link the old world with the new,
interested her less than the galleries of Florence. She
surveys the grand array of tombs in St. Peter's, and
remarks nothing but some peasants feeling the teeth of
Canova's lion.

Travel supplied the later books with the materials
which came at first from home. The *Spanish Gypsy*
was derived from a Venetian picture. The celestial
frescoes in Savonarola's home at San Marco suggested
the argument of *Romola*. A Dresden Titian haunted
her for years. It became the portrait of her latest

hero, whose supposed resemblance to our Lord gives intensity to the contrast between a Jew who sacrificed his people for religion, and a Christian who goes back to Judaism, renouncing his religion in obedience to the hereditary claim of race.   When she was writing *Adam Bede* at Munich, a Moldavian Jew came with introductions to her friends, intent on the same vague errand of national redemption upon which Deronda disappears from sight.   Liszt, whom they had known at Weimar, became Klesmer ; and a young lady over whom George Eliot wept in the gambling rooms at Homburg, and who remembers the meeting, served as the model of Gwendolen.

After many years characterised by mental independence and resistance to control, George Eliot inclined to that system which is popular among men who " yield homage only to external laws."   The influence of Comte began early and grew with the successive study of his works, until the revolutionary fervour of 1848 was transformed into the self-suppression of the *Spanish Gypsy,* and the scorn for Liberality and Utilitarianism which appears in *Felix Holt.*   It was the second Comte, the dogmatising and emotional author of the *Politique Positive,* that she revered, and she has not a word for the arch-rebel Littré. Positivists deem that she never thoroughly conformed. But she renounced much of her unattached impartial freedom for an attitude of doctrinal observance, and submitted her mind to discipline, if not to authority.   She continued to analyse and to illustrate with an increasing fertility and accuracy ; but she was in the clasp of the dead hand, and the leading ideas recur with constant sameness.   That the yoke was ever shaken does not appear. We learn from the Life that she never became a party politician, and refused to admit that political differences are, what religious differences are not, founded on an ultimate diversity of moral principles.

Comte, who was averse to popular Protestantism, who excluded the reformers from his Calendar, and acknowledged the provisional services rendered to the mediæval phase of the progress of society by the Church, encouraged the growing favour which she showed to Catholicism. *The Imitation*, which is the most perfectly normal expression of Catholic thought, as it bears the least qualifying impress of time and place, and which Comte never wearied of reading and recommending, prepared the sympathy. It had been in her hands when she translated *Spinoza* and afterwards when she wrote the *Mill on the Floss*. No thought occurs more often in her writings than that of the persecuted Jews; but she spares the persecutors. *Romola* suggests that Catholic life and history is guided by visions; but the stroke is aimed at other religions as well. The man who, for the pure love of holiness, became a brother of the Order of Torquemada, led up to the central problem of Catholicism, how private virtue and public crime could issue from the same root. Comte has extolled De Maistre, the advocate of the Inquisition; and when, in her next work, George Eliot approaches the subject, it was done with reserve, and without advancement of learning. Although she preferred the Protestant Establishment to Sectarianism, Catholicism to Protestantism, and Judaism to Christianity, the margin of liking was narrow, and she was content to say that the highest lot is to have definite beliefs.

George Eliot's work was done before Lewes died. A year and a half after his death she married Mr. Cross, and went abroad for the last time. Her husband's illness at Venice was a severe shock to her; but when she came back to her home, released from the constraint of so many years, a new life began. She was able to indulge her own tastes, choosing retirement, reading the Bible and the *Divina Commedia*, and hearing the Cardinal at Kensington. There was no return to literary composition. The crowding thought had outgrown her control—"E sulle eterne pagine Cadde la stanca man."

Before the summer was over her health gave way. In one of the last letters, written in an interval of recovered strength, she says that she has been cared for with something better than angelic tenderness. "I do not think I shall have many returns of November, but there

is every prospect that such as remain to me will be as
happy as they can be made by the devoted tenderness
which watches over me." During this afterglow of
tranquil happiness, George Eliot suddenly fell ill and
passed away, silent and unconscious of her approaching
end. There has been no deathbed to which the last
words of Faust are so appropriate :—

> Zum Augenblicke dürft' ich sagen :
> Verweile doch ! Du bist so schön !
> Es kann die Spur von meinen Erdentagen
> Nicht in Äonen untergehn !
> Im Vorgefühl von solchem hohen Glück
> Geniess' ich jetzt den höchsten Augenblick.

George Eliot did not believe in the finality of her
system, and, near the close of her life, she became uneasy
as to the future of her fame. True to the law that the
highest merit escapes reward, she had fixed her hope on
unborn generations, and she feared to make sure of their
gratitude. Though very conscious of power and no
longer prone to self-disparagement, she grew less satisfied
with the execution of her designs, and when comparing
the idea before her with her work in the past, her mind
misgave her. She was disconcerted by ignorant applause,
and she had not yet poured her full soul. Having seen
the four most eloquent French writers of the century
outlive their works, and disprove the axiom that style
confers immortality, she might well doubt whether
writings inspired by distinct views and dedicated to a
cause could survive by artistic qualities alone. If the
mist that shrouded her horizon should ever rise over
definite visions of accepted truth, her doctrine might
embarrass her renown. She never attained to the
popular pre-eminence of Goethe, or even of Victor Hugo.
The name of George Eliot was nearly unknown in
France ; she had lost ground in America, and at home
her triumph did not pass unchallenged, when men like
Beaconsfield, Ruskin, Arnold, Swinburne denied her
claims. Lewes himself doubted the final estimate, for
he announced with some excitement that she had been

compared to Wordsworth, and that somebody thought the comparison inadequate. Men very far asunder—the two Scherers, Montégut, Mr. Spencer and Mr. Hutton, Professor Tyndall and Mr. Myers—have declared with singular unanimity that she possessed a union of qualities seldom, if ever, exceeded by man, and not likely to be seen again on earth ; that her works are the high-water mark of feminine achievement ; that she was as certainly the greatest genius among women known to history as Shakespeare among men. But George Eliot did not live to recognise, in the tribute of admiring friends, the judgment of history.

She has said of herself that her function is that of the æsthetic, not the doctrinal teacher—the rousing of the nobler emotions which make mankind desire the social right, not the prescribing of special measures. The supreme purpose of all her work is ethical. Literary talent did not manifest itself until she was thirty-seven. In her later books the wit and the descriptive power diminish visibly, and the bare didactic granite shows through the cultivated surface. She began as an essayist, and ended as she had begun, having employed meanwhile the channel of fiction to enforce that which, propounded as philosophy, failed to convince. If the doctrine, separate from the art, had no vitality, the art without the doctrine had no significance. There will be more perfect novels and truer systems. But she has little rivalry to apprehend until philosophy inspires finer novels, or novelists teach nobler lessons of duty to the masses of men. If ever science or religion reigns alone over an undivided empire, the books of George Eliot might lose their central and unique importance, but as the emblem of a generation distracted between the intense need of believing and the difficulty of belief, they will live to the last syllable of recorded time. Proceeding from a system which had neglected morals, she became the pioneer in that movement which has produced the *Data of Ethics* and the *Phänomenologie*. Her teaching was the highest within the resources to which Atheism is restricted, as the teaching of the *Fioretti* is the highest within the Christian limits. In spite of all that is omitted, and of specific differences regarding the solemn question of conscience, humility, and death, there are few works in literature whose influence is so ennobling ; and there were people divided from her in politics and religion by the widest chasm that exists on earth, who felt at her death what was said of the Greek whom she had most deeply studied—σκότον εἶναι τεθνηκότος.

X

MR. BUCKLE'S THESIS AND METHOD [1]

MR. BUCKLE is a gentleman who has had the rare fortune
of jumping to celebrity at a bound, by the publication of
an elaborate book on a profound subject. The success
of the published portion of his *History of Civilisation
in England* has been hitherto far above that which usually
attends such efforts; and it must be conceded, that a work
which could thus seize on the public ear must be, at any
rate, a remarkable production. It must have powerfully
appealed to something or other in the public mind, or
tell something or other very important, which people
wanted to know, in order to have won so rapid a
popularity.

The object which he proposes to himself is, to prove
that history may be reduced to a science. To comprehend
the full meaning of this proposition we must ask, what is
" history," and what is " science "? History is a generalised
account of the personal actions of men united in bodies
for any public purposes whatever; and science is the
combination of a great mass of similar facts into the
unity of a generalisation, a principle, or a law, which
principle or law will enable us to predict with certainty
the recurrence of like events under given conditions.
Now, then, can there be a science of history? Can we
ever arrive at such a complete knowledge of all the
motives and laws of human conduct as to be able to
predict with certainty of any bodies of men what their

---

[1] " History of Civilisation in England, by H. T. Buckle. London, J. W.
Parker." *The Rambler*, 1858.

conduct in given circumstances will be? Mr. Buckle thinks we can. Not that he ever hopes to be able to predict the actions of individual men; but for men in masses, for humanity in general, for large races, for nations, he supposes that pretty close approximations may be arrived at.

The "history" which Mr. Buckle proposed to write is not history in general, nor history of such kind as biography, or accounts of families, but the special history of civilisation. Now, what is civilisation? It is the progress of mankind measured by "the triumph of mind over external agents." It is the conquest of nature by man. In thought, it is the gradual weaning of the mind from a superstitious veneration for, and deification of, nature; in action, it is the use of nature, the making matter and its forces obedient to our behests, and using them for our needs and convenience.

It is important to settle that this is *all* that Mr. Buckle means by civilisation; for on this definition depends the whole logical value and consistency of his book. Among many passages that might be selected, the following, from p. 205, where he announces the plan of his future volumes, includes all that we want to show :—

> In a great and comprehensive view, the *changes* in every civilised people are in their aggregate dependent solely on three things : first, on the amount of knowledge possessed by their ablest men ; secondly, on the direction which that knowledge takes, that is to say, the sort of subjects to which it refers ; thirdly, and above all, on the extent to which the knowledge is diffused and the freedom with which it pervades all classes of society.

The word *changes* indicates that the fundamental idea in the writer's mind is that of *progress*. The *knowledge* which he requires for this progress must be either religious, moral, or scientific. He proves, with great care, that it is neither of the two former; it must, therefore, be the last. Not that he denies the power of religious and moral convictions, but he says that their action ceases with individuals, and leaves no permanent result on society. Vices and virtues, like plus and minus quantities in an equation, eliminate each other, and leave the residuum to be attributed to some other cause; they are equivalent opposing forces, neutralising each other, therefore contributing nothing to *progress*, therefore not to be considered in the history of civilisation, according to the terms of the definition. The following passage immediately succeeds that quoted above:—

These are the three great movers of every civilised country; and although their operation is frequently disturbed by vices or the virtues of powerful individuals, *such moral feelings correct each other*, and the average of long periods remains unaffected. Owing to causes of which we are ignorant, the moral qualities do, no doubt, constantly vary; so that in one man, or perhaps even in one generation, there will be an excess of good intentions, in another an excess of bad ones. But we have no reason to think that any permanent change has been effected in the proportion which those who naturally possess good intentions bear to those in whom bad ones seem to be inherent. *In what may be called the innate and original morals of mankind, there is, so far as we are aware, no progress.* Of the different passions with which we are born, some are more prevalent at one time, some at another; but experience teaches us that, as they are always antagonistic, they are held in balance by the force of their own opposition. The activity of one motive is corrected by the activity of another. For to every vice there is a corresponding virtue. Cruelty is counteracted by benevolence, sympathy is excited by suffering, the injustice of some provokes the charity of others, new evils are met by new remedies, and even the most enormous offences that have ever been known have left behind them no permanent impression. The desolation of countries and the slaughter of men are losses which never fail to be repaired, and at the distance of a few centuries every vestige of them is effaced. This is the ebb and flow of history, the perpetual flux to which, by the laws of our nature, we are subject. Above all this, there is a far higher movement; and as the tide rolls on, now advancing, now receding, there is, amid its endless fluctuations, one thing, and one alone, which endures for ever. The actions of bad men produce only temporary evil, the actions of good men only temporary good; and eventually the good and the evil together subside, are neutralised by subsequent generations, absorbed by the incessant movement of future ages. But the discoveries of great men never leave us; they are immortal, they contain those eternal truths which survive the shock of empires, outlive the struggles of rival creeds, and witness the decay of successive religions. All these have their different measures and their different standards; one set of opinions for one age, another set for another. They pass away like a dream; they are as the fabric of a vision, which leaves not a rack behind. The discoveries of genius alone remain : it is to them we owe all that we now have, they are for all ages and all times ; never young and never old, they bear the seeds of their own life ; they flow on in a perennial and undying stream ; they are essentially cumulative, and, giving birth to the additions which they subsequently receive, they thus influence the most distant posterity, and after the lapse of centuries produce more effect than they were able to do even at the moment of their promulgation.

Let us not allow the emotions stirred up by Mr. Buckle's eloquence to blind us to the real meaning of his grand words. We must note that the "eternal truths" do not concern morality, or that "flux and reflux" of human action which neutralises itself and forms no element of progress. They have still less to do with religion ; for they "outlive the struggles of rival creeds, and witness the decay of successive religions," but they are "the discoveries of genius"—not barren truths regarding intellect and will, and such-like metaphysical matters, which yield no fruit, but truths which teach man how to conquer and make use of nature, which tell him what he may do with water, and steam, and electricity, and wood, and coal, and iron, and gas, and skins, and horns. They are "essentially cumulative" : one man begins where the last ended, and adds improvement on improvement—not as in morals, where all men begin afresh, and no real advance is made. Again, it is evident that individual happiness or misery forms no element in Mr. Buckle's computation : he eliminates both vice and virtue, not only because they balance one another, but because, after a century or two, no vestiges are left of the greatest crimes or most splendid acts of goodness. Mr. Buckle, therefore, does not contemplate the action, but the result ; not the life or thinking of the man, but the work he has done, or the theory he has thought out. Where no trace remains of the work, nothing was done worth speaking of.

Having thus made the individual soul of no account in his investigations on the history of human progress, it is clear that only one manner of looking at mankind remains : if they are not to be viewed as persons in detail, they must be considered as bodies in mass. Hence not individual acts, but their statistics engage his attention. It is not personal doings, but sums total, that he seeks. But here we will let him speak for himself :—

The actions of individuals are greatly affected by their moral feelings and by their passions, but these being antagonistic to the passions and feelings of other individuals, are balanced by them. So that their effect is, in the great average of human affairs, nowhere to be seen, and the total actions of mankind, considered as a whole, are left to be regulated by the total knowledge of which mankind is possessed.   And of the way in which individual feeling and individual caprice are thus absorbed and neutralised, we find a clear illustration in the history of crime.   For the amount of crime committed in a country is, year after year, reproduced with the most startling uniformity, not being in the least affected by those capricious and personal feelings to which human actions are too often referred.   But if, instead of examining the history of crime year by year, we were to examine it month by month, we should find less regularity, and if we were to examine it hour by hour, we should find no regularity at all ; neither would its regularity be seen if, instead of the criminal records of a whole country, we only knew those of a single street, or of a single family.   This is because the great social laws by which crime is governed can only be perceived after observing great numbers of long periods ; but *in a small number, and a short period, the individual moral principle triumphs, and disturbs the operation of the larger and intellectual law.*   While, therefore, the moral feelings by which a man is urged to commit a crime, or to abstain from it, will produce an immense effect on the amount of his own crimes, they will produce no effect on the amount of crimes committed by the society to which he belongs ; because, in the long-run, they are sure to be neutralised by opposite moral feelings, which cause in other men an opposite conduct.   Just in the same way, *we are all sensible that moral principles do affect nearly the whole of our actions,* but we have incontrovertible proof that they produce not the least effect on mankind in the aggregate, or even in men in very large masses, provided that we take the precaution of studying social phenomena for a period sufficiently long, and on a scale sufficiently great to enable the superior laws to come into uncontrolled operation.

The doings of individual men, of families, of the inhabitants of single streets, are nothing to Mr. Buckle ; they must be divested of all personality, of all reminiscences of personality, before they are of use to him.   That is to say, in his view of civilisation, he looks at men not as persons, but as machines ; and the result he contemplates is not the action of these machines, but their productions.

This is all that Mr. Buckle's design includes, all that logically he has any right to pretend to discuss.   Defining, as he does, civilisation to be that mass of ideas, knowledge, and production which remains over and above when you have abstracted all transitory actions, all the results of politics, war, or religion, of course his history of civilisation ought to be confined to the genesis of this product, and the rules on which he proceeds to such as are applicable only to such a history.   For instance, as virtues, vices, and all transitory actions are excluded from his view, of course he has nothing to do with the question of the force on which they depend ; hence he is quite right in eliminating free-will from his laws of civilisation.   Man's knowledge depends not on his will, but on his intellect ; now it is his will, not his intellect, that is free.   A man cannot refuse to see that which he does see, nor force himself to disbelieve that which is demonstratively proved.   It is only when he has to decide whether he will open his eyes to see, or whether he will act on that which is proved to him, that he is free to do as he chooses.   Again, it is only to men as persons that free-will belongs : look at them in masses, and they become machines ; with their personality you abstract their freedom.   Looking, therefore, at mankind as Mr. Buckle does, not as individual persons but as masses of producers, he could not allow free-will to come into his calculations.   So again with Providence. Providence dealing with the world is that creative and preservative force which conducts the universe according to " a law which shall not be broken " ; the expression of Providence is this law, wherein no personality can be proved.   But Providence dealing with persons is the action of a Personal God upon his personal creatures ; warning them, teaching them, judging them.   Eliminate personality from your science, and of course your science has nothing to do with the personal providence.   Nothing can be clearer.

But then, again, nothing can be clearer than this, that when you have cut off a part from anything, the thing is no longer a whole.   This very clear truth Mr. Buckle, with the most charming simplicity, not only forgets, but tries to make his readers forget also. Having arbitrarily settled the limit of his history ; having, in so many words, recognised that things do exist outside of these limits, which, however, do not require his attention, as they do not influence the precise matter on hand ; having confessed that the constant variation of moral qualities in men is "owing to causes of which we are ignorant"; that to individuals, or a small number of persons his rules will not apply, because there "the individual moral principle triumphs, and disturbs the operation of the larger and intellectual law," and that "we are all sensible that moral principles do affect nearly the whole of our actions,"—yet he goes on to treat his science as exhaustive, as including every possible kind of human actions, and as furnishing the true key to the only real "history" of the human race. Let us see how Mr. Buckle manages to turn this wonderful intellectual somersault. We must suppose that the man who has written so remarkable a book had the whole plan of it in his mind. He knew that he was to write about men, not as individuals, but in masses. He knew that all his proofs were to be statistical, that is, winnowed from all personal detail, lumped together, averaged, and reduced to mathematical symbols. Yet, for all this, he pretends to begin from persons. The fundamental question of his book is thus stated : "Are the actions of men, *and therefore of societies*, governed by fixed laws, or are they the result either of chance or supernatural interference ?"[1] He discusses these latter alternatives, not mathematically, or metaphysically, or logically, but by means of a fanciful theory, illustrated by an apologue. He imagines man to have been originally a wild and savage hunter, sometimes finding game, sometimes starving, and attributing his good or ill success only to chance ; next the savage becomes agricultural, and seeing that seasons succeed regularly, and that the crop answers to the seed, the first notion of "uniform sequence" arises, and ripens into that of "law of nature".

[1] P. 8.

and " necessary connection." These doctrines of the people give rise, among the men of leisure, or thinkers, to two corresponding doctrines of the learned—free-will and predestination ; founded one on a metaphysical, the other on a theological hypothesis. Mr. Buckle rejects both doctrines : the second, as unproved, and if proved only a barren hypothesis ; the first, free-will, as " in reality resting on the metaphysical dogma of the supremacy of the human consciousness. Every man, it is alleged, feels and knows that he is a free agent ; nor can any subtleties of argument do away with our consciousness of possessing a free-will." This *supremacy* of consciousness he denies : first, because we cannot prove that consciousness is a faculty ; secondly, because if a faculty it is fallible, or, as he explains in a note, infallible as to the *fact*, but fallible as to the *truth* ; infallible in testifying the presence of a phenomenon to the mind, fallible in affirming the substantial reality of the phenomenon. Now the consciousness is often deceived in affirming the existence of ghosts and the like, therefore it may be deceived in affirming the existence of free-will. This is literally the whole proof which Mr. Buckle deigns to give us of the premiss of the fundamental proposition of his book.

It is almost too absurd to controvert. He foists the unnecessary word *supremacy* into his adversary's statement, in order that he may object that, consciousness not being a faculty, there is no supremacy. Possibly not. Yet consciousness being the mind's knowledge of its own acts, and of the motives upon which it acts, either consciousness is true, or all our knowledge of our own thoughts is possibly false—*i.e.* possibly I am thinking exactly the contrary of that which I know I am thinking. Next, the mind may be infallibly conscious of its acts and motives, and, among the rest, of its own freedom. Put the case of every imaginable motive of interest and pleasure, temporal and eternal, being offered me to determine me to a certain act : I know that if I choose, I may do exactly the reverse, simply to prove my freedom. I am conscious not only of my freedom to act, but also that the assertion of this freedom may be a motive outweighing all other motives together. We are all conscious that we often will not do what we ought, simply because we are commanded: "If you tell me I may, I won't; if you tell me I must, I will see you hanged first,"—that is, egotistical freedom asserts itself by not brooking permission, and by defying command. Mr. Buckle has no right to object to this, that our consciousness may be wrong, for he himself appeals to it in a passage quoted above: "We are all *sensible* that moral principles do affect nearly the whole of our actions." *Sensible* means *conscious*; he therefore puts himself out of court by producing in his own behalf the witness whose truth he had before impeached. To compare our *consciousness* of ghosts with our *consciousness* of our own freedom, is to confound the mind's *self-consciousness* of itself with its *consciousness* of a false sensation, or false nervous impression; one is outward, the other inward. It is to argue that because a blind man cannot *see* colours, therefore he cannot *see* the validity of a syllogism. So that Mr. Buckle utterly fails to establish the premiss of his fundamental proposition: "the actions of men, and therefore of societies, are governed by fixed laws, and not by free-will."

Again, why make an "alternative" between fixed laws and free-will? God is absolutely free and absolutely immutable. Freedom is not instability. The liberty of the children of God does not consist in holding an even balance between obeying and disobeying God, now inclining to one side, now to the other. True liberty is a self-determined, self-chosen perseverance in the way we deliberately think the best. Fixedness, then, is not really opposed to freedom. But further; let us assume as an hypothesis the existence of an immaterial soul, having perfect and even capricious freedom,—such that there is no fixity in its intentions, no possibility of predicting the changes of its self-determination. Yet as soon as this soul is united with body, as soon as it manifests its acts in time and space, it must follow the laws of time and space. It must work "in number, measure, and weight." It cannot enclose a space with two straight lines; it cannot find a shorter way of joining two points than by a straight line. So also in moral acts; it cannot do anything that may not be referred to the seven virtues, or the seven sins; nay, there must be an average in its sins or virtues; it must either attach itself to all equally, or it must now prefer one, now another. Its acts must be capable of numeration; and every thing that is numerable becomes at once a subject of statistics,—it has its average, its maximum, and its minimum, and is ticketed as belonging to a "fixed law." Yet, by the hypothesis, it was perfectly free. Therefore perfect freedom, and subjection to a fixed law, are quite compatible even in the individual soul, working in space and time. In its inner self-determination it may be perfectly free; yet in the manifestations or results of its free action it is bound by the fixed laws of number, space, and time. Again, these results, before they become appreciable, are done; they have become facts, and as such are removed from the influence of free-will. Not even God, says the poet, can make a fact not a fact, can render undone what is done. That which is done is become a material external product, altogether independent of the interior determination, or free-will, which motived or gave the first occasion of its existence. Hence no examination of these facts, apart from the consciousness of the doers of them, can possibly give us the element of freedom; they are mere material external facts, as subject to numeration and measurement as a crop of wheat, or the velocity of a bullet.

And if this is true of the acts of an individual, how much more true will it be of the acts of a mass of men? The laws of number are capable of a much more varied manifestation in large than in small numbers. There is no regularity in throws of dice taken ten and ten together; but in 10,000 throws we can predict with great confidence how many times sixes will be thrown. There is no possible certainty that any given individual will commit murder; but take a population of 100,000, and in a given time some one or other is sure to be found committing murder. All double things are done at intervals; and though there is the greatest uncertainty when they will be done, yet give laxity enough, allow a thousand, a hundred, or fifty years, and it may be confidently predicted that the thing will be done in that time; and this by no quality inherent in the thing or the doer, but by the law of numeration. Hence we cannot say, as Emerson somewhere says, that " if one man in thirty thousand eats shoes, or marries his grandmother, then one man in every thirty thousand must eat shoes, or marry his grandmother," for there is no necessity in the case. Take the dice. The mathematician will tell you exactly how often he will throw aces in 10,000 throws. But suppose by some very possible accident you had made 9990 throws without turning aces the average number of times, are you in any conceivable way surer of having aces in the last ten throws than if you were only just beginning the game? Not a bit. The former throws have nothing to do with the latter. The law is a law of numbers, a law of chances applicable to numbers and *on the average* applicable to all numerable things; but not implying any force, or cause, or reason why the things themselves should be thus rather than otherwise. Hence, in the first place, we should never be surprised if facts, the origin of which is free-will, are numbered; nor, secondly, if they are found capable of being averaged, so that a given number of them take place in a given time, but from this to make the third step, and to say, because they are numerable, because they can be averaged, therefore they happened by necessity, by a fixed law, is absurd in any man, and in Mr. Buckle dishonest.

It is dishonest in Mr. Buckle, because he must be aware that he is using the words *law* and *necessity* in a sense quite different from that intended by ordinary mortals. When we say " law," we always think of some force, or command, which is the cause of the thing being done. But Mr. Buckle, by *law*, only means *numerical average.* Now it is clear that when a thing has an average, it has an average ; you may call this a *fixed law* if you please ; but use your terms in such a way that we may not be led into the mistake of concluding that *fixed law* means a necessity inherent in the essence of the thing, and that therefore whatever has an average is necessary, and could not be otherwise. So, again, the word *necessary.* Common thinkers mean by it that which cannot be thought to be otherwise without self-contradiction ; thus it is necessary that two and two make four, that the three angles of a triangle equal two right angles, and the like. Now, is there any *necessity* of this kind in averages ? Clearly not, or they would not be averages, but identical numbers. If there were any fixed law, or necessity of murder, the annual number of murders would not be merely approximate, but identical, or varying directly as the population. As they are not thus identical, there clearly is no fixed law in the usual sense, no necessary average of murder ; and Mr. Buckle has no right to mislead his readers by using the word in his sense.

And now let us see what Mr. Buckle says on these points.

> Rejecting the metaphysical doctrine of free-will, and the theological dogma of predestined events, we are driven to the conclusion that the actions of men, being determined solely by their antecedents, must have a character of uniformity, that is to say, must, under precisely the same circumstances, always issue in precisely the same results.

Here, we observe, Mr. Buckle contradicts himself ; for though he expresses so confidently that the law of individual action is, that it is " necessarily determined by antecedents," he concedes in another place that the variation in human conduct is " owing to causes of which we are ignorant." But let us proceed :—

> To state some of the most decisive proofs we now possess of the regularity with which mental phenomena succeed each other, . . . murder, one of the most arbitrary and irregular of crimes, is committed with as much regularity, and bears as uniform a relation to certain known circumstances as do the movements of the tides and the rotations of the seasons.

The great authority for this statement, and for the theory he derives from it, is M. Quételet. Now although he conceives that because he calls M. Quételet " confessedly the first statistician in Europe," his conclusions will therefore pass unchallenged, we must observe that a very different opinion of him prevails among those who are more competent judges than either Mr. Buckle or ourselves. His way of applying the theory of probabilities to statistics is rejected even by the French writers ; and the following observations made with reference to him by one of the most celebrated political economists of the age, show the estimation in which his method is held in Germany :—

Of late years an opinion has been gaining ground that statistics have only to deal with political and social facts expressed in figures, without being confined to any particular time. Calculations are made with tables, etc. ; and meanwhile the signification of the figures virtually disappears from the mind, which becomes conscious of it only when the result is obtained. Now for all those facts which are susceptible of it, the mathematical form of expression is undoubtedly the most perfect, and we must endeavour, therefore, to make the mathematical branch of statistics as comprehensive as possible. But one branch of a science is not the science itself. Just as there is no special science in natural philosophy called *Microscopia*, which combines all observations made through the microscope, so the principle of a science ought never to be deduced from the character of its principal instrument. This restriction would deprive statistics of al scientific unity and interior coherence.[1]

But to return to Mr. Buckle—

" This," says he, " will appear strange to those who believe that human actions depend more on the peculiarities of each individual than on the general state of society."

So suicide; the number of suicides in every year is about the same, therefore—

. . . in a given state of society a certain number of persons must put an end to their own life. This is the general law ; and the special question as to who shall commit the crime depends of course upon special law ; which, however, in their total action, must obey the large irresistible social law to which they are all subordinate.

[1] Roscher, *System der Volkswirthschaft*, i. 29.

Alas, then, if one person in our village is to commit suicide, if nobody else will, I must! And why? Simply because one person has committed suicide there yearly for several years past. Nothing can withstand the simple rules of arithmetic! But fortunately this "irresistible social law" allows of a considerable *laxum* in its operation; *about* two hundred and forty persons a year must kill themselves in London, but the special number may vary between two hundred and sixty-six and two hundred and thirteen. Our readers, too, may take comfort from hearing that "suicide is more frequent among Protestants than among Catholics."

Nor is it merely the crimes of men which are marked by this uniformity of sequence. . . . In England the experience of a century has proved that marriages, *instead of having any connection with personal feelings*, are simply regulated by the average earnings of the great mass of the people. . . . Year after year the same proportion of letter-writers forget to direct their letters, so that we can actually foretell how many will do it next year.

The chief things we note here are, the utter worthlessness of the reasoning itself, and its formal contradiction by the author's admissions previously quoted. What can we think of the judgment of a man who allows statistics to make him believe that marriages *have no connection* with personal feelings! or that can use a few imperfect returns about murders, suicides, and undirected letters, to upset all the affirmations of personal consciousness, the whole common sense of the world, as expressed in human language, and his own common sense to boot! For we do not forget, that though at p. 26 he tells us that the question who, what individual, shall commit suicide "depends upon special laws, which in their total action must obey the large social law to which they are subordinate," at p. 208 he tells us that this is only true for great numbers of men, and long periods of time; for "in a small number, and a short period, the individual moral principle triumphs, and disturbs the operation of the larger and intellectual law": we must study "social phenomena for a period sufficiently long, and on a scale sufficiently

great, to enable the superior laws to come into uncontrolled operation."

Now this very contradiction should have taught Mr.
Buckle that he was involved in a fallacy. In nature
totals are made up of parts similar to the whole. A block
of stone is made up of stony molecules; a kidney of
several little kidneys; a wave is an accumulation of little
waves. Every chip of wood has the same construction as
the block. Yet Mr. Buckle pretends to show us a long
period and a great number made up of a quantity of short
periods and small numbers, which are ruled by principles
contradictory in their action to the principle which rules
the total. In other words, the repetition of an individual
law destroys that law! Individual moral principle manifests itself so often that it is never seen! A thing, by
being multiplied, is annihilated! Addition, instead of
increasing, diminishes the sum!

Mr. Buckle's fallacy consists mainly in this: that
whereas his whole conception of the object of his work
required him to abstract his consideration entirely from
all persons, and to consider man only in the mass, as so
much productive machinery, oiled indeed, and kept in
working order by a due amount of virtue, but intended only
to produce intellectual truths capable of teaching how more
and more to subdue nature,—he has chosen to apply the
rules, applicable exclusively to man under this aspect, to
man as a person, as an individual; though he knows and
confesses that they are not so applicable. We are sorry
that we are thus reduced to defend either Mr. Buckle's
understanding at the expense of his honesty, or his
honesty at the expense of his understanding. In fact,
man, as person, cannot be added to man; soul cannot be
mixed with soul; each individual stands apart, or loses his
individuality by addition.

History, therefore, on Mr. Buckle's plan, is impossible.
For as soon as we seek simply statistics and averages, we
have lost sight of man, and are contemplating only his
works, his products. The true historian takes the individual for his centre; he describes the typical man, whom

all others more or less resemble ; he recounts the adventures of the ruler, to whose will multitudes bow.   If he treats of mobs, or armies, or bodies of men, he invests this multitude with a kind of personality of its own,—its own wishes, passions, character, will, and conscience.   Mr. Buckle's history, if he *could* write a history according to his programme, would be the reverse of all this : he would merge the individual in the company, the person in the body ; wishes, passions, character, conscience, all would be abstracted ; for those things either balance, and so neutralise each other, or else are transient in their effects, and so immaterial to the total.   History would consist in tabular views of births, deaths, marriages, diseases, prices, commerce, and the like ; and the historian would be chiefly useful in providing grocers with cheap paper to wrap up butter in.   But Mr. Buckle knows better than to reduce history to such dry chaff; when he writes history he makes persons his centres, and reduces it to what it must always be, an intricate and interlacing tissue of biographies, so far as men advanced some particular movement on which the historian is writing.   Thus Louis XIV., Richelieu, and Burke crop out in Mr. Buckle's volume as the centres of his political speculations.

Mr. Buckle's practice herein is utterly contrary to his theory.   History can only be reduced to a science by excluding individualism and personality.   Persons act, if not by free-will, at least by unknown laws, which are in opposition, as Mr. Buckle owns, to the great statistical laws on which he would found historical science.   The reason of this opposition is manifest ; and an explanation will clearly show why it is, and always will be, impossible to write a history upon Mr. Buckle's programme, and why he must be disappointed in his expectation of reducing history to a science.

All sciences are either inductive or deductive.   We need not waste time in arguing with Mr. Buckle that history is not a deductive science, for he himself spends several pages in proving this proposition.   It must, therefore, be a science depending upon induction.   Now what is induction ? Though essentially the same as of old, this act of reason is differently conducted now. Formerly, if two or three instances suggested a principle or a generalisation to the mind, this principle was said to be gained by induction. Or if a mere guess or fancy could be strengthened by a few instances or analogies, this might readily be turned into an inductive argument : " It is the case in this, and a second and third instance, therefore in all." But this loose unscientific induction is now changed; the instances have to be well manipulated before they can be used for a true induction ; and not only similarities but dissimilarities have to be investigated. We must abstract all points of difference before adding the various elements ; induction therefore is not only addition but subtraction also. Before we can include two things under a general law, we must subtract all that makes them different from one another ; otherwise we should include contradictions in a pretended unity.

Now, if we submit men and human actions to the crucible of induction, they must be " prepared," like everything else, for the process. The unlike must first be abstracted. Take any two men : what is the first element that constitutes their difference ? Clearly their personality; John is not Robert ; not because they have a different nature, but because they have a different personality. If we wish to include John and Robert under a single generalisation, the first thing we must divest them of is personality, with all its distinctive characteristics, the chief of which is usually said to be freedom of the will. Man, then, in this induction is not real man ; he is no longer a personal free agent, but a machine, subject in his movements to those laws of action which remain after personality and free-will have been subtracted.

Thus, if free-will is the source of action in men, it will be impossible ever to reduce all the sources of human action to an inductive generalisation, such as will enable us to predict how men will act. Free-will refuses the inductive process. The only chance is, to prove that free-will does not exist, or is not such a source of action.

Y

This Mr. Buckle has attempted to do in various ways. In his first chapter he tries to prove that "the actions of men, *and therefore of societies*, are governed by fixed laws"; how weakly, we have shown above. We reproduce the thesis here to show that even Mr. Buckle allows that individuals are the primary elements of societies, and that the laws of society may be deduced from the laws that govern individuals. In other places, before quoted, Mr. Buckle asserts that the moral actions of men depend on particular laws, to him unknown, which laws are in their operation *antagonistic* to the great laws that govern society. And elsewhere he says that the laws of society are the rule for the individual, the actions of men are regular because "they are *governed* by the state of the society in which they occur."

Here, then, we see that there is a fundamental impossibility, because a self-contradiction, in Mr. Buckle's method and system, when applied to anything beyond the limits to which he himself is conscious it should be confined. If he would really eliminate all the moral actions of men, all the "flux and reflux" of society, all war and politics, from his speculations, and apply his theory to the "discoveries of genius" and to the progressive knowledge and subjugation of nature alone, he would escape all contradiction. But if he insists on applying his method to history, in the usual acceptation of the word, we are forced to tell him that his pretensions are untenable. These pretensions may perhaps be traced to that characteristic which Socrates holds up to such ridicule in his speech in the *Apologia*. Every artisan, he says, because he is expert in his own art, thinks he knows every other art. The tendency of the intellect is to complete its own circle; whatever gaps a man finds in his knowledge are filled up by an unwarrantable stretching of the next subject which he knows. The whole system of positive philosophy is the work of under-educated, or half-educated men, adepts in physical science, but ignorant of the principles of any other, who insist that all science must have the same method as theirs, and that metaphysical realities must be measured and explained by physical laws. We state this to show that Mr. Buckle's absurdities and dishonesties are not his own, but those of his school.

We are quite conscious that in this article our criticism does not reach over the whole extent of the work under review ; but as the limits of a monthly journal are so narrow, we thought it better to confine our remarks to one or two points, rather than to dissipate our attention over the multitude of subjects that ought to be discussed. We have, however, attempted to discover the fundamental and leading idea of the book, which we have proved to be untenable. We do not deny all merit to the work ; we only say that the mass of information, collected with immense labour, and put together with great acuteness, a boldness fearless of consequences, and in a captivating style, does not exactly prove that which he undertakes to prove ; for nothing can prove a proposition that contradicts itself.

We shall have to return to the book, to make observations on Mr. Buckle's detailed proofs. Hitherto we have only attacked his general thesis, the conclusion which he proposes as the end of his induction ; we shall hereafter have to examine some specimens of the terms of his inductive argument, and to inquire into the validity of his claims to respect for the extent and accuracy of his learning.

XI

MR. BUCKLE'S PHILOSOPHY OF HISTORY[1]

IN our last Number we explained the theory which Mr. Buckle's book is written to prove, and estimated his merits as a philosopher. We have now to consider his attainments as a scholar. We have to examine his competency for the task he has undertaken, and the degree of success with which he has executed it. This is the more imperatively necessary, that it would be very unfair to Mr. Buckle to judge him by the merits of his system only; for the system is not his own. We may praise him or blame him for his judgment in adopting it, certainly not for his skill in devising it. His view of "the principles which govern the character and destiny of nations" is borrowed partly from Comte and partly from Quételet, and has already been applied, not indeed by historians, but by natural philosophers. We find it stated, for instance, by the celebrated physiologist Valentin, as follows (*Grundriss der Physiologie*, 1855, p. 10) :—

Chance, to which we ascribe the event of an isolated case, must make way for a definite law as soon as we include a greater number of cases in our observation. No fixed rule appears to regulate the proportion of the sexes to each other, or the relative number of twins that are born, or the kind of crimes committed within a given period. But if we extend our range of observation over millions of cases, certain regular quantities constantly recur. Where this is not the case, the causes of the fluctuation can often be ascertained by the rule of probabilities. Here, as everywhere, chance vanishes as a phantom of superstition,—as a result of that short-sightedness which has burdened the history of human opinion with so many apparently higher, but in reality degrading and erroneous, ideas.

---

[1] *The Rambler*, 1858.

This nearly describes the theory which Mr. Buckle has transferred from the history of nature to the history of man. He can hardly be said to challenge inquiry into its truth. He is at small pains to recommend it to those who are not predisposed in its favour. He is more inclined to dogmatise than to argue; and treats with placid scorn all who may not agree with him, and who are attached to one or other of the creeds and systems which have subsisted amongst men. It is a characteristic of certain diminutive parties to make up by the confidence and doggedness of their language for the small support they are able to command in public opinion. It is the same spirit in which Coleridge used to be worshipped at Highgate, and Jeremy Bentham at Westminster.

Taking a survey of literature from the pinnacle of his self-esteem, Mr. Buckle repeatedly affirms that history has been generally written by very incapable men; that before his time there was no science of history; that "the most celebrated historians are manifestly inferior to the cultivators of physical science" (p. 7), and much more to the same purpose *passim*. He gives us, moreover, to understand that he is as much at home in ethical as in historical literature; and delivers the valuable opinion, "that a man, after reading everything that has been written on moral conduct and moral philosophy, will find himself nearly as much in the dark as when his studies first began" (p. 22). Having thus cleared the way for his own appearance on the neglected fields of history and philosophy, he leaves us to infer that there are very few people capable of appreciating his performance, or for whose judgment he cares a pin. He writes for a school; and uttering its oracles to the world, he may question the competency of any tribunal which does not in some degree admit his premises and consents to judge him out of his own mouth. But if we are unworthy to judge his theories, his facts at least are common property, and are accessible to all men; and it is important to see what they are worth, and how much Mr. Buckle knew about the matter when he endeavoured to make history subservient to his philosophy.

The attempt to reconcile philosophical speculation with the experience of history, and to harmonise their teachings, is perfectly natural, and, at a certain stage, inevitable. Both are unbounded in their range, and in some sense they may be said to include each other. Neither science is perfect till it obtains the confirmation of the other. " Man," says Jacobi, " requires not only a truth whose creator he is, but a truth also of which he is the creature." Yet the comparison could take place only at an advanced period of the progress of philosophy and of the knowledge of history. Philosophy must be seen by the light of history that the laws of its progress may be understood ; and history, which records the thoughts as well as the actions of men, cannot overlook the vicissitudes of philosophic schools. Thus the history of philosophy is a postulate of either science. At the same time, history, unless considered in its philosophic aspect, is devoid of connection and instruction ; and philosophy, which naturally tends to embrace all the sciences, necessarily seeks to subject history, amongst the rest, to its law. Hence arose the philosophy of history. " In history," says Krug, " philosophy beholds itself reflected. It is the text to which history supplies the commentary." [1] Both sciences had attained a certain maturity of development before they sought each other. " Philosophy," said Schelling, " ought not to precede the particular sciences, but to follow after them." [2] Generalisation in history was not possible until a great part of its course was run, and the knowledge of its details tolerably complete. Nor could the history of philosophy be written before it had passed through many phases, or before it had attained a considerable development. Thus it naturally happened that the philosophy of history and the history of philosophy, as they proceeded from the same causes, began to be cultivated about the same time. They are scarcely a century old.

The mediæval philosophy had taken no cognisance of the external world until, in the sixteenth century, a

[1] *Handwörterbuch der philosophischen Wissenschaften*, ii. 217.
[2] Salat, *Schelling in München*, i. 60.

reaction took place. As theology had predominated in the Middle Ages, now physiology prevailed in its stead. The study of nature became the first of sciences, and in the age of the supremacy of the Baconian system, Kepler and Galileo and Newton were considered philosophers. To the philosophic investigation of nature was added, in the eighteenth century, the philosophic contemplation of history. The method by which Bacon had revolutionised natural science "ab experientia ad axiomata, et ab axio-matibus ad nova inventa," [1] came to be tried on history. Since that time a philosophy of history has been attempted upon the principles of almost every system. The result has not always been to the advantage of history, or to the credit of the philosophers. "When things are known and found out, then they can descant upon them ; they can knit them into certain causes, they can reduce them to their principles. If any instance of experience stands against them, they can range it in order by some distinctions. But all this is but a web of the wit ; it can work nothing." [2]

The first attempt to give unity to universal history by the application of a philosophic system was made by Lessing, in his celebrated fragment on the *Education of the Human Race*. It was his last work, "and must be considered the foundation of all modern philosophy, of religion, and the beginning of a more profound appreciation of history." [3] He employs the ideas of Leibnitz's *Théodicée* to explain the government of the world. Condorcet's *Sketch of the Progress of the Human Mind* is inspired, in like manner, by the sensualist doctrines of Condillac. Kant, though perfectly ignorant of the subject, was incited by the French Revolution to draw up a scheme of universal history in unison with his system. It was the entire inadequacy of Kant's philosophy to explain the phenomena of history which led Hegel, "for whom the philosophical problem had converted itself into an his-

[1] *De Augmentis*, iii. 3 : "From experiment to axioms, from axioms to new discoveries."
[2] Bacon, "In Praise of Knowledge," *Works*, ed. Bohn, i. 216.
[3] Schwarz, *Lessing als Theologe*, p. 79.

torical one," [1] to break with the system altogether. Thirty
years later, when the supremacy of Kant had long passed
away, and Hegel was reigning in his stead, he too set up
his philosophy of history as the crown and end of his own
philosophy, and as the test of its absolute truth.[2]   " It is
for historical science," says his latest biographer, " to enjoy
the inheritance of Hegel's philosophy." [3]   In like manner,
the transcendental system of Schelling resulted in a
Christian philosophy of history, of which a late able
writer says that by it " the antagonism of philosophy and
history, proceeding from a defective notion of the first,
and an utterly inadequate view of the latter, was removed." [4]   So, again, the system of Krause presents a
combination of philosophy and history in which their
respective methods are blended together.[5]   Especially
since the publication of Hegel's *Lectures*, history has been
generally considered by philosophers as belonging to
their legitimate domain.   And their dominion is such,
that even a moderate acquaintance with the events of the
past has ceased to be deemed a necessary or even a useful
ingredient in the preparation of a philosophy of history.
No system will confess itself so poor that it cannot reconstruct the history of the world without the help of
empirical knowledge.   A Pole, Cieszkowski (*Prolegomena
zur Historiosophie*, 1838), has a physical scheme for the
arrangement of historical phenomena.   According to him,
light is the type of Persia, mechanism of China, Athens
represents dynamic electricity, Sparta static electricity.
The electro-magnetic system answers to Macedon, the
expansive force of heat to the Roman Empire.   The

---

[1] Haym, *Hegel und seine Zeit*, p. 45.

[2] "Gewissermassen, die Probe des ganzen Systems" (Michelet, *Entwicke-
lungsgeschichte der neuesten deutschen Philos.*, p. 304).   " Die Wahrhafte Theo-
dicee, die Probe von der Wahrheit des ganzen Systems" (Huber, *Deutsche Viertel-
jahrs Schrift*, 1853, ii. 50).   " Die unwidersprichlichste Bewährung des Systems "
(Haym, *Allgem. Encyclop.*, art. "Philosophie," sect. iii. vol. xxiv. 176).

[3] Haym, *Hegel, etc.* 466.

[4] Schaarschmidt, *Entwickelungsgang der neuesten Speculation*, p. 194 ; and
Schelling, *Werke*, i. 480, 481.

[5] According to his disciples, "der harmonische Haupttheil," "die Blüthen-
knospe," of the system (Erdmann, *Entwickelung der Speculation seit Kant*,
ii. 676).

dualism of Church and State in the Middle Ages corre-
sponds to the antithesis of acid and alkali, etc. etc. The
same ingenious person argues from the analogy of the
natural sciences, in which, with the help of an old tooth,
you can reconstruct an antediluvian monster, that history
has to deal with the future, and cannot submit to be
confined to the knowledge of the past. Twenty years
ago, the well-known novelist Gutzkow was in prison, and
not having books at hand to help him in writing a novel,
beguiled the time by writing and publishing a philosophy
of history.

These recent examples may serve to show us that it is
not to be wondered at that an attempt should be made to
obtain for a new system the sanction of history ; or that,
having been made, it should have produced a ludicrous
result, and should have furnished the most complete
confutation of the system it was meant to confirm. But
we have already said that the theory is not the most
remarkable part about Mr. Buckle's book. It is by his
portentous display of reading that he will impose upon
many in whom the principles in their naked deformity
would simply excite abhorrence. The theoretical portion
is completely overgrown and hidden by the mass of
matter which is collected to support it, and on which
Mr. Buckle has brought to bear all the reading of a
lifetime. The wonderful accumulation of details and
extravagance of quotation have the manifest purpose of
dazzling and blinding his readers by the mere mass of
apparent erudition. " So learned a man cannot be mistaken in his conclusions," is no doubt what they are
expected to say. We cannot, therefore, consider the
success of Mr. Buckle's work as a fair indication of the
extent to which the peculiar form of infidelity which he
holds prevails in this country. To accept his conclusions,
we must be prepared to say, *Credo quia impium* ; but in
order to be overawed by his learning, it is enough to have
less of it than Mr. Buckle himself.

It is for this reason worth while to inquire briefly
whether Mr. Buckle is in this respect so great an authority

as he professes to be, and as it is commonly taken for granted he is—whether he really possesses that knowledge of his subject which justifies him in writing upon it, or whether, in a word, he is an impostor.

Apart from the historical excursions of modern philosophers which we have spoken of, and with which Mr. Buckle has not thought fit to make himself acquainted, the great problems of civilisation which he tries to solve have been discussed within the last few years by three eminent men, whose works have some points of similarity with his own. In 1853 a French diplomatist, M. de Gobineau, published the first portion of a work which he has since completed in four volumes, *Essai sur l'Inégalité des Races humaines.* Familiar with all the latest researches of French and German writers, he investigates in great detail the laws which regulate the progress and the decline of civilisation. He finds that it depends entirely on purity of blood. The deterioration produced by the mixture of races is the sole cause of decline : " A people would never die if it remained eternally composed of the same national elements " (i. 53). The fate of nations is unconnected with the land they inhabit ; it depends in nothing on good government or purity of morals. Even Christianity has no permanent influence on civilisation : " Le Christianisme n'est pas civilisateur, et il a grandement raison de ne pas l'être " (p. 124). Whether we admit or reject these conclusions, it is unquestionable that they are founded on most various and conscientious research, and an abundance of appropriate learning, strongly contrasting with the dishonest affectation of knowledge by which Mr. Buckle deludes his readers. There is, moreover, a learned appendage to Gobineau's book, in the shape of a pamphlet of 275 pages, by Professor Pott. About the same time an anonymous work appeared at Marburg, in three volumes, bearing the somewhat obscure title, *Anthropognosie, Ethnognosie und Polignosie,* in which also the laws which influence the political and social progress of mankind are explained with uncommon erudition. It was by a well-known political writer, Dr. Vollgraff ; and, though disfigured by endless subdivisions and an obscure arrangement, it is undoubtedly one of the most comprehensive and instructive works that have appeared in our time. All the principal points of Mr. Buckle's theory are here discussed and illustrated with infinitely greater fulness of knowledge than in the work of our English author ; and although the conclusions to which the German philosopher would lead us are not much better, at least there is much more to be learnt on the road.

The third work to which we allude is very different in style and spirit, and bears a motto which at once deprives it of any considerable resemblance to Mr. Buckle's work : *Lo bueno, si breve, dos vezes bueno.* It is the work of the most eloquent and accomplished philosopher in Germany,[1] and passes in review, in 168 pages, all the great questions which constitute the philosophy of history. The wisest sayings of the ancients, and the latest discoveries of the moderns, are brought together with incomparable taste and learning ; since Schlegel, so brilliant a work had not appeared on the same field.

We have drawn attention to these works because they treat of exactly the same questions as Mr. Buckle's *History of Civilisation,* and are all written by men of distinguished abilities—the last by one of the greatest modern scholars ; because, moreover, they are the only works which, during the last ten years, have really advanced the study of philosophy of history, and are therefore the first books to which anybody would naturally turn who is employed upon the subject. None of them, we may add, are written from a specifically Catholic point of view, yet Mr. Buckle has never once alluded to any of them.

We may attribute this monstrous neglect of what has been done and is doing in the field which he is cultivating, either to simple ignorance of the present state of learning, or to a wary dislike of whatever might not help to support his own views. There is no other alternative, and either supposition is equally fatal to his credit.

---

[1] Ernst von Lasaulx, *Neuer Versuch einer alten auf die Wahrheit der Thatsachen gegründeten Philosophie der Geschichte.*

As Mr. Buckle despises the historians, and knows nothing of the principal philosophers, it may be asked, where, then, are his authorities?   The answer is given in a note (p. 5), where we are told that Comte is the "writer who has done more than any other to raise the standard of history."   This is the key to the whole book, and in general to Mr. Buckle's state of mind.   His view seldom extends beyond the bounds of the system of that philosopher, and he has not sought enlightenment in the study of the great metaphysicians of other schools.   The limits of his knowledge in this respect are curious.   Of Aristotle, though he frequently mentions him, and in one place even places him on a level with the French physician Bichât (p. 812), there is no proof that he knows anything at all.   He tells us, for instance, that the chief writers on the influence of climate are Hume, Montesquieu, Guizot, and Comte.   It never occurs to him that his favourite theory on this point is to be found in Aristotle (*Problemata*, xiv.), or that Hippocrates wrote a work on the subject.   Plato, though sometimes quoted, seems hardly better known.   Nobody familiar with his works and life would venture upon the statement that it is doubtful whether he ever visited Egypt (p. 81) ; still less would a scholar with any self-respect have cited Bunsen as an authority on the matter.   In reality, the only question is how long he remained there.

This is a fair instance of our author's habit of going to the wrong place for information, and ignoring the obvious authorities.   Altogether Mr. Buckle, who does not commonly put his light under a bushel, exhibits acquaintance with scarcely four or five of the most common writers of antiquity.

It is not to be expected that the Christian writers should come off better ; there is a good deal said about them, but it is borrowed at second-hand, generally from Neander, sometimes from Mosheim or Milman.   For it makes no difference to Mr. Buckle whether a thing is true, or whether somebody has said that it is true.   It is enough that it should answer some particular purpose of the moment. Indeed, although his reading appears excessively promiscuous, it is in reality selected with great discrimination. So far as we have observed, the standard work which is the real and acknowledged authority on each particular subject is never by any chance or oversight consulted for the purpose. We have shown how the case stands relatively to the general subject of civilisation. For the history of philosophy we have continual references in Tennemann, who was greatly esteemed at the time of Kant's supremacy in the schools. The progress of learning has long since displaced his works, as well as those which immediately succeeded him. Sometimes we find reference to Ritter's *Ancient Philosophy*, the most antiquated portion of his highly unsatisfactory work. The vast literature on this subject which has arisen within the last few years is never noticed. So, for the history of medicine we have Sprengel and Renouard, whose books were long since superseded by the works of Hecker, Häser, and others. On India, again, we are referred to a number of obsolete publications, and the great work of Lassen is never mentioned. The same ignorance prevails upon almost every branch of learning that is ostentatiously brought forward ; but we should be following Mr. Buckle's very bad example if we were to go on giving lists of books which he ought to have consulted.

The title of the sixth chapter, " Origin of History, and State of Historical Literature during the Middle Ages," excited our expectations. To a man of Mr. Buckle's industry, the hundreds of folios in which the historical works of the Middle Ages are contained offer a splendid and inexhaustible field for the exhibition of his powers of research. Here was to be found, in the history of European civilisation for a thousand years, the secret of its subsequent progress. But Mr. Buckle's method is the same here as elsewhere. He shows himself acquainted with just half a dozen of the commonest mediæval historians ; and these, if we remember rightly, with only one exception, all English. On the other hand, whatever

is to be found about them in the most ordinary books—
Hallam, Warton, Turner, Palgrave, Wright, etc. — is
diligently repeated. The vulgar practice of reading the
books one is to write about was beneath so great a
philosopher. He has read about them, but very little in
them. They could not greatly attract him ; for the
Middle Ages must be a mere blank to one who writes the
history of modern civilisation without taking into account
the two elements of which it is chiefly composed—the
civilisation of antiquity, and the Christian religion.
Having to utter a few generalities upon the subject, it
was obviously more convenient to know nothing about it,
and to take counsel of a few writers who knew very little
about it, than to run the risk of finding an imprudent
curiosity rewarded by the unexpected discovery of
unpalatable and inflexible facts. This safe and timely
ignorance, which he has discreetly cherished and preserved,
has made him fully competent to declare " that not only
was no history written before the end of the sixteenth
century, but that the state of society was such as to make
it impossible for one to be written " (p. 299).

Agreeably to the materialistic character of his
philosophy, Mr. Buckle examines with special pre-
dilection the physical causes which influence mankind.
His second chapter, which is devoted to this inquiry, is
the most interesting and elaborate part of the volume.
In these regions he is somewhat more at home. It is
but an act of justice, therefore, to give some attention to
this chapter. Nowhere do the ignorance and incapacity
of the author more visibly appear.

The subject here treated has very recently been raised
to the dignity of a separate and distinct science ; and it
has been cultivated on the Continent with extraordinary
zeal and success. In no department was so much
assistance to be derived from contemporary writers.
Ritter, the founder of the science of comparative
geography, began forty years ago the great work of
which he has not yet finished even the Asiatic portion.
He was the first among the moderns to determine in detail

the connection of the material world with the history of man. In his footsteps a numerous school of writers have followed—Rougemont, Mendelssohn, Knapp, etc.,— and a variety of able writers have made it a popular study.

As Ritter first established a bridge between history and geography, the link between geology and history was discovered by the Saxon geologist Cotta. Another branch of the same subject—the connection between the vegetable world and the civilisation of man—has been treated by the celebrated botanist, Unger of Vienna.[1] Finally, Professor Volz[2] has produced a most learned work on the influence of the domestic animals and plants on the progress of civilisation. Yet Mr. Buckle is totally ignorant of the writings and discoveries of these men ; and he has therefore written a dissertation which not only does not exhaust the subject, but is of no value whatever at the present day.

The proposition that out of Europe civilisation is dependent chiefly upon physical causes, and man subordinate to nature, is proved, among other examples, by that of Egypt (p. 44). The instance is infelicitous, inasmuch as it is cited by Ritter in support of precisely the contrary view.[3] The original inhabitants of the valley of the Nile were not better off or more civilised than their neighbours in the deserts of Libya and Arabia.

It was by the intelligence of the remarkable people who settled there that Egypt became the richest granary of the ancient world. The inundation of the Nile was rendered a source of fertility by the skill of those who made use of it. But when the vigour of the nation died away under the wretched government which succeeded upon the fall of Rome, that fertile valley relapsed in great measure into its old sterility ; the Thebais became a desert, and the Mareotis a marsh. Instead of proving Mr. Buckle's case, Egypt is the best instance of the subordination of nature to the intellect and will of man.

[1] *Botanische Streifzüge auf dem Gebiete der Culturgeschichte.*
[2] *Beiträge zur Culturgeschichte.*
[3] "Ueber das historische Element in der geographischen Wissenschaft," 1833, in his *Abhandlungen*, p. 165.

Pursuing his idea of the influence of the aspect of nature on man, Mr. Buckle, who has a theory for everything, discovers that the cause of Catholicism lies in earthquakes :—

" The peculiar province of the imagination," he informs us, " being to deal with the unknown, every event which is unexplained as well as important, is a direct stimulus to our imaginative faculties. . . . Earthquakes and volcanic eruptions are more frequent and more destructive in Italy and in the Spanish and Portuguese Peninsula than in any other of the great countries, and it is precisely there that superstition is most rife, and the superstitious classes most powerful. Those were the countries where the clergy first established their authority, where the worst corruptions of Christianity took place, and where superstition has during the longest period retained the firmest hold."

In other words, sequence is cause, as Hume proves ; whence *post hoc, ergo propter hoc,* the great logical principle of the positivists.   But increase of Popery follows increase of earthquakes ; therefore, the consequence is clear.   And not only is Christianity extracted out of earthquakes, but also, by a similar chemistry, Providence is derived from the plague.

Our ignorance about another life, he says, is complete :—

On this subject the reason is perfectly silent ; the imagination, therefore, is uncontrolled. . . . The vulgar universally ascribe to the intervention of the Deity those diseases which are peculiarly fatal. The opinion that pestilence is a manifestation of the Divine anger, though it has long been dying away, is by no means extinct, even in the most civilised countries.   Superstitions of this kind will, of course, be strongest either where medical knowledge is most backward, or where disease is most abundant.

It is in tropical climates that nature is most terrible ; and here, says our author, " imagination runs riot, and religion is founded on fear ; while in Europe nature is subject to man, and reason rules supreme."   This theme he illustrates by the extreme instances of India and Greece ; and he generalises his conclusions into the statement that " the tendency of Asiatic civilisation was to widen the distance between men and their deities ; the tendency of Greek civilisation was to diminish it." Hence " in Greece we for the first time meet with hero-worship, that is, the deification of mortals "; this could not take place in tropical countries. "It is therefore natural that it should form no part of the ancient Indian religion ; neither was it known to the Egyptians, nor to the Persians, nor, so far as I am aware, to the Arabians "; but it was part of the national religion of Greece, and has been found so natural to Europeans, that "the same custom was afterwards renewed with eminent success by the Romish Church."

Perhaps no writer of pretension ever made a more disgraceful exhibition of ignorance and unreason than Mr. Buckle in these passages. Unreason : for if the Catholic cultus of saints is to be identified with the Greek deification of heroes, then certainly this deification is not simply European ; it is as natural to the Indian Catholic as to the Italian or German, not to mention the Orientals. Exactly the same thing is found in Mahometanism, wherever it spreads. If Allah alone receives divine honours, anyhow the chief cultus is paid to the tomb of the prophet, and to the graves of the various holy person-ages with which Moslem countries are so thickly studded. But if this cultus is not what Mr. Buckle meant by the Greek hero-worship, then his mention of the Catholic practice is invidious, impertinent, and utterly irrelevant to his argument. Ignorance : for the "deification of mortals," so far from forming no part of the ancient Indian and Egyptian religions, was their very central idea and foundation. The fearful, terrible gods that Mr. Buckle's imagination is so full of, were only elemental deities, rising and falling with the world, destined to be annihilated ; while the human soul was to last for ever, and was in its essence superior to all those beings that kept it in a tedious but temporary thraldom. The whole idea of the Vedas is the power of the Brahmin over the elemental deities, exerted by means of the sacrifice. The deities in question, though vast in power and wonderfully large, are by themselves undefined and vague ; they want personality, and therefore require personal direction ; though they are in some sense universal intellect and

Z

soul, yet they are formless and void ; they are mere
blunderers till they are directed by the more sure intelligence of minds akin to those of man.   Hence, in the
Vedantic genesis of things, the elemental deities are the
matter of forces which compose the universe ; while the
intelligent agents who conduct the creative process are
the seven primeval sages, Rishis, or Manus, whose very
name attests their human nature.[1]   It is by the sacrifice
of these Rishis, and by the metres they chanted, that the
mundane deities received their place and office in the
world ; and, what is more, the sacrifices of the Vedantic
religion are all identified with this primitive creative
offering.   The seven priests who offer the Soma sacrifice,
so often mentioned in the hymns, are only the successors
of the primitive Rishis or Angiras, whose work they carry
on.   The Sama Veda was their ritual ; and they pretended that this ceremonial was necessary for the preservation of the universe, by continuing the action of the
seven creative forces which first formed the world.   In
the more modern system of the Puranas the same agency
is found.   The world is successively destroyed and re-
constructed ; there are seven such revolutions each day of
Brahma, and each time the world is restored by a Manu
and seven attendant Rishis.   Here, instead of the sub-
serviency of man to nature, we have the inferiority of
nature to man, and the deification of men in as exaggerated a form as can possibly be conceived.   The
same may be said of the Buddhist system ; the seven
human Buddhas are successively the great rulers of the
universe.   And here the facts are so directly contrary to
Mr. Buckle's crude speculations, that in the very country
where nature is most intractable, and where natural forces
exert the most terrific influence on man—in the great
frozen plateau of Thibet—there the deification of man is
carried to the farthest extent, and the Grand Llama, or
living Buddha, is actually identified with the Supreme
God.   With regard to the Egyptians, Mr. Buckle founds

[1] See the fable of Purusha, *Rig Veda*, lib. viii. cap. iv., hymns 17, 18, 19 ;
and *Yadjur Veda*, cap. xxxi.

a hasty conclusion on a few words of Herodotus, and cares nothing for the universal and most ancient worship of Osiris, the human god, with whom every man is identified at death in the ritual. In Egypt the human soul, or man, was superior to the elemental deities. " I am your lord," says the soul to the mundane gods in a monumental inscription :[1] "Come and do homage to me ; for you belong to me in right of my divine father." The same doctrine may be found in the Egypto-Gnostic lubrications of the pseudo-Hermes Trismegistus. In the Persian system, Mithra seems to have held a place somewhat similar to that of Osiris in Egypt. At any rate, so far from its being true that the deification of mortals was unknown, the fact is, that the king assumed successively the insignia of each of the seven planets, and was adored by the people as the incarnate presence of each.[2] Of the ancient Arabian religion, Mr. Buckle professes his ignorance ; the name, therefore, is only inserted to swell his catalogue to the eye, without any corresponding increase in the value of his induction. As we have shown each of his other assertions to be exactly the contrary of the truth, we need not trouble ourselves with disproving one that he owns to be a mere guess. In a later page he says, that in Central America, as in India, the national religion was "a system of complete and unmitigated terror. Neither there, nor in Mexico, nor in Peru, nor in Egypt, did the people desire to represent their deities in human forms, or ascribe to them human attributes." On the contrary, we can prove, in all these countries, the gods —at least the human-formed gods—are in sculptures only distinguishable from men by the addition of their respective symbols ; while, on the other hand, the Egyptian kings and queens are continually represented by the characters of the various gods and goddesses whom they patronised. As to human attributes being ascribed to these gods, it is more difficult to prove this point against Mr. Buckle from the scarcity of poetical legends. But he will find his negative still harder to prove against us. In

[1] Champollion, *Grammaire*, p. 285.   [2] Dabistan, p. 42.

Mexico, the progenitors of our race, Cihuacohuatl (the woman-serpent, or mother of our flesh) and her husband, are placed among the thirteen great gods; and, as such, take precedence of all the elemental deities, coming next after Tezatlipoca, the creator, and Ometeuctli and his wife, the progenitors of the heroes. In Peru the Aztec sovereign was, as in Egypt, worshipped as the sun. Again, Mr. Buckle's principle is as false as his facts. Religious terrorism is in direct proportion to the humanitarianism of a religion. As among men, according to Mr. Mill, and therefore according to Mr. Buckle, cruelty is in proportion to inequality—as the despot sheds more blood than the constitutional sovereign, and as the despot by divine right, who claims not only the civil homage but the religious veneration of his people, is obliged to be more severe than the mere military adventurer; so, when we go a step further, and raise a living man, or a caste, into the place of God, we are obliged to hedge them round with a fence of the most bloody rites and laws. The real cause of Brahmin and Mexican cruelty was not because the Divine nature was so separated from mankind, but because it was so identified with a certain class of men, that this class was obliged to maintain its position by a system of unmitigated terrorism. The farther we remove God from humanity, the less we care about Him. We could not fancy an Epicurean fighting in defence of his indolent deities. As a general rule, those who persecute are willing to suffer persecution, we cannot fancy anybody willing to suffer in defence of an abstract divinity: hence we suppose that the more abstract, intangible, and unreal a religion is, the less cruelty will be perpetrated in its name. This, it appears to us, is the true account of the cruelties of the religions Mr. Buckle enumerates, and not the mere influence of climate and the aspects of nature.

The origin of Mr. Buckle's mistakes here, as in other subjects, is his learned ignorance. He never goes to the best authorities; he scarcely ever consults the originals. If he had given himself the trouble to read and understand the Vedas, which he so ostentatiously quotes at second-hand, the Puranas, the collections of Egyptian monumental inscriptions, the Zendavesta, and to understand the documents about America by M'Culloch, he might have given a rather more rational account of the religions which he pretends to philosophise upon.

In the same unlucky chapter Mr. Buckle declares, what on his principles was inevitable, that "original distinctions of race are altogether hypothetical " (p. 36) ; in support of which view that eminent positivist Mr. Mill is very properly quoted. As we have to deal now with Mr. Buckle's false learning rather than with his false theories, we can only glance at this great absurdity. For the same race of men preserves its character, not only in every region of the world, but in every period of history, in spite of moral as well as physical influences. Were not the Semitic races everywhere and always monotheists ; whilst Japhetic nations, from Hindostan to Scandinavia, were originally pantheists or polytheists. Epic poetry, again, is distinctive of the Indo-Germanic race alone. The most amusing example of a nation's fidelity to the character which it obtained on its first appearance in history is afforded by France. Lasaulx has collected the judgments of the ancients upon the Gauls : " Gallia," said Cato, "duas res industriosissime persequitur, rem militarem et argute loqui. Mobilitate et levitate animi novis imperiis studebant" (*Caesar, B. G.* ii. 1). "Omnes fere Gallos novis rebus studere et ad bellum mobiliter celeriterque excitari" (*Ibid.* iii. 10). "Sunt in consiliis capiendis mobiles, et novis plerumque rebus student" (*Ibid.* iv. 5). "Galli quibus insitum est esse leves" (*Trebellius Pollio Galien.* 4). "Gens hominum inquietissima et avida semper vel faciendi principis vel imperii" (*Flavius Vopiscus Saturninus,* 7).[1]

---

[1] "Gaul pursues two things with immense industry,—military matters and neat speaking." "Through instability and levity of mind they were meditating the overthrow of the government." "Almost all men of Gaul are revolutionists, and are easily and quickly excited to war." "In council they are unstable, and generally revolutionary." "The French, to whom levity is natural. A most restless kind of men, always wanting to set up a king or an empire."

But we must conclude. We have said quite enough to show that Mr. Buckle's learning is as false as his theory, and that the ostentation of his slovenly erudition is but an artifice of ignorance. In his laborious endeavour to degrade the history of mankind, and of the dealings of God with man, to the level of one of the natural sciences, he has stripped it of its philosophical, of its divine, and even of its human character and interest.

When an able and learned work appears, proclaiming new light and increase of knowledge to the world, the first question is not so much whether it was written in the service of religion, as whether it contains any elements which may be made to serve religion. A book is not necessarily either dangerous or contemptible because it is inspired by hatred of the Church. " Nemo inveniret, quia nemo discuteret, nisi pulsantibus calumniatoribus. Cum enim haeretici calumniantur, parvuli perturbantur. . . . Negligentius enim veritas quaereretur, si mendaces adversarios non haberet "[1] (Augustin, *Sermones ad Populum*, lib. xi.). Theodore of Mopsuestia, Julian of Eclanum, Calvin, and Strauss, have not been without their usefulness. An able adversary, sincere in his error and skilful in maintaining it, is in the long-run a boon to the cause of religion. The greatness of the error is the measure of the triumph of truth. The intellectual armour with which the doctrine of the Church is assailed becomes the trophy of her victory. All her battles are defensive, but they all terminate in conquest.

The mental lethargy of the last generation of English Catholics was due perhaps not a little to the very feebleness of their adversaries. When a formidable assailant arose at Oxford, he found an adversary amongst us who was equal to the argument. In like manner, when the Duke of Wellington was the no-popery champion of Toryism, a very sufficient opponent appeared in the person of O'Connell. And now that Mr. Spooner is the repre-

---

[1] No one would discover, for no one would discuss, unless roused by the blows of misrepresentation. For while heretics misrepresent, the little ones are scandalised. . . . Truth would not be sought so industriously, if it had no enemies to tell lies of it.

sentative of anti-Catholic politics, by a similar admirable dispensation and fitness of things he too finds among Catholic statesmen foemen who are worthy of his steel.

It is not, however, on such grounds as these that Mr. Buckle had a claim on our attention. He is neither wise himself, nor likely to be the cause of wisdom in others ; and with him

Bella geri placuit nullos habitura triumphos : [1]

for we could not allow a book to pass without notice into general circulation and popularity which is written in an impious and degrading spirit, redeemed by no superiority or modesty of learning, by no earnest love of truth, and by no open dealing with opponents.

We may rejoice that the true character of an infidel philosophy has been brought to light by the monstrous and absurd results to which it has led this writer, who has succeeded in extending its principles to the history of civilisation only at the sacrifice of every quality which makes a history great.

[1] We understand a war where victory is no triumph.

XII

GERMAN SCHOOLS OF HISTORY[1]

MACAULAY once lamented that there were no German historians in his time worthy of the name; and now M. Darmesteter tells us that they are ahead of other nations by twenty years. A perplexed person might read Professor Wegele's *Deutsche Historiographie*[2] without being quite sure which is right. Nine-tenths of his volume are devoted to the brave men who lived before Agamemnon, and the chapter on the rise of historical science, the only one which is meant for mankind, begins at page 975, and is the last. Before this century the Germans had scarcely reached the common level even in the storage of erudition. Their provincial histories could not be compared with those of Burgundy, of Brittany, or of Languedoc; they had nothing equal to the Annals of Bologna or of Milan, to Mamachi's *Life of Saint Dominic*, or even to Secousse's *Charles of Navarre*. History was subordinate to other things, to divinity, philosophy, and law; and the story worth telling would be the process of emancipation by which the servant of many masters rose to be a master over them, and having become a law to itself imposed it on others. The beginning was made by Niebuhr, and none of those who followed and strengthened the powerful impulse which he gave rival the best of their countrymen in perspicuity and grace.

When Germans assert that their real supremacy rests with their historians, they mean it in the sense of Bentley

[1] *English Historical Review*, 1886, vol. i.
[2] *Geschichte der deutschen Historiographie*. Von Dr. Franz X. von Wegele. Munich: Oldenbourg, 1885.

and Colebrooke, not of Machiavelli and Saint-Simon, in
the sense in which the Bishop of Durham [1] and Sir Henry
Maine take the lead in England, the sense in which
M. Fustel de Coulanges calls history the most arduous of
the sciences.   A famous scholar, enumerating the models
of historical excellence, named Humboldt, Savigny,
Grimm, and Ritter, not one of whom had ever written
history proper, in the common, classical, literary use of
the term.

The better part of the ground has been occupied
already by those who have celebrated German achievement in other branches of literature.   Neander, Böckh,
Baur, Schwegler, Lassen have their record elsewhere.
Excepting Niebuhr and Ranke, Professor Wegele has had
to deprive himself of his best materials.   The division of
labour removes almost every man who was an historian
and something more.

Historical writing was old, but historical thinking was
new in Germany when it sprang from the shock of the
French Revolution.   Condemnation of history had been
the strongest plank in the platform of 1789.   The evils
exposed in the *cahiers* were not accidents of the age, but
the bequest of malignant forces at work for centuries.
Irresponsible power, the caprice of war, slavery, intolerance, arbitrary arrest, the deadly prison, the inhuman
aggravation of the pains of death, had been the steady
produce of elaborate design.   The men who struck at the
misery inflicted by traditional authority believed no dogma
so firmly as that of the folly of their ancestors.   The
supreme object of their striving was to depose and to
degrade a tyrant who, at his best, was blind and ignorant
and cruel, and who, moreover, was dead.   Their sternest
resolve was that generations of astrologers, sorcerers, and
torturers, of legislators unable to read, of sovereigns only
able to kill, that the wisdom of the *code noir* and the
statute book of George II. should not be suffered to reign
over Watt and Hunter, over Lavoisier and Laplace, Smith
and Kant ; and the most vigorous of the revolutionary

[1] Dr. Lightfoot.

thinkers, Jefferson and Sieyès, studied both to banish the past and to prevent the present from again overshadowing the future.   It was under this flag that the armies conquered Germany, destroying and transforming, and left no institution standing but the monarchy of Frederic the Great.

The romantic reaction which began with the invasion of 1794 was the revolt of outraged history.   The nation fortified itself against the new ideas by calling up the old, and made the ages of faith and of imagination a defence from the age of reason.   Whereas the pagan Renaissance was the artificial resurrection of a world long buried, the romantic Renaissance revived the natural order and restored the broken links from end to end.   It inculcated sympathy with what is past, unlovable, indefensible, especially with the age of twilight and scenes favourable to the faculties which the calculators despised.   The romantic writers relieved present need with all the abounding treasure of other times, subjecting thereby the will and the conscience of the living to the will and conscience of the dead.   Their lasting influence was out of proportion to their immediate performance.   They were weak because they wanted strictness and accuracy, and never perceived that the Revolution was itself historic, having roots that could be profitably traced far back in the ages.   But they were strong by the recovery of lost knowledge, and by making it possible to understand, to appreciate, and even to admire things which the judgment of rationalism condemned in the mass of worthless and indiscriminate error.   They trifled for a time with fancy, but they doubled the horizon of Europe.   They admitted India to an equality with Greece, mediæval Rome with classical; and the thoughts they set in motion produced Creuzer's *Comparative Mythology* and Bopp's *Conjugations*, Grimm's enthusiasm for the liberty and belief of Odin's worshippers, and Otfried Müller's zeal for the factor of race.

As long as the romantics were a literary school, running æsthetical canons in opposition to Goethe, they remained unconscious of the active principle within. Dante and Calderon, Nibelungen and Sakuntala, were not so near the core as Burke's maxim that wisdom and religion dictate that we should follow events, and not attempt to lead, much less to force them. When their ideas came to be taken up by reasoners, they were found to involve a system of scientific definitions charged with interminable consequences. Their philosopher was Schelling, who married Schlegel's wife, and who, condensing the vapour of the school into something like solid propositions, taught that the State does not exist for purposes of men, and is not governed by laws of their devising, but by the cosmic force above.

Upon this aphorism, Savigny, the jurist of the party, developed the historic method of jurisprudence. The sovereign legislator is not the government, but the nation. Law, like language, proceeds from its primitive nature and its experience and is part of its identity. The deliberations of lawgiving consist in ascertaining not what is best, but what is consistent with usage. Laws are found, not made, for the treatment adapted to successive emergencies is already latent in the public conscience, and must be evolved from precedent. Laws and constitutions expand by sustenance drawn from the constant and original spring ; the force preparing the future is the same that made the past, and the function of the jurist is to trace and to obey it faithfully, without attempting to explain it away.

Learning and eloquence long effectually concealed the logical effect of this doctrine. It assorted so well with the spirit of the age that it predominated for half a century against Bentham, and Hegel, and the year 1848, and is yielding slowly to the keener dialectics and deeper philosophy of Ihering. It is the strongest of all the agencies that have directed German effort towards history, viewed as a remedy for the eighteenth century and the malady of vain speculation. When Laboulaye described it as a school that had no masters in France and only one disciple, who was himself, it was controlling Germany.

In the mind of Savigny and his followers their doctrine made for progress and independence, but not for liberty. The notion that each generation of men is powerless over its own fortunes, and receives them subject to inherited conditions, combined well with the rooted conservatism of the country.   But it possessed that property of the works of genius, that it could be carried out in opposite directions.   If the nation is the source of law, it is reasonable to infer that national consent is a normal element in legislation, and that the State ought legitimately to take its limits from the nation.   Niebuhr, in unguarded moments, drew one of these inferences, and Dahlmann the other.   And it came to pass that the historical school, having abolished the law of nature which was the motive of 1789, instituted the law of nationality, which became the motive of 1848.

Bishop Stubbs informs us that history is likely to make men wise, and is sure to make them sad.   In the long chapter of the melancholy historians no figure is more tragic than Niebuhr, the politician, as Savigny was the civilian, of the school.   He had flashes of admiration for the English Government as it appeared under Eldonian auspices ; but when the world went off the ancient ways, he lost his temper and his spirits, and his end was a warning to weaker men to keep their studies apart from the hopes and fears of life.   Had he survived, he would have been what Radowitz became, the king's intimate adviser.   The inflexible qualities which repelled his colleagues and spoilt him for a statesman fitted him for a critical historian.   His passion for truthfulness was such that he defied Stein to show that he had ever subscribed himself the obedient servant of a man he did not respect. With his high notions there was no writer whom he could trust, and neither ancient nor modern veracity could stand before him.

The first edition of his *Roman History*, afterwards repudiated, began the evolution of historic science.   It exhibited the theory that truth is not buried underneath tradition—that, although the Romans had forgotten the

early state of their institutions, the processes of history
are so well defined that it is possible to work back from
the known to the unknown, from effect to cause, and so
to recover the unrecorded past.   This was the visible sign
of the new doctrine of fixed lines, invariable laws, and
overruled action of men.   It indicated a mode of certainty which did not depend on the credit of historians.
When they have been tested to the breaking-point, the
critic comes in and begins his proper work.   The right
sphere of these operations is the primitive obscurity.
They could not flourish in the daylight, and Niebuhr
never showed that he knew how to apply them to events
and characters told by contemporaries.   When he filled
the meagre outline of Manlius by transferring to him the
character of Mirabeau, he gave the example which Stanley
followed when he put Lord Shaftesbury into the Reformation, and Mr. Golightly into the Jewish monarchy.   The
weighty volumes, crowded with doubtful but suggestive
matter, won so little popular success that he laid them by
for many years.   When he rewrote them, under the spur
of contradiction, and in the midst of a vigorous intellectual
movement which was partly his work, they found less
favour than the finished productions of Savigny.   The
historical school penetrated everywhere and remodelled
every branch of legal study excepting ecclesiastical and
comparative law, which resisted the national principle.
But the work of Niebuhr's life stood still.   There was a
temporary reaction in favour of Roman views of Roman
history ; and he had been dead for twenty years before
he began to be superseded by innovators bolder and
better appointed than himself.   Schwegler's early death
deprived Germany of the one man who combined real
philosophic talent with the rarest critical faculty.   Mommsen, whose book was begun at the same time as Schwegler's,
realised that union of qualities which Macaulay described
when he said that Niebuhr would have been the first
writer of his time if his talent for communicating truths
had borne any proportion to his talent for investigating
them.

The fruit of the *Roman History* ripened for Greece. The men who made it known in this country were Thirlwall and Grote ; it sent Otfried Müller to historical studies ; and Böckh dedicated to Niebuhr a work which has stood the test of time better than his own.   Under the powerful sway which Böckh exercised in Prussia for fifty years, Hellenic studies obtained the lead.   A deeper scholar than Niebuhr, an historian, which the Saxon philologists disdained to be, he abandoned Rome to jurists and politicians, and primitive times to romantic theorists. His own taste was for the hardest possible facts and the clearest proofs.   Like Niebuhr, he believed that antiquity is covered over with error, which will shrivel like a parched scroll, and that hidden truth will be brought to light. But instead of the incommunicable genius of conjecture he set to work with a new organon, and substituted improved evidence for dazzling guesswork.

Inscriptions had been always a source of dire con- fusion, for it paid local antiquaries to forge them, and two hundred consuls were invented by a single impostor. Niebuhr dismissed this branch of inquiry wholesale, saying that nobody could be expected to master it. Böckh showed that it could be made an instrument of discovery as efficacious as the boldest ingenuity, and it became, in his firm and patient hands, the corner-stone of the building.   Besides showing the way of reaching truth even beyond Thucydides, he was an illustrious example of the historian who puts himself out of sight and displays what is certain, suppressing rigidly his personal senti- ments.   The tone of elegiac and cathartic poetry is one thing : the epic tone is another.   After hearing his course on ancient philosophy, I asked him why his lectures were more interesting than his books.   Böckh answered benignly, " Because I give my finished researches to the public, and keep my own views (*die ideale Anschauung*) for the students."

The *Public Economy of the Athenians* is almost the only history produced before the critical epoch which still stands, unshaken and erect.   The critical epoch lies between 1824 and 1828.   To mark the distinction between what was planted in those five years and the wild growth that preceded them, is half the work that Professor Wegele had to do.

In natural gifts and in acquirements the earlier writers were not, upon the whole, inferior to those who, with better opportunities, have made them a prey to dumb forgetfulness.   It is matter of legendary notoriety that Schlosser consumed so many thousand volumes in a given time.   The *Symbolik* of his colleague Creuzer is a mine of learning animated with ideas.   Voigt was among the first who, either from the easy indifference of rationalism or from the manifold interest of romanticism, released the mediæval Papacy from the dilemma of good or bad.   Few of those who have come since Luden can write so well.   Raumer earned the praise of having written readably on the Middle Ages, and made it known that there was much to be learnt from the Italians.   Many writers of this epoch had qualities not cultivated afterwards by men of sterner stuff, and addressed their style to readers less learned than themselves, who preferred a clean text to perpetual dissertation.   All the works of Schlosser deserve the malediction which Mr. Morley pronounced on one of them ; yet there was a blunt integrity about him, and his influence upon men so superior to himself as Gervinus, Rothe, and Bernhardi proves, what his writings do not, that he possessed some higher quality.   Luden made a name for patriotism ; and Raumer was a liberal, often in tepid water for his opinions. Of the three periods into which the attitude of Germans towards the Middle Ages has been distributed,—the contemptuous, the admiring, and the intelligent, these men generally represent the second.   In point of trust-worthiness they are near the level of their French contemporaries ; of Thierry amplifying *Ivanhoe*, Barante transcribing Monstrelet, and Michaud flogging all the dead horses of the First Crusade.   Waitz and Leo said of them that they could read texts but never studied them ; and they stand condemned as men who did not know how to distinguish authentic knowledge from second-hand, and were at the mercy of their informants. They are gathered to the geographers who made charts before Columbus.

A new art of employing authorities came in with Ranke in 1824. Müller's *Introduction to the Science of Mythology* quickly followed ; Gieseler and Neander began their histories of the Church ; and Menzel, after an inferior book on the Middle Ages, published the first volume of what was long the best modern history of Germany. Niebuhr prepared the new edition, which is the pillar of his fame, in 1827 ; and in 1828 Stenzel adapted to the Gregorian epoch the canons of criticism which Ranke had made obligatory on every serious writer. These seven or eight works were the symptom of a great transition.

Ranke has not only written a larger number of mostly excellent books than any man that ever lived, but he has taken pains from the first to explain how the thing is done. He attained a position unparalleled in literature, less by the display of extraordinary faculties than by perfect mastery of the secret of his craft, and that secret he has always made it his business to impart. For his most eminent predecessors, history was applied politics, fluid law, religion exemplified, or the school of patriotism. Ranke was the first German to pursue it for no purpose but its own. He tried to make the generality of educated men understand how it came about that the world of the fifteenth century was changed into the Europe of the nineteenth. His own definite persuasions regarding church and king were not suffered to permeate his books. It was meritorious in Böckh, but not heroic, to contain his feelings about the Attic treasure and the setting of Arcturus ; but Ranke was concerned with all the materials of abiding conflict, with every cause for which he cared and men are willing to kill or die.

He expects no professional knowledge in his readers, and never writes for specialists. He seldom probes to the bottom the problems of public life and the characters of men, and passes dryshod over much that is in dispute.

As he writes history, not biography, he abstains from the secrets of private life ; and as he writes history, not dogma, he never sorts men into black and white according to their bearing in vital controversies. His evil-doers escape the just rigour of the law, and he avoids hero-worship as the last ditch of prehistoric prejudice. He touches lightly on matters pertaining to the jurist and divine, but he has not their exclusiveness. His surface is more level than theirs, but his horizon is wider. The cup is not drained ; part of the story is left untold ; and the world is much better and very much worse than he chooses to say.

Ranke was profoundly influenced by Niebuhr ; and the example of so wise a man sinking under the load of political disappointment impressed him with the belief that it is well for people generally to disconnect their scientific and their practical life. Niebuhr's treatment of history required men as able as himself, and as familiar with the play of institutions, but boded disaster in weaker hands. Ranke brought his art down to a lower capacity. In the preliminary measure of testing authorities, he showed that it is possible, by careful analysis, to learn whence a writer obtains his facts ; and this part of the work is often almost mechanical. It depresses the study of history to a level with the collation of texts, and admits a large and useful body of workers who would make a mess of the three first Muses, or the first decade of Livy.

The task of analysing character is more complicated. There is a peculiarity about the revision of historians that excludes them from the benefit of the common law that innocence must be assumed until guilt is proved. The presumption which is favourable to makers of history is adverse to writers of history. For history deals considerably with hanging matter, and nobody ought to hang on damaged testimony. The life of the witness must be subjected to closer scrutiny than the life of the culprit. He is condemned when he is suspected ; doubt is decisive against him. When Father Paul relates that Luther's arguments were thought to be unanswerable at the court of Rome, but were resisted in order that authority might be upheld, he appeals to the diary of Chieregato, which has not been produced. The story, therefore, stands and falls with his own credibility. Nobody has a right to adopt it who is not able to vindicate the character of Sarpi. There is a test of credibility, and consequently a rule of right and wrong, which everybody must acknowledge, because without it there is no such thing as evidence, and the code which is applied to books applies to events. The maxims by which we judge the statements of Cæsar or of Clarendon enable us to judge their actions. The principles are the same, though the rigour in employing them is unequal.

True impartiality is no respecter of persons, and judges resolutely regardless of the judgment of others. Ranke's merciful abstinence from strong language, his reserve in passing sentence, correspond to two governing facts in the movement to which he belongs. Germans, like other people, have certain hereditary landmarks not good to disturb, certain names too closely associated with national glory to be exposed to profanation. Luther is one of them, and Frederic, and Goethe. Döllinger's double-edged saying, that the nation recognises its own nature in Luther (*ihr potenzirtes Selbst*), became popular; and the passionate temper of the Reformation tracts no more repels his countrymen than the violence of More, of Milton, or of Grattan interferes with their credit here. Gratitude to the king, pride in the poet, tell in the same way to exclude the vulgar standard and to check unruly speech touching such matters as divine right, arbitrary power, and ethical neutrality. There is, if not depreciation of the moral currency, impatience of the language men utter in censuring equals. The public feels a shock of incongruity when the President of the Bavarian Academy accuses an emperor of the murder of a Bavarian prince, or when Dahlmann crudely says that the sovereigns who divided Poland were as guilty as the Terrorists.

The infallible conscience, the universal and unwritten law, the principles of eternal justice, are precisely those eighteenth-century phantoms against which the romantic and historical school rose in defiance. The belief that men carry about them the knowledge of good and evil is the very root of revolution. Those who, in the words of De Maistre and the Prussian conservatives, desired, not the counter-Revolution, but the contrary of revolution, decreed that the mighty past shall not be measured by present rules and the categorical imperative. Mankind varies and advances in ethical insight ; the virtue of to-day was once a crime, and the code changes with the latitude. If King James burnt witches, if Machiavelli taught assassination as an art, if pious crusaders slaughtered peaceful Jews, if Ulysses played fast and loose, we are exhorted to remember the times they lived in, and leave them to the judgment of their peers. Mobility in the moral code, subjection of man to environment, indefinite allowance for date and race, are standing formulas from Schlegel to the realistic philosophy.

Although Ranke practises moderation and restraint, and speaks of transactions and occurrences when it would be safe to speak of turpitude and crime, he kept himself above the indifference and the incapable neutrality of those who held, with Gerard Hamilton, that there are few questions on which one may not vote conscientiously either way. This was the infant shape of impartiality. The Italians, said Raumer, justify the cities of Lombardy ; the Germans justify their emperors : both are right and both are wrong. Raumer was not a strong man ; but there were many in his day who admired such abdication as the triumph of fairness, and discarded human responsibility. On a solemn occasion Ranke declared that the modern to whom, after Niebuhr, he was most in debt, was Fichte. Of Fichte's philosophy there is little either in Ranke's sixty volumes or elsewhere now. But as the most advanced apostle, since Butler, of the efficacy of conscience, he opposed submission to impersonal forces, and no doubt strengthened Ranke in his resistance to more than one of his most famous colleagues.

Ranke acquired very early an unrivalled knowledge of historical literature, but towards 1840 he began to say that the last five centuries cannot be understood from printed books only. He did not lead the way to the archives. When an Englishman or Scotsman took a side in the revolution of 1688, he was accustomed to support himself with new documents. Austria was before the rest of Germany ; and Mignet's incomparable fragment on the foreign policy of Lewis XIV. surpassed all that the rest of Europe was doing. At first the narrow opening of archives was not an unmixed boon. The partial use of manuscripts was as misleading as the partial use of books. When Stein planned the *Monumenta*, Gentz avowed the opinion that truth is not always a desirable thing, and a Würzburg professor denounced the under-taking as a scheme of obscuration. 'Tis sixty years since, and now every state reveals its inner life : the Vatican and the *Affaires Étrangères* are as easy of access as the Frari, or the Hofburg under the generous management of Arneth ; the chief archivist of Prussia, after declaring that his country has nothing to conceal, proves his sincerity by the publication of twenty-six volumes ; and Treitschke adds the substantial reason that the enemies of Prussia have told the worst, making concealment at once needless and impossible. Ranke has gone along with the progress which has so vastly extended the range and influence of historians. After starting without manuscripts, and then lightly skimming them, he ended by holding that it is not science to extract modern history from anything less than the entire body of written evidence. Touching which, there are two opinions. One is, that history would be all right but for historians ; that nothing is certain but what is secret and official ; and that no man is so safe to punish as he that is condemned out of his own mouth. Others deem that we cannot realise events without know-ing how they seemed to those who saw them ; that letters deceive as much as memoirs or chronicles ; that rulers of men, not uncommonly, are rogues, provided with a set of false bottoms as a precaution against curious impertinence.

Ranke was at once acknowledged by Niebuhr as the

first of historians, but he did not storm the position. At the university he was outshone by Gans, the mouthpiece of Hegel, and afterwards by Droysen, the mouthpiece of Imperialism. Böhmer, who so much disliked Berlin exports that he could read neither Duncker nor the *Life of Stein*, delighted to quote the description given by satirical students of Ranke lecturing, with his jerky manner, his chin pointing upwards, his fingers catching the air. There was a conspiracy in high quarters to raise up a rival to him in the person of Raumer, whom even Jaffé at first pronounced perfection; whilst Humboldt declared in favour of the Dryasdust grotesquely treated by Carlyle, and abetted the sneers of Varnhagen. Leo used to call Ranke a vase-painter, and denied that truth is hidden in the correspondence of envoys. Gervinus preferred Schlosser; and Droysen, his only rival in influence, derided his flexibility and kinship with the variable romantics. Eichhorn deplored that there was so little to learn from his *Reformation;* Wuttke published a tract against the *Servian History*, and Ritter against his ways generally. Rehm, dimly remembered by the light that shone from his Arabic studies on the Middle Ages, considered his books unfit for a place in the library of Marburg University. Sybel thought him too lenient to Austria; and Reimann accuses him of partiality in the affairs of Poland. Whilst a Prussian conservative complained that he was neither fish nor flesh, a liberal Saxon declared that he was too good a legitimist to master the problems of parliamentary states. His *Memoirs of Hardenberg* have not satisfied critics who knew the inside of the Berlin archives. The *English History* was received with cold but decent respect; and the *Grenzboten* published a hostile article on the first and weakest volume, by Bergenroth, then a new man, unfurnished with a horoscope. It has been a grievance with Villari that Ranke said, and misled Sybel's *Zeitschrift* into repeating, that he had overlooked manuscripts in his own town of Florence, which he, in fact, had cited scores of times. Panizzi objected that one of his books was not

original ; Green, that another was dull.   Macaulay ended
by resenting the threatened invasion of his prerogative, and
was less favourably disposed than in the glowing days of
the purple New Zealander.   There was a brief opposition
from the Catholics.   Höfler attacked the *Popes ;* a garbled
manuscript of the sixteenth century was sent to press for
the diminution of his credit ; and Theiner assured the
King of Bavaria that he had done less than justice to
Gregory XIII.   *Grand talent, petit esprit*, was the adverse
verdict of the *Correspondant.*   The Frenchman might have
defended his point if it was a distant allusion to stature.
When Lord John Russell was on his way to Vienna, it
was reported that Frederic William IV., by a refinement
of flattery, invited four eminent men to meet him who
were all smaller than himself ; and Ranke was one of
them.

He outlived all rivalry, and well-nigh all antagonism.
He lived to hear Arneth declare, before the assembled
historians of the South, that he alone among writers of
prose had furnished a masterpiece to every country.   He
was hailed by Döllinger as *praeceptor Germaniae.*   In his
own home the dissent of militant patriotism was expressed
in the words of Dove, that pure history cannot satisfy the
need of a struggling and travailing nation ; and when
Mommsen says that the only ascertained maxim of
research is that hearsay evidence is as good as the source
it comes from, I understand him to mean that genius is
better than schooling.

In very early days it seemed that philosophy possessed
an adept who would surpass Ranke, and bridge the
afflicting chasm between fact and law.   Leo had belonged
to the most turbulent set of students in the time of Sand,
when he came to Berlin, obtained the friendship of Hegel,
and disparaged Ranke by reviews, and by encroaching on
his domain.   With other men the question is, how they
came to succeed : the wonder in the case of Leo is, how
such abilities contrived to miss not only the first place
but the first rank.   He scorned the tame spirit, the
obscure labours, the negative results of fleshless scholars

whose cares are bounded by scholarship, who aim at no target, and are incurious of things to come. He was always combative, homiletic, clamorous for quick returns, and, like men too eager, verbose and violent. He shed his Hegelian skin in the Middle Ages, and emerged from them detesting the three last centuries as an epoch of selfishness and decay. History became subservient to politics, to a policy of reaction against economists, humanitarians, and all men seeking happiness before authority. Having written too many books not destined to live, he made up his mind to abandon a hemisphere that was going wrong, and set about reducing his baggage and packing all he knew in a traveller's kit. This was the origin of Leo's *Universal History*, still, after half a century, the most thoughtful of the books that bear that ambitious title. What more he did during the restless remainder of his life for royalism and religious union is written in water. He is the most remarkable of all the men who, being partisans where partiality is discredit, failed through the want of discipline. Gfrörer, who was superior to him and perhaps to all men in historic grasp, is equally destitute of authority. But Gfrörer, though the most reckless and unsafe of guides, is as vigorous a stimulant in mediæval study as Germany has possessed, and of the fourteen or fifteen volumes which he wrote from Charlemagne to Hildebrand, not one can be spared.

Without the training and habits of the new school even the learning of Neander fared not much better than the talent of Gfrörer and Leo. He was probably the best-read man living towards 1830 ; and he introduced into the permanent literature of his country a serious spiritual element that was wanting. For the romantic scholars were still incurably tainted with the vice which, outside of morals, bears no harsher name than inaccuracy ; while the church historians in possession considered religion with a professional eye and were more secularly minded than professors of profane arts, such as Lachmann or Carl Ritter. He not only tried to bring within reasonable compass and under the control of ideas what used to straggle through forty-five and even eighty-five volumes, but he was profoundly in earnest ; and it was of him that Tholuck said that the orthodox are generally the most pious.   He had more heart for the interior life of saints than for the border history of Church and State. His knowledge, deep and massive as that of a later Benedictine, was seldom new, and with his traditional habits he was like a ghost in the company of Böckh and Ranke.   Among books which he took faithfully as he found them, deeming with Mr. Freeman that manuscripts begin to be useful after they are printed, many were interpolated, incorrect, assigned to the wrong men.   Schweighäuser's saying that for centuries no real care had been taken of classical texts was almost equally true of ecclesiastical ; and the work of Wolf and Bekker scarcely began for them until Neander was dead.   When the *Annals* of Baronius were reprinted, De Rossi reminded the editor that the primitive church presented no longer the same outlines as in 1567, or in the days of Pagi, and offered, unfortunately in vain, his aid as an annotator. Since Neander a deeper spirit of inquiry has possessed itself of his topic and is working changes as considerable as in all the time since Baronius.   He spent his last days in a forlorn endeavour to trace the Bohemian revolution to Bohemian causes, telling much that nobody knew about a very obscure time.   For, like all men before Shirley, he entirely mistook Wyclif.   In our day Lechler and Arnold, Matthews, Buddensieg, and Loserth have published a new Wyclif, and a new pedigree of Hus, and the same transforming effect of the scientific approaches has befallen or yet awaits every chapter of Neander.

The tendency of the nineteenth-century German to subject all things to the government of intelligible law, and to prefer the simplicity of resistless cause to the confused conflict of free wills, the tendency which Savigny defined and the comparative linguists encouraged, was completed in his own way by Hegel.   He displayed all history by the light of scientific unity, as the manifestation of a single force, whose works are all wise, and whose

latest work is best. The *Volksgeist* of the new jurisprudence was less dazzling than the *Weltgeist* of the new
philosophy, with the smallest allowance of hypothesis for
the largest quantity of phenomena. Science was pro-
pitiated with visions of unity and continuity ; religion, by
the assurance of incessant progress ; politics, by the ratification of the past. Liberty and morality were less well
provided ; but it was the epoch of the Restoration.

An ambiguous use of terms concealed the breach
between pantheism and Christianity so well that the most
learned catholic layman of the time rejoiced at the coming
of a new era for religion. The breach with experimental
science betrayed itself by the contempt for Newton in
which Hegel was of one mind with Goethe and Schelling
and Schopenhauer ; but there were scientific men who, to
the disgust of Humboldt, accepted the *Naturphilosophie.*
Its defects were visible when Hegel's lectures appeared
after his death, and the system went down under the
assault of inductive science. But his influence on historical study has not gone down, and it is the one thing
on which he retains his grasp. The *lex continui* was a
central idea with Leibnitz, who discovered it, for it was
the point in common between his anticipation of Darwin
and his anticipation of Hegel. In the same double sense
it was renewed by Haller, and obtained some superficial
acceptance through Herder, until it came to govern
entirely the Hegelian notion of history.

Hegel did not shine in expounding public transactions,
excepting cases like the French Revolution, where the
individual is swallowed up in the logic of events. He
moved awkwardly in the presence of human agents, and
was unskilled in playing his pawns. The quest of the
vera causa failed with men, but it was beyond measure
successful, away from the world of sense, in explaining
the action and succession of ideas.

The history of philosophy had taken rise before
Hegel was born, and was secreted in books not desti-
tute of plodding merit, but unreasonably dead and dull.
Under the magic wand systems fell into an appointed

and harmonious order: λαμπάδα ἔχοντες διαδώσουσιν ἀλλήλοις. The progress of speculative thought has been made, by less systematic and coercive successors, one of the luminous spots in literature, to the damage and exclusion of more essential things. For the marrow of civilised history is ethical not metaphysical, and the deep underlying cause of action passes through the shape of right and wrong. Hegel did not promote the study of morals, and Germany fell behind the French eclectics, until, in the revolt of the last ten years against utilitarians and materialists, the growth of ethical knowledge has become, for the first time, the supreme object of history.

The main line of the Hegelian succession passed to the divines. It was of the essence of pantheism to transcend national limits and the conditions dear to jurists. Where one considers the British constitution as a plant of Teutonic growth, drawing life from ideas common to all the conquerors of Rome, or traceable to hazy customs on the Elbe, the other accounts it a phase of monarchy, a fragment from a sphere that is above race. In the same way, Hegel regarded Christianity as an episode in a natural process that began before the Christian era, and continued beyond the uttermost boundaries assignable to churches, as one step among many to be taken by mankind. The propositions issuing from this view of religion supply the work of the Tübingen school. They teach that the origin of the Christian faith is in the gradual action of antecedent causes; that it has been substantially true to itself in the formation of dogma, and has accomplished its mission of providing fuel for the flame of a higher philosophy.

On his first acquaintance with Hegel's writings, Strauss ceased to believe, and the motive of his book was to justify his disbelief with arguments derived from the scholarship of the day. But the soil that reared him was philosophic not historic. His reason for rejecting the gospel was metaphysical, though his argument was historical. The newest discovery was that certainty may be attained behind the back of historians, after finding

whence they get their facts and with what mind they
state them.   Strauss renounced the attempt, and denied
the possibility.

But the critical phase, if it did not prompt the *Leben
Jesu*, contributed to its success by encumbering the business of reply.   In those days the Nepaul transcripts were
bewildering Europe with the spectacle of a lasting and
widely spread religion sprung from an obscure and
legendary, if not a mythical origin.   Stapfer, the Swiss
apologist, levying an argument from the lake and the fell,
likened Strauss to the inventor of paradox, who presumed
to doubt the story of William Tell, and was confounded
by the indignant scholarship of Uri.   Just then, that
vivacious ghost was for ever laid by the reverent hand of
a zealous conservative, ultramontane, and patriot, who
exposed the fable and restored the real history of Swiss
independence in a manner which showed that the lessons
of Bonn and Berlin had penetrated to the forest cantons.
A greater man than Stapfer objected to Strauss that
the first century of the Church was too enlightened
for mythology ; but the study of the New Testament
apocrypha, still in its infancy, showed that the apostolic
age was rich in poetic and theological fiction.

The credulity of the last generation was put to a
severe strain.   The clearances went on at a pace that drove
people to despair, and it appeared that the crop of falsehood grew too fast for the reapers.   One is tempted to
suppose that the conspicuous fabrications like those of
Shapira, of Simonides, of the deft deceiver of Chasles,
are exceptional.   It is a new revelation to learn that a
crust of designing fiction covers the truth in every region
of European history.   The most curious of the twenty-
two thousand letters in the correspondence of Napoleon,
that of 28th March 1808, on his Spanish policy, by which
Thiers was taken in, proves to be a forgery, and the
forger is Napoleon.   Whole volumes of spurious letters
of Joseph II., Marie Antoinette, and Ganganelli are still
circulated.   Prince Eugene should be well known to us
through his autobiography, the collection of six hundred

of his letters, and the *Life* by Kausler. But the letters are forged, the *Life* is founded upon them, and the autobiography is by the Prince de Ligne. The letter from the Pruth, which deceived the ablest of the historians of Peter the Great, is as fabulous as his political testament. So too are the *Monita Secreta*, the Life of the Almirante by his son, one of the trials of Savonarola, Daru's acts of the Venetian inquisitors, the most famous of the early Italian chronicles, the most famous of the early privileges and charters of almost every European country. The ancient monuments of Bohemian literature, edited in 1840 by the two best scholars of the Slavonic world, were a very recent imposture; and Saint Cyril, the apostle of the Slavonians, is credited with an account of his own life, a confession of faith, and an introduction to the gospels, none of which are authentic. At his first step in epigraphic science, Mommsen rejected one thousand and three Neapolitan inscriptions.

In the fervour of detection men were tempted to conclude with Goethe that poetry is the only form of truth, and that all history might with advantage go the way of Raleigh's book. The doctrine of the hopeless uncertainty of human testimony recommended the study of ideas instead of events, for we can follow the ideas of Abelard or Descartes under their own undisputed hand, with less risk than the secret councils of kings. A disposition to run riot, not only to doubt where doubt means safety, but to reject where there is only ground for doubting, appeared in several directions: the *Laws* and the *Parmenides* were written by the second Plato; many of the *Odes* were not composed by Horace; and Saint Patrick became an imaginary personage.

This excess prevailed in Germany less widely than is supposed. The restoring purpose, the craving for positive results, grew strong amid the devastation; exaggerated doubt was succeeded by activity in preserving, and the fictions unduly spared outnumber the truths unduly questioned. Methodical doubt had no affinity with a universal scepticism. Niebuhr, unlike Sir George

Lewis, who represents him to us, passionately believed in the resources of his art, accepted the discoveries of Champollion when many hesitated, and looked forward to like results in Assyria, six years before Lassen appeared.   Wolf wished his treatment of Homer to be applied to the Bible, but he stopped far short of the hypothesis of Graf.   In spite of his weighty advocacy, Markland's attack on the *Epistles to Brutus* and the *Four Orations* did not prevail.   Many things which the French reject are accepted by Germans who uphold Buddha against the solar interpretation of Senart, the Pragmatic Sanction of Saint Lewis against the doubts of Paul Viollet, the tables of Malaga and Salpensa against objections which Laboulaye would not abandon until the close of his life.   There is a state paper on the Juliers succession in 1609 which was admitted by Ranke, Droysen, Treitschke, and never disputed until it went to pieces in 1883.   Not very many years ago a monument was erected at Pforzheim by the Baden legislature in commemoration of an event that never occurred ; and the purchase of the Moabite antiquities in 1873, advised by Schlottmann in spite of Ganneau's warning, exhibits the softer side of Prussian criticism and economy.   The eagerness of juniors in urging every element of improbability has been rebuked by the master, Waitz ; and Giesebrecht, the only critical historian of the Middle Ages who is a popular classic, who occupies a moderating position between extremes, is peculiarly cautious against the solicitations of doubt.   His rare mistakes have come from conservative leanings, and he has rescued letters of Sylvester II. denounced by his French editor, has reinstated Lambert as a main authority for Gregory VII. against a host of detractors, and has maintained in the midst of much opposition the *Dictatus* of the pope himself.   The severest repressor of overmuch doubting is Sickel, the prince of critics, who has been able to demonstrate that the skill of the forgers is less than was imagined, and that many pieces suspected thirty years ago were suspected wrongly.   In earlier stages of the progress of knowledge the proper attitude is suspense, and when Maurenbrecher failed to establish the authenticity of Charles V.'s *Commentaries*, he rightly laid them aside until Ranke satisfied him.

While open questions of criticism diminish, new documents raise new problems, and nobody gets the last word.   Much has come lately to light touching the partition of Poland.   Who proposed it?   The answer is continually shifting, and the truth goes farther off.   It was Catharine or Prince Henry in 1771, Bibikoff at Christmas 1770, Joseph II. in July, Wolkonsky in March. It was Count Lynar in 1769, or a mightier personage wearing his mask.   Or it was Kaunitz in 1768, if not Choiseul in the same year.   Panin started the idea in 1766, Czernitcheff or the electress of Saxony in 1763, Lord Stair in 1742, the King of Poland himself in 1732, or the crown prince of Prussia one year earlier.   There is the same difficulty as to the man who shattered the empire of Napoleon by advising the retreat to Moscow. The idea is claimed for Alexander and Count Lieven, for five German officers at least, for the lesson of Torres Vedras, for Barclay, by whom it was executed.   Or again, who was it that induced the allies, in March 1814, to advance on Paris?   For that there are five competitors, a Russian, a Livonian, an Austrian, a Prussian, and a Corsican.   Where we now stand, in the year 60 of renovated history, it does not seem impossible to settle some of these matters.   But things were less clear during the procession of rival witnesses ; and this is one of the elements which made the science of historians seem a solace for the imagination, a gallery of dissolving views, a museum of illusions in which a man of strong convictions was free to take or to leave.   It was under this empire of instability that a group of Wirtemberg divines obtained the lead in critical research and kept it for twenty years.

A theologian who trod the paths of Hegel had lately introduced the study and the name of symbolism.   Men who were not passionately addicted to the solutions of the

sixteenth century were the better for knowing, as a matter
of fact, without ulterior purpose, what it was all about,
and why Erasmus, Luther, Calvin, and Socinus differed.
Marheineke explained it to readers more curious of
historic than dogmatic truth, who could enter heartily
into every system not their own.   Peace had been concluded between Lutheran and Calvinist, and a suspension
of hostilities between Catholic and Protestant ; and it was
the time when a Protestant publisher circulated Stolberg's
Church History, and Schlegel wrote to him : " Let us shake
hands like Christians across the narrow stream between
us."   The first object of the new science was to explain
the division of Christendom, not to justify, and not to heal
it.   The usefulness of this necessary chapter of history
depended on the fidelity of the writer in refusing favour to
his own side ; and when Möhler took care, like Johnson,
that the Whigs should have the worst of it, Marheineke
called his book a treatise of controversy under the name
of symbolism.   The absence of the purely historical spirit
gave Möhler his six editions and his immediate celebrity.
Men came after him who restored the former tone,
indifferent to peace or war.   Koellner, being a Protestant,
wrote an exposition of Catholicism, and, being a Calvinist,
an exposition of Lutheranism, on the plan of describing
them from within ; but the public interest languished.
The steps that had led up to the religious crisis of the
present century were of more vital significance than the
distant and inelastic formulas of the sixteenth.   History,
which already occupied other domains, was laying its hand
on theology, and history is the knowledge of things that
live and move.   The process attracted more than the
definition.   Comparative dogmatics took the place which
had been filled by the narrower treatment, and the history
of Protestant theology was discussed in a series of books
by Dorner and Gass in Germany, and by Schweizer and
Schneckenburger in Switzerland, that carry matters a
good deal beyond the point reached when the conflict
raged round the *Symbolik*.

While the Protestants were interested in tracing

dogmas down to their own day, it was the object of the Catholics to trace them upwards to the seed-time of the Church, in order that what was imputed to them as genuine might be tested by time. The generation of 1830, which in a variety of converging ways assigned the property of growth undetermined by will or wit of man, of development without forfeiture of identity, to the civil law, the academic philosophy, and the Aryan grammar, was not tempted to deny an analogous prerogative to Christianity. The principle had already found a home in the Church, and received new vigour from the mental revolution effected by the anti-revolutionary Germans. When Möhler, moved by the asperities of controversy, left Tübingen to teach ecclesiastical history at Munich, Döllinger made way for him and lectured on divinity. He directed his own historical method on theological system, and exhibited the faith of Christendom at successive stages, so that a man should stand at all the crossways, realise each problem as seen at its rising, and pass in his own mind through the experience of the Church.

The men who, at Munich, were working out the law of development within their communion, lived in acute and unappreciating hostility to the Suabian divine who was digging a theological bed for the teaching of the Suabian philosopher. The real importer of pantheism with its consequences into history, the man who grafted Hegel on Ranke, was Strauss's master, Baur, the colleague whose sarcasms drove Möhler from Tübingen. He was a convert from Creuzer's nebulous method, which looks for analogy and resemblance, and he adopted with uncommon energy the view which denies the supernatural, suspects marvels and coincidences, and adjusts spiritual life to the prosaic level of daily experience. Baur would give no opinion on the *Leben Jesu* until that which had been for ten years the law of profane history was thoroughly applied to sacred. He undertook the work and accomplished it himself, with the aid of those whom he called the critical school, implying that all others are uncritical, and, if they admit dogmatic motives, insincere. His postulates were that the gospels must be examined as profane books are, without presumption of truth, and that space must be given for Christianity to evolve itself from the combination of exceedingly dissimilar elements. According to Baur the business of history is not so much with facts as with ideas ; and the idea, not the fact, of the Resurrection is the basis of the Christian faith. Doctrines are developed out of notions, not out of events. Whether or no the belief is true, he refuses to inquire. In the most characteristic passage ever written by a German historian, he declares that it is a question beyond the scope of history.

The view of the New Testament which the critics of Tübingen built up with an expenditure of intellectual force greater than Strauss had applied to demolition, was too deeply influenced by the specific negations of pantheism to live apart from their esoteric tenets.   What was speculative in their system not only isolated them from the bulk of European science, but brought about divisions, and at last the dispersion of the school.   Wherever their purpose was exclusively historical, they threw much light on matters which have been discussed for centuries ; and their sagacity in the investigation of details has been fruitful for all men.

Their permanent action is less acknowledged in the foundation than in the development of Christianity. Baur's mastery in tracing the march of ideas through the ages, over the heads of men, was a thing new to literature. He maintained that the formation and growth of doctrine is consistent and normal, not accidental or arbitrary ; and the impression made by his histories of the central dogmas appeared in many directions.   Nearly half the books that have been written on dogmatic history came out in a space of six or seven years, under his impulse, and were often the work of men far from sharing his opinions.   The inner circle of Lutheran orthodoxy has adopted from Tübingen the term — the Formation of truth (*das Werden der Wahrheit*), a notion which would have astonished Luther.

2 B

Baur's bitterest adversary was Ewald, whose competence in Old Testament studies was not then contested.
But it is the last and most original of his disciples, a
man better known amongst us than most German writers,
who has set in motion that Mosaic controversy which has
so much analogy with the views of Tübingen.   From the
days when he mingled imprecations against Gesenius with
his prayers until he denounced the *Culturkampf*, Ewald
had been steeped in dissent, and his fame had suffered
diminution before the treason of Wellhausen.

The low political vitality of the Thirty Years' Peace
was favourable to calm studies.   It was the time when
Goethe was amazed that any sane person should think
the revolution of July a topic of interest, and when William
Humboldt, the most central figure in Germany, the confidant of Schiller and Goethe, of Wolf and Niebuhr, who
had fought Talleyrand at Vienna on the memorable day
on which legitimacy was born, who had forged the link
between science and force by organising a university at
Berlin, and who, until the murder of Kotzebue, had been
the pride and the hope of intelligent Prussia, devoted the
maturity of his powers to Malay roots.   Those were the
days in which the familiar type of the German scholar
was generated, of the man who complained that the
public library allowed him only thirteen hours a day to
read, the man who spent thirty years on one volume,
the man who wrote upon Homer in 1806 and who still
wrote upon Homer in 1870, the man who discovered the
358 passages in which Dictys has imitated Sallust, the
man who carried an electric telegraph from his house to
the church and carried it no farther.

Primarily, he was a Greek scholar, bounded by ancient
horizons, and his mind was not seldom shaped by some
favourite classic, as were Böckh by Plato, Creuzer by
Plotinus, Trendelenburg by Aristotle, and Roscher by
Thucydides.   More rarely he carried the dry powder of
philology into the early Christian conflicts, or the chaos
of the first, the Teutonic, Middle Ages.   On the modern
world, with its unsettled and unsettling questions,

and its inaccessible information, he sternly turned his back.   He loved to settle on a space he could hope to exhaust by giving his life to it, unmindful of Godfrey Hermann and his dictum : " Est quaedam etiam nesciendi ars et scientia."   Like Hegel, who comfortably finished his book at Jena during the battle, and, starting for the publisher's in the morning, was surprised to observe that the streets were full of Frenchmen, he did not allow the voices of the striving world to distract him.   Often he had risen, by mere energy and conduct, from crushing poverty, had gone barefoot to school, or had begged his way like Hase across the Fatherland ; and he remained frugal and austere, cultivating humble obscurity and the golden gift of silence, and marrying, as Feuerbach did, upon an income of forty pounds.   With that genius for taking trouble which Ritschl called the way to everything, he was not sensitive to genius of any other sort.   The extreme subdivision of labour narrowed his view, and gave an unusual scope and value to diligent mediocrity. Dull men built themselves an everlasting name at which we wonder as we wonder at the glory of Grant ; and the excessive talent of Stahl and Lassalle was suspected, as a Jewish glitter, wanting substance.   Walter, standing still on the old ground of Niebuhr, scoffed at that marvel of ability, the *Geist des römischen Rechts ;* and W. Sickel's *Verfassungsgeschichte*, the most brilliant account of early institutions ever written, is scorned by the accepted teachers.   " Too clever to make a good administrator " is a judgment of Napoleon's ; and Metternich invokes the international epigram, " L'esprit sert à tout et ne mène à rien."

The scholar of the old school was an open adversary and a candid friend.   Aristotelian Brandis, who was remarkable for social amenity, writes of his early fellow-ship with Bunsen that they disputed " without effeminate sensibility " (*ohne wehleidige Schonung*) ; and the Breslau students were gratified with the sight of Passow in the *Professorencarcer* for insulting Menzel.   Thiers said to Senior : " I may call my opponent a villain, though I know him to be honest." Not so in Saxony, where the courts have decided that it is lawful to call a book foolish, but not to call the author a fool.

The leaders of the movement that sprang up in the second quarter of the century were animated by the conviction that the genius and learning of the modern world went to work the wrong way, and missed its aim, not from incapacity, but from interest, influence, and prejudice. It was their belief that literature had long been an arduous and comprehensive conspiracy against truth, and that much envenomed controversy could be set at rest by exposing the manifold arts that veil substantial falsehood —suppression, distortion, interpolation, forgery, legend, myth. The Germans came late upon the scene, and did not claim to be better than those who went before them ; but they would begin their work over again—" expurgata jam et abrasa et aequata mentis area "—warned by example to escape the sources of error. By extreme patience and self-control, by seeking neither premature result nor personal reward, by sacrificing the present to the far-off future, by the obscure heroism of many devoted lives, they looked to prepare the foundation of the kingdom of knowledge. " Plurimi transibunt et multiplex erit scientia." They trained themselves to resist the temptations by which others had suffered, and stood to win by moral qualities. There was so much rough material to hew, so much time to recover, that they renounced making points and drawing conclusions. The politic Briton, with a practical object in view, avoids needless provocation to dissent ; and the studious German tried to exclude contentious matter, and to adjust theory to fact, on the maxim, " On s'arrange plus facilement sur un fait que sur un principe."

Their literary dogma, that truth is worth living for, and honesty, in fact, is the best policy, yields to nobody now the fresh emotion of discovery. Lanfrey writes that the only patriotism of historians is sincerity ; and the best of the French reviews has said the same thing in its prospectus. " Nous ne prétendons servir qu'une cause,

celle de la science—Le livre seul est l'objet de la critique ;
l'auteur pour elle n'existe pas." A clever fellow assured
Lasker that he lied no more, having observed that it is
less profitable than it used to be, and that truth, on the
whole, answers better. Half a century ago, when every
member of an election committee was understood to vote
with his party, when a cry of derision went up at the
hyperbole that property has duties as well as rights, when
one prime minister considered that rich men ought to
know how poor men vote, and another said, " On ne
trompe personne quand on trompe tout le monde," such
principles were not yet trivial, and were enjoying the short
span which Schopenhauer assigns to truth, between the
paradox of yesterday and the commonplace of to-morrow.

Late in his life Thiers said of Napoleon, " Il faut con-
venir que c'était un scélérat et un fou." He had concealed
his opinion in twenty volumes. Guizot having discovered
certain scandal about a queen (who was not Queen
Elizabeth), by the advice of the Duchess de Broglie suppressed it. Quite lately, the president of a great assembly
avowed that impartiality is a merit only in presidents.
When Tocqueville spent a lifetime in declaring the advent
and the natural history of democracy, without betraying
the intensity of his fears, and kept his religious opinions
so well out of sight that the suppression of one or two
letters has been enough to conceal them altogether ; or
when the Bishop of Chester [1] mentions, with becoming
pride, that a man may read his books and take him for a
radical, they illustrate a phase of literary character which
was specially developed by the Germans in the studious
and pacific days before 1848. And Mr. Freeman's proposition, that historic criticism and historic fairness are
hardly possible when a man writes simply as a partisan
of the Papacy, would be accepted by them without the
implied restriction. By what secret channels error filters
into the mind, most people have read in Bacon, and may
read much better in Spencer. The ideal historian adum-
brated by Rothe, Kampschulte, Roscher, Dümmler,

[1] Dr. Stubbs.

374 ESSAYS ON MODERN HISTORY

Löning, Gierke, Gass, is a man armed at all these points, and the discipline that makes him opens further visions of penetrating ethics, not obvious on the beaten track.

Among the historians of that epoch the most eminent, though he never wrote a page of history, was Böhmer, the librarian of Frankfort. Dumas's enthusiasm for the author of the *Girondins* broke out in the words: " Il a élevé l'histoire à la hauteur du roman " ; and of Böhmer it can be said that he raised drudgery to the rank of a fine art. For the centuries to which he confined himself, from the eighth to the fourteenth, he made it a precept that truth dwells in documents, and not in chronicles or lives. The author of a grant or a state paper knows what he is doing ; the author of a book does not. In one case history is told by those who make it ; in the other, by those who hear of it from other people. The chronicle is a mixture of memory, imagination, and design. The charter is reality itself. When Thierry was over-worked, he refreshed his mind with the glossary of Ducange ; and there is no better reading in German than the prefaces of Böhmer, and his *Regesta* as completed by the Innsbruck professors. He makes all mediæval literature subsidiary to the charters, and relieves his terse and telling abstract with illustrations from the historians as well as with points of his own. As the citizen of a republic, whose mental life was spent among the records of mediæval empire, as a Protestant who sought the society of Catholics, he had the advantage of a central and independent position. But his warmest sympathies were with the institutions which had vanished in his lifetime, with the church whose tenets he rejected, and he delivered his sentiments with a petulance and malice which no other reputation could have withstood. Waitz, and the northern scholars whose modes of thought he flouted, voted him a prize, as the foremost historian of the day ; and Ficker, who has carried forward his work with better training and at least equal solidity, devised a theory for his benefit, which maintains that prejudice is consistent with veracity. Like Stälin, who had his

Wirtembergische Geschichte, the best of provincial histories, corrected by a priest, Böhmer gravitated towards the Catholic south, and was the chief of a scattered party of Guelphic scholars which has not survived. When he died, in 1863, the romantic school to which he had imparted the dignity of exact learning went below the horizon.

The chief promoter of mediæval studies was the modern Ranke. He had been famous for ten years before his influence was established, for the strongest men who came up were carried away by Hegel. In 1834, when the lieutenants were dividing the empire, Ranke set the reign of Henry I., the imaginary Fowler, as a subject for an essay. Giesebrecht and Köpke competed, and were defeated by Waitz, who has just revised the third edition of his biography, fifty years after it gained the prize. This was the foundation of what has been for so long incomparably the first school of history in the world, not for ideas or eloquence, but for solid and methodical work. Ranke discouraged men from approaching the passionate discussions and buried materials which were his own domain, and directed them to the times before the thirteenth century, the sources of which occupy a limited compass, and were just then in process of being threshed out for Pertz. It was a time that could be studied in the same cool temper as the weights and measures of Babylon, and had some analogy with the things taught by Böckh. But no philologist had Ranke's mastery of the detective arts. Even Drumann, when he came to Boniface VIII., proved ignorant of technical rules, while, on the other hand, the canons which Nitzsch and Nissen applied to Rome were formed in the mediæval school. It supplied the best editors of the *Monumenta*, eclipsing Pertz and his legal coadjutors, beat up all the libraries of Europe, and gradually obtained the control of the historical reviews. The Annals of the mediæval empire are the most perfect achievement of these men. They were slow to quit the libraries for the archives ; but a younger generation, working at Munich on the sixteenth

and seventeenth centuries, and laying half of Europe
under contribution, has solved the harder problem of
making state papers the backbone of modern history.

The weak place was the nineteenth century until the
revolution of 1848 compelled attention to the problems
of the day.   Droysen had already proposed a series of
books on recent times, to be laid down on the lines
of Dahlmann, which should fuse past and present, and
treat politics and history as one.   In connection with
this plan, which was not carried out, Häusser produced
the first serious work on the fall and the rise of Germany,
between the death of Frederic and the overthrow of
Napoleon, a work which hardly justifies the considerable
influence which the author exercised without his pen, but
which marks a new era as a plea for Prussia from a
southern and avowedly liberal hand.

The next Heidelberg writer prophesied a democratic,
not a Prussian future.   Gervinus personates the average
German, the average middle-class German from the
smaller towns of the smaller States, crowded with indisputable information, sceptical and doctrinaire, more
robust than elastic or alert, instructive but not persuasive,
with a taste for broad paths and the judicious forcing of
open locks.   He began his *History of the Nineteenth
Century* at the lowest ebb of national sentiment, and he
left it, a fragment in eight volumes, when reviving
nationality discarded his dogmas.   Schlosser, the master
in whom he persistently believed, confessed that the
world moved away and left him superfluous and obsolete.
The same experience darkened the last days of Gervinus,
who thought that Cavour must fail, that Bismarck was a
new Polignac, who kept his place among the vanquished
of 1866, and died disowning the results of 1870.   He
had been a power in the land before 1848, when he
applied the reigning theory to literature, and exhibited
every writer limited and bound to fixed surroundings, and
every poem a barometer.   He rescued the realm of
imagination from the wild will of poets and the incalculable
sceptre, and brought a new region under scientific cultiva-

tion.   Julian Schmidt and other vigorous men have enlarged his notions.   The better part of the nation's mind works in pursuit of truth, and its thought, its knowledge, its errors, constitute the object of literary history as well as those things which may be lawfully told in verse.   The flowery empire of æsthetics did not flourish under this amalgamation as it had done in less practical days.   The best work is a history of Italian literature ; but of the greatest living critics—Haym, Bernays, and Scherer—not one is great alike in the tracing of ideas, in perfect knowledge of biographical and bibliographical fact, and in taste.

Gervinus and Sybel exhibit the contrast between north and south, and between the time before and after 1848. Sybel had learnt to make war on confusion and fiction in the strict mediæval school ; but his mind was essentially modern, his interest lay in practical directions, and he opened the way to the later, inexhaustible, and almost unattempted centuries.   He studies the Revolution in the light of a vast disturbance of the permanent policy of cabinets, without mercy on its picturesque and passionate element.   The Reformation was in fact a blow struck at reforming Catholicism, more than at the supine advocacy of things as they were ; and this historian, without unction or sympathy, deplores the Revolution as a catastrophe that threw back intelligent progress for half a century. He began these studies forty years ago with two essays on Burke, whose letter to Mercer embodies much of his philosophy.   Both in his history and in his review, Sybel adopts the dogmatic terms of Burke and Savigny ; but he is never lost in theory.   Although his introductory chapter anticipated the *Ancien Régime* with no better help than Tocqueville's article in the *Westminster Review*, the depth and soundness of his work was not perceived until his gradual discoveries in many archives awakened controversy and provoked a flood of answering matter.

The year 1848, which sent more than one hundred professors to Frankfort, had been detrimental to the British and Baconian maxim, that knowledge is power. In Sybel they were united ; for he was learned in the wisdom of universities, and eminently conversant with the working of political forces ; a man of life and action, an expert such as had not been seen.   He became the first classic of imperialism, and helped to form that garrison of distinguished historians that prepared the Prussian supremacy together with their own, and now hold Berlin like a fortress.   If any one will make a list of their names, he will see that such a phalanx was never arrayed before, and will also detect one of the *arcana imperii*, by which the rude strength centred in a region more un-genial than Latium was employed to absorb and to stiffen the diffused, sentimental, and strangely impolitic talent of the studious Germans.

Things were different heretofore, when history, not yet woven into the web of national greatness, was carried on by private enterprise.   Men living in a small way, with a dim political background, were not often practical, but were generally disinterested.   Göttingen, Tübingen, and Heidelberg had some advantages for historical teach-ing over Berlin, where " William Tell " was a forbidden play.   Among their leisurely professors were men who found, like Dahlmann, that the great Frederic stuck in their throats ; like Gervinus and Ewald, who repudiated Dahlmann's precept, that what their country wanted was force before freedom.   The disconcerting verdict of events ruined their credit as readers of the signs of the times. Apart from the convenient popularity of the maxim, " Die Weltgeschichte ist das Weltgericht," it was appa-rent that the past had not revealed to them its inmost secret, and they were disparaged, as investigators of irre-claimable dry bones.   The men who took betimes the side of the big battalions, showed superior penetration into the things beneath the sun.   They brought history into touch with the nation's life, and gave it an influence it had never possessed out of France ; and they won for themselves the making of opinions, mightier than laws. The most clear-sighted of those who resolved, after the failure of the Revolution, that the future of Germany belonged to Prussia, was Droysen.

Ten years before the fire-and-sword despatch revealed
Count Ferro, while intelligent adherents of Greater Germany argued that without Austria there could be nothing
but a magnified Prussia, Droysen affirmed that unity
could never come from liberty and the vote of parliaments, that it required a power strong enough to crush
resistance at home and abroad. The rest of his life was
devoted to Prussian politics and the imperial arts ; and
he was one of that central band of writers and statesmen
and soldiers who turned the tide that had run for six
hundred years, and conquered the centrifugal forces that
had reigned in Germany longer than the commons have
sat at Westminster. He had learnt classical scholarship
in the school of Böckh, and had acquired from Hegel
the habit of abstract thought and that preference for the
Hellenic empire which is adversely noted in the *History
of Federal Government.* In spite of his Macedonian proclivity, his earliest pupil testifies that he was always a
liberal, meaning a promoter of secondary liberties.
Whatever element of the kind was in him, was fostered
by his residence at Kiel, in a land flowing with political
excitement, the early home of gratuitous education. To
sustain the faith and the practice of patriotism, he published his lectures on the time between the Stamp Act
and Waterloo, a book full of views and turbid cleverness.
He passed on to his own domain with the biography of
the grim warrior whose defection prepared the ruin of
Napoleon, and whose son fell in the last action of the
revolutionary war, refusing quarter, and exclaiming that
his name was Yorck. The long *History of Prussian Policy*
followed, and brought popularity and power. Being asked
by what subtle charm he and the intimate advisers had
changed the plain soldier of the last generation into the
mightiest of conquerors, Droysen replied that it was
nothing but the stern sense of duty (*die verfluchte Schul-
digkeit*). He made this the note of Hohenzollern history.
Their success lay in diplomacy and war, and the narrative
is international, not domestic. The affairs of Europe
from the Great Elector to the eve of the Seven Years'

War have never been told with so large a knowledge of
politics ; and the later volumes are more effective than
the parallel work of his illustrious rival.   Ranke, who
discards the teleological argument of history, whose feelings are so well under control that he dilates on the
disasters of 1806 more than on the triumphs of 1757,
had neither his popular fibre nor his official sanction.
Fastidious readers doubt at last the swiftness of Achilles
and the piety of Æneas ; but to those who do not require
conviction, the sagacious advocate of Prussian monarchy
is as persuasive as the avowed defenders of other causes,
of parliamentary government or federal democracy.

The one writer of history who is more brilliant and
powerful than Droysen is Treitschke.   Droysen's grasp
of his materials began to relax when he came to Frederic;
but Treitschke never flags, and is always vehement, certain, and overwhelming.   As a political essayist, long ago
he broke the spell of superiority which, until the death of
Stahl, belonged to the religious and the strict conservative
world.   He was predestined for Berlin by his first conspicuous act ; for he had attacked, and it was thought
had refuted, the notion of a separate science of society,
as the sphere of religion, morality, economy, and knowledge, as a vast community, organically distinct from the
State, and able to control it.   The idea, which comes
from Harrington, and was pronounced by John Adams
the greatest discovery in politics, had been made by
Lorenz von Stein the key to the Revolution, in a work
exposing the economic cause of political science, with
Hegelian formalities which contrast unhappily with
Treitschke's gleaming style.   For he writes, with the
force and the fire of Mommsen, of a time remembered by
living men, and pregnant with the problems that are still
open.   He marshals his forces on a broader front than
any other man, and accounts for the motives that stir the
nation, as well as for the councils that govern it.

Treitschke's *History of Germany* belongs to a series
that has made up for the long delay in approaching the
present century, in which England, from the regency to

Victoria, was allotted to Pauli.   Reluctance to compete
with Ranke had led him to abandon his former work,
and in the stronger currents of his own country he drifted
from his English moorings.   In the last year of his life
he was thinking of a compendium embracing his thirty
years' study of every part of the history of England in
one or two volumes.   His book on the nineteenth century
suffers by comparison with the powerful mixture prepared
by Mr. Cory for the patient Asiatic, and is not equal to
the Spanish or Russian histories in the same collection.

Bernhardi's *Russia* carries us from the unrealities of
scholastic history, from the complacency of satisfied
philosophers and the adoration of *Bonus Eventus*, to the
most penetrating and relentless censure of the thoughts
and deeds of men.   The author combines what was never
combined before by a writer of history, long and intimate
initiation in secrets of state, with military science and the
knowledge of an original and profound economist.   He
represses the inclination to think that what is explained
is excused, that all ideas are reasonable and all events
opportune, and gives a prominence, suggesting early
contact with the dissatisfied Heidelbergers, to the im-
ponderable and unaccountable elements of human weakness and folly.   His principal work is oddly diversified
with episodes on the British constitution and on Adam
Smith, besides a slight sketch of universal history ; and it
is time that his account of 1815, composed without the
papers of Talleyrand and Metternich for the congress, or
of Gneisenau and Grouchy for the campaign, should be
rewritten.   Bernhardi is the ablest of the German writers
on Napoleon.   The affinity that may be discovered
between the first consul in the plenitude of his own ideas,
before the peace of Amiens, and much that is peculiarly
Prussian, does not disarm this admirer of Frederic and
friend of Moltke, and he dispels even the illusion of the
war in Champagne.   He also gives literary expression to
the judgment of the Prussian staff on Wellington.   At
Vienna the duke departed from the policy of Castlereagh,
joined Talleyrand in pleading the Saxon cause, and

assured Metternich that Prussia was likely to become the
most dangerous Power in Europe.   Talleyrand recorded
the scene twenty years later with satisfaction tempered
with surprise at so gross a mistake.   This was the feeling
which Wellington took with him to Belgium ; and
Gneisenau informed the officer sent to attend him that he
was an excellent commander, but as false as the wiliest
Hindoo.   From that day until his administration in 1830,
it was a standing maxim at the Berlin foreign office that
the duke might always be counted upon to desert a
friend.

Probably there is no considerable group less in
harmony with our sentiments in approaching the study of
history than that which is mainly represented by Sybel,
Droysen, and Treitschke, with Mommsen and Gneist,
Bernhardi and Duncker on the flank.   Up to this moment
it is the best found and the most energetic of all ; and as
there is no symptom of declining favour and authority, it
is important to understand along what lines of reasoning
men so eminent, so quick to inquire into every new
thing, have adhered to maxims which it has cost the
world much effort to reverse.   The theory of the political
historian is distinct from the plea of the partisan.   The
historian displays the laws governing human life : it is
not his duty to expound a private view, or to explain,
like the wise Castilian, how much better the universe
would be contrived if he had been consulted in time.   He
attends to the ship's course, not to the passengers.   The
forces to be reckoned are those which, in the long-run,
prevail.   The historian justifies only that which is just by
the judgment of experience.   It is the heresy of history
to choose a side that seems good in our eyes, to reject the
appointed course and the dominion of law, in order to
degrade the life of nations under the anarchy of casual
and disconnected causes.   Consistency in the powers that
direct the world is the supreme acquisition of all German
thought.   It is not partiality, but renunciation of party
feeling and personal preference, to hold that the world
works well, that what lives permanently in the light and

strife of civilisation lives rightfully, that whatever perishes
has earned its fate.   Wyclif revived a very ancient saying
when he wrote : " Ponat talis fidelis spem et causam suam
in adiutorio altissimi, et non est compossibile quod vel
persona vel causa pereat."   It is the philosophy of
Emerson proclaiming " the skill with which the great All
maketh clean work as it goes along, leaves no rag, con-
sumes its smoke."   And does not a living classic write :
" Somehow or other it is always the Eternal's wisdom
which at last carries the day " ?

There is no escape from the dogma that history is the
conscience of mankind unless for those who reject the
collective growth, the canons that rivet the future to
the past, and take their stand aloof with Archimedes.
All the successions of thought during three generations
constitute the shaft whose shining point is made by the
Berlin interpreters of enlightened and triumphant Germany.   They are the legitimate dynasty, reigning by
right as well as by force, inheritors of the line that comes
down from Burke to the last stage of evolution and
selection, who have set up the reign of imperishable moral
forces for an intermittent Providence, the play of passion,
and the blind will of man.   Their doctrine proceeds as
logically from the scientific as from the political experience
of the country.   And it is held, practically, even by men
who do not stand with both feet within the charmed ring
that binds history to politics ; by Mommsen, when he
scouts the idea of explaining Roman conquests by Roman
perfidy ; by Waitz, when he said that a censor of the
Reformation had no right to pit himself against his
nation ; by Kurtz, who establishes a presumption in
favour of the Church against the sects because the sects
came to unspeakable grief, and in favour of the Reformation against Rome because the reformers were successful.

To be without party is to be without principle, according to that saying of an English statesman, that a man
who denies party belongs to a party he is ashamed of.
To be impartial is to follow a very wide induction, to
acknowledge the manifest destiny of monarchy, with a

mind prepared, if it must be, to follow "the tramp of democracy's earthquake feet."

There is no palliation of inaccuracy; but there are no men more accurate than these, and few more watchful of the springs of error within. Renan has said that hardly any one but Littré could confess a blunder without loss of dignity. If that Napoleonic sentiment prevails in France, it is a point of inferiority to the neighbouring rival. The puerile temptation of consistency, the weak reluctance to contradict what disciples are repeating on their authority, is inevitable among the chiefs of the many schools into which German scholarship is apt to crumble. Stronger still is the assurance that historical science is moving with the vigour and rapidity of a natural law, and that its teachers can no more stand still than chemists or biologists.

Ranke read before the French Institute his retractation of a mistake about the memoirs of Richelieu. Treitschke elaborately corrects an error into which Arndt had led him, an error concerning the disappearance of spoons, which had been exposed with insult. Gervinus used to call the *Philosophie der Griechen* a singular instance of a faultless book; hundreds of improvements in the last edition show that Zeller is himself of a different opinion. When Berghaus said that Humboldt had "invariably fixed" the longitude of Callao, the philosopher required him to strike out the word. There are, he said, no invariable fixtures. Albrecht, the jurist, was a man of one book, and his literary position depended on a treatise concerning a difficult point of early law. In 1858, 1869, and 1872 his conclusions were successively demolished by three different writers. To the first he wrote that the ruin of essential portions of his structure did not in the least interfere with his satisfaction. The next time he said that he did not mind even if it was to be the death-blow of his book. At last he admitted his defeat, and added that he had long expected it. So pleasant a temper has not been granted to every German. When Reinhold said that a philosopher should bear in mind that he may err and be ready to learn from others, Fichte told him that he spoke like a man who had never been convinced in his life.

The last twenty years have made the Germans careful in the economy of force, and they waste less powder in salutes. Their soldiers were on the Loire when they began to say that their scholars were to be no more the humble servants of the foreigner. Nothing, said Mommsen, is so hollow as the pretence of humility. " We are not modest by any means, and do not wish it to be thought of us." The *National-Zeitung* confessed that its countrymen, though not envious, are slow to acknowledge merit, and added that hundreds of Germans remain unknown, who in France would lead science and society. Würtz's exaltation of Lavoisier, and Schérer's highly discriminating estimate of Goethe, were received with indignation ; and Rümelin's able but unceremonious book is one among many signs of rising impatience at the old enthusiasm for Shakespeare.

As early as 1849, Prince Albert said to Bunsen that self-sufficiency was the German rock ahead. The historians generally escaped this peril and welcomed every proof of superiority. During many years Pauli regularly introduced the Rolls publications which were undermining the work of his life, and admitted that there were points on which the *History of the Norman Conquest* surpasses everything yet written on the Middle Ages. Ewald preferred Selden to all his followers in Syriac. Lehrs declared that he could make nothing of the political life of Greece until he read Grote. The Prolegomena to Tischendorf's last text have, I believe, been committed to an English hand ; and Bailleu says that the best lives of the greatest modern Germans, of Frederic, Stein, and Goethe, are those which have been written in England. Rosenkranz thought Damiron superior to the German historians of philosophy ; Böhmer rated Delisle's *Philippe Auguste* above every German book of the same kind ; and Böckh, irritated just then by the absurdities of Gerlach and the temerities of Mommsen, said that Wallon's

Histoire de l'Esclavage dans l'Antiquité was better than what his own countrymen were doing in philology.   A reviewer of Guerry declares him at least the equal of Roscher in learning ; and Roscher places the *Réforme Sociale* of Le Play at the head of books on social science. The best Frenchmen—Rénier, Rougé, Le Blant, Molinier, Riant, A. Rambaud—stood or stand just as well on one side of the Vosges as on the other, although Bekker never forgave Cobet's utterance that Germans were *doctiores quam saniores.*   Madvig's supremacy among Latinists was admitted by Halm, in spite of the Danish depreciation of Mommsen.   Harnack, writing in the principal theological review, judges that his country possesses no history of early Christianity as good as that of Renan, nothing equal to Hatch on the primitive constitution of the Church, or to the *Introduction to Ecclesiastical History* of a Flemish Jesuit.   A less perfect courtier than Bunsen would perhaps have made a better fight.

When the euthanasia of metaphysic anticipated by Carlyle was setting in about 1850, physical science came forward as its rival, and history as its heir.   The philosophers themselves turned into historians, and beat their speculations into facts.   Their lecture-rooms were empty, and Schelling confessed to a traveller that the end had come : " La pensée allemande est aujourd'hui dans un cul-de-sac, et je ne vois pas qui pourra l'en tirer." Braniss conceived that religion, which had been brought low by the negations of thinkers, would be restored by the affirmations of scholars ; and others said that history is the only unassailable revelation.   Belief and unbelief both led to the same conclusion : Kuno Fischer opened his great work on modern metaphysics by defining philosophy as the self-knowledge of history ; and Schaarschmidt, on the opposite side, calls philosophy and history one and the same thing.   One of the philosophical reviews declared that the history of the systems was a substitute for the systems themselves ; and even the laggards of *a priori* science were won by the assurance that the philo-

sophical idea is the substance of all history. The historic
mind had always glowed beneath the metaphysical ice
cap. Goethe described it as one of his last steps in
mental progress to have the unseen past always present ;
and he had approved the fine piece of idealism, since
copied by Renan, in which Humboldt denounced the
prosaic improvements which would make Rome a place
unfitted for the spectres who are its worthiest inhabitants.
Gerlach, the leader of the Prussian conservatives, used to
say that what he had admired most in England was Mr.
Speaker's wig. For when he spoke of it as a time-
honoured relic, an historical-minded Englishman told him
that it was nothing of the sort, but quite a modern
institution, not two centuries old. At Göttingen one day
a Protestant was defending the celibacy of the clergy, and
saying that without it Catholicism would lose its identity.
A Catholic replied : " We were used to married priests so
long that it is the law of celibacy which we feel as an
innovation."

The scientific era had its own lesson for historians.
The world proceeded on its new path with increasing
velocity, there was no stopping, and no step backward ;
and the law of progress, which had been a crude and
vague speculation, became a manifest reality. With this
new aspect of the life of men and of societies, a conception
of history arose of which Du Bois Reymond is the prophet.
The future depends on truths and forces being, and to be,
discovered. The past survives only by supplying available material that may be a guide for science and an
equivalent of power. The function of history is to reveal
its own futility, to display the conquest of the ancient
realm of uncertainty, probability, inheritance, by irresistible
demonstration. Bourbons and Habsburgs go over to the
Egyptian kings, and make room on earth for the monuments of a dynasty that begins with Copernicus and will
never pass away. All else is ballast to be discharged,
and the Greek exercise must surrender to conic sections.
As mere denial of history, the new conception is an old
one. But by promoting the neglected history of scientific

388 ESSAYS ON MODERN HISTORY

ideas, it promises greatly to enrich both historians and philosophers.

Forty years after Savigny's *Vocation* made Germany a nation of historically thinking men, every branch of knowledge had felt its influence. It had penetrated jurisprudence by the end of the French war ; language, with the first volume of Grimm's *Grammar* in the edition of 1822 ; geography, when Ritter drew the spark from Humboldt ; philosophy, when Hegel lectured at Berlin ; art, with Schnaase's *Letters from the Netherlands;* theology, with Baur's work on the Atònement ; and canon law when Richter was made, instead of Stahl, the adviser of the Prussian government in Church and State. Until 1840, political economy was almost the only science in which Germany followed, with unequal steps, the lead of France and England. The change came when Roscher, who had been the ripest of Ranke's scholars, a man more perfectly endowed with historic instinct than Niebuhr or Baur, was set to train practical economists for the kingdom of Hanover. He united in an eminently receptive mind the better strains of the German character—the wide and not absorbing sympathy, the impartial attentiveness to the several sides of questions, the notion that error is not done with until it has been made to yield a residue of truth, confidence in the general reasonableness of things, regulation of private opinion by universal experience. Abstraction was already losing its strong grip, and experimental methods were obtaining sway. " The history of a science," said Goethe, " is the science itself " ; Trendelenburg spoke of definitions as the end, not the beginning, of knowledge ; and Say told de Candolle that he had acquired the art of observing social physiology from the naturalists. These fluid notions were much in the air. Hermann, the strictest of dogmatists, being asked what to read, advised men to learn the making of the science in the economic articles which appeared from the beginning in the *Edinburgh* and *Quarterly Reviews.* The prodigy of Roscher's reading and his historic bent of mind urged him to detach propositions from their place in the system, in order to trace their career in literature and the experience of nations. He required that the inductive argument shall meet and justify the deductive.   He turned from the solid conclusion to the process which led up to it, from the discovered law to the law of discovery, the ineffectual anticipation, the simultaneous attainment, the contested reception, the disputed priority.   If the full - blown precepts of developed science which accompany the mature, the normal, and therefore industrial epoch of national life were not clear formerly, Roscher explains the defect not by the fault of men groping in the dark, but by the fact that political economy, which exists for mankind, varies with the progress of events, and is subject to the conditions of youth and age.   He distinguishes physiology from pathology, insists on the phenomena proper to epochs of decline, and notes with especial care the teaching of nations that have carried the experiment of existence to its conclusion.   Starting with the idea that the ancients understood distribution better than we do, and that truth is often older than error, he has expanded and enriched professional literature with the study of all the economic notions in the civil and the ecclesiastical code, in Erasmus and Luther, Bacon and Burke.   The worst use of theory is to make men insensible to fact ; and facts, as they existed before Salmasius vindicated 5 per cent, or Gournay spoke the winged words, are nearly as good for instruction as the things that have been since the discoveries of 1776, 1798, 1815, and 1835.

With little less than Buckle's appreciation of Adam Smith, Roscher's memory, crowded with instances of the power of self-sacrifice, disinclines him from the doctrine which refers economic facts to the simplest and most universal of human motives, and he derives laws and theories from causes deep in the entire structure of society, and from combinations of human and spiritual influence. He came at a time when several candid generalisations of primitive liberalism were withering under the mathematical touch of comparative statistics, and is always ready to find a grain of wisdom in the oddities of our ancestors ; and

the saying of ancient practitioners that the lancet produced much the same results upon the generation that is
past as its disuse upon the generation that is passing, is
Roscher all over. Though he deems protection a mark
of weakness, and its prolongation a mark of incapacity,
he admits the use of temporary sacrifices in the training
of resources. With Adam Smith he rejoices at the enactment of the navigation laws, and with Cobden at their
repeal ; he feels with Garrison about emancipation, but is
vividly conscious of conditions in which slavery is an
instrument of civilisation. He expounds with intelligent
admiration the colonial system by which this country has
changed the face of the world, but he studies with equal
care, he admires in another way the system by which
Spain preserved where we destroyed. Absolute monarchy is the note of first or second childhood, but absolute
monarchy rescued the peasants. Monopolies are a mistake ; but the monopoly of the Oporto Company saved
port wine.

The best of the economists who last preceded Roscher
admitted that in dealing with poverty their science failed.
Mill thought that want in any sense implying suffering
may be completely extinguished ; and Roscher added that
precept must be modified by fact. His disciples went
on to argue that the principles of the classic teachers
on the theory of population, of rent, of the source of
wealth, lead beyond their conclusions. With Roscher's
doctrine of relative truth, the impregnable stronghold was
hard to keep against the assault of sympathy and the
prickings of that delicate conscience which is defined, a
conscience unequal to the struggle of life. He dwells
complacently on the immeasurable progress of this age,
on the enlarged sphere and accepted duties of the State
in respect of misery, education, overwork, health, and help
to the weak, and judges that the social advance cancels
the socialist programme. "Socialism," said Dunoyer, "is
merely the present system logically carried out." On the
other side, if it is right that the State should do so much,
the reign of the log was usurpation and the ancient ways

were wrong. Then the indictment brought by Considérant and Engels against the society of 1840 is just,
and the order of things which produced so much sorrow
was criminal. So vast a change is not development but
subversion, the departure of one principle, the development of another. In all that pertains to the past, the
party now dominant in the universities, and destined,
after calculable intervals, to dominate in literature and
law, pursues the ideas of Roscher, and completes his work.
In practical things it does not accept, as he does, the
Frenchman's saying, " Je n'impose rien ; je ne propose
même pas : j'expose." His contemplative, retrospective
spirit, borne backward by sheer weight of knowledge, is
not easily roused by the spectacle of error, suffering, and
wrong, and is slow to admit the guilt of omitted acts and
the responsibility of States for all they might prevent or
cure. He has attended as much to problems and their
solution in other times as to the problems and solutions
of his own ; and the service done by his enormous influence to political economy, which Mr. Cliffe Leslie and
Mr. Ingram have described, is far less than his services to
the cause of intelligible history. A large number of the
most valuable works on England proceed from the movement he has promoted. The academic socialists are
proceeding to reconstrue history, making property and the
social condition the determining factor, above the acts of
government or the changes of opinion ; and this is by
many degrees the most important addition made of late
years to historic science.

The successive schemes have been less a modification
than an enlargement of the definition, and the best would
be one that should complete and combine them all. The
idea that the fine arts are a result of all that is at work
in nations led to an attempt to focus their entire life,
and the design of a history of civilisation grew out of
the history of art. Burckhardt's *Renaissance* and Friedländer's *Sittengeschichte* are the only works in which the
intellectual view of the subject has been adequately
studied ; and in both, the political, and therefore the

practical, element is weakest. One man is living who has an equal grasp of the moving and the abiding forces of society. More than thirty years ago, before Burckhardt or Friedländer, Buckle or Symonds, Riehl, a scholar quickened by journalism, a student of art, an original political writer and teacher of social sciences, began to lecture on the history of civilisation, revealing to his fortunate audience new views of history deeper than any existing in literature. There is always much going on in lecture rooms beyond what is yet deposited in books ; and if Professor Riehl has gone on as he began in 1854, there are materials for a new and curious chapter of German historiography. The newest chapter, and one of the most curious, should concern the histories which the Germans have not written, the threads they have dropped, and the points on which they yield to the superiority of other nations. My object has been to show neither their infirmity nor their strength, but the ways in which they break new ground and add to the notion and the work of history.

XIII

TALLEYRAND'S MEMOIRS [1]

THE reality of History is so unlike the report that we continue, in spite of much disappointment, to look for revelations as often as an important personage leaves us his reminiscences. The famous book which has been so eagerly expected and so long withheld will not satisfy those who, like the first Queen of Prussia, demand to know *le pourquoy du pourquoy*. The most experienced and sagacious of men discourses about certain selected events that concerned him, and passes sentence on two generations of contemporaries ; but he betrays few secrets and prepares no surprises. Nothing could increase the lustre of the talents which he is known—by the malevolent testimony of Vitrolles—to have displayed at the first restoration, or which are proved by his own correspondence from Vienna. But we are made to know him better ; and all that he says and much that he conceals brings into vivid light one of the wonders of modern politics.

Three months after the fall of Napoleon, Talleyrand went out of office, opposed by Russia, disliked by the King, hated by the triumphant Royalists. Under that constellation, mainly in the year 1816, he wrote these Memoirs. The undercurrent of motive is to explain, or to explain away, the earlier part of his career ; to expose his incomparable services to the crown, the country, and the dominant party ; to show that nothing in the various past disqualifies him for the first place in the councils of the monarchy he had restored. It is not the plea of a

---

[1] *The Nineteenth Century*, April 1891.

vulgar competitor ; for, with all his sleepless ambition, he writes with studied moderation and reserve. He has not the tone of a man contemplating from aloft his own achievements, his immense renown, his assured place in the central history of the world. Talleyrand is dissatisfied, satirical, and almost always bitter in his judgment of men. The better to dissociate himself from evil communications, he interpolates a laboured attack on the Duke of Orleans, which would be a blot on the composition but for the redeeming paragraph on Sieyès, the best of all the characters he has drawn. He slurs over his own share in the work of the National Assembly, justifies his attitude under Napoleon by the pressing need for monarchy, and by his breach with him on the affairs of Spain, and puts himself straight with the Church by a detailed narrative of the disputes with Rome.

He was reputed too idle a man to be a good writer, and it was supposed that Des Renaudes held the pen for him at one time and La Besnardière at another. Chateaubriand, who devoted his most tremendous sentences to the business of denouncing him as a traitor in politics and religion, and who insisted that the last action of his life was a deceitful comedy, quotes a letter to himself as evidence that Talleyrand was deficient in ideas, and wrote an unsubstantial style. These volumes are composed with much art, and, in the passage which is an express vindication, with uncommon power. Sometimes the author shows that he is accustomed to careless converse with inferior minds. He has more good sense than originality, and few gleams of unexpected light, like his friend Hamilton, or his master Machiavelli.

Although Talleyrand was in the habit of showing portions of the Memoirs to many persons in his time, his literary executor, Bacourt, determined that they should not be published until the year 1888. At that time they were the property of M. Andral, who would have liked to protract the suppression. This excessive caution has not been explained. Andral, the grandson of Royer-Collard, who presided over the Council of State under MacMahon, and, in the struggle for class government, was once thought of as the head of an extra-parliamentary Ministry on the American model, was much consulted as a shrewd adviser, steeped in the knowledge of public and private affairs. The business of the day left him without time or care for remoter things, and he lightly eluded inquiry into his precious deposit. He communicated the manuscript to the Count of Paris, though he refused it to his friend Thiers ; and he died, bequeathing it to the distinguished writer, who is at the same time a party leader and the bearer of an historic name.

Talleyrand is not favourable to men in authority, or to precepts of attachment and respect. His Memoirs forcibly proclaim that there is no such thing in reason as personal loyalty to a party or a man ; that whoever serves one order of things, does well to be preparing for the next ; that it is the note of a strong man to employ principles, and of a weak man to obey them. They are especially injurious to the house of Orleans ; and a passage relating to Philippe Egalité is the one portion of the manuscript which has been allowed to disappear. This hiatus of several sheets raises the question of the second copy. The Duke de Broglie publishes the final and authentic text ; but an earlier transcript exists, and bears marks of having been retouched by the author himself. For appreciable reasons, its possessor has never chosen, hitherto, to make any use of it ; but it will now be known whether it completes the published text and throws light on the successive growth of the Memoirs. Two or three passages are evidently later insertions ; some were written earlier ; and it will be interesting to inquire whether the Spanish and the Roman chapters are entirely the work of Talleyrand himself. One of them is hardly in keeping with the usually secular turn of his mind, and both are out of perspective.

French critics will easily detect inaccuracies, besides those which the editor has pointed out and corrected. It is not true that the Austrians were defeated in Germany in 1796 ; Carnot never was at Cayenne ; Oudinot was not a marshal in 1808. In one of his letters, Talleyrand showed how little he knew about English politics, when he says that the Whigs were seldom in power for more than a short time since 1688. Slips of memory and involuntary mistakes will not discredit the Memoirs. The omissions are more suspicious and indicate design. The remark that Marengo almost made Hohenlinden superfluous, curiously ignores the treaty with St. Julien, one of the less creditable transactions in the life of the French negotiator. But it would be unjust to insist on things untold; for if the author, sweeping a vast horizon, passes discreetly over treacherous places, he has not sought opportunities for vainglory, and is too well bred to record the scenes which exhibit his promptness in emergencies and the ease with which he disconcerted opponents. He describes neither the deliberations of the provisional government nor the arts of management by which a senate peopled with regicides was brought to declare for the Bourbons. He does even less than justice to himself when he relates that Napoleon, refusing to preserve his crown by reducing the territory, said, " Find other masters—je suis trop grand pour vous." This saying, made known last year, and bearing the mark of the lion's claw, proved that the mysterious duplicate is authentic. What Talleyrand does not say is that Napoleon, after these heroic words, assented at last to the conditions offered at Châtillon ; and that he himself, in May, signed peace on more favourable terms. Instances of this kind are so many, that the Duke de Broglie esteems that the work he has published was not designed for an apology.

He complains that Madame de Staël is not mentioned among those who procured the author's recall from proscription. But Talleyrand acknowledges that he owed to her his introduction to Barras, and his first appointment to the Ministry of Foreign Affairs. He affirms that he, for his own part, would have preferred to stand aloof, and that he yielded reluctantly to her influence. He allows full credit to her initiative in a step which was to lead so far. The story has been told in another shape. Talleyrand, it is said, declared to Madame de Staël that his money was exhausted, and that he would have to blow out his brains if, in a month, she could not find him a way to supplies.   This is the version of Barante, the least inventive of men, who knew them both well, who had seen the Memoirs, and who goes on to describe the meeting with the director and the scene at Suresnes, as they do. If the well-informed and disinterested historian deserves credit, the Memoirs must be discarded as a concatenation of insincerity.   But he is not a sufficient witness to carry such a verdict.   For he says that the friends soon afterwards quarrelled, that Talleyrand never ceased to detest the woman to whom he owed so much, and that she, in her anger, never again dreamed of a reconciliation.   Nevertheless, in February 1809, she entreated his intervention with the Emperor, in terms which would have been barely dignified in any circumstances, and are incompatible with unforgiveness.   The breach on her side cannot have been as incurable as Barante has described it.   Yet the occasion was one which might have justified strong feelings.

The American envoys made it known that they had been invited to bestow a present of money on the French minister, and Talleyrand had laughed at the idea of being challenged to repel the accusation.   The reproach of official corruption is, perhaps, the most difficult to meet of all those that he incurred.   Count Senfft, who, when I knew him, was an inmate of the Jesuits' College at Innsbruck, but who had been Talleyrand's warm admirer and friend as early as 1806, relates that he caused a sum of four millions of florins to be returned to the Poles, when he found that he was unable to serve their cause ; but that he accepted gifts of money from the German princes, whose interest he promoted, including one payment of forty thousand pounds from the King of Saxony.   Senfft himself was Saxon Minister, and as such in the secrets both of Dresden and Warsaw.   Bacourt, who has been careful to ascertain that Metternich and Nesselrode received no millions from France, says nothing in exoneration of his chief and patron.   The next volume, which will contain Talleyrand's account of the execution of Enghien, may possibly give some reply to this more formidable imputation.   In one of his earliest despatches he censures the venality of Thugut ; but his papers, so far as we have them, say nothing of his own.   It might be urged that what he did was not really done in secret, that the reconstruction of the European ruin after the revolutionary war, during the confederation of the Rhine and at the Congress of Vienna, afforded opportunities so exceptional that they amount to excuses ; that Napoleon, who allowed his brother to bring back bags of diamonds from Madrid, admitted the practice of diplomatic *douceurs*, and distributed enormous sums in that way.   Enemies of the United States used to affirm that the Ashburton treaty was carried by a method which may be traced in the books of Barings.

Talleyrand gives himself all the advantage to be got by depreciating others.   He speaks warmly of Hamilton, and respectfully of Lansdowne and Fox in England, of Mollien and Caulaincourt in France ; and he is above the vulgar and inefficacious error of reviling enemies.   Friends enjoy no immunity from his satiric temper ; and he is severe towards his tutor, Langfois, his secretary, Des Renaudes, and his intimate associate, Narbonne.   He says that the choice of Necker was the worst the King could have made ; Lafayette is beneath the level of mediocrity ; Breteuil is fit for the second place anywhere ; Sieyès would not be a rogue if he was not a coward ; the hands of Carnot are dripping with blood ; Fesch is a corsair disguised as a cardinal ; Joseph and Jerome are inglorious libertines ; the most prosperous of the marshals, Suchet, is *quelque peu bel esprit* ; his own successor, Champagny, begins every day trying to repair his blunders of the day before ; Humboldt is a bore ; Metternich is tortuous and second-rate ; Wellington has no head for principles ; Castlereagh strains the Englishman's prerogative of ignorance.

Most historical characters will probably suffer if we try them fairly by a fixed standard ; but Talleyrand displays no such thing as a standard of public or private morality. He tells how, greatly to his honour, he remonstrated with the Emperor upon his Spanish policy, saying that much evil-doing may be condoned, but that a mere cheat becomes contemptible. He was ready to make sacrifices to his sense, not of duty, but of propriety. The thing that shocks him is the indignity offered to the royal family, not the wrong done to the Spanish nation, for he himself had proposed that France should annex Catalonia. This passage, jointly with one or two others, gives the measure of his notion of right and wrong. He relates that, as a student at the seminary, he was silent, resentful, and morose, and was rescued from this unhealthy condition by an actress, whom he met under an umbrella, and with whom he lived for two years. He confesses that she was stupid; but he adds, with unmixed complacency, that the improvement of his manners and disposition was very much her work, and that the authorities had learned not to interfere with a youth of good family, predestined to become a Minister of State, a cardinal, perhaps even the dispenser of Crown patronage. To write like this in Memoirs addressed to the society of the Restoration shows more than a flaw in his knowledge of good and evil. Elsewhere he tells how a lady, whose intimacy with himself had not been free from scandal, requested him to stay away from the place where she was residing, as his presence might hinder her intended marriage. He publishes her name, and adds that the marriage came off without impediment, although there were others about who might have been as much in the way as himself. Here it must be admitted that the great master of ceremonial and the social art touches low-water mark, and we learn to suspect that a low moral vitality had as much to do with the stains on his life as violent passions or extreme temptation.

Talleyrand means it to be understood that, in all his versatile career, he was not the mere servant of opportunity, but that he was a man steering by fixed stars, applying principles to policy, occupied and possessed by certain general ideas superior to time and place. Many volumes of his letters produced in the last ten years show what truth there is in this thesis of the Memoirs. They show that Talleyrand accepted the essential philosophy of Liberalism, construed from Montesquieu and Turgot, Smith and Bentham. In 1786 he defends the Commerical Treaty as a policy based on the true natural laws that will put an end to the rivalry of nations. He believes, even then, that France and England ought to be inseparable in the cause of reason and justice against the world of divine right. A little later he declares that the traditional alliances terminate with the traditional monarchy ; and anticipating in 1792 the language of James Mill, argues that arbitrary governments labour for their own good, and free governments for the good of mankind. At a time when it was said that there were only two tolerant prelates in the Church of France, he was one of them. If it cost a sceptic no meritorious effort to emancipate the Jews, the ex-Bishop of Autun attested his sincerity in an hour of passion and peril, by insisting that the State has no authority over the conscience of citizen or monarch, and that the priest who refused the oath must be protected against the popular rage. He deems it the interest and the duty of France to rest content within her own wide borders, and to respect the integrity and independence of other countries by the same law as her own. He pleads for non-intervention in 1792, and still more in 1798, as plainly as in 1830. He acknowledged more and more that every people has the right to shape its own government, and maintained that France would have done well to create a united Italy, an independent Poland. As an avowed convert to the doctrine of Nationality and Revolution, he doubted the supreme masterpiece of political compromise and half measures, the Orleanist monarchy, and exhorted Lamartine to reserve his genius for a worthier cause than the support of a baseless throne. At the height of authority and fame he defies the wrath of his Government, and compels Louis Philippe to refuse for his son the proffered crown of Belgium.

When we touch the hard formation and come to the

convictions he expressed when circumstances did not sway him, and his language was apart from his interest, this is what we find. His Memoirs, letters, and State papers contain a buried picture not unlike the familiar one on the surface of history. The old lines are not effaced. We have not got to expunge from memory the unscrupulous priest, the money-getting Sybarite, the patient auxiliary of the conqueror and the tyrant, the Royalist who defended the tenth of August, the Republican minister who brought on the Empire, the imperial dignitary who restored the Bourbons, the apostle of legitimacy who hailed its fall. The Talleyrand of manifold tradition remains, and he remains a more valuable study than the most consistent doctrinaire.

But the doctrine is there as well as the policy, and the contrast gives an import to his life beyond any measure of practical success. It was characteristic of his public conduct repeatedly to undo his own work, and the problem is to find any constant motive under the glaring outer inconsistencies. Principles, in his easy philosophy, depended a good deal upon circumstances for their available use; and his saying that non-intervention is a term that means about the same thing as intervention, was more than a jest. Accustomed to hold dogmas loosely and conditionally, even in the science of which he was master, he described his own principle of legitimacy as nothing more than a supreme expedient. He gives the keynote at once by declaring that he will not call his Memoirs " My view of the events of my time," because that would be too positive a title for the work of a man *qui a autant que moi douté dans sa vie.* He understands the economists and believes in their doctrines, but he confesses that, having found human nature a poor material to carry them out with, he cheerfully ceased to care about them. Wessenberg records that he heard him say, " *Le seul bon principe est de n'en avoir aucun.*" The interior Talleyrand is a man with a nucleus of distinct opinions, which have not enough sanctity, or even certainty, to be worth the waste of an existence. He knows his short-

2 D

comings, his failures, his mistakes, but he assigns most of the blame to others. He brings an indictment against the many resisting and disturbing influences under which he strayed ; and the times he lived in, like nothing else in history, have to answer for much deviation. The first enemy was his father.

The accident that lamed him robbed him both of his birthright and of his home. During boyhood he never spent a week in the house of his parents. They not only showed him no affection, but gave him no encouragement, lest success should awaken importunate hopes and claims. They did not even inform him that the meaning of all this coldness, humiliation, and neglect was that he had been dedicated to the service of God. At last he was sent to Rheims, to his uncle the coadjutor, that he might be made aware of the sweets of episcopal life ; and he went through his course at St. Sulpice and the Sorbonne. He never had the choice of an alternative or the opportunity of escape. His father would give him no other provision, and the cost of his education was paid out of his first benefice. The family insisted absolutely on putting him into the Church ; and the Church received him as he was, without moral fitness, and apparently without religious faith. He was not more unworthy than others of the French clergy in his time, and he was far the ablest. His narrative, with measured but repeated touches, produces an impression stronger than his words. It is not he that sinned, but his parents. If, by taking orders without vocation he became a sacrilegious priest, destined in his long life never to know the security of a tranquil conscience, the crime was theirs. In this man, yet more than in Mirabeau, the ancient order of society, operating in conformity with accepted usage, prepared its doom.

When he last appeared before the world, mindful of his early training, he said that theology imparts certain qualities to the mind—*une force et en même temps une souplesse de raisonnement*—conducive to political excellence. He names the example of Lionne, who, having been educated for the Church, became the chief organiser

in France of that diplomatic subtlety and finesse which
Richelieu and the Père Joseph developed between them.
He had in mind that which divines learn on the benches
of the schools, the extreme subdivision of thought, the
habit of threshing out all the contents of a proposition,
the dialectics verging on hair-splitting and sophistry,
inherited from long ages that were undeterred by observation ; not the advantages of a system with imposing
traditions, fixed maxims, and a constant policy, whose
agents are never taken by surprise and know the uses of
time. He was thinking of the priesthood negotiating
more than governing. He had seen in his own vicinity,
in his own person, things more memorable than the
diplomatic art of Cardinal du Bellay and Cardinal de
Bernis. The Revolution had been started by one priest ;
the Republic had been proposed by another. Three out
of eight in the Constitutional Committee were ecclesiastics.
The Constitution of the year III., as well as that of the
year VIII., were chiefly devised by divines. The four
ministers who, at the Restoration, inaugurated parliamentary government belonged to the clergy.

His own studies were principally profane. The first
book he mentions is the *Memoirs of Cardinal de Retz*, a
man often compared to him in point of character and
ability. He tells us that he read political writers and
historians ; but when he puts Polignac next to d'Ossat
among negotiators, he betrays the limits of his knowledge
in that sort of literature. He had read Montesquieu, and,
like all the best minds of that age, he was influenced by
the *Esprit des Lois.* He pays Machiavelli the tribute of
intelligent imitation, and fortifies his legitimacy by the
authority of a grim passage from *The Prince.* He collected
a choice library ; but he was too much a man of the world
to resign himself to study and the dominion of silent
masters. Books, he says, have enlightened him ; he has
never allowed them to govern him. He describes how
much he owed to conversation in chosen society and how
he picked the brains of specialists.

In old age Talleyrand used to say that life had never

had so much to recommend it as at Paris in his youth.
In the Memoirs he speaks of a diminution of refinement
and a falling-off from what had been before the approach
of revolution.   He regards himself as belonging to a
higher and earlier epoch of good manners, and describes
as bearing an inferior stamp men who were the guide of
contemporaries and their mould of form.   Choiseul, the
man he liked best, gesticulates too much, and has a cold
heart.   Narbonne's cleverness is all for show, and is
exhausted by a joke ; his spirits are higher than good
taste allows, his familiar grace makes him friends,
especially among rather vulgar men.   *Il a une politesse
sans nuances.*   Nevertheless, they were all such good
friends that their intimacy, in the course of five years, was
never disturbed by tittle-tattle or misunderstanding.   He
attributes his own reputation for wit a good deal to the
power of holding his tongue.   He explains what he
considers that the best conversation should be, by the
example of his mother, whose charm consisted in pleasing
and passing on, without saying a word that could strike or
remain.   *Elle ne parlait que par nuances ; jamais elle n'a
dit un bon mot : c'était quelque chose de trop exprimé.*
Much of the thought, the talent, the discipline, the exertion
which goes, with other men, to the conduct of affairs, the
making of speeches, the writing of books, was concentrated,
by him, on the business of pleasant intercourse.   His
perfect mastery of so much that makes mere society
enjoyable, acquired among men who had beheld the
evening rays of Louis the Fourteenth, became one of the
elements of his superiority ; and he spoke with meaning
when, after an outbreak of Napoleon's fury, he said that it
was a pity so great a man had been so ill brought up.
An ambassador described him in 1814 as one "*qui
posséda si éminemment l'art de la société, et qui en a si
souvent usé avec succès, tantôt pour en imposer à ceux
qu'on voulait détruire, en leur faisant perdre contenance,
tantôt pour attirer à lui ceux dont on voulait se servir.*"
The prestige of his grand manner, of his lofty distinction
was a weapon both for attack and defence.   The Emperor

himself recognised the political force residing in the region where his aristocratic minister was supreme, when a report from Madame de Genlis on the conversations of the Faubourg St. Germain, which Talleyrand read to him, put him beside himself with anger, on the evening of Austerlitz.

The young Abbé de Perigord was so obviously marked out for promotion that he was made agent-general of the clergy before he was ordained.   In that capacity he relates that he endeavoured to be more than a man of his cloth, and attempted measures of general use   He generally failed ; and he professes to have failed because of that common vice of inexperienced men, too much idealism, and an artless belief in human nature.   He was so conspicuous that he was spoken of for the Archbishopric of Bourges, and looked forward to a position which would have given scope to his talents as an administrator. The Pope, urged by Gustavus the Third, who came to Rome in 1784, consented to make him a cardinal.   But Perigord, being connected with the Rohans, shared the disgrace which the Diamond Necklace brought upon them ; and the Queen, through Count Mercy, who calls him a scoundrel, prevented the appointment.   Louis the Sixteenth hesitated for months before nominating him to the See of Autun, which happened just before the meeting of the States-General.

Talleyrand appeared at Versailles with the reputation of a man of business, expert in money-matters.   By his management of the affairs of the clergy and his associa- tion with Calonne, he was better known by his head for figures than as a master of ecclesiastical policy.   Mirabeau, with whom he had had a serious quarrel, meant to offer him the department of Finance.   At that time he is described as a man without enthusiasm or illusions, pliant, patient, and calm, sure of rising to the greatest elevation. He was no orator, and obtained no popular ascendency. In his address to his clergy, he demanded the Habeas Corpus, trial by jury, free trade, a free press, and the codi- fication of the law.   But he thought it madness to double the Third Estate, and wished that the King would dissolve the Assembly and summon another on different lines, with a definite plan of action, which Talleyrand had prepared. He took the lead in discarding instructions and the division of the orders ; but, after the fall of the Bastille, he, with his friends, called on Louis the Sixteenth to adopt their policy.   At midnight, on the 16th of July, he roused the Count of Artois, explained to him during two hours what would happen if the unresisted Assembly was allowed to send France down the entire cataract of deductive logic, and made him get out of bed and carry the ultimatum to the King.   Louis, judging that this was a bid for office by a man who had given no extraordinary proof of capacity, and who in public had taken the opposite line of submission to the majority, rejected the warning, and the Count came back, protesting that the game was lost and that he would be off for the frontier in the morning. Talleyrand vainly dissuaded him from emigrating.   At last he said, " Then, sir, as the King and the princes abandon the monarchy, nothing remains for us but to shift for ourselves."   Twenty-five years later when, as head of the Government, he invited the Count to return, he was able to remind him that the advice he had given at their last meeting was good.

The famous decree with which Talleyrand is identified, though it altered fundamentally the conditions of religion in France, was a financial measure, not the outcome of a scheme of Church government.   At a Conference held in May, the Archbishop of Arles made, with applause, the insane proposal that they should take the opportunity to have the debt of the clergy paid by the State.   It was soon apparent that the clergy would be called on to supply the deficit of the State, and after the 4th of August, and the abolition of tithes, the property of the Church could not be saved.   As soon as the assembly had removed to Paris, the Bishop of Autun, quick to recognise the inevitable, moved that the nation should take over the Church property, allowing a pension exceeding by a million sterling that which is now paid,

which, while reducing the income of prelates, improved
the situation of the parish clergy.   The effect was not
what he intended, for he did not save the public credit,
and he ruined the Gallican Church.   The Assembly
would neither leave the patronage to the executive, nor
salary a body of men to be nominated by the Pope.   It
therefore adopted the principle of election, which was the
substance of the *Constitution Civile.*   In questions of
Canon Law, ancient or modern, Talleyrand was neither
competent nor interested.   The scheme was not of his
devising, but it was executed by his instrumentality ; he
consecrated the first of the new bishops.   Writing amid
the environments of 1816, he states his reason.   Nearly
all the bishops had refused the Constitutional oath.   If
none had accepted, and if there had, consequently, been
nobody to transmit the succession, the State might have
lapsed into Presbyterianism, which was a form that
harmonised with the spirit of the new institutions, and
Calvinism would have been established.   This far-fetched
argument may have been a genuine reminiscence of
Bossuet, and of the doctrine familiar to Gallican divines,
that a Huguenot is a Republican, that a Presbyterian is
the same as a Whig, and that hierarchy in the Church
responds to monarchy in the State.

It may be that the bishop employed schism as a
supreme preservative against Democratic heresy.   The
establishment of the new episcopate gave him a welcome
opportunity of abandoning his position in the Church and
seeking a new career.   There was no French abbé on
whom his orders sat more lightly, or who was so secular
in his conduct.   But though he wore no mask of hypocrisy,
and submitted to little restraint, when he could not win
twelve hundreds at play without being made the talk of
the town, the falseness of his position became intolerable.
He resigned his bishopric, and refused to have himself
put forward for the See of Paris.   Three years later, when,
riding at night in an American forest, he called out to his
servant, and a voice answered, " Here I am, Monseigneur,"
he could not help laughing at this reminder of distant

Autun.   In 1802 Pius the Seventh, although he loved
his excommunicated brother less than he will have it
secularised him for his services to the Concordat.   The
Memoirs specially observe the tone of ecclesiastical
decorum ; and once, addressing Louis the Eighteenth,
Talleyrand is aghast at the incredulity of the age.

For a short time, when his Parisian rival, Narbonne,
became Minister, he obtained considerable influence, and
came to England early in 1792 on an acknowledged, but
necessarily unofficial, mission, to ensure the neutrality of
Pitt.   In August he was again in Paris, and witnessed
the overthrow of the monarchy.   He induced Danton to
send him back to London, under cover of some scientific
negotiation, and was thus able to declare that he had
not incurred the pains of emigration, and yet to assure
Grenville that he was not in the service of the Republic.
But with all his dexterity and coolness he could not hold
a position between the upper and the nether millstone.
He was outlawed in France, he was expelled from
England ; and having sold his books in London, he
sailed for Philadelphia.   He would have been glad to get
a passage to India, to be shrouded in sufficient obscurity
until his time came.

It came at the end of two years.   In 1796 he found
himself restored to France, in the embarrassing company
of a lady who had got Francis into trouble before him, and
having no position but that of a member of the Institute.
In the scheme for a national system of education, which
he presented to the Assembly, the whole was to have been
directed by a central board composed of the ablest men
in France ; so that the idea of the Institute may be said
to belong to him.   The Duke de Broglie, following his
father's *Souvenirs*, believes that Talleyrand's Report was
not his own work ; while Jules Simon affirms the contrary,
and the Memoirs claim that he drew it up after consulting
Lavoisier, Laplace, and the scientifie men of the day.   In
his new character he read two papers exposing the wisdom
he had gathered in exile.   During his two years' stay in
England he had made a friend of Lord Lansdowne, and

in the Bowood circle had met men who were working
the problems of the hour on different lines from those he
had learned at home.   In the United States he came under
the influence of Alexander Hamilton.   He had gone away
a disciple in economics of Dupont de Nemours, without
his dogmatism and without his fervour.   He came back
a believer in the doctrine of Utility, in the colonial system
of Adam Smith ; and he informs his countrymen that
nations act by self-interest, not by gratitude or resentment, and that nothing can divert the trade of America
from England to France.   He said afterwards that a sound
political economy was the talisman which made England,
for thirty years, the first of European Powers.

Academic exercises were not the road to greatness ;
and Madame de Staël rescued him from penury by telling
Barras what manner of man he was.   Talleyrand's fortune
was made that day.   He grasped his opportunity; fascinated
the director by that pleasant talk which aged men still
remember with admiration ;   and was appointed Minister of
Foreign Affairs by a bare majority over the most obscure
of competitors.   With an interval of four months in 1799,
he held the office during the ten extraordinary years from
Campo Formio to Tilsit.   His despatches, written for the
Directory, have been published by M. Pallain, who, but
for names and dates, would be an excellent editor, and they
are not worthy of his later fame.   As the executive agent
of a deliberative and fluctuating body, he is not seen to
advantage.   His employers distrusted him, and he despised
his employers.   The Swiss and Italian questions were
decided without him ;   the question of the negotiations at
Lille was settled against him.   He made way slowly, and
carried to extremes the compliance which is expected in a
subordinate and in a colleague.   He tried in vain to be
elected one of the directors, and the Prussian envoy writes
that his elevation would put an end to the convulsions of
Europe.   He craved for a master more intelligent than
the directors, or at least firmer and more constant.   Together
with Sieyès he thought of Moreau, of Joubert, of the Duke
of Brunswick, the grand illusion of the time.   Together

they contrived the Eighteenth of Brumaire. He had seen
from the beginning that Bonaparte had more than a military genius. He felt for monarchy like the Vendéan chief
who, when he was asked in whose name he fought, replied,
" In the name of the King, that is, of any man who may
occupy the throne."

He had found what he wanted, a master worthy of such
a minister. By the account which he gives of his own
system, his endurance in office during all the ascending
years is a prodigy of suppleness. Talleyrand at all times
wished to restrict the limits of France to the Rhine. He
would have made terms with England by the sacrifice of
Malta, and thought us justified in the breach of the peace of
Amiens. He regarded Austria as the natural and necessary
ally, and would have granted overwhelming compensation,
by the partition of Turkey, for her losses in the sphere of
French influence. He advised the restoration of Venice,
and exposed the folly of surrounding the Empire with a
girdle of helpless Bonapartes. On the topics of agreement
with Napoleon he does not enlarge, and asserts some merit
for sympathy and generosity shown to the vanquished
Hohenzollerns. But in his political construction Prussia
was the inevitable adversary. He constantly described it
as a neighbour on whom there was no reliance, with a barren
territory and an open frontier, compelled by nature to be
ambitious and aggressive, and to scheme for the subjugation
of Germany. *Tout prétexte lui est bon. Nul scrupule ne
l'arrête. La convenance est son droit.* His encounter at
Vienna with the Prussian statesmen, when he got the better
of William Humboldt, must have been a prouder moment
than when he set up his chancery at Berlin.

From his entrance into office he pursued the policy of
secularisation. From Salzburg all round to Liége Europe
was covered with ecclesiastical proprietors and potentates,
and it was an opportune and congenial resource to
suppress them in order to satisfy the princes who had
to be consoled for the conquests of Bonaparte. This
process of ecclesiastical liquidation was Talleyrand's element. He had destroyed the Church of France as a

privileged and proprietary corporation ; and by the like
impulse he helped to deprive the clergy of the Empire of
their political prerogative.   And he was still on the same
ground at the Congress, when he reduced political right
to the hereditary rights of families, and the Prince of
Reuss was a weightier personage than a doge of Venice
or an Archbishop of Cologne.   There was little to boast
of in following with a despatch-box where the sword of
Napoleon cleared the way ; but Talleyrand claims to have
done his best for the victims, and he angered his master
by drawing clauses from which he could not escape.   He
had to submit to be the instrument of violence, to see his
State papers transformed ; and, as in the Lauderdale
correspondence, to publish as authentic letters he had
been too wise to send.

Not much in the description of Napoleon is new.
There is a good deal between the lines of the grotesque
account of the Spanish princes at Valencay ; and in the
complacent details of the interview at Erfurt, the point
of the dialogue with Wieland has been lost.   But the
portrait of the Emperor by the most intelligent man in
the Empire will always retain its value.   The idea it
suggests is that Napoleon failed by excess of talent.   The
flaw in the reckoning was that he calculated too much, and
carried his thinking too far.   He set himself to provide
against contingencies which he could detect, but which
were so remote that they practically did not exist, and
weakened himself by defences against dangers not likely
to take shape amongst obvious-minded men.   He brought
on perpetual war because the increase of France having
been the work of other generals, he was afraid of their
renown.   Therefore he annexed Piedmont as a trophy of
his own campaigns.   In the same way he thought that
Spain could never be reduced to a trusty satellite, as the
King would some day remember who the Bourbons were,
and how they came to reign beyond the Pyrenees.

In 1807, when the Empire was at its best, Talleyrand
resigned his office ; but as a great dignitary of State he
continued to be consulted and employed.   His proper

412 ESSAYS ON MODERN HISTORY

place at that time was in opposition. He implored
Alexander not to ruin his master by too much yielding.
His advice to Metternich was an encouragement to
Austria to prepare for the war of 1809. Napoleon
proposed to send him to Warsaw in 1812, and made the
mistake of changing his mind. In the following year he
again offered him the Foreign Office. Talleyrand refused ;
he was not good on a sinking ship. It does not suit
everybody, as he said to Savary, to be buried in the
impending crash. Before Napoleon started for the
campaign in France, that scene of violence occurred
which Molé described to Dalling. Talleyrand offered to
resign his dignities. Insult had released him from
personal obligation ; and when the fortune of war turned,
after the victories of February, he allowed his friends to
open communication with the invaders. Their emissary
made his way through the French lines to headquarters,
carrying two names as a password, names which had a
meaning for Stadion ; and, for Nesselrode, these dangerous
and significant words traced in invisible ink : " You march
on crutches." The bearer of these credentials was the
most acute, the most alert, and the boldest of Royalists.
He found, in the middle of March, less than a fortnight
before the capitulation of Paris, that the allies were agreed
in rejecting the Bourbons. This mission of the Baron de
Vitrolles, of which there are three narratives in the second
volume, is an epoch in the life of Talleyrand. When he
knew that Louis the Eighteenth, who was forgotten in
France, was repudiated by Europe, he resolved that he
should be king. It was the one solution entirely his own.
And he made him king, imposing his choice with
invincible ease on an Assembly of Republicans and
Bonapartists, and on the wavering and bewildered master
of twenty legions. It is the stroke of genius in his career.
The conquerors of Napoleon found themselves at Paris in
the hands of a gracious cripple in powder, who, without
emphasis or exertion, crumpled up their schemes, and
quietly informed them that the Bourbons alone were a
principle.

With those words he legislated for Europe. By that law, so convincing to his generation, he was providing an organic force that enabled him at Vienna to subdue the Congress, to scatter the victorious allies, and to achieve his own chosen scheme of an alliance between England, Austria, and France. The implacable analysis of history has since made known that the doctrine which makes hereditary right paramount in politics is unscientific, and cannot combine with the rights of nations. Talleyrand was no advocate of arbitrary power, either at Paris or at Vienna. He was disgusted with those who sent Ferdinand the Seventh to reign without conditions. Although it was not his hand that drew up the Charte, it was his mind chiefly that inspired it. In 1815 he denounced the reactionary counsels of the Count of Artois before the King and the Count himself, and insisted on the principle of a homogeneous and responsible ministry ; and he retired before the Holy Alliance. The Bourbons, if they had reigned by his advice, would not have fallen. When he wrote his narrative of the events in which he performed the part of king-maker, he did not see that he had made a blunder. The dynasty he had enthroned persisted for fifteen years in excluding him from power. After 1830 he regrets that he had forgotten Fox's saying that the worst sort of Revolution is a Restoration. When Madame de Lieven affected surprise that the man who had crowned Louis the Eighteenth should appear in London as the plenipotentiary of Louis Philippe, he replied that the King he served would have been the choice of Alexander in 1814. They do not seem to have remembered who it was that prevented it.

XIV

THE LIFE OF LORD HOUGHTON [1]

To the present generation the name of Lord Houghton represents, in the apt terms of his biographer, a social moderator and leisured literary expert. But the original Monckton Milnes was known as something more than this, as a serious and effective writer and a busy and apparently dissatisfied politician. Mr. Wemyss Reid renders full justice to him in his earlier character. Lingering survivors will prefer the anticipated judgment of posterity, and will be inclined to think less of his real success in literature or his supposed disappointment in politics than of those qualities which made him the centre of a vast circle of friends, and gave him a singular and brilliant position at the point where letters, politics, and society met.

He was the son of a country gentleman, who, having refused to be Chancellor of the Exchequer at twenty-five, lived to decline the offer of a peerage forty-seven years later. The remainder of his career does not maintain the level of his lofty abnegation. In early youth he convinced both friends and rivals that he was equal to the best of his contemporaries ; but he never afterwards cared to live up to that reputation. A remark of Lord Palmerston on his second speech in the House of Commons, a remark of his own, after following the army from Brussels to Paris, to the effect that the Prussians were of no use at all at Waterloo, make it doubtful whether his early fame or his later obscurity was better earned. He became a man of

[1] " *The Life, Letters, and Friendships of Richard Monckton Milnes, First Lord Houghton.* By T. Wemyss Reid, London, Cassell & Co., 1890." *The Nineteenth Century*, December 1890.

pleasure, seldom losing a thousand at a sitting, but thinking
five hundred pounds a reasonable price for the waistcoats
of the year.   Mr. Wemyss Reid, who produces the father
as a foil to the son, says, in allusion to this item of
account, that Pemberton Milnes was " not altogether free
from the spirit of dandyism."   This felicity of understatement and sobriety of colour is one of his merits as a
biographer.   He used to be a guest at Fryston, and
writes as a personal friend.   His best act of friendship
is the lucid good sense with which he assigns the just
proportions to his hero, marking the limit and the drawback, and indulging in no word of praise that will not
amply be confirmed by all who remember him.

The elder Milnes, who died in 1858, did not transmit
his parliamentary talent to his son, and was disposed to
look down on him for spoiling his political position with
desultory literature.   But there was a wayward instability
and fastidiousness which seems to have run in the blood.
The son never threw away such a chance or deceived the
expectation of others, as his father did.   The family
history, perhaps, influenced him at another point.   They
were Unitarians who, not long before his time, exchanged
the meeting-house for at least an occasional conformity.
In religion, as in other things, he showed not the zeal of
a convert, but an impartial eclecticism, a vivid and inconstant curiosity, a semi-detached adhesiveness, which tended
towards isolation.

His university life was active and useful to his mental
development, if not positively studious ; but before
Thirlwall and Niebuhr shaped him he began to display one
quality which had much to do with the enmities and the
friendships of later times.   He treated his disreputable
uncle like a schoolfellow, and his aunts as if they were
his sisters ; and he told his respected father that he
thought he must be insane.   Before settling down to Pall
Mall and Parliament he was so long abroad that he was
a pretty good linguist, and could detect the English
accent in our best French scholars.   He always continued
his connection with France, and many of his best friends

and best stories were French. He went to Italy and
Germany for curiosity and amusement; but for the society
of Paris he had a real preference. His Orleanist sympathies were one of the chief factors in his career. They
were not interrupted by his acquaintance with his London
comrade Napoleon, and neither of them suffered by his
attachment to Lamartine, from whom, in despite of Lord
Aberdeen, he raised a sum of money. There was no
exaggeration in Disraeli's joke about his entertaining
royalties and revolutionists. Once, walking away with
one of his guests, I was stopped by a friend who asked
me who the small boy was. The small boy was Louis
Blanc, who was explaining his belief in the survival of
Lewis the Seventeenth. For a man who loved varieties
of character and cultivated the art of conversation, there
could be no doubt of the pre-eminence of France.

When he was eighteen, Spurzheim drew his horoscope
in terms which amounted to saying that he would never
do much harm or much good. Aubrey de Vere, who
remembers him in 1831, fills in the outline as follows:
" He had not, as it seemed to me, much of solid ambition,
nor did he value social distinction as much as intellectual
excitement and ceaseless novelty." Houghton said of himself with much point and candour: " Having no duties
to perform, I am obliged to put up with pleasures." When
he appeared in London, the worldly sage of the day, Sam
Rogers, seeing that he was a fine gentleman, but also a
scholar and a wit, drew a shaft from his ancient experience
which did not fall wide: " Get on by pleasing the women,
the men will hate ye."

M. Taine, when he said that the English were dull
talkers—" Ils ne savent pas s'amuser avec la parole "—
can have known very little of Milnes. Others of his set
talked as well or better, and had more of their own to
say; but there was no other man who made the pleasure
of conversation the business of life. His philosophy of
society was not fanciful or frivolous, as, in the outer circle,
men supposed. He took a warm and intelligent interest
in many things, in which conversation was the common

denominator. He conceived that one who, having the time to surround himself constantly with the best, to spend his time with Macaulay and Carlyle, Tocqueville and Guizot, even with Sherman and Moltke, prefers the casuals of life, is mean and incompetent.

He once propounded a sublime and self-denying definition of a good dinner as civility without consumption. As to company he was less exacting. The severe orthodoxy which requires that a man shall prefer the topics and initiative of others to his own ; that he shall neither insist, nor repeat, nor contradict ; that he shall speak of things, not of persons, and never of himself; that he shall restrain the use of witticism and anecdote, would have been tiresome and ruinous in his eyes. He knew how to draw out of each guest what was in him, to make the talk general, and discourage the eddies and hole-and-corner whisperings which are the grave of good company. He sought not only talent but diversity ; and not only diversity but contrast. He loved the flavour of antagonism, and held that a gentleman is one who can live with adversaries. Vambéry once related at his table things since made public — his journey in disguise to the Mahometan centre of Asia, and the inscription of the Christian captive which nearly betrayed him. Another Eastern traveller chafed visibly under these revelations of the deceitful dervish, uttering gutturals which could be nothing else than Turkish imprecations. When a certain suave prelate, putting on to perfection the Bishop in *Little Dorrit*, asked the Hungarian by which road he meant to take his next journey, and was answered, "That, my lord, is my secret," everybody felt that Milnes had not lost a day.

He had known what it is to be over-sensitive, to have tender spaces and antipathies, and he knew that these things are to be overcome. Therefore, when you wrote a book, you went to him prepared to find your reviewer ; and if you were the reviewer, you found your victim. The man who shrank from facing a critic or a rival, the lion afraid of a louder roar, was a thing below par, and only fit to be improved away. At the risk of some

annoyance, at the price of some mistakes, he very
deliberately strove to raise and humanise the social tone,
and his house was not only a school of colloquial art, but
of proper self-control.   He had the opportunities, the
large acquaintance with men, the versatile interest in ideas,
the international position.   Above all, he had the purpose
and the energy.   In this sense it is not an exaggeration
to say that the object he sought was influence.

The rare and subtle essence which constituted so
much of the enjoyment of his life was evanescent.   If
Houghton was distinguished as a brilliant conversational
centre and extractor of men's thoughts, it was a gift which
has left no permanent trace behind.   Sir George Trevelyan,
in the life of the best English talker of his time, has little
to record, and Mr. Wemyss Reid has no description of a
Symposium—nothing as interesting as Hawthorne's breakfast on the 11th of July 1856, where he met Ticknor
and the Brownings, Lord Lansdowne and Macaulay.
Unfortunately Milnes, who heard so much, wrote down
very little.   He stays at Val Richer, but only tells us
that Guizot's grandchild preferred jelly to hare.   He pays
a visit to Tocqueville and has nothing to report.   His
memory was better furnished than his correspondence.
He used to relate that at Tocqueville somebody incautiously spoke of people who marry beneath their rank.
There was a moment of chill silence, until the host, taking
his wife's hand, said, " Moi aussi, j'ai fait une mésalliance ;
et Dieu ! que cela m'a réussi."   Milnes has written somewhere what he remembered of the man whom he complacently called his French double.   The papers to which
his biographer has had access leave all this to perish,
and it is hard to believe that there were no notebooks
left and forgotten under lock and key.   For it is to the
life of Houghton that Englishmen would look for something that they could compare to the dialogues of the
dead preserved by Roederer and Villemain and Falloux.

His biographer knew him well in later life, and was
drawn to the sturdy Yorkshire Liberal who was not always
apparent behind the self-caricaturist of Brook Street.   He

thinks of him as a politician, of his want of success and happiness in politics, and affirms that he was a disappointed man.   Milnes was at different times a candidate for public employment.   As he spoke French and was a familiar friend of the House of Orleans and its chief adherents, he would have liked to be First Secretary at Paris.   He was even more persuaded of his claim to represent the Foreign Office in the House of Commons, and there is no doubt that he was wounded when the place was given to a man who must be described as his personal enemy.   Ten years later he got up Irish questions, expecting to be sent to Ireland, but Palmerston only offered him a junior lordship. Afterwards he thought that a blunder was committed when he was not made an *Alabama* Commissioner.   Although he had neither the craving for office which comes from pride and greed, nor the legitimate ambition to carry measures and impress opinions, he thought it stupid of Peel to imagine that a poet is unfitted for politics.   When Palmerston had few personal adherents Milnes was one of them, but by October 1860 his liking for him " has very much gone off."   He consoled himself for his American disappointment by administering much private advice to those who did not send him, and his Liberal feelings became tinged with Imperialism.   On the day when Lord Derby, by taking his seat below the gangway, proclaimed his resignation, and there was the smell of gunpowder in the air, he could scarcely contain his exuberant delight. He was firmer in resisting the latter developments of Liberalism than his letters show, and his nightmare took the shape of Mr. Gladstone pursuing him in a hansom. His dread of Socialism and his contempt for the Greeks are recorded here ; but there was also a growing coolness towards the Poles which German sympathies may explain, but which was unexpected in a member of the Polish Committee.   For a man whose views were influenced by foreign thought, he was a steady politician, and the wish to be an under-secretary was a modest aspiration in a life so rich and varied that, by common consent, two large volumes can hardly do justice to it.

In that life the main interest was not political loss and gain.   Milnes was not easily irritated by opposition or satire, but he was extremely susceptible about anything like a want of regard or reciprocity, and above all suspicious of a disposition to take him as a mere ornament.   He had deserved well of all men.   He had made it a point of honour to be generous and helpful with very many, to be patient and good-humoured with everybody.   As time passed and shadows lengthened, he found that there were some who repelled his advances and depreciated his merits. These were the failures which he felt, which he resented in private life quite as much as in public.   There was more wounded good-nature than wounded ambition in his regrets. There were some, too, in a further circle, of whom he thought or experimentally found that he could make nothing, and who thought themselves just as good, or as bad, as his miscellaneous society.   Certain feuds, such as those with George Smythe and Panizzi, are mentioned by Mr. Wemyss Reid.   Those who shared his confidence could no doubt show a longer and more characteristic list of men who were not in harmony, who sneered at or obstructed him, and on whom he avenged himself by the perfect perspicacity of his spoken or written judgments. He speaks of Thackeray's occasional perversity, and thinks that Sidney Herbert ought to have prospered, because he had both wealth, grace, tact, and not too much principle. One of his gravest and probably most sincere utterances is this: " As one gets on in life, one of the most annoying reflections is the little good one has done by what people call benevolence ; in fact, how little man can be benefited by others."

It would be absurd to accept with Philistine gravity the extravagant sayings in which Houghton vented his dislike of the social enemy, of prejudices and idols, of impostors and bores, or to confound riotous paradox with explosions of genuine conviction.   We often remember Lord Tennyson's warning : " Every fool will think he meant it."   It occurs to us where he speaks of the mendacity of Orleanist ministers, as well as in the passages where he says probably more than he thought of Cardinal Newman and the late Lord Derby. The most characteristic story is that of his saying to Lord Stanhope, in the severe dulness of the Lords, "You and I are the only men in this place who can read and write." To which Lord Stanhope replied, "Pardon me ; you forget Lord Lytton." There is an inevitable perplexity in determining his real thoughts ; and this very perplexity is the triumph of his many devices to startle and to bewilder. The concealment of lofty ideas and deep emotion beneath hyperbole and affected cynicism has made it a difficult task to lift the veil from his inner spiritual life.

Mr. Wemyss Reid insists much upon Lord Houghton's feeling towards Rome ; and even heard him say that he might have been a Catholic but for the Oxford Movement. It must have gratified him to think that he went the contrary way to other men, and that the XC. Tracts which led so many away from the Church of England were to the author of *One Tract More* the motive of his remaining in it. From early Bonn days he had many Catholic friends, here and abroad, and during the hottest No-Popery agitation he attended the Cardinal's receptions as if he had been in Italy, and bent over his ring with every mark of ceremonious respect. He was quite in his element at Rome during the Council, discussing policy and doctrine with the Princess Wittgenstein and the Archbishop of Tuam. He told his best friend that he had no right to find fault with Lord Ripon for adopting the faith held by nineteen-twentieths of the Christian world. Carlyle, who was not generally tolerant of such things, says that he talked *dilettante* Catholicism. When he had Catholic guests on Friday, he was scrupulous about the fish, and did not like his care to be vain. Perhaps irony sometimes mingled with his solicitude. Mérimée was settling down to a plate of turtle when Milnes exclaimed : "No, no ! give him the other ! M. Mérimée, il y a une soupe maigre pour vous !" The academician answered : "Merci ! j'aime autant celle que j'ai."

With his large power of sympathy and inclusion he

had neither head nor heart for strict denominational studies. Not to be in living touch with the immense phenomena of Catholicity, with the teaching of Wiseman, as with that of Guizot or Heine, would have seemed to him a lapse into ancestral sectarianism or national insulation. At Paris he would visit the veteran Chouan Rio, who was affectionately attached to him, and then go straight to another Breton, Renan. He was as intimate with Montalembert as with any foreigner ; but he resented his attitude towards the *coup d'état*, and repeated the malicious stories spread from the Elysée. Neither Thirlwall nor Aubrey de Vere took his theological demonstrations very seriously, and he himself, when he was asked, used to say that he was a professed crypto-Catholic.

Without being a recluse, or even a strict economist of time, he had read widely, and possessed a very unusual knowledge of unusual things in literature and history. His studious curiosity and zeal in collecting rare books blossomed into a society of literary Epicureans called the Philobiblion Club, which was an enlarged edition of Monckton Milnes. He wished it to be looked upon as a society of idle men—of men so indifferent to the shortness of time that they would go out breakfasting, not only at each other's town houses, but, by preference, at Twickenham or Wimbledon, at Highgate or at least at St. Dunstan's. They were the owners of unique copies, of bindings bright with the arms of Mazarin, and titlepages defaced by priceless signatures. Though reputed enemies of profitable knowledge, in a luxurious way they issued volumes of recondite and exquisite matter ; but when one of them published a mere life of Shakespeare, stiff with the solidity of facts and dates, others felt like an epicure invited to dine on condensed egg. The unwritten law forbids profane intrusion into the life of clubs, but the Philobiblion exists no more, and Mr. Wemyss Reid was justified in pleasantly describing an association peculiarly characteristic of Lord Houghton's tastes, in which he spent many of his happiest hours, and where those who had the privilege of meeting him found him at his best. He also follows him to Grillion's, which was the occasion of some of his literary work, and he says with truth that no place suited him better. For it was originally a parliamentary club, founded on the practice of pairing for dinner ; so that men who had spoken at each other from five to eight might drink wine with each other between eight and ten. It was enriched by a very choice flavour of unparliamentary intellect. Lord Houghton was also a member of the club, but he was elected late in life —so late that he was insensible to the compliment, and it contributed little to his pleasure.

Most of his early associates died before him, and he had not the faculty of attaching himself to new people. Sir Charles MacCarthy, his most trusted confidant and correspondent of his prime, died in 1864. At that time Lord Houghton had already become acquainted with a Liverpool merchant, of whom he writes, " I look on him as the last of my friends of mature life." Henry Bright was a man whose refined charm of manner and excellent attainments made him an invaluable companion, after the death of Sir William Stirling Maxwell, whom Houghton was with difficulty dissuaded from pronouncing, in the lifetime of Carlyle, the first of literary Scotsmen. He wrote to Bright : " He, I, and you were the only real men of letters in Great Britain." In spite of the habitual exaggeration, all those who knew the man to whom these words were addressed will recognise the truth that was in them. He was a more careful scholar than his friend, but he loved literature for its own sake, without profit or display, and not in quest of hard-working truths. He had not health for sustained effort, and he spent on reviews of the books of the day, and in running to ground topics cast up in familiar table-talk, knowledge sufficient for a considerable reputation. Four weeks before his death he dictated a letter informing Houghton that he was very seriously ill, and he added with his dying hand this postscript : " Should we not meet, let me here thank you for a friendship of nearly twenty-five years, which has added so greatly to the brightness and happiness of my life." This was the simple farewell which closed an intimacy that had done much to cheer and comfort Houghton when the loss of his wife, the marriage of his daughters, the burning of Fryston had turned his happy life to gloom.

At this time his own health was breaking, and he had received a warning which he perfectly understood. He had always felt deeply ; he was ἀρτίδακρυς, and was as easily moved by things great and good as by sorrow. But in regard to himself he was tranquil. Neither increasing infirmities, nor the certainty of impending death subdued his spirit. He insisted on writing my name on a book that he borrowed, and explained that he might, at any moment, be carried off in a fit. He became anxious not to be left alone, clinging to his friends, and especially to his sister, Lady Galway, who devoted herself to watching over him in the declining years. Mr. Wemyss Reid found him very ill one day, and asked what was the matter. "Death," he answered gravely ; "that is what is the matter with me. I am going to die." And then his face was illumined by a smile of serene resignation. The end for which he had been preparing came, as he expected, swiftly, in August 1885.

He was accustomed to describe his career as an unsuccessful one, and loved to be thought a failure. But as a poet he attained his full stature very early, and turned away satisfied with his work.[1] He lived long enough to know that the one thing for which his many faculties and virtues unfitted him was power. He had cultivated too attentively the art of being misunderstood, and it was not easy to defend effectively a man so easy to misrepresent. Drudgery, pretentious commonplace, dense prejudice, invincible dulness, which make up the larger half of average politics, were things which no middle-age training could ever render tolerable to a mind fed daily on every refinement and every exotic. If he wished for

---

[1] I was once dining at a party with him and Tennyson, when, turning to me and pointing to the poet, he said, "Ah! a great deal of him will live for ever, and so will some of me" (Ed., *Nineteenth Century*).

that which was denied him, he desired it as material for that which his life richly afforded, a position of almost unique social usefulness and enjoyment. He leaves a memory nobler and more enduring than that of the ordinary successful politician, as one who, having gifts and opportunities above almost all other men, employed them throughout a long life in personal service, striving far less for his own ends than for the happiness of others.

XV

A HISTORY OF THE PAPACY DURING THE PERIOD OF THE REFORMATION [1]

MR. CREIGHTON'S new volumes tell the story of the Papacy as an Italian power during the last half-century that preceded and prepared the rise of Protestantism. Next to the merits of moderation and sobriety which the preface rightly claims, their first characteristic is the economy of evidence, and the severity with which the raw material is repressed and so kept out of sight as not to divert the reader's attention or turn his pleasure into toil. The author prefers the larger public that takes history in the shape of literature, to scholars whose souls are vexed with the insolubility of problems and who get their meals in the kitchen. The extent of his research appears whenever there is a favourite point to illustrate ; but he generally resembles a writer on the Long Parliament who should treat Rushworth and Clarendon as too trite for quotation, or Mr. Walpole if he were to strike out several hundred references to *Hansard* and the *Annual Register*. There is some risk in attempting a smooth narrative of transactions belonging to an age so rich in disputed matter and dispersed material, and quick with the causes of the Reformation. As the author rarely takes stock or shows the limit of his lore, the grateful student, on whom proofs are not obtruded, cannot tell whether they abound, and may be led wrongly and injuriously to doubt whether

---

[1] By M. Creighton, M.A. Vols. III. and IV.—The Italian Princes, 1464-1518. *English Historical Review*, 1887.

the sources of information and suggestion have been fully
explored.   Nobody should stand better with Mr. Creighton than Ranke.   The late John Richard Green used to
complain that it was from him that he had learnt to be
so dispassionate and inattentive to everything but the
chain of uncoloured fact.   In reserve of language, exclusion of all that is not history, dislike of purple patch-
work and emotional effect, their ways are one.   At the
same time, the chapter on Savonarola has been more distinctly a labour of love than any other part of these
volumes.   Yet the essay on Savonarola, which is among
Ranke's later writings, has not been suffered to influence
the account of the friar's constitution and of the challenge.
Burckhardt, the most instructive of all writers on the
Renaissance, is missed where he is wanted, though there is
a trace of him in the description of Caterina Sforza.
The sketch of Gemistus Pletho is founded on Alexandre's
edition of his *Laws*, irrespective of Schulze's later and
more comprehensive treatise.   Schulze is as well known
to Mr. Creighton as Ranke or Burckhardt, and his
studious exclusion needlessly raises a question as to
whether this book is written up to date.   It relates from
the usual authorities the story of the ancient Roman
corpse that was discovered in 1485, carried to the Capitol,
and tumultuously admired by the enthusiasts of the revival.   Another account, written by an eye-witness, at
the time, has been published by Janitschek, and reproduced by Geiger in works only second to those of Voigt
and Burckhardt.   The *Regesta Leonis X.* should be an
indispensable aid in the study of his pontificate, and
should have roused a suspicion that the act confirming
the legitimacy of Clement VII. has long been known, and
that the page of Balan's *Monumenta* to which we are
referred for it is misprinted.   They also prove (p. 323)
that the *Bullarium Magnum* cannot be trusted by critical
scholars.   In the character of Paul II. there is no notice
of a statement made by Gregorovius (vol. vii. p. 212), whom
Mr. Creighton has studied carefully, though not, I think,
in the last edition.

To make this good and to strengthen confidence, we
have many valuable extracts from unpublished works,
such as the history of the Augustinian, Cardinal Egidius of
Viterbo, one of the least inefficient among the Italian
priesthood of that age, and the diaries of the master of
the ceremonies and Bishop of Pesaro, whose manuscripts
have been the mainstay of papal historians from Panvini
and Raynaldus to Hergenröther. But the desire to reject
superfluous notes and paraded erudition has influenced
the author's manner in another way. No scrupulous and
self-respecting writer will speak his mind or say things
that challenge inquiry unless the proof is prompt. To
relieve his text of the burden of incessant quotation, he
must understate his meaning and lose in definiteness and
precision what he gains in lightness. His chisel is
necessarily blunted, and he cannot work in high relief.
It has cost Mr. Creighton but little to accept this drawback on his method. He is not striving to prove a case,
or burrowing towards a conclusion, but wishes to pass
through scenes of raging controversy and passion with a
serene curiosity, a suspended judgment, a divided jury,
and a pair of white gloves. Avoiding both alternatives
of the prophet's mission, he will neither bless nor curse,
and seldom invites his readers to execrate or to admire.
His tints are sometimes pale, and his tones indecisive. I
do not refer to such ambiguous sayings as that Matilda
left all her lands to St. Peter, or that the sudden death of
Paul II. was regarded as a judgment upon him for his
want of faith, or that Julius II. felt the calls of nature
strong at the last. But there are places where, in the
author's solicitude to be within the mark, the reader
misses the point. There was a time when the schemes
of ecclesiastical reform found a last refuge in the sacred
college itself. In letters written from Rome on 23rd and
28th September 1503, we read : "Li Signori Cardinali
essendo in Conclavi, hano ordinati multi Capituli tendenti
a proponere de la Sede apostolica, et del Collegio, et creato
el Pontefice, li hano facto giurare de observarli. . . .
Tutti li Signori Cardinali furno chiamati per N. S. in

Congregatione a Palatio, et per farse mentione de
Concilio et de reformatione de la Corte neli Capituli del
Conclavi, La Santità Sua propose et concluse, se habi a fare
el Concilio, et se habi ad intimare ali Principi Christiani.
Ma circa el loco et lo tempo de esso Concilio se reservò
a deliberare un altra volta.   Fu bene ragionato che lo
ultimo Concilio fu facto in Basilea, et per Monsignor de
Rohano fu ricordato, quando se tractarà del loco, se habi
a chiamare lo Procuratore del Christianissimo Re, dimon-
strando che essendo stato facto lo ultimo in Allamagna,
seria conveniente questo farse in Franza.   La Santità
Sua anchora propose la reformatione dela Corte, et
concluse se havesse a riformare."   Mr. Creighton, who
has no faith in the conciliar and spiritual movement, and
is satisfied with the printed edition of Giustinian, merely
says that Pius III. "spoke of reforming the church."   The
flavour has evaporated.   A patriotic Florentine, Boscoli,
compassed the death of the Medicean monopolist of
power, and suffered, reasonably, for his crime.   We are
told that the great question for his friends was the
opinion of Aquinas on the sinfulness of tyrannicide ; and
that his confessor declared afterwards that his soul was in
peace.   The difficulty for his friends was to make him
believe that St. Thomas condemned tyrannicide utterly,
and what his confessor afterwards said was that they
had contrived to deceive him.   There is a report that
Alexander objected to the ordeal of fire, because he
feared it might succeed.   We are only told, in a note,
that it would have been very awkward for him if by any
chance Savonarola had been successful.   Cæsar Borgia
"awakened the mingled terror and admiration of by-
standers."   This is true of others, besides Machiavelli.
When the news of Cæsar's most conspicuous crime
reached Venice, a citizen who hated him, and who kept
in secret a diary which has not seen the light, made this
entry : "Tutto il mondo cridava contro di lui ; tamen per
questo li morti non resusciteranno, e dimostrava haver un
gran coraggio, e di farsi signor di tutta l' Italia."   And
somewhat later :   "Di quanta riputatione, e fausto, e

gloria s' attrovava all' hora il Signor Duca Valentino in
Italia, non lo posso per hora dichiarire, perche l' effetto
delli suoi successi, delli sue vittorie, e del stato acquistato,
lo dimostrava.   Onde di lui si parlava variamente : alcuni
lo volevano far Re dell' Italia, e coronarlo ; altri lo
volevano far Imperator."   The picture of Julius at the
Lateran council, when " he had forgotten to prepare a
speech," and when he " could only stammer through a
few sentences," is less vivid than the account of his
oratory given by Paris de Grassis : " Non facio mentionem
de Julio, qui cum oraturus esset semper per triduum ante
actus occupatus erat in studio memorandi sermonis ; et
tamen cum in consistorio publico dicere vellet semper
semimori videbatur, ita ut mihi esset necesse occurrere et
excitare eum in stupore membrorum occupatum et
exinanitum, sicut omnes viderunt, et Sua Sanctitas saepe
mihi hoc idem dixit."

Mr. Creighton has a decided opinion on the question
whether Alexander VI. died a natural death, but the
arguments on either side might be strengthened.   " Contemporaries saw a proof of the effects of poison in the
rapid decomposition of the pope's body, which grew black
and swollen. . . . It was evidence only of the state of
the atmosphere."   Compared with the report in Sanuto,
this is a tame description : " El sangue ge abondava da
le rechie, da la bocha e dal naso, adeo che non potevano
tanto sugar quanto l' abondava : i labri erano più grossi
che 'l pugno di un homo : era con la bocha aperta, e ne
la bocha ge bogliva il sangue, come faria una pignata che
boglisse al focho, e per la bocha ge saltava el sangue a
modo de una spina, e sempre abondava : e questo è de
visu."   Alexander fell ill on the 12th, not on the
13th, of August.   The error may be due to the omission,
by Villari, of the first sentence in a despatch of 14th
August.   In the original it begins with the following
words : " Sabato passato, dovendo andare N. S. in signatura, secondo el consueto, la signatura fu' destinata.   Et
de la causa non se ne intese altro per quella sera.   Ma fu
ascripto ad uno pocho de indispositione havea havuto el

Signor Duca, el dì inante." The despised Leonetti has
the right date. "It is not surprising that two men, living
under the same conditions and in the same place, should
suffer from fever at the same time." It is a case, not of
two men, but of three; for Cardinal Hadrian afterwards
assured Jovius that he had been poisoned. When three
men who have dined together are seized with such illness
that the oldest dies, and the youngest is prostrated during
the most critical week of his life, we even now suspect
verdigris in the saucepan or a toadstool in the mushrooms.
Villari, whose authority stands high, maintains that the
suspicion of poison arose when the pope was dead. But
on 18th August Sanuto writes: "Si divulga per Roma
sia stà atosegado"; and Priuli has the following entry on
the 16th: "Furono lettere da Roma volantissime, per le
qual s' intendeva come il Sommo Pontifice essendo stato
a solazzo a cena del R^mo Cardinale chiamato Adriano,
insieme col Duca Valentino et alcuni altri Cardinali,
havendo crapulato ad sobrietatem, essendo ritornato al
Pontificale Palazzo, s' era buttato al letto con la febre
molto grave, per la qual infermità si giudicava fosse stato
avvelenato, e questo perchè etiam il giorno seguente il
prefato Duca Valentino et il Cardinal s' erano buttati al
letto con la febre." On the other hand, the only direct
authorities available—Giustinian, Costabili, and Burchard
—report that Alexander died a natural death, and it
would appear that the famous supper took place nearly a
week before the guests were taken ill. Giustinian writes
on 13th August: "Uno di questi zorni, e fo ozi otto di,
andorno a cena ad una vigna del R^mo Adriano, e stettero
fin a notte; dove intravennero etiam altre persone, e tutti
se ne hanno risentito."

Mr. Creighton warns us against the credulous
malignity of the writers he is compelled to use. It must
be appraised, he says, as carefully as the credulity of
earlier chroniclers in believing miraculous stories. It will
not do to press the analogy between Cæsarius or the
Liber Conformitatum, and Infessura or Burchard. Mr.
Creighton accepts the most scandalous of the scenes

recorded by the latter; he assuredly would not accept
what is gravely testified in the Beatification of Ximenes,
that he stopped the sun at Oran, so that several Moors,
seeing the prodigy, asked to be baptized.   But his
reluctance to rely on common gossip is justified by the
rank growth of myths in the journals of the *cinque cento*
Grevilles.   On the death of the Venetian Cardinal
Michiel in April 1503, Priuli writes: " Fù discoperto,
come qui sotto appar, che 'l detto Cardinal fù attossicato
per intelligenza del Duca Valentino per haver li danari, e
fù squartato et abbruciato questo tale, che era Cameriere
del detto Cardinale."   In August the same story is
repeated: "Morse da morte repentina un Cardinale
nepote del Pontefice, chiamato il Cardinale Monreale,
huomo di grandissima auttorità, in due giorni, al qual fu
trovato tra argenti e denari 120 M. ducati, e si diceva, e
giudicavasi per certo, il detto povero Cardinale esser stato
avvelenato dal Duca Valentino per li suoi danari, che al-
l' hora era consueto ammazzare le persone c' havevano
danari a Roma da questo Duca."   The news of the pope's
illness suggests the following reflections: " Si dubitava
assai che 'l detto Pontefice non dovesse da questa
infermità morire, perche, ut vulgo dicebatur, questo
Pontefice havea dato l' anima et il corpo al gran Diavolo
dell' Inferno; e però che non potesse morire ancora per
far delli altri mali."   Another relates that an ape was
caught in the apartments of Alexander, who exclaimed,
" Lasolo, lasolo, chè il diavolo."   Sanuto has a detailed
account of the supper party, according to which there
was no mistake; but Hadrian, knowing his danger, gave
the butler a heavy bribe to make the exchange.   " El
Cardinal, che pur havia paura, se medicinò e vomitò, et
non have mal alcuno."   A ghastly tale is told in the life
of a man who, fifty years later, rose to the summit of
power and dignity and historic fame, but who was then
an obscure prelate about the court.   When Alexander
came to the villa of Cardinal Hadrian, it was found that
the box containing a consecrated host, which he wore as
a protection, had been forgotten.   The prelate, who was

sent for it, on arriving at the Vatican, beheld the pontiff lying dead in his chamber.

No authority is more often cited for the early part of the sixteenth century than the diary of Marin Sanuto. Mr. Creighton quotes sometimes from the printed edition, sometimes apparently from the Vienna transcript, which does not always agree with the original. In the conspiracy of the cardinals in 1517 his reliance on the fidelity of Marin Sanuto's *précis* of despatches raises an interesting problem of historical criticism. The statement of Pope Leo, as quoted vol. iv. p. 245, is inaccurate. There is no question of a letter written by Sauli, or of a promise made by him, or of a prisoner having confessed that the cardinal had actually plotted the death of the pope. The text of the despatch, which, upon all these points, has been distorted, is as follows : " Sapiate che za alchuni giorni io feci retenir uno de i suo, apresso dil qual furono ritrovate alchune scritture, et tandem alchune lettere che lui scriveva al Cardinal, per che 'l non si havea potuto exeguir quanto lui li havea commesso cum molte altre parole ; per modo che si poteva judicar ditto Cardinal haver trattato di voler avenenar Sua Bne. et posto de tormento confessò la verità, et etiam chel Cardinal de Sauli era conscio di tal ribaldaria." This prisoner, who was in the service of Petrucci, not of Sauli, confessed under torture ; but the words *auto corda assai* do not apply to him, as Mr. Creighton supposes. They describe the fate of the physician whom he denounced. Marin Sanuto writes in the passage which seems to have been misunderstood : " Quel Zuan Baptista di Verzei a confessato il tutto, qual a auto corda assai." On the next page Leo is made to say : "4 zorni poi fussemo fatti Papa tramono questi di darmi la morte." The Venetian copy of the diary has : " 4 zorni poi fossimo Papa tramono questi darne la morte." The words actually reported by the envoy are : " Quatro giorni da poi la nostra creatione questi Cardinali tractorono de far un altro Pontefice, da poi la nostra morte." Of Riario, whom the Venetians call the cardinal of St. George, Mr.

Creighton writes : " Riario denied all knowledge of the matter till the confessions of the others were read to him ; then he said, ' Since they have said so, it must be true.' He added that he had spoken about it to Soderini and Hadrian, who laughed and said they would make him pope."   Marco Minio says : " Per le depositione del Sauli et etiam de qualche uno de li altri si vede come etiam haveano communicato questa cum li R^{mi} Cardinali Voltera et Adriano, et quel Adriano, intesa la cosa, si messe a rider stringendosi nelle spalle, che è uno atto solito per lui farsi molte volte, et il R^{mo} Volterra disse, ' Faciate pur presto.'   Si che tutti loro dimostrar haver grandissimo odio al Pontefice.   Ma San Zorzi dimostra haver havuto più presto grande desiderio al papato che altro ; et loro promettevano di farlo papa."   It does not appear that Riario admitted having sounded Soderini and Hadrian, nor that it was proved by the evidence of others, nor that the two cardinals implicated made any promise to elect him.   All this is taken from Sanuto's summary : " Quando fo letto al Cardinal San Zorzi quello havia detto Siena e Sauli, qual primo negava, disse, za che lhoro hanno dito cussi el dia esser el vero, et chel comunichoe con Voltera et Hadriano Cardinali quali se la riseno come solito è a far Hadriano, et Voltera disse, ' Faziate pur presto,' e che li prometteva far esso San Zorzi Papa."

Mr. Creighton judges his half-century as an epoch of religious decline, during which the Papacy came down from the elevation at which it was left by Pius to the degeneracy in which it was found by Luther.   With Paul II. it starts well.   Then the temptations of politics, the victorious creation of the temporal state, bring his successors into degrading and contaminating rivalry with wicked statesmen, and they learn to expend spiritual authority in exchange for worldly gains, until at last, when they have to face new antagonists, their dignity is tarnished and their credit gone.   At each pontificate the judgment becomes more severe.   Sixtus is worse than Paul, and Alexander than Sixtus.   But worst of all are those prosperous pontiffs who, in their ambition to become great monarchs, sacrificed their country and their church. The reformers rose up in opposition to a vast political machine, to a faggot of secular motives, which had usurped the seat of Gregory VII. and Innocent IV. The Papacy to which they were untrue had become untrue to itself.

This increasing rigour and occasional indignation, as the plot thickens, is assuredly in no wise due to the irrelevant detail that Cambridge does not elect its Dixie professor among the adherents of Rome. Religious differences do not tinge his judgment or obstruct the emollient influence of ingenuous arts. If Mr. Creighton, as a theologian, does not accept the claims of the pre-reformation popes, as an historian he prefers them to their adversaries. The members of the Council of Pisa are renegades and schismatics. When Paul II. refused to be bound by the compact he had signed with the other cardinals, he was not to blame. " The attempt to bind the pope was a legacy of the schism, and rested upon the principles laid down by the conciliar movement. Such a proceeding was entirely contrary to the canonical conception of the plenitude of the papal power." The character of Pius III. " stood high in all men's estimation, though he was the father of a large family of children." Mr. Creighton insists on the liberality of the popes, not only at the time of which he treats, but generally. " Fanaticism had no place in Rome, nor did the papal court trouble itself about trifles. It allowed free thought beyond the extremest limits of ecclesiastical prudence. The Papacy in the Middle Ages always showed a tolerant spirit in matters of opinion. We cannot think that Roman inquisitors were likely to err on the side of severity." The last sentence shows that in varying dis-interested history with passages which might be taken from the polemics of Cardinal Newman, Mr. Creighton is not unmindful of the Inquisition. But he shows no strong feeling for the liberty of conscience. He speaks coldly of " writers who themselves regard toleration as a virtue," and say that Pomponatius " was judged in the papal court with a judicial calmness and impartiality which the modern advocates of religious tolerance might well admire." When speaking of Gemistus, the last original thinker of the tolerant eastern church, he passes unheeded the most curious passage of the *Laws :* οὖ καὶ σοφιστῶν, ἥν τις παρὰ τὰς ἡμετέρας ταύτας δόξας σοφιζό-μενος ἁλῷ, ζῶν καὶ οὗτος κεκαύσεται. He declares that it is unjust to brand Sixtus IV. as a persecutor because he granted the powers asked for in the shape of the Spanish Inquisition. And this is prompted by no tenderness for the memory of Sixtus ; for we find elsewhere that " he allowed himself to become an accomplice in a scheme for assassination which shocked even the blunted conscience of Italy." It may be safely said that Mr. Creighton esteems Ximenes a better specimen of the Christian priest than Julius or Leo, with all their religious liberality.

The spirit of retrospective indulgence and reverence for the operation of authority, whether it be due to want of certitude or to definite theory, is an advantage in writing on this portion of history. From a less conservative point of view the scenery is more gloomy, and the contending parties, tarred with the same brush, are apt to prove less interesting. Mr. Creighton is able to be considerate and appreciative both to popes and reformers. He has no love for the Italian humanists, and may reserve his harshest censures for the pseudonymous liberalism of More and Socinus. It is not necessary, he says, to moralise at every turn ; and he neither worries and vilipends his culprits, like Carlyle and Taine, nor adapts his judgments to dogma, like Hook and Mozley. He goes farther, and declares that it is not becoming to adopt an attitude of lofty superiority over any one who ever played a prominent part in European affairs, or charitable to lavish undiscriminating censure. Of course this does not imply that justice has one law for the mighty and another for the fallen. If it means that every age ought to be tried by its own canons, the application of that sliding scale is a branch of ethical and historical inquiry that is yet in its teens, and practically of no avail. Or it may mean that power goes where power is due, that the will of Providence is made manifest by success, that the judgment of history is the judgment of heaven. That is undoubtedly a theory of singular interest and influence as the groundwork of historic conservatism ; but it has never been brought to the test of exact definition. Mr. Creighton perceives the sunken rock of moral scepticism, and promises that he will not lower the standard of moral judgment. In this transition stage of struggling and straggling ethical science, the familiar tendency to employ mesology in history, to judge a man by his cause and the cause by its result, to obviate criticism by assuming the unity and wholeness of character, to conjure with great names and restore damaged reputations, not only serves to debase the moral standard, but aims at excluding it. And it is the office of historical science to maintain morality as the sole impartial criterion of men and things, and the only one on which honest minds can be made to agree.

I dwell on the spirit and method and *morale* of the *History of the Papacy*, not only because it is difficult to contend in detail with such a master of solid fact, but because it is by the spirit and not the letter that his book will live. Studious men who have examined the hidden treasures of many Italian libraries, and have grown grey with the dust of papal archives, are on the track behind him. Pastor's history has only just reached Pius II. ; but it is dense with new knowledge, and announces a worthy competitor to Ranke, Gregorovius, and Creighton. But not a hole must be left unpicked ; and there are several particulars on which reader and writer may join issue. The account of the conclave of 1471 seems scarcely just to Bessarion. According to Panvini, he lost the tiara not from national or political jealousy, but because he refused an uncanonical compact: " Res ad Bessarionem, tum senatus principem senem doctrina et vitae integritate clarissimum, spectare videbatur. Quem Ursinus obtinendi pontificatus spe deposita, Mantuanus, Cancellarius convenientes certis sub conditionibus pontificatum se ei daturos polliciti sunt.

Quumque ille se ea ratione pontificem creari velle perne-
gasset, ut scilicet pacto aliquo intercedente papatum
obtineret, illi, intempestivam senis severitatem stomachati,
ad Cardinalem Sancti Petri ad Vincula, Magistrum
Franciscum Savonensem, sunt conversi, virum doctrina
praestantissimum." In a passage apparently inspired by
aversion for the irreligious renaissance, Savonarola is
called " the most sincere man amongst the Italians of the
time." It is invidious to disparage a man whose faith
was strong enough to resist authority both in Church and
State, and who impressed a doctrine which was newer if
not more true then than now, that an awakened conscience must be traced and proved in public as much as
in private life, so that a zealous priest is, normally, a
zealous politician. And it may be that the shrill utterance of opportune prophecy is not always inconsistent
with integrity. But the man who described in the pulpit
his mission from Florence to heaven, and what he heard
there, and afterwards explained that this was all a trope,
cannot well be pronounced perfectly sincere on any
hypothesis of sanity. How far the plea of partial insanity,
which is gaining ground in society, may serve for the
interpretation of history, is a problem which should
commend itself to a writer so slow to use hard words and
to associate *dolus* and *culpa*. Mr. Creighton describes
the constitution of Julius against simony as a bold
measure, showing a strong sense of the need of amend-
ment. But he speaks of it as an incident in the annals
of the year, a feature in the portrait of a pope, a plant
sprung from no buried root. The prohibition of bribery
at conclaves was old in the law of the Church. Four
hundred and sixty years before, one of the popes wrote
that he had been raised to the papal throne in place of
three others, deposed for bribery—" explosis tribus illis,
quibus nomen papatus rapina dederat." The rising
against Alexander VI., the coalition between Julian and
Savonarola to eject him, would hardly be intelligible if
the law against simony had been no more than an abrupt
innovation. It is not quite accurate to say that the first

care of the cardinals on the death of Julius was to lay hands on the treasure which he left behind. The Venetian envoy wrote, 25th February: " Alcuni Cardinali voleano partir questo tesoro tra tutti li Cardinali, tamen li altri non hanno voluto, et si riserverà al novo Pontefice." On 2nd March he adds: " Hanno tratto li Cardinali di Castello ducati 30,000; et perche li Cardinali che non hanno intrada ducati 600 per uno, Julio fo una constitution di darli di danari del Papato fin a quella somma, perhòse li darà perlio se." The letter of the protonotary Marcello from which the dubious words are cited—" siche partivano duc. 120,000 tra lhoro "—goes on to say that they got less than this. The election of Leo X. is told with the aid of extracts from Paris de Grassis; but neither text nor note speaks of the capitulations in which the future pope pledged himself to revoke, under pain of excommunication, the sale of indulgences for the fabric of St. Peter's. " Promittet, iurabit, et vovebit, statim post assumptionem suam omnes et singulas indulgentias revocare fratribus Sancti Francisci ordinis minorum, pro fabrica Sancti Petri concessas, sub quibusvis verborum formis, eisque mandabit, sub excommunicationis latae sententiae poena, ne illis ullo modo utantur." The terms of this covenant are not very comprehensive, yet they should possess some significance for one who thinks that a pope weak enough to keep an oath taken in conclave would betray his trust. They show that Rome was in some measure aware of present evil and impending danger; and that the refusal of remedy and precaution was not due to the corruption of courtiers, but to the plenitude of sovereignty.

Although it is not easy to detect a wrong quotation, a false inference, or an unjust judgment in these records of discredited popes, whoever consults them for the key to the coming Reformation will go away conscious of things left out and replenished with more political than religious secrets. He will know by what means the Papacy, borne on the stormy tide of absolutism which opens modern history, established an independent state on the

subjugation of Italy.   But the marrow of things does not
lie in the making of a distinct principality, or in the price
paid for it, or in the means by which its makers wrought.
Other causes changed the axis of the world.   Within the
folds of temporal monarchy an ecclesiastical process was
going on of more concern to us than the possession or
the partition of Italy.   De Maistre's argument that those
who deem absolutism legitimate in the State have no
foothold to resist it in the Church, had been proclaimed
already by a writer favourably known to Mr. Creighton :
" Nemo est tam parvae urbis dominus, qui a se appellari
ferat : et nos Papam appellationi subiectum dicemus ?
At si me, ais, Pontifex indigne premit, quid agam ?   Redi
ad eum supplex ; ora, onus levet.   At si rogatus, inter-
pellatus nolit subvenire misero, quid agam ?   Quid agis,
ubi tuus te princeps saecularis urget ?   Feram, dices, nam
aliud nullum est remedium.   Et hic ergo feras ! "   The
miscarriage of reform left the Holy See on a solitary
height never reached before.   It was followed by indifference and despair, by patient watching for a new departure,
by helpless schemes to push philosophy across the margin
exposed by the religious ebb.   We are familiar with the
antipathy of Machiavelli and the banter of Erasmus ; but
the primary fact in the papal economy of that age is not
the manifold and ineffective opposition, but the positive
strengthening of authority and its claims.   The change is
marked by the extremity of adulation which came in
about the time of Alexander.   He is *semideus, deus alter
in terris*, and, in poetry, simply *deus*.   The belief that a
soul might be rescued from purgatory for a few coppers,
and the sudden expansion of the dispensing power, facts
that alienated Germany and England, throve naturally
in this atmosphere ; and between the parallel and con-
temporaneous growth of the twin monarchies a close and
constant connection prevails.   From that last phase of
mediæval society to modern, there could be no evolution.
But Mr. Creighton's second title is *The Italian Princes*.
He describes the things that vary rather than the things
that endure.   We see the successive acts, the passing

figures, the transitory forms, to which the spiritual element imparts an occasional relish; but we see little of the impersonal force behind. The system, the idea, is masked by a crowd of ingenious, picturesque, and unedifying characters, who exhibit the springs of Italian politics more truly than the solemn realities of the Church. We are seldom face to face with the institution. Very rarely, indeed, we are sent to the *Bullarium Magnum;* but that work, unwieldy as it is, contains an infinitesimal proportion of the acts of the mediæval pontiffs. The inner mind of the Papacy has to be perused through many other collections pertaining to the several countries, churches, and religious orders; and these are so voluminous that three large folios are filled with the bulls that belong to St. Peter's alone. By giving us life and action for thought and law, Mr. Creighton lifts an enormous burden. The issues which he has so far deliberately avoided will force their way to the front when he reaches the commission given by Leo to the master of the sacred palace, Cajetan's expedition into Germany, and the pilgrimage of Eck to Rome. Without reversing his views, or modifying any statement, he has yet to disclose the reason, deeper and more interior than the worldliness, ignorance, and corruption of ecclesiastics, which compelled the new life of nations to begin by a convulsion.

XVI

A SHORT HISTORY OF NAPOLEON THE FIRST. By John Robert Seeley

THE FIRST NAPOLEON: A SKETCH, POLITICAL AND MILITARY. By John Codman Ropes [1]

A CONDENSED biography of Napoleon ought to make the richest and most interesting volume in profane literature. Frenchmen find it a difficult book to write, because they feel both the excess and the deficiency of essential information. The correspondence of the Bonapartes, though it occupies more than sixty volumes, is mutilated and incomplete. Materials for an ample supplement are known in France; a collection of the emperor's autograph letters was offered for sale in London not long ago; and the priceless bundles that passed through Mr. Murray's hands passed into concealment. The papers of imperial ministers are lost or kept back. Those of Fouché are said to have been burnt at Trieste; those of Talleyrand were partially destroyed, and the few readers of his memoirs foretell disappointment. Barras and Sieyès, Cambacérès and Caulaincourt, Molé and Pasquier left memoirs which are at least difficult of access to most people except M. Taine. Some are printed but unpublished. The task may be fitly undertaken at a distance by men resolute not to be distracted by the pursuit of detail or baffled by mysteries that resist inquiry.

Two such lives written in English at the same time

[1] *English Historical Review*, vol. ii. 1887.

are better than anything of equal compass on the continent. Alike in ability and industry, they differ widely
in the choice of materials and still more in their conclusions, and so conveniently complete each other. Both
are worth reading, apart from the views they are meant
to serve. Mr. Seeley's rapid sketch tells of things not
easily found in French books, avoids detail, and judges
austerely. Mr. Ropes, his rival, discourses more on
military affairs, and is not only an admirer but an advocate. We shall not go far wrong if we take the good of
Napoleon from Mr. Ropes, and the bad from Mr. Seeley.
It is difficult to exaggerate either. The American lives
afar from the temptation of wrongs that cry for vengeance, and pride not yet appeased. He inherits no part
or partnership in the inorganic Europe which it was
Napoleon's mission to destroy, likes the French quite
as much as the English, and prefers the enlightened
emperor to the Wellesleys, who called the liberals
Jacobins, and supported the Spanish *Serviles*. He urges
how much he was sinned against, and how much the
nations might have profited by his sway. Canning once
said : " I would not myself, if I were a rascally Portuguese, or Prussian, or Dutchman, hesitate one moment to
prefer the French " ; and Mr. Ropes improves this text.
Mr. Seeley surveys from a patriotic elevation the career
that did so much for the expansion of England, and
treats it as an episode in the long duel for the prize of
distant empire. A force more constant and irresistible
than human will impels Napoleon to a hopeless struggle
with manifest destiny, and his wars are subsidiary to the
supreme national purpose of crippling England. It is a
development of Rapetti's thesis that, in occupying maritime Europe from the Adriatic to the Baltic, the emperor
pursued the fixed lines of ancient rivalry ; a commentary
on the words spoken to Molé, that it was the English only
that he meant to attack in Russia ; on the subtler speech
to Schwarzenberg, that he cared for nothing but the war
with England, which all other fighting hindered and
retarded ; on the pithy sentence recorded by Mollien :

"La France n'a étendu ses conquêtes que pour enlever des tributaires à l'Angleterre."

The practised observer of history is apparent in many places. The *Constitution Civile* is described as the ruin of the Revolution; but the Concordat is set forth as a contrivance to dissociate the clergy from both of the preceding orders of things, and make it subserve the new. So close a student of Marmont could not miss the defect in Napoleon's generalship, the forward eagerness that would not provide for ill-fortune. But it is a merit in a biographer of Stein to recognise as he does the prodigious success of Metternich's ministry during the war of liberation. He is not blinded by the glare of Russian snow-fields, and knows what Jomini explained long ago, that the army was destroyed by its commander, and not by the cold. He does not fall into the extinct error of thinking that the Congress of Vienna was going to pieces when Napoleon escaped; but he does not make it clear that the emperor started for France in that belief, and that the settled concord of Europe was a surprise to him. The spirit of nationality, the propeller of so much later history, is derived by Mr. Seeley from the imperial wars; but he is not careful to distinguish national from liberal opposition, or the effect of resistance to Napoleon in Spain from the direct influence upon his Italian countrymen of his political forecast: "L'Italie est une seule nation. L'unité de mœurs, de langage, de littérature, doit, dans un avenir plus ou moins éloigné, réunir enfin ses habitants sous un seul gouvernement.—Rome est, sans contredit, la capitale que les Italiens choisiront un jour." In other ways he at least does him strict justice, showing that the destruction of popular liberties had been the nation's own act, and that the emperor was continually forced to defend himself against aggression. More stress might have been laid on the policy of making Europe pay the deficit of France which Napoleon disclosed when, in answer to a minister pleading that his finances wanted repose, he said: "Au contraire, elles s'embarrassent; il leur faut la guerre."

His excellent materials would often justify Mr. Seeley
in being more sure of things than he appears ; and when
he is not sure he employs precautions which a compendium ought, if possible, to avoid.   He doubts whether Bonaparte showed any remarkable firmness of character in
Vendémiaire ; whether Carnot chose him for the command in Italy ; whether he bribed Sieyès, as he boasted,
with public money.   He does not know whether Monge
suggested the expedition to Egypt ; whether the marriage
with an archduchess was part of the original plan ;
whether the sudden illness at Pirna and the poisoning at
Fontainebleau are real ; whether or no the allies resolved
upon the march to Paris on 24th March.   Nearly all
these things are ascertainable.   When there was some
hesitation about using force against the rising of Vendémiaire, Bonaparte said : "Attendez-vous que le peuple
vous donne la permission de tirer sur lui?"   The Italian
appointment does not rest on the unsupported word of
a Terrorist.   La Réveillère, whose memoirs are an apology
for Fructidor and an attack on the *Réponse à Bailleul*, who
reviles Carnot for the favour he enjoyed during the
empire, affirms that the nomination was not the act of
Barras.   If he could have said that it was not the act of
Carnot, he would have said it.   We learn from Lavallette
that Monge discussed Egypt, not that he proposed the
expedition.   Bonaparte is not our only authority for the
gift of public money to Sieyès.   The other consul, Roger
Ducos, informed Gohier that Sieyès had taken £16,000,
and he himself £4000, and that the First Consul had said
to him : "Il faut gorger ce prêtre de biens pour en avoir
raison."   The Austrian match was so little part of the
original plan that Napoleon preferred a Russian grand-
duchess.   Alexander himself directed his thoughts
towards Vienna, and Metternich had proposed the
marriage before the divorce.   In February 1810 a French
diplomatist wrote to him that Talleyrand had done the
most to alter the emperor's choice, adding : "We shall be
on bad terms with Russia in less than five months, and at
war in eighteen."   Thiers and Bernhardi support the

doubt whether the fatal inaction on 28th August 1813 was really due to sudden illness. They say that Fain is the only witness, and Fain notoriously cannot be trusted. The fact is known on the better testimony of Maret, Caulaincourt, St. Cyr, and Senfft ; to say nothing of Ségur, Fézensac, and Pelet. Ségur's narrative of the attempted suicide was confirmed to many people still living, by Count Flahaut, who was at Fontainebleau at the time. Our witness for the date of the momentous conference at Sommepuis is Lord Westmorland, the officer accredited at headquarters, who was present, and whose statement in his book, and in his letter published in Toll's memoirs, can scarcely be disputed. The assertion that, in Napoleon's boyhood, " his abilities do not seem to have excited wonder," is an instance of excessive caution. His mother said to Prokesch : " Au début de ses études, Napoléon fut celui de mes enfans qui me donna le moins d'espérances ; il resta longtemps avant d'avoir quelque succès." And it is rather a balk to be told that the creation of the university " gave Napoleon the occasion for some striking and original remarks." He remarked that it was to be " un moyen de diriger [otherwise, surveiller] les opinions politiques et morales," and that there is no safety for the state " tant qu'on n'apprendra pas, dès l'enfance, s'il faut être républicain ou monarchique, catholique ou irréligieux." The studied vagueness of the author's style is inadequate at times to the intense definiteness of Napoleon's thought and speech. Oncken, who has been of some service to Mr. Seeley, might have satisfied him that the memorable interview with Metternich took place on 26th June, not 28th June, and lasted eight hours and a half, not ten. As to the dramatic passage, the best reason for thinking that Metternich reports it faithfully is that the emperor said the same thing both to Caulaincourt and to Narbonne.

The scheme of interpretation which contemplates the wars of the empire from the point of view of the continental blockade and the British shopkeeper falls short in Spain. When Mr. Seeley says that the invasion was an act of insensate violence, that the Spaniards were entirely subservient to France before, and unanimously hostile after, he passes over some essential elements of the case. We learn nothing of the technical provocation which had been given, nothing of the strong French party which, but for the Russian expedition, had nearly accomplished the pacification of the peninsula, or of the statesman's argument for thinking the suppression of the Bourbons as desirable for the Bonapartes as the suppression of Murat was afterwards for the Bourbons. There were Spaniards who, as early as 1805, had foreseen that the extinction of one family would be needful for the elevation of the other. Napoleon admitted that he could not leave in Bourbon hands a country that might be one day formidable, not to himself but to his successors. The solidity of ancient thrones, the gathered force of long prescription, filled him with a mysterious awe which forbade him to be content with making vassals of that craven dynasty. At Smorgoni, on the night on which he abandoned his army, he exclaimed : " If I had been born to the throne, it would have been easy to make no mistakes." And he added : " Les Bourbons s'en tireraient." During the invasion of France he expressed the same thought thus : " If I were my son, I could go on fighting until I stood with my back to the Pyrenees." Towards Sieyès Mr. Seeley entertains the sentiments which Burke and Mallet du Pan have bequeathed to their successors. He loves to impute the new absolutism to the destroyer of the old, and distinguishes but faintly between his work and the suppression of his work by Napoleon. He even attributes to the backwardness and timidity of Sieyès the mismanagement which nearly wrecked the enterprise of Brumaire. The performer who flinched in the drama of St. Cloud was not Sieyès but Bonaparte. When he turned pale with the terror of outlawry, Sieyès calmly said : " Ils vous mettent hors la loi : mettez-les hors la salle." So the scene was told not many years since by one who had lived among the actors in it. Montrond was present, and his account, virtually the same, is preserved by Rœderer.

There we read how, when all was over, Talleyrand said
that it was time to dine; and how, during dinner,
Montrond was observed to shake his head and mutter:
"Général Bonaparte, cela n'est pas correct." There too
we read that the "yoke of the S" in Lucien's pamphlet
meant not Soldiers, as Mr. Seeley infers, but Sieyès. The
First Consul was angry with his brother for attacking so
useful a man, sent Talleyrand with an apology, and had
an edition printed with the word *militaires*. Like the
German writers of whom he makes great use, he denies
to the Russians the merit of design in the successful defence of 1812. He thinks that they had learnt from
Wellington the value of retrograde movements, but that
the retreat was not based on strategic calculations of the
benefit of space. We know from Dumas and Ségur that
the idea of retreating into the interior had struck a
Russian officer during the campaign of Eylau, and that
he executed it afterwards, against the feeling of the army,
whilst he held command. Alexander had previously
assured a Frenchman that nothing would be lost if he
had to retire beyond Moscow; and the Frenchman
had answered politely that he would still be the first
Power in Asia. Mr. Seeley is doubtless right in thinking
that the Austrian terms ought to have been conceded at
Prague; but it is not so clear that, when Austria turned
against him in 1813, Napoleon's doom was sealed. He
was outnumbered in the proportion of ten to nine; but
he deemed that his presence doubled his force. It was
worth an addition of 50,000 men, says St. Cyr; and
Wellington thought that it was equal to 40,000. Even
at Leipzig the odds were not greater than at Dresden,
where he gained a complete victory. Three of the best
judges, Jomini, St. Cyr, and Bernhardi, do not agree that
the struggle on the Elbe was hopeless. In the defence
of Champagne, Arcis, which is as decisive a date as Lodi,
deserved better treatment than to be passed over in
silence whilst Hagelberg is duly recorded. Having been
repulsed at Laon by the Prussians, Napoleon tried his
fortune against the Austrians, and was defeated at Arcis.

It was there he understood that the end had come, and that he rode forward and stood over a shell about to explode. An officer, on the point of uttering a warning cry, was stopped by another, who said : " Don't you see that he is doing it on purpose, and wants to have it over ? " Mr. Seeley states that, in 1814, Fouché was weaving a military plot. The proceedings of that exceedingly able man barely fit in to so plain a form of words. He made a merit of trying to maintain the Bourbons, and, in a secret interview, had given some remarkable advice : " Servez-vous à la fois de la vertu qui a éclaté dans l'oppression, de l'énergie qui a été développée dans nos désordres, et des talents qui se sont produits dans le délire. On ne gouverne pas plus les états avec les souvenirs et les répugnances qu'avec les remords." Blacas of course replied that legitimacy can no more coalesce with revolution than truth with error. Then Fouché, exclaiming that the king, if he had ten crowns with such an adviser, would lose them all, tried the younger branch. That is how Napoleon afterwards told Meneval that he had dethroned not Lewis XVIII., but the Duke of Orleans.

In such a mass of facts and allusions there are probably not a few which a vindictive Bonapartist would mark with a sign of interrogation. He might object that the French at Acre were not reduced to musketry fire ; that the primate of the confederation did not hold the See of Mentz ; that Moreau was in the Russian, not the Austrian camp ; that the Holy Alliance did not come into existence for three months after the Hundred Days ; that the first indication of the policy of the concordat dates not from Tolentino in February 1797, but at least as far back as the previous October, when Bonaparte wrote : " J'ambitionne bien plus le titre de sauveur que celui de destructeur du Saint-Siège " ; that if the story of his getting drunk with punch at Campo Formio is derived from Hüffer, it is right to add that Hüffer warns us against believing it ; that the institutions which " brought the country to bankruptcy, civil war, and almost barbarism," from 1795 to 1799, were not more pernicious than what had gone before.

The passage asserting that the discovery had recently been made in America that a republic must have a president is not written in earnest. So eminent a student of politics knows that the Americans discovered no such thing, but adopted a president, being used to a governor in the several States, and that " Oranje boven ! " and " Down with the pensionary ! " was not the formula of a new philosophy. Republics since then have prospered without presidents, and have perished by them. Any reader impervious to irony whom the authority of a great name might tempt to take the remark for an axiom, may profitably meditate Félix Pyat's speech of 5th October 1848, comparing it with Tocqueville's reply in defence of the presidential theory. If I may quote a demagogue against an imperialist, here is the sort of thing he would find : " Qu'est-ce que la république des Etats-Unis ? Le mot l'indique ; une république fédérale, girondine, passez-moi le mot, une agrégation d'états ou corps divers, une nation d'alluvions et d'attérissement, composée successive-ment des parties hétérogènes, insolidaires. Le danger, en France, est en sens inverse des Etats-Unis. Aux Etats-Unis il est dans la dispersion des provinces, et il fallait un président : en France, il est dans la concentration ; il ne faut qu'une assemblée."

The philosopher of national greatness, when he cele-brates the triumph of British arms, has a manifest peril to shun. It would be congenial to him to adopt Pitt's last speech, proudly graven on the medal commemorating the peace : " Se ipsam virtute, Europam exemplo." But he is guarded not to inflate the glory and the spoil of England, not to remind us of the time when an Englishman scorned to fight less than three Frenchmen starving on their diet of frogs. He yields no countenance to Wellington's gratifying contention, that Napoleon was driven out of Germany by his own movement on Vittoria. The familiar names, Vittoria, Salamanca, Toulouse, do not occur on his pages. In one or two places, the American, advocate as he is, shows greater impartiality. It may be that Bonaparte miscalculated the naval power of England in the Mediterranean as much as Mr. Seeley believes, but the grand audacity of that six weeks' voyage with transports, in the presence of Nelson, deserves warmer recognition. An almost imperceptible confusion of dates would make it appear that the invasion of England failed through the terror that went before the face of Calder, rather than through the combinations of continental Powers. "In the last days of August, Admiral Villeneuve, issuing from Ferrol, took alarm at the news of the approach of an English fleet, and instead of sailing northward faced about and retired to Cadiz. Then for the first time Napoleon admitted the idea of failure, and saw the necessity of screening it by some great achievement in another quarter." Villeneuve issued from Ferrol, not in the last days of August, but on the 14th. At that time Napoleon was quite unable to avoid war with Austria, and was already preparing for it. On the 13th he had written : "Cette puissance arme. Je veux qu'elle désarme ; si elle ne le fait pas, j'irai avec 200,000 hommes lui faire une bonne visite. Mon parti est pris ; je veux attaquer l'Autriche, et être à Vienne avant le mois de novembre." Talleyrand was to inform the Austrian ambassador that he had abandoned his design : "Il a compris qu'il ne pouvait se porter en Angleterre avec 150,000 hommes lorsque ses frontières du midi étaient menacées." Whilst he was turning his back on England and facing Austria he continued to entertain hopes of his fleet : "J'ai de bonnes nouvelles de mes escadres du Ferrol et de celle de Rochefort." On 22nd August he writes to Talleyrand : "Une fois que j'aurai levé mon camp de l'océan, je ne puis plus m'arrêter ; mon projet de guerre maritime est tout-à-fait manqué. Du 20 au 25 Fructidor, je suis obligé de faire une contre-marche pour m'opposer aux progrès des armements de l'Autriche." This was ten days before he knew that his fleet had retired to Cadiz. The sudden change of front was caused by the forward policy of Mack and

Czartoryski, not by the backwardness of Villeneuve. It was not contrived to scatter dust in the eyes of Europe and to screen discomfiture, but to resist attack. It is not safe to say positively that Napoleon had no means of getting at England. She was saved, as it is the way with islands, by a change in the wind, such as determined her history in 1588, 1688, and 1798. If a man like De Ruyter or Farragut had been in Villeneuve's place when Magon, in a fury, flung his wig into the sea, the landing in Kent would have come into measurable distance. So indeed it would have been if the Institute had not laughed at the crazy projector who came with a plan to give Napoleon the empire over sea and land—the plan of a steamboat. Nobody reading the account of Moore's expedition would gather that it was a disastrous failure. Rather it would seem that the thwarted and disconcerted combatant was Napoleon. "He had missed his mark, and professed to receive information which showed him that he was urgently needed in Paris." The information he had received concerned the material fact that Austria was again arming to attack him. Metternich had gone over to the war party on 4th December. "He would have made short work," wrote Lord Grey, "if he had not been called off by Austria."

In the campaign of 1815 the American is superior both in fulness and fidelity to the Englishman. He cherishes the forlorn hope of justifying the orders to Grouchy, and he makes the absence of Davout too prominent, for Napoleon purposely rejected the four best generals in France ; but he shows that the plan which so nearly succeeded was not foiled by the skill of the allies. Mr. Seeley esteems that victory was out of the question, that the emperor was incapacitated for war, that Waterloo was won, as Marmont said, by the English alone, whose advance decided the victory. Not a word of Bülow's disproportionate loss, of Ziethen's timely arrival, of the sight seen by Colonel Reiche when he came upon the field and was told both by Müffling and Scharnhorst that the French were gaining the day. The English generals

were not so extravagant as Napoleon, who complained of
treason, and Gneisenau, who published that the French at
Ligny were 150,000 strong ; but they started that warm
patriotic colouring against which General Chesney delivered the warning which Mr. Ropes observes more
heartily than Mr. Seeley.   Lord Anglesey averred that
the issue had never been doubtful ; Lord Raglan believed
that the English were outnumbered by 20,000 men ;
Wellington knew nothing of the Prussian attack on the
right rear of Napoleon until about an hour before he
advanced.   We are invited to believe that Napoleon
showed himself, on 16th June, "an indolent and inefficient
general," but we are not told that he gave orders to turn
the Prussian right, which would effectually have divided
his enemies and enabled him to overwhelm the Duke of
Wellington.   Those orders, everybody knows, were not
obeyed.   D'Erlon says : " Le maréchal Ney, étant au
moment d'être forcé aux Quatre Bras, ne tint pas compte
des ordres envoyés par l'empereur, et rappela à lui mon
corps d'armée."   Napoleon saw the consequences in all
their gravity when, on the 17th, he said to D'Erlon, " On
a perdu la France."   It is true that his officers found
fault with his conduct of the campaign, and Grouchy even
ventured to say : "Il a oublié l'art de la guerre."   But
this burst of criticism was no new thing.   Besides the
envy of Masséna, the bitterness of Marmont, and Berna-
dotte's audacious boast that he had won a great battle by
disobeying orders, clear-sighted officers were never wanting who knew the limitations of his talent as accurately as
the vices of his character.   Campredon considered with
dismay even the tactics of Austerlitz.   After Pultusk
and Essling his prestige fell considerably, at Borodino
even the fanatic Davout found fault with his manœuvre ;
even Eugene and Murat did not know him again.
Decrès and Duroc confided to friends that he was
losing his head.   The most intellectual of the marshals,
St. Cyr, declares that he had committed errors of
which no ordinary man would be capable.   He says :
" Dans ce génie, sublime pour certaines parties de la

guerre, il n'entrait aucune des qualités propres à la conservation."

Considering the end, the sub-chapter headed " Was he Invincible ? " was scarcely needed. Napoleon himself thought that this question was set at rest before 1809. Rebuking a flatterer, he declared that he had been repeatedly defeated, and instanced Acre, Essling, and the first day at Arcole, for it was then, in November 1796, not, as is here implied, in an earlier crisis, that he sent orders to Milan to prepare for the worst. He admitted to Davout that his plan was faulty at Eylau ; and he assured Cambacérès that the new energy of resistance revealed at Essling changed the whole direction of his policy. At Dresden he confessed with magnanimity that the worst blunders of the Russian campaign were his own. Although he despised Masséna for his cupidity, he insisted that he possessed military talents *devant lesquels il faut se prosterner.* He pronounced himself equal to St. Cyr in attack, but his inferior in the science of defensive war.

Mr. Seeley denies to Napoleon the merit of originality. The art of engrossing power, the kindred art of applying it, had been already brought to high perfection, and he had great models to study. When Madame d'Outremont offered half her fortune that her son might be released from conscription, he answered that the whole of her fortune and her son too were his already. This is no more than a brightly pointed repetition of the assurance given by the Sorbonne to quiet the conscience of Lewis XIV., and of Richelieu's stupendous words to the father of Pascal : " Je vous le recommande." Once he seemed to rise above himself when at the marching of his legions he was heard to say, " Tout cela ne vaut pas les institutions." But he had been warned repeatedly by at least two of his shrewdest advisers that he had founded nothing until he had founded something strong enough to resist him. Having first to account for public and outward events, Mr. Seeley has no leisure to study the emperor in council and conversation. He is visibly impatient of

the literature of St. Helena, and of his recorded talk.
The disposition common in France and Germany to
reject the *Mémorial* seems to have affected him. We
miss the catena of characteristic utterances with which
Napoleon struck fire, from the night at Cherasco when he
assured the Piedmontese negotiators that he might lose
battles but would never lose minutes, down to the last
dictation in which he calls history the only true philosophy. The gross and graceless tyrant of these pages is
not the man who said : " Je ne suis pas un homme, mais
une chose."

Whilst the republican New Englander deplores and
despises the triumph of Castlereagh and Metternich, it
is the note of the Cambridge history not only to judge
their cause just, but their enemy infamous, and to dwell
on the slaughter of Jaffa, the bequest to Cantillon, and
the execution of Enghien. If we must judge a man's
intellect by the highest level which he reaches, and his
morality by the lowest, this is the deciding test of
Napoleon's character, and fixes his place in the seventh
circle. His action at Jaffa was not worse than the action
of an English worthy to whom even recent opinion has
been very lenient. The disgraceful codicil only shows
that the testator died unreconciled, and that the companion who, on hearing him speak of Providence, reported to Sir Hudson Lowe that his captive was breaking,
understood the real habits of his mind. It raises perhaps
a doubt whether it was in derision that he whispered at
Weimar a question as to the existence of Christ, which
drew from Wieland the prophetic answer that men might
as well deny the existence of Napoleon. But there is
nothing in the Vincennes tragedy to mitigate the bare
guilt of murder, or to turn away the historian's wrath ;
and his judgment stands, if the particulars are open to
dispute. He makes a point by saying that the duke
was tried and shot for having borne arms against his
country, and was not even charged with complicity in the
plot. The sixth article of accusation was : " d'être l'un
des fauteurs et complices de la conspiration tramée par

les Anglais contre la vie du Premier Consul, et devant,
en cas de succès de cette conspiration, entrer en France."
On this point he was examined and unanimously condemned, and it is certain that his participation in the
flagrant conspiracy was believed at the time.   Nor is
it distributively fair to represent this act as one that
seemed almost normal in the light of revolutionary
experience.   European opinion did not stand so high
above French, or royalist above revolutionary.   We do
not forget what the Austrians did at Rastatt, and the
English at Naples, the undisguised design of La Roche-
jaquelein, Gentz's indignation when Fox denounced
Guillet, and the ferocious despatch in which the Russian
protest was met by asking whether Alexander would
have hesitated to seize his father's murderers if they had
ventured within striking distance of his frontier.   Whilst
Austria gave assurance that she was ready to accept
without discussion the motives of the arrest, the applause
of the revolutionists was less decided than Mr. Seeley
implies.   The Jacobins, says Garat, were as indignant as
the royalists.

Although Mr. Ropes rises on the other side avowedly
to plead a cause, it is the interest of science that the
reason of things should be reasonable, and that interpreters of history should not resort prematurely to mere
folly and passion, and the psychology made common by
Tacitus.   The produce of late years, even of the brief
interval since these artists mixed their colours on both
sides of the Atlantic, will not allow the mighty figure
ever again to shine with excessive light.   It is well to
have his enemies watched through the same lens, and
weighed in the same scales as himself ; to see how much
failure and evil in his life is explained without his fault,
by the wiles of foes, by the legacy of time, by the necessity of defence, and the extremity of peril which the new
order suffered from the girdle of ancient forces ; to mark
the regenerating hand, the gratitude of nations, like the
Swiss, that did not thwart him, the gift of fascinating
good men.   The use which Thiers made of the finest

opportunity ever afforded to an historian has not resisted
the assault of hostile time. Even that undaunted pane-
gyrist enumerates six grave errors. Napoleon acknowledged many more. If he displayed emotion of the
better kind at Dandolo's last appeal for Venice, and when
early friends were torn by cannon shot, if his firm nerves
gave way utterly at Ebersberg when he saw the fighting
done by a lieutenant sterner than himself, yet there is no
evidence of remorse. Few things denote him more than
the manner of his regret for his greatest crime : " La
mort méritée du duc d'Enghien nuisit à Napoléon dans
l'opinion et ne lui fut d'aucune utilité politique." An
entire book of Retractations might be made of avowals
such as this. In 1805 he said to Talleyrand : " Je me
suis tant trompé en ma vie que je n'en rougis pas." And
in 1813 to Rœderer : " Une faute ! C'est moi qui ai fait
des fautes." He confessed at various times that he had
done wrong in crowning his relations, in raising his
marshals above the level of their capacity, in restoring the
confiscations. The concordat was the worst fault of his
reign ; the Austrian match was his ruin ; the birth of his
son an onerous complication. The unlucky attack upon
Spain was not only a wholesale blunder, as the irrevocable
event proved, but a series of blunders in detail. The invasion of Russia was hopeless during the Spanish war.
He ought to have restored Poland ; he ought not to have
remained at Moscow ; he ought to have stopped at
Smolensk ; he ought not to have crossed the Niemen.
At the Beresina he cried : " Voilà ce qui arrive quand on
entasse fautes sur fautes ! " He regretted the attempted
conquest of San Domingo, the annexation of Holland, the
rejection of Talleyrand's warning that France would show
less energy than himself. He wished that he had not
concluded the armistice after Bautzen, that he had
followed up his victory after Dresden, that he had made
peace at Prague, at Frankfort, at Châtillon. It would
have been better if he had employed Sieyès, if he had
never trusted Fouché, if he had not sent Narbonne to
Vienna. When he heard of the treaty of February 1815

between England, Austria, and France, he said that that
would have been his true policy.   He repented his
moderation as sincerely as his violence.   He lamented
that he had twice shrunk from making himself dictator,
and had swerved too soon from the scheme of making
his dynasty the oldest in Europe, which it might have
become if he had had the resolution to dethrone the house
of Brandenburg after Jena, and to dissolve the Austrian
monarchy after Wagram.

There is that which bars the vindication of his career.
It is condemned by the best authority, by the final judgment of Napoleon himself.   And this is not the only
lesson to be learnt from the later, unofficial, intimate and
even trivial records which the two biographers incline to
disregard.   They might have enabled one of the two
to admire without defending, and the other to censure
without disparaging, and would have supplied both with
a thousand telling speeches and a thousand striking traits
for a closer and more impressive likeness of the most
splendid genius that has appeared on earth.

XVII

MABILLON ET LA SOCIÉTÉ DE L'ABBAYE DE SAINT-GERMAIN-DES-PRÉS À LA FIN DU XVIIE SIÈCLE. Par EMMANUEL DE BROGLIE.[1]

IN his *Life of Mabillon*, which appeared within a week of *Marie-Thérèse Impératrice*, Prince Emmanuel de Broglie takes a handsome revenge on the French Benedictines who assailed his father. Whilst the duke explains the rising pride of Prussia and the reasons of the *Maison du Roy* for reserving their fire, his youngest son, overcoming difficulties which would disable any ordinary man, displays the obscure labours of the Champenois peasant who became the glory of the Congrégation de St. Maur. The academic *éloge* has long developed the art of redeeming the monotony of praise with pinches of salutary censure. This, however, is not a criticism on the famous critic. There is no attempt to overdo, scarcely even to describe, his special merit as an investigator of the past, or to ascertain how far he contributed to progress, in matter and method, and how far it has left him behind. Mabillon is presented as the equal of men like Ducange and Baluze, whilst the most learned of the Dominicans and of the Jesuits, Quétif and Hardouin, are not taken into comparison, and the amiable weakness of biographers appears, if at all, in admiration of the monk, not of the scholar. The worth of the book consists in extracts from the archives of the abbey of St. Germain, now in the congenial custody of M. Léopold Delisle. Its defect is that this

---

[1] *English Historical Review*, vol. iii. 1888.

inappreciable reservoir of curious knowledge has been too much neglected in favour of books always familiar to students of the growth of erudition. For Mabillon belongs to the family of pioneers, and his is one of the best and best-known names in the line of discoverers, from Valla and Sigonius to Borghesi and Morgan, who have made history a science. His branch of the order admitted study as a sub-genus of manual labour. Blameless providers of raw material, they placed texts above facts and facts above thoughts. He himself paid heavy tribute to the humble cumulative purpose which was still the foremost need in that stage of knowledge. He slaved in the mine, and belongs, one half of him, to the useful but unostentatious army of editors, compilers, and transcribers. But although disciplined and repressed by the strict reform of St. Maur, he rose above his brethren to be, as an historian, eminently solid and trustworthy, as a critic the first in the world ; and his thoroughness and individuality brought on disputes in which he was as often right as any man who embarks in much contention.

The portrait here given is taken from these characteristic controversies more than from the study of his greater works. He is heard speaking to contemporaries, not addressing the future. His work was confined to those centuries, from St. Benet to St. Bernard, during which the Benedictine order was the foremost association in Christendom, and a leading force in the civilisation of the West. History, as he found it, was shrouded in fable. Others were content, in reverent indifference, to accept the fable with the fact, and shrank from the coarse touch which dispels illusions and gives sterile and unaccommodating fact for religion in poetic garb. Mabillon undertook to rescue the work of his founder from the reproach of uncertainty, to bring it out of cloudland into shape fit for daylight, to carry the machinery of positive knowledge into the darkest and most doubtful of the ages of faith. Historical criticism was reduced to an art for the sake and honour of the Benedictines. Mabillon's first care was for the title-deeds of his order. Nobody before him had shown that it is possible to prove beyond dispute that an early document is genuine ; and the uncertainty of history was a welcome ally to those who resisted the tests of truth that were taught by the Cartesian and the inductive philosophers. Abbot Hirnhaim wrote : " Nihili curanda est nobis hominum authoritas, quos constat plerumque falsitatis esse authores.—Diminutae sunt veritates a filiis hominum, et de ipsa veritate vix aliquid veri tenemus.—Nec mundus regitur scientiis sed opinionibus." Some hoped or professed to elevate spiritual authority by the repression of human testimony ; and Huet, with the name and aspect of a Christian apologist and divine, wrote things that might have gone into the article " Pyrrhonisme ": " Il ne se trouve point de faculté naturelle par laquelle on puisse découvrir la vérité avec une pleine et entière assurance." There were men who, anticipating a controversy which reappeared at the cradle of statistical science, declared that the evidences of Christianity would become invalid by lapse of time, and would expire about the year 3154—or, as it came to be amended, in 1789. To this scepticism Mabillon offered the remedy of criticism ; and his great quality is that the criticism he founded was constructive and did not rest at the exposure of error. M. de Broglie adopts a saying of Leibnitz, that the defence of history was really a defence of religion. Mabillon's antagonist in the endeavour to drown history in legend, the Bollandist Papebroeck, was convinced by the treatise *De Re Diplomatica ;* and its doctrine, less opposed at the time than that of Simon or of Newton, has remained unshaken and as fruitful as theirs. It covered a small part of a very large field, leaving much for later determination. Thierry says, with more or less justice, of Guizot : " Il a ouvert, comme historien de nos vieilles institutions, l'ère de la science proprement dite ; avant lui, Montesquieu seul excepté, il n'y avait eu que des systèmes." What Mabillon did was to pass from fiction to reality, not from system to science.

My own copies, made many years ago from the manuscripts which M. de Broglie has consulted, do not authorise me to dispute readings taken with the aid of such a master as Delisle.   But some passages of interest have been over-looked, and the want of attentive revision in small things is a drawback in a book of this academic kind.   It is not very difficult to read the conundrum contained in the words " M. de Leybum, auditeur de mgr. le cardinal de Montfort."   But the " Libellus de expeditione sacra sub Urbano II." is an account of the first crusade, not of a pilgrimage under Urban the Fifth ; Johannes Diaconus ought not to be confounded with Paulus Diaconus, though both wrote lives of the same personage ; Christine of Sweden was not the daughter of Charles XII. ; in 1686 Burnet was not Bishop of Salisbury ; and the rejoicings over the reported death of William III. took place after Boyne Water, not " au moment où il venait de détrôner Jacques II."   A hasty reader of the words " Comme Pierre Victor l'écrit dans le deuxième livre de sa Rhéto-rique" would take the commentator for the author.   In the account of Allatius's emotion at the loss of the Greek pen which had lasted forty years, " ne versa pas une larme" does not give the sense of " tantum non lacry-masse."   Mabillon wrote " Animadversiones " on a book which claimed the *Imitation* for Kempis.   We are assured that the title of the book is *dans nu Latin un peu barbare*.   The title is *Vindiciae Kempenses*, without any barbarism.   Madame de Guise is counted among those who urged Rancé to write against Mabillon.   If it is so, authority should be given, for there would appear to be some the other way : " Le P. Abbé avouoit dans une de ses lettres que ces avis lui venoient de plus de vingt endroits.   Madame de Guise, entre autres, lui écrivit fortement sur ce sujet ; mais c'étoit pour lui une affaire de conscience."   It is scarcely accurate to say simply that the dispute touching the orthodoxy of the Benedictines of St. Maur, provoked by Mabillon's preface to St. Augustine, was silenced by the pope in 1700.   The king imposed silence in 1699.   In March 1701 the question was re-opened at Rome ; in January 1708 Massuet wrote his defence against the Bishop of Beauvais ; it was even proposed to dissolve the congregation. The preface was less successful than the biography implies. Fénelon declared it equally offensive to Catholics and to Jansenists ; and one of the Benedictines accuses the writer of trimming, and says, "Cette préface donne quelque atteinte à la réputation de Dom Mabillon."

Though slow to admit the justice of attacks, the biographer does not care to refute them. When Mabillon, whose function it was to write correct and copious Latin, became revealed, under stress of controversy, as a master of unsuspected French, it was believed that his friend Nicole stood at his elbow and revised his style. This, we are told, is untrue. Nevertheless, the authority for it is Rancé, an adversary, no doubt, not to be trusted in speaking of character, but so richly furnished with sources of information, that his word, on matters of fact, deserves the compliment of refutation. Richard Simon, being, like Fénelon, a Molinist, disliked and disparaged Mabillon. According to Simon, there was so much opposition in the abbey to his special studies that he wished to escape from it ; several of the monks became Protestants ; and one, after scoffing at the new criticism, fled to Berlin. The superior himself was not at ease with such a fish in his net : "Il a toujours été dans cette pensée, que les lettrez de sa maison n'apportoient que du désordre ; et s'il en avoit été crû, on les auroit obligez aux exercices de la communauté comme tous les autres Religieux." Threatened with an action for libel—"de injuriis lege postulatus"—Simon withdrew certain of his statements, which are furthermore contested in the posthumous volume of the *Annales ordinis S. Benedicti.* The report of internal dissension at St. Germain does not appear to have been either confuted or withdrawn, and, coming from one who, in the view of posterity, was the most important divine then living, who did more for the advancement of religious knowledge than either Bossuet or Mabillon himself, calls for verification. All this we are not suffered to know or to perpend. Neither attack nor defence is set forth.

Perhaps the most curious document in these volumes

is the letter in which Lamy describes his interview with Rancé at the height of the strife between scholar and ascetic. The whole of it, indeed, only transposed to the third person, was published a century and a half ago ; and it should be pointed out that its drift is contested. Lamy represents Rancé as conceding a good deal. But Rancé says : " Je ne suis convenu de rien avec le père Lami, mais je n'ai point voulu disputer avec lui sur rien, car je ne veux disputer contre personne." The question of precedence which perplexed Lord Castlemaine at Rome is told in a letter of 21st January here printed. We are not told what came of it, which would have been found in the letter of the 28th. There is much in this correspondence about England, not to say about the Nag's Head. Durand, in one of the omitted letters, touches as follows upon the prospect opened by James II., and on one of the problems which it raised : " J'ay même desjà vu quelques personnes de considération qui mettoient en question, si l'on devoit réordonner les évesques d'Angleterre, en cas qu'ils se reconciliassent à l'Eglise ; et de la manière que ces personnes s'expliquoient, il semble qu'on devoit espérer en peu quelque changement considérable en cette Isle, touchant la religion." These Maurine fathers, when they settled in Rome, struck no root. One of them writes : " Tout me scandalise dans Rome.——Je suis persuadé que les Romains n'ont ni dévotion ni religion. Ils se contentent d'en faire paroistre à l'extérieur dans la magnificence des Eglises ; surtout les monsignori et les gens de la cour Romaine, qui fourbent Dieu aussi bien que les hommes." This might be rejected as trivial and unscrupulous. But after Sergardi's censure of Roman ignorance given in vol. i. p. 192, we might expect Germain's tribute to Roman learning, which not only expresses the judgment of Mabillon himself, but is remarkable in the pen of a man notorious for petulance and satire : " Je reconnois tous les jours qu'il n'est pas vrai qu'on étudie si peu les bonnes choses à Rome, qu'on s'imagine à Paris. C'est une illusion de croire que toute l'habileté des savants de cette ville se termine au droit civil et canonique. Je

vous assure qu'ils sçavent fort bien la théologie, et que
dans la De Propaganda Fide, et dans leurs autres acadé-
mies, il se fait des conférences sur les Conciles et sur
l'Histoire ecclésiastique, où l'on dit des choses aussi belles
et aussi foncières qu'on puisse faire à Paris. Il est vray
qu'ils ont tort de ne pas écrire sur ces matières ; mais ils
ne laissent pas de les sçavoir."

In the seventeenth century the purposes of controversy were dominant ; ecclesiastical history was more
developed than civil, and polemical motives underlie even
the writings of Mabillon. Thinking sometimes of his
order and sometimes of his church, he rejoices especially
in the eleventh century " ex restitutione ecclesiasticae
disciplinae, quae a Romanis pontificibus ex ordine nostro
assumtis facta est." When he contends with Daillé for a
date, he is defending the very citadel of the theology of
tradition. Yet his canons of good history were not
injured by devotion to a cause : " Donner pour certain ce
qui est certain, pour faux ce qui est faux, pour douteux ce
qui est douteux.—Mon but n'est autre, que de faire
rechercher simplement la vérité par l'examen des raisons,
qui les auteurs de différent parti ont apportées de part et
d'autre.—Nec satis est, tamen verum amet et investiget,
nisi is insit animi candor, quo ingenue et aperte dicat
quod verum esse noverit." The maxim that mischief
lurks oftener in praise than in blame, that it is better to
dwell on evil than on good, is one of the rare points on
which his sage and lucid but not prophetic mind saw two
centuries ahead. His position towards other schools is
defined by the *Traité des Études*, in which he counsels the
young Benedictine to read the *De Officiis* in preference
to various Christian writers on morality. " On étudie
l'Ecriture et les sentimens des Conciles et des Pères dans
leurs sources, et non pas seulement dans de méchans
extraits que les scolastiques empruntoient les uns des
autres, et s'en servoient bien souvent contre le sens des
auteurs.—A force de raisonner, on a perdu quelquefois la
raison, et on a vû avec douleur, que la morale des payens
faisoit honte à celle de quelques casuistes.—Il n'y a presque

2 H

point de crimes, auxquels on n'ait trouvé des palliations et des excuses." He quotes with approval the words of Godeau : "Les Docteurs se sont multipliez et la bonne doctrine s'est presque toute perdue. On a traité exactement des cas de conscience ; on a tout examiné, on a tout réglé ; et l'on a perdu la conscience." On his travels he is careful not to commit himself about the authenticity of relics, rebukes superstition, and tells with a touch of humour the tricks that were played with " Corpi Santi. Catenae beati Petri de more ostensae sunt.—Miranda majorum nostrorum pia simplicitas, a moribus nostrae aetatis longe diversa, qui ejusmodi ossa pro veris reliquiis habebant.—Utinam hanc (Baronii) religionem imitarentur, qui sanctorum recens absque certis nominibus inventorum fictas historias comminiscuntur, atque in lucem obtrudunt ad confusionem (ne quid amplius dicam) verarum historiarum : immo et qui paganorum inscriptiones aliquando pro Christianis vulgant.—Recurrisse in mentem Sixto quod Felici acciderat, ac meditari coepisse quo pacto Canonicos Sancti Hieronymi corpore, quod in ea cappella asservatur, spoliaret. Ideo sub Sancti Doctoris patrocinio ecclesiam, quae Sixto titulus Cardinalitius fuerat, ad ripam Tiberis a fundamentis instaurasse, ut in eam sacras reliquias transferret. Sed Canonicos fraudem subodoratos, eas in locum secretum abdidisse : sicque dolum dolo fuisse delusum." At a time when Petavius could not be reprinted in England, lest the Socinians should help themselves to his ante-Nicene quotations, Mabillon speaks of Rome in such terms as these : " Apostolicam sedem paullo minus reveriti sunt fideles praecipue aliarum Ecclesiarum episcopi etiam religiosissimi, atque saeculares Principes, quantumvis perditae famae et vitae essent Romani antistites. Hinc Sergius Coloniensis archiepiscopus, et Rogerus Hammaburgensis, pallium a Sergio III. (Deus bone quali monstro !) modeste petierunt." Nor is this an utterance of anti-Roman spirit, for he goes on to say of the Bavarian bishops : " Sic illi sedem Petri tamquam errori haud obnoxiam suspiciebant." Having convinced himself on his visit to Rome that there was a practice of

finding the remains of imaginary saints, to be sent forth
with lying legends attached, he exposed the abuse. His
treatise gave offence, and the pope required that he should
rewrite it. Mabillon submitted, and produced an enlarged
and amended edition, which was published with approbation. In a preface of genuine moderation and humility,
he assumes the bearing of one who has undergone correc-
tion : " Eo tendit ut emolliam si quid durius, ut explicem
si quid obscurius, denique ut emendem et corrigam si quid
secus quam par sit a me hac in epistola scriptum non-
nullis videatur." To the world, and even to his own
brethren, he appeared to have confessed his error. Dom
Thuillier says that he condemned himself and was only
too long about it. In fact he had sacrificed his credit
rather than his judgment. To a friend he writes of this
book : " Je l'ai donc retouchée sans l'affoiblir en rien, et
l'ai augmentée de près de la moitié." The historian who
says that the finest moments in Church history are the
resistance of Luther and the submission of Fénelon, might
find room for a third type in the example of Mabillon.

The moral that distils from these pages is that Mabillon
and his companions were not only learned and able, but
veracious and sincere ; that history, which intellectually
makes giant strides, makes none morally ; that the rules,
the limitations, the observances that guarded the compilers
of so many folios are safer than the maxims of an age in
which Renan, Havet, Hauréau, occupy the seats of Gallican
learning, when unattachment is more honoured than
authority, and a man is less esteemed for equity towards
opponents than for alacrity in turning against friends.
" Les érudits d'autrefois valaient bien ceux de notre
temps.—Tous . . . portent dans leurs études et leurs
recherches une bonne foi, une liberté d'esprit et de jugement, qui frappent singulièrement." There is a problem
here of historical psychology and progressive ethics that is
worth thinking about. At first sight it should seem a
paradox to say that two centuries which have accomplished so much for the science of conscience, for the
theory of morals, for the testing of certainty and the

analysis of motive, which have learnt to probe the springs
of error with instruments of precision as little known to
the logic of Port Royal as fluxions to Hipparchus, have
added nothing to the notion of truth.   Men without
fastidiousness in their political tastes imagine that liberty
flourished under Alfred, under Charlemagne, or even in
the Hercynian forest.   Probably the conception of historical veracity has been as greatly expanded, modified,
fertilised by culture and experience as that of political
liberty, and we may be as far from what the seventeenth
century meant by good faith as from that which it understood by freedom.   What are we to think of a man who
declares that the enemies of the Church come to an
inevitable bad end : " Mira Dei in ecclesiae gubernatione
procuratio, occulta et ineluctabilis divinae vis Providentiae
ad perdendos ecclesiae hostes " ?   Or who makes a theological argument out of the existence of a Latin liturgy in
France in the seventh century ; or who thinks that one
who denied the legend of Veronica, "ex suae sectae praejudicio impugnavit ? "   At Naples Mabillon beheld some
custom which he thought Protestants right in denouncing.   " Detectio haec fit cum dignitate et modestia, non
cum iis ritibus quos alibi in Italia observatos vidimus, non
satis fortasse ad gravitatem religionis compositos.   Ejusmodi ritus Neapoli nobis superstitionis nomine objecerunt
quidam Hollandici haeretici, quibus, ut par erat, satis-
fecimus.   Cum vero ea de re ad quemdam nobilem verba
haberemus, respondit ille non decere, ut quod fidei
domesticos aedificat, in gratiam exterorum et segregum
facile abrogetur."   Taking the lesson home with him, he
employed it in defence of the " Sainte larme de Vendôme.
Il faut voir si la suppression que l'on prétendroit faire ne
causeroit pas plus de scandale que l'abus même que l'on
prétend oster ; et s'il ne seroit pas plus à propos de tolérer
ce que l'on ne peut supprimer sans causer un plus grand
mal.——On doit s'en tenir à la bonne foy des Eglises,
jusqu'à ce que l'on ait des preuves certaines et évidentes
qui obligent de porter un autre jugement."   He is not
far from applying this rule to the head of St. John, of

which there are several. The earliest mention of the
Vendôme relic is late in the twelfth century. No matter ;
we need no testimony where we have prescription : " Ce
principe peut bien servir pour prouver un point de dogme,
de morale, ou de discipline : mais d'en vouloir faire
dépendre la vérification des reliques, c'est réduire presque
toutes les Eglises à l'impossibilité d'en montrer de véri-
tables." The silence of authors is no objection, for
Fulbert nowhere mentions the similar relic of Chartres,
which is known to have existed in his time : " Nous en
avons une preuve indubitable sur la fin du neuvième
siècle, lorsque Rollon, chef des Normans, ayant assiégé la
ville de Chartres, l'evesque ayant fait une sortie et porté
la chemise de Notre Dame, Camisiam S. Mariæ in mani-
bus ferens, mit en fuite Rollon et son armée."

That such reasoning as this can have been seriously
meant and published by the supreme scholar of the age of
Lewis XIV. is not absolutely impossible, because nothing
is impossible to historians ; but it is hard to believe.
Mabillon was not his own master. He had to consider
the credit of two hundred French monasteries, the feelings
and the interests of the studious body among whom he
lived. To be checked and winnowed by Sammarthanus,
Coustant, and Massuet is a servitude we all should envy ;
but it is not conducive to originality or to integrity, which
imply isolation. And there were other ordeals, civil and
ecclesiastical, to pass before honest manuscript could get
into deceitful type. Thuillier gives a cue when he says of
Mabillon, " que souvent il faut deviner son sentiment, et
qu'il ne l'insinue d'ordinaire que par un peut-être, pourrait-
on dire." But our author's admiration extends generally
to the group of which Mabillon is the centre. One of the
ablest of these men wrote in defence of the revocation of
the Edict of Nantes. When it was doubted whether
Innocent XI., who was labouring as no pontiff had done
before him for conciliation and reunion, would approve
that measure, the Benedictines grew impatient. Durand
expresses their inner mind when he writes : " On a
d'autant plus de sujet d'espérer que le Pape fera quelque

ordonnance sur ce sujet, que Grégoire XIII. tint consistoire exprès sur l'affaire de la St.-Barthélemy, et qu'on a comme voulu éterniser cette action si honteuse à la France, en la faisant dépeindre dans la salle royale du Palais Vatican." As this was by no means the universal sentiment of the French clergy at the time, it cannot be excused by the argument from environment. And the allusion to Gregory XIII. shows that it was inspired neither by the rapture of religious zeal, nor by respect for authority. Another sinister symptom among these men is their extreme sensibility to contradiction and their anxiety not to be answered. Huet, who stands in the front rank as a scholar if not as a thinker, hit thus wildly at certain Protestants : "Ces gens-là, par leurs médisances et par leurs calomnies atroces, font bien voir qu'ils n'ont guère de Christianisme. Ils ont fait une critique sur le dictionnaire de l'Académie." Valois writes that Germain tried to induce him by threats to give up his intention of answering a particular publication of the Benedictines : "Il me dit d'une voix émue : Si vous le faites, nous vous perdrons ; et dans la même conversation il me répéta plus de douze fois ces mots : Nous vous perdrons." As the struggle against Jansenism was not confined to scientific arguments, it raised a crop of equivocation. One of the ablest of the French priests wrote : "J'ai signé contre M. Jansénius des faits dont je ne suis pas persuadé, et qui me paraissent au moins fort douteux et fort incertains.— Je n'ai souscrit aux formulaires simplement et sans restriction, principalement la dernière fois, qu'avec une extrême répugnance, par une obéissance aveugle à mes supérieurs, par imitation, et par d'autres considérations humaines." Nisard has described a writer "qui louvoye entre plaire et déplaire, et pour qui concevoir une idée et s'inquiéter de ce que l'on en dira, est une seule et même opération d'esprit." Under pressure of dependence and solidarity they learnt to speak what was not precisely their opinion, and to shelter themselves behind insinuations and ceremonious ambiguities. "La politesse est à la fois la fille de la grâce française et du génie jésuite." To this

day a Frenchman who indicates disagreement by some
deferential suggestion, instead of calling his friend a
Serbonian plunger or a hog from Tartarus, is told : " Il
n'y a qu'un élève du Petit Séminaire pour être poli comme
cela." Malebranche, having to give an opinion about a
magical performance, says : " Je crois que c'est une four-
berie ou une diablerie ; mais un peu plus le premier que
le dernier." And Thuillier, speaking of the enemy at La
Trappe, says quite seriously : " Les saints ne nous instrui-
sent pas moins par leurs défauts que par leurs vertus."
The fact is that these men were devoted, exact and temperate, but indirect and given to a simple irony. The
praise of sincerity should not be squandered. M. de
Broglie touches the right note when he writes the wary
words : " Mabillon ne parle même plus de cette attaque
qui était venue le chercher si loin, et le silence était peut-
être aussi habile que chrétien."

XVIII

A HISTORY OF ENGLAND, 1837-1880.[1] By the Rev. J. FRANCK BRIGHT, D.D., Master of University College, Oxford.

GENERAL GARFIELD wrote in his diary : " No country has made nobler progress against greater obstacles than this heroic England in the last hundred years." At the same time, Gratry described the admirable spectacle of a nation turning from its sordid carnal ways to make reparation for centuries of profitable wrong. Just then, too, Prévost Paradol, with the same scene before him, said that we all know at what stage of existence people begin to feel remorse, settle their affairs, and try to atone for their misdeeds. Dr. Bright has seen these things, and has found in them the keynote of the reign of the queen. He crowns the history of England with the age of conversion and compassion, of increased susceptibility in the national conscience, of a deepened sense of right and wrong, of much that, in the eye of rivalry, is sentiment, emotion, idealism, and imbecility. He has shown how the nation, the constitution, the empire were formed ; but his heart is not in the striving, stumbling past, in the siege of Ascalon and the coronation at Paris, with Drake and Clive, but with those who administer the inheritance of power and responsibility, the treasured experience, and the imperial arts, to the needs and claims of three hundred millions of men. He is the historian of living forces and present cares. His intense consciousness of duty and

---

[1] *English Historical Review*, vol. iii. 1888.

difficulty in the discharge of such a trust makes this book vivid and impressive beyond his former volumes, although it lacks the dramatic element. We do not keep the weary watch on the rampart of Jellalabad for the army that is no more ; and when O'Connell is saved by a flaw we do not learn how the error which had escaped the law officers and the judges, the Irish bar, and the cunning prisoner himself, was detected by a young lawyer in London who had nothing to do with the case, and whose fortune it made to this day.

Gneist pleasantly describes us as floundering in a transit of socialism. What he calls " Uebergang in das Jahrhundert der Socialreformen und der Socialbills," Dr. Bright designates as the democratic age. To call it the liberal age would be to court a party triumph ; and we should have to define liberty, which resembles the camel, and enjoys more definitions that any other object in nature. Democracy, if not the most scientific notation, is the one that divides us least. The two ideas are not always kept apart, and a veil hangs over the question how they come out in respect of class government, equality, imperialism, education, toleration, slavery, nationality, federalism, conquest, the right of minorities, the reign of the higher law. Zeller has thought it worth his while to open the *Archiv für Geschichte der Philosophie* with the admonition that history should explain as well as narrate. The advice is not addressed to the master of University, who knows the unpolitical cause of much political effect, and always looks beneath the surface of vacant debates for the derivation, if not for the original root of things. But he never sails under the bare poles of theory, and pronounces as little as he can upon party dogmatism. He shows himself a partisan like Keble when he asked whether Disestablishment was not just ; or Quesnay when he said, " Quand on parle pour la raison et la justice, on a bien plus d'amis qu'on ne croit." He deserves the high praise that he will not satisfy inferior minds of his own or any other way of thinking. For the sincere liberal he is full of weighty lessons, meaning by sincere one who knows his cargo and his course, who both thinks and acts with a mind applied to consequences, who can appraise the saying of the philosopher, that liberalism will lose India, and the Prussian minister's speech to our countryman : " You will cease to be a nation before you have time to put your hand into your breeches-pocket." He avoids glaring contrasts and exact definitions, and abstains with excessive abnegation from the statement of private opinion. The Oxford movement was a wave of conservatism, and a Liberal is by the hypothesis an enemy of the Church, a man who wants to set the bishops' house in order, a follower of Colenso.   Men like Cardinal Newman and the Dean of St. Paul's still interpret the term in that sense, and German Lutherans, for their own constitutional reasons, do the same.   Dr. Bright accepts the Tractarian nomenclature without remonstrance, regardless of men who would thereby surrender the ground beneath their feet, and who, believing that the doctrines of Laud are to those of Bradlaugh as heaven to hell, yet glorify the Providence that sent the primate to the Tower and the atheist to the House of Commons.   With the same extreme reserve, he likes to speak conditionally of foreign countries.   " Whatever may be thought of the political aspect of the *coup d'état*," is the form of his judgment upon it.   The want of sharp outlines reminds one of the Prague poet who went to see Béranger in 1847, and had to answer a few questions.   Was Prague in Hungary or in Poland ?   In neither one nor the other.   Was Bohemia in Austria or in Germany ?   In both.   Was the Prussian monarchy absolute or constitutional ?   Partly one, partly the other.   At last Béranger lost patience.   " Frenchmen," he cried, " like things to be clear.   What is not clear is not French."   The scruples and qualifications and optatives of this history would not be admitted in a French compendium.

All this caution is dismissed at the approach of transactions which betray the faults of the national character, and are subject to considerations by which we all are bound, not those for which man is not accountable to man.

"Such was the natural result of the position occupied by the English in India. The rightfulness of the position may well be questioned. . . . At no time, it must be confessed, did they show in more cruel fashion their fixed belief in themselves and in the rightfulness of their cause, and their incapacity for understanding the rights or feelings of those opposed to them. . . . The contest seemed to lie between two savage races capable of no thought but that, regardless of all justice or mercy, their enemies should be exterminated." The right to applaud, and even to exult at times, is justified by the generous integrity of such judgments as this. History of a higher tone has never been written ; at the death of Cavour, Doudan writes : "Ceux qui l'appellent un scélérat ne savent guère de quel bois se sont chauffés la plupart des libérateurs des nations." Dr. Bright knows it well, and it nowhere mitigates the gravity of his avenging sentences. If there is an exception, it is a tendency to be complacent in the Crimea, and to share some of our discredit with the French. He follows Kinglake even on the boulevards, and in his account of the plan of Paskiewitch, which led to the disaster at Silistria, omitting his really historic advice to march upon Constantinople through Vienna. But when Kinglake assigns to the allies at least 24,000 men more than the enemy at the Alma, he scarcely allows an excess of more than 5000. At Inkerman a somewhat unsteady regiment of the French line is aided by the invincible courage of the English. If the fact is so, the tone is not that of the sergeant's speech in giving the health of the French. "Don't you remember when we saw them coming over the hill?"

The Duke of Wellington, who is buried and eulogised in 1852, is the conventional hero with powers mellowed by age, loyal, trustworthy, too good for party ; and the opportunity is lost of strengthening the shadowless Elizabethan portrait with the colours of prose. We have to estimate his fitness as a statesman by his encouragement of Ferdinand VII., his refusal to allow the elevation of the house of Orleans, his fancy for Charles X. and

Polignac, his objection to constitutional government in Poland on the ground that it would imperil the tranquillity of Europe at a time, September 1814, when there was too much liberalism about. While Canning was straining all his resources to stay the invasion of Spain, the duke showed his fidelity as a colleague by exhorting the French Government to push on boldly and defy him ; and when the first faltering steps were taken towards popular education, Wellington gives the measure of his superiority to the narrowness of party feeling by the *dictum* " that money ought not to be levied upon the subject, or granted by Parliament, for the purpose of educating the people in popery, in the tenets of the Unitarians, in those of the Anabaptists, in those of any sect not in communion with the Church of England ; or at all, excepting in the tenets of the Church of England." In Peel's great administration—great because it included ten men of the rank and substance of premier—he ceased to be listened to, and came to be treated as an august bore.

Masters of expediency and compromise, like Peel and Palmerston, are convenient to the political historian who writes for all readers. Lord Palmerston especially, as a sort of medium Englishman, fares well at his hands. He deems that he was prejudiced in his judgments and material in his aims, and in a characteristic paragraph on the war for the sale of " a noxious and poisonous drug," austere morality wrestles uneasily with an acquiescent patriotism. The garbled Portuguese and Afghan despatches he does not touch. It is only from 1835 onwards that he makes Lord Palmerston prominent as the manager of our foreign policy. " In the period between November 1830 and the autumn of 1834 it was much governed by the then prime minister, Lord Grey." When Kinglake wrote those words there were men living who could bear witness that they were not only true, but considerably within the mark. Too much is made of the British triumph in the fall and submission of Mehemet Ali. To be in perfect keeping it should be said that, having been deposed by the sultan, he was formally reinstated, and was even made hereditary Pasha of Egypt. So far, therefore, France under Guizot recovered her influence. The marriage of Queen Isabella would hardly have provoked so loud an outcry against the offending French, or so serious a rupture, but for the previous enmity between Louis Philippe and Lord Palmerston. Dr. Bright traces it back as far as the quadruple treaty, and the date is confirmed by what King Leopold writes, in 1840, on the authority of Melbourne: " Seit er vor vier Jahren in der spanischen Frage einen ihm empfindlichen Widerspruch von Seiten des Königs Louis Philippe erfuhr, ist er noch nicht versöhnt, und aus Rachsucht geneigt, Frankreich schonungslos zu behandeln." The ill-feeling began when they were younger men ; and the outrageous memorandum in which Palmerston justified his attitude towards the *coup d'état* expressed sentiments of long standing.

It belongs to the friendly treatment of Lord Palmerston to be severe on the Spanish marriages ; but to say that so scandalous a breach of morality has seldom occurred, and that the queen was doomed to an unfruitful union, is excessive. The choice lay, at last, between two brothers, of whom the elder, for no good reason, was the candidate of France, and the younger, who was a *progresista*, was preferred by England. The French carried their point. They also wished the queen's sister to marry the Duke de Montpensier, and England assented ; but it was agreed that the second marriage should be postponed. The French contrived that they should be simultaneous. That is the extent of the breach of faith which broke up the western alliance. Having conceded to England that the husband of the Queen of Spain should not be a French prince, France stipulated at least for a Bourbon, and informed the English Cabinet that they would hold themselves absolved from their engagements if any candidate was brought forward who did not descend from Philip V. The warning had scarcely been conveyed to Lord Aberdeen when negotiations were opened for a match with Leopold of Coburg. It was rejected by the Government ;

Lord Aberdeen threatened to recall our minister at Madrid, and Lord Palmerston was committed to the Spanish Liberals and to their candidate Don Enrique. Having kept faith absolutely, they had a right to hold France to her bargain. But the French were able to reply that Sir Henry Bulwer was responsible for Prince Leopold; that the court, if not the Ministry, were interested in his success; that he was encouraged by the Kings of Portugal and Belgium. After three months of hesitation, Palmerston induced Prince Albert to decline the proposal of Queen Christine; but the French employed their plausible materials so well that two generations have believed that the scheme which he in fact demolished was his own; and as late as last June, M. de Mazade wrote that Lord Palmerston's first care on taking office in 1846 was to revive the candidature of Leopold. Duke Ernest, on the contrary, testifies that he was incapable of harbouring a design favourable to the house of Coburg. The rejection, not by France but by England, of a prince connected with the royal family, who was the fittest candidate, who was preferred by the Queen of Spain, opened that conflict between English and German notions of the function of monarchy in free States which the dynastic literature has exposed. Accepting without challenge Prince Albert's action in this country, Dr. Bright passes by the revealing allusions of the Duke of Coburg to what he feels as failure in his brother's career: "Ob Prinz Albert in seinem Verkehr mit dieser Nation gleich von vornherein den richtigen Ton zu treffen wusste, will ich nicht entscheiden. Ich habe über diesen Punkt oft in aller Liebe mit meinem Bruder gehadert und immer die Empfindung gehabt, dass ihn ein schweres Loos getroffen, sich dem grossen Inselvolke verständnissvoll einfügen zu müssen. . . . Man hätte streben müssen ihn freundlicher zu stimmen. . . . Die grösste Wärme und opferfähigste Neigung vermochten sich zuweilen in schmerzliche Kälte zu verwandeln, und oftmals sah man ihn an jener Grenze, die für Mächtige und Hochgestellte so verführerisch sein mag, in Urtheilen und Anschauungen

sich gefallen, die einem gewissen Hange zur Menschen-
verachtung entspringen. . . . Es war eine ewige Gedan-
kengährung in ihm, darauf gerichtet, die Menschen zu
beglücken, und er konnte gegen den Menschen sich so
hart wie möglich zeigen. . . . Man steigerte sich in abfäl-
liger Beurtheilung der vornehmen, sowie der niedern
politischen Halbwelt, welche sich vermass zu praktiziren
und in das Leben einzugreifen." This last sentence is
from the panegyric of Stockmar.

Mr. Ruskin came from Hawarden rejoicing that he
had solved the great Gladstonian mystery. Dr. Bright is
less confident, and might perhaps suspect a momentary
illusion. His own key is assimilation ; and he thinks
that Mr. Gladstone absorbs in the shape of popular vapour
what he gives back in scientific showers. Consequently
he has some difficulty and indecision in dealing with a
letter, I presume to Dr. Hannah, which was cited as
evidence of a too rapid conversion to Disestablishment.
The change was neither sudden nor subject to external
cause. My own testimony is needless, because Lord
Selborne's knowledge reaches farther. The Oxford
supporters had due warning in 1863, and there were
Whigs who, as early as April 1864, knew what was
coming, and were enabled, without help from prophecy, to
forecast the fortunes of the party through many later
years. I even questioned the guarded doubt whether the
government in 1873 were conscious of diminished power.
After the Church and the land, one of the ministers most
interested in the upas tree said, " Now comes education,
and that will soon turn us out." According to Dr.
Bright, the Tories did wrong to refuse office after their
victory. It may be a question whether opposition is to
be considered before administration, whether it is the
higher function to govern or to prevent misgovernment, to
exercise power or to control it. If he is a little strict
with Mr. Disraeli at this point, he speaks of him with
respect after the time of his attacks on Peel. Having
spoken of Lord George Bentinck, he adds : " The fire, the
venom, and the acute parliamentary tactics were supplied

by his less distinguished henchman." Hard words towards a statesman who, if he left few friends on one side of politics, was honoured with a public monument on the other, and who had a higher right than the Duke of Abrantes to say that it is better to be an ancestor than a descendant. Apparently there is a reminiscence of the story that Peel wanted to challenge Disraeli, whose violence was caused by the inconceivable neglect of his fitness for office, and whose wife answered the consoling Milnes, " The worm will turn." In truth he repels the considerate and sympathetic treatment which Dr. Bright extends all round, for he liked to accentuate antagonism and to make it very real. He resisted the polite habit of saying " my right honourable friend," when the friend was an enemy, and objected emphatically to the incongruous friendships of Northcote. Too much amenity he feared would teach the audience that what does not affect fellowship does not affect character, and that parliamentary contention is exaggerated and insincere. The pleasant conciliation of the *History of England* would not have been to his liking.

The actual mistakes are few and trivial; and in several doubtful places the author indicates opinions which, without being argued or final, are worthy of attention. Earl Fortescue did not become lord-lieutenant of Ireland in 1841, but the lord-lieutenant became Earl Fortescue ; Mr. Bayne is Sir Edward Baines ; the Duke d'Aumale was the fourth son, not the eldest ; there are no archdukes in Russia ; the Duke de Gramont was not war minister, unless figuratively ; the elector of Hesse, in 1850, did not take flight before an insurgent chamber; "Paulo's younger son " should be " Francisco de Paula's younger son " ; the treaty of 1866 was signed at Berlin on 8th April, not on 27th March. It is confusing to read that in 1871 " Grévy was elected president, and Thiers put at the head of the Ministry." One was president of the assembly, the other head of the government. The imprecations of Sir John Hay do not fitly represent a large section of opinion towards Lord Palmerston ; for the indignant orator had

personal motives of a kind that compelled respect. That
the reform debate of 1859 was memorable for the speeches
of Bulwer and Cairns is well said, by virtue of the prerogative, to mark the force of arguments that are none the
worse because they did not persuade, and the rights of a
cause that has failed ; but it is out of proportion. Bulwer
far surpassed himself on 26th April in the following year,
when he so impressed opponents that Ayrton turned in
astonishment to Bernal Osborne, saying that it was the
finest speech on the representation of the people he had
ever heard. Sir Hugh Cairns never acquired in the
Commons anything like the reputation and authority
which his splendid gift of intellectual speech brought him
in the other House, where some say that the great
tradition which comes down from Mansfield and Chatham
ended at his death and, by the law of demand and supply,
is likely not to revive.

One of the disputed passages which Dr. Bright settles
by implication concerns the marriage of the queen. He
praises Lord Melbourne for bringing about an event which
involved his own abdication, and evidently does not assign
to him any part in the arrangement by which the marriage
was to have been put off for three years. He says that
Prussia, by the treaty of Prague, obtained all that it
desired ; thereby rejecting the story that the king desired
more, by several millions of souls, and was restrained by
the moderation of his son. It was supposed that Lord
Russell, to screen the convention of Plombières, obtained
false assurances from Turin, and conveyed them to Parliament. Clearly, Dr. Bright does not believe it. Nor does
he admit that Lord Russell, when asserting our neutrality
and resisting the confederate proclivity of Napoleon III.,
spoke without conviction, as the mouthpiece of an over-
ruling Cabinet led, while he lived, by Lewis. He does
not even hold England guilty of avoidable delay in the
affair of the Alabama. Thus, he drops more than one
figure in the American calculations. For those Englishmen whose sympathies were southern he has scant respect.
He says of the wealthier classes : " With their usual mis-

apprehension of the true meaning of the word, they supposed that the southerners came nearer to satisfy the ordinary definition of gentlemen than their northern brethren." Dives perhaps might reply that he was only adopting a saying of Burke, which Pinckney, I think, quoted in congress ; and he would find solace in a northern criticism of Arnold's latest utterance, to the effect that distinction is a correlative of snobbishness, and incompatible with genuine equality. The thing cannot be explained by the suspected thoughts of men too unintelligent to know a gentleman when they see him. Macaulay, at least, was not an aristocrat. He had done more than any writer in the literature of the world for the propagation of the Liberal faith, and he was not only the greatest, but the most representative Englishman then living. Yet Macaulay, in 1856, spoke this remarkable prophecy : that the union would not last ten years ; that it would be dissolved by slavery, and would settle down into several distinct despotisms.

In the three wars which between 1860 and 1870 determined the isolation of England, and generated Jingo, Dr. Bright does all that a few solid sentences can do to make the issues impartially intelligible ; although each contending party might add a rectifying word. He dislikes slavery, but is not far from agreeing with Mr. Oliphant, that a dog with a master is as good as a dog without one. He thinks the abolitionists fanatical, and shares that phase of federal opinion which was expressed by President Buchanan : " The original and conspiring causes of all our future troubles are to be found in the long, active, and persistent hostility of the northern abolitionists, both in and out of congress, against southern slavery, until the final triumph of their cause in the election of President Lincoln." Whilst he barely admits the strength of the pledges which Lincoln gave against abolition, the disinclination to assign grave practical consequences to impalpable dogma leaves a haze on the other side. That the theory which gave to the people of the States the same right of last resort against Washington as against Westminster possessed a certain independent force of its own, that northern statesmen of great authority maintained it, that its treatment in successive stages by Calhoun and Stephens forms as essential a constituent in the progress of democratic thinking as Rousseau or Jefferson, we are not told. The confederates are presented as men who adopted a certain political theory because it suited their interests and their passions. But beyond this, the immediate cause of secession, the duration of the war, its balanced fortune, its historic grandeur, were very much due to four or five men, most of whom took arms under compulsion of an imperative law, in obedience to duty in its least attractive form. To the cogency of the unwritten law, to the stern power of the disinterested idea for which men died with a passion of sacred joy in the land of the almighty dollar and the cotton-king, justice is not done. That which made the conflict terrible, and involved Europe in its complications, was not the work of premeditating slave-owners, but of men to whom State rights, not slavery, were supreme, who would have given freedom to the slaves in order, by emancipation, to secure independence. Many good officers, before resigning their commission, before, in Douglas's phrase, they checked their baggage and took a through ticket, hesitated like Lee and like A. S. Johnston, who wrote, " I suppose the difficulties now will only be adjusted by the sword. In my humble judgment, that was not the remedy." From the Seven-days' Battle to Appomattox, during three years, the defence of the confederate capital rested upon Lee ; and although M'Clellan believed that he knew him by heart, and that the South had better men, without him the end would have come in 1862 or 1863, as surely as it would have come to the revolutionary war in 1796 or 1799 but for Bonaparte and Masséna. General Lee delivered the following opinion : "In addition to the great political advantages that would result to our cause from the adoption of a system of emancipation, it would exercise a salutary influence upon our whole negro population." The *History of England* has not to estimate the political effects which would have ensued if the corrections of the federal constitution adopted at Richmond had been completed in timely pursuance of this advice ; but it ought to note that there was more at work than fanaticism and ambition on one side and provincial pride and private cupidity on the other.

That Austria took the final step towards war in 1866, by refusing to consider territorial changes at the congress, is technically correct. But the terms of the refusal were not so peremptory. Count Mensdorff made it a condition "qu'on exclura des délibérations toute combinaison qui tendrait à donner à un des états invités aujourd'hui à la réunion un agrandissement territorial ou un accroissement de puissance. Sans cette garantie préalable qui écarte les prétentions ambitieuses et ne laisse plus de place qu'à des arrangements équitables pour tous au même degré, il nous paraîtrait impossible de compter sur une heureuse issue des délibérations proposées." This cautious language does not prohibit exchanges ; for Austria had attempted, too late, to neutralise Italy by the offer of Venetia, with a view to compensation in Silesia. Dr. Bright doubts whether Bismarck was unscrupulous enough to use the duchies throughout as the means of a quarrel with Austria. That statesman explained his purpose to General Govone with the same laudable candour with which he spoke of ceding the Rhine-frontier down to Coblenz. The duchies were too weak a basis to justify a great war in the eyes of Europe, but they served to irritate King William and to detach him from legitimacy : "Chiamare l' Austria a parte della guerra danese e vedere di cementare cosi l' alleanza austro-prussiana. Questa esperienza essere completamente fallita, o direi piuttosto completamente riuscita, . . . e l' esperienza avere guarito il rè e molte persone sull' alleanza austriaca." Govone's despatches were published by La Marmora, and suggested to that distant countryman of Machiavelli the pertinent gloss : "In politica come in tutte le faccende della vita, il migliore modo di essere furbo è di non ricorrere mai alle cosi dette furberie."

The theory of the war of 1870 is not so sound as that

of 1866. The agitation in France is described as a phase of that vulgar patriotism which protects the feeble neighbour and detests the strong, as Thiers objected to the consolidation of Italy, and every French politician, excepting Ollivier, deprecated the consolidation of Germany. The candidature of the Prince of Hohenzollern becomes a mere pretext, inasmuch as he was the grandson of a Murat, the grandson of a Beauharnais, and nearer to the French court than the Prussian. Germany resents the arrogant demands, and the French ambassador meets with a somewhat rough reception. With all their faults, the proceedings of the two Powers were more politic and more reasonable. The candidate for the crown of Spain was a Prussian officer. He had been recognised as a prince of the Prussian house. His father had been quite lately prime minister to the King of Prussia, and had contributed, as a trusted adviser, to the elevation of Bismarck. The French argued that with such a man on the Spanish frontier they would have to guard the Pyrenees in the event of war on the Rhine. They required that he should withdraw, and expressed a hope that he would, by his own act, prevent a conflict. When the French Government had declared that a voluntary withdrawal was all they demanded, the prince, by the advice of Prussia, refused the proffered crown. Émile Ollivier at once proclaimed that all ground of quarrel was removed. The constitutional empire had won a great diplomatic triumph, after the absolute empire for ten years had endured the humiliation of failure. The success of the liberal and pacific statesman was a check to the imperial tradition and to the men who desired that the power of Napoleon should be transmitted to his son undiminished by conditions of popular debate. Without his knowledge the question was reopened. Whilst Ollivier declared himself satisfied, Gramont asked for more. The Hohenzollern candidature, known to be offensive to France, had been off and on for a year and a quarter, and had been matured in secret. They asked to be assured that the prince, whose mind had wavered so long, and had changed so suddenly, would waver and change no more. They had carried Europe with them in protesting against his election, even when, knowing what they knew of German opinion and preparation, for their agents served them well, the words of Molé to Baron Werther were repeated, forty years later, to his son, " La guerre est au bout de mes paroles." But until that despatch was written to Benedetti France had not resolved to go to war.

Prussia had taken no irrevocably hostile part. While the confidential reports of French officers found their way to the Wilhelmstrasse in the original, the Government could not be ignorant that France was discussing with Austria the place where their armies were to unite. At the same time an old man of rare political experience and sagacity, out of office, but deeply initiated, was missing from the tea parties of Berlin, on a tour in the peninsula. But the Spanish crown was surrendered with a good grace, and even the arrogant demands were not at once resented. The correct Prussian showing the door to the gilded envoy, who may still be seen in picture-books for the use of the Philistine, was never seen but there. But the seething waters were lashed by the ambiguous *communiqué*, which was instantly hailed as a studied insult to France. The leading organ of cultured Prussia said of it, " Die fortgesetzte Insolenz hatte endlich die allerderbste Zurückweisung erfahren. Die bisher erlittenen Beleidigungen waren reichlich wettgemacht." Self-command was not wanting at Ems or at Berlin, nor the faculty of entirely dispassionate calculation, which debate impairs, but which no statesman even of the second rank ever permits to fail him in office hours. To give way, without sulking, before the direct action of hostile force is a lesson in elementary politics which no civilised government finds it difficult to learn. Prussia might have accepted her diplomatic repulse as England bore the dismissal of Crampton, America the surrender of the prisoners, France the disavowal of Drouyn de Lhuys, Northern Germany itself the dismantling of Luxemburg. There remained in reserve the means of satisfying national feeling by

demanding explanations of the haughty language of
Gramont. But they could not lose the advantage of
being attacked. The assured neutrality of Europe, the
union of all the German armies, were at that price. The
telegram indicating the rebuff of Benedetti secured them
against the risk of a pacific reaction at Paris. Dr. Bright
who has related what came to Palmerston when he
received in silence the complaint of Walewski, backed by
the chorus of colonels, could tell what fate would have
attended Ollivier if, while Germany rang with the tidings
of insult, he had protested that there was no offence either
meant or taken.

He thinks that we lost ground by our conduct during
the war in France, and lost it unjustly. If we were censured for having failed to prevent or to abridge hostility,
and for having made no friends by our neutrality, this
judgment would be correct. But it is not enough to
obtain defence against wild hitting. Even in the age of
experimental science, the area which reason commands is
not extensive, and history, by further contracting it,
sacrifices itself. We go to historians for the sake of what
is reasonable : passion, and folly, and sin, we find better
in the poets. The cool reception of Thiers, or the sale of
arms to the French, is the declamation, not the real complaint. But we had not taken note of the double train of
gunpowder laid after the *plébiscite*, and our agents did not
ascertain what the mysterious travellers, Lebrun, Bernhardi, and Salazar, carried about them. Therefore, when
the crisis came, we had forfeited somewhat of our weight
and competence in advice, and were like watchers of a
game whose eyes have strayed from the board. The
decisive moment was when the emperor demanded
security against the reappearance of Hohenzollern. Four
days earlier Gramont assured us that France would be
content with the voluntary renunciation which he asked
our aid in obtaining ; and when it was obtained he pronounced it worthless, and gave an opening for effective
remonstrance. Lord Lyons only informed him that,
although we might be disappointed, deceived, and even

slighted, it would make no difference, so that he might strike for the Rhine without risking the loss of our friendship.   Again, after Ferrières, when a good deal depended on coolness, and temper, and accuracy, and the government of defence was in need of a judicious bottle-holder, our ambassador was away.

A dozen lines, from first to last, in the 570 pages would meet every grievance.   The question would remain whether it is best, with effacing fingers, to make history with individual character, class interests, and the fortuitous changes of opinion, or with the ceaseless conflict of defined forms of thought.   We begin to see daylight in the Cromwellian era when we know what a Calvinist meant and an Arminian, a Presbyterian and an Independent, a Baptist and a Socinian.   It would be a luminous moment if, for the perpetual round of violence and weakness, folly and crime, somebody would display the operation of the original materials that supplied the French Revolution, the distinct systems that divided the three assemblies and governed the several constitutions : the eighteenth-century law of nature, the American rights of man, English parliamentary institutions, the abstract constitutionalism of Montesquieu, Voltaire's humanitarian code, Protestant toleration, Jansenist theories of Church and State, the perfectibility of the encyclopædists, the whiggism of Holbach, the Helvetian doctrine of equality, Rousseau's democracy, the socialism of Mably, Turgot's political economy, the unguarded sentence in the *Wealth of Nations* which gave to the Provençal priest the fulcrum to overturn the monarchy of Lewis XIV., the conditional contract which Marat transmuted into a theory of massacre, the policy of the four Genevese who worked Mirabeau ; and our times might be clearer if, instead of our own devices, the historian explained what it is really all about, wherein a Conservative differs from Whig and Tory, where a Liberal draws the line against Whig and Radical, how you distinguish a philosophic from an economic Radical, or Manchester from Birmingham, at what point democracy begins, how it combines with socialism, and why some socialists are Liberal and some democrats Tory. Impartiality would remain intact, for the strength of a doctrine, that which has to be accounted for, is its truth or semblance of truth ; its errors make themselves known by its consequences and variations. The difficulty is that political symbolism implies symbols, and a party seldom produces or obeys its charter. No manifesto or election programme has the defining authority of a Shorter Catechism ; and political teachers are not representative in the same sense as Hammond or Chillingworth, Baxter or Barclay. Theology differentiates towards exclusiveness, while politics develop in the direction of comprehension and affinity. Men who move along plain lines, like Seward and Castelar, are not often the most efficacious ; and the alchemy that could condense Thiers or Bismarck or Frère Orban into a formula, as Bulwer's French cook put the Prize Durham into a pomatum-pot, is a lost art. History does not work with bottled essences, but with active combinations ; compromise is the soul, if not the whole of politics. Occasional conformity is the nearest practical approach to orthodoxy, and progress is along diagonals. Most of the maxims that have made the times since 1776 different from what went before are international. Criminal and philanthropic and agrarian legislation is simultaneous in many countries ; the Reform Bill was carried in the streets of Paris, and purchase fell between Metz and Sedan. Pure dialectics and bilateral dogmas have less control than custom and interest and prejudice. The German loves abstractions and the Frenchman definitions, and they are averse from whatever is inconsistent and illogical. But the earliest history which is still read in Germany begins, " There was once a count " ; and Ranke is always concrete, seldom puzzling over predestination or the balance of trade. Almost the only man who in France has succeeded with deductive history is the Milanese Ferrari ; even the best historian of the Revolution, Sorel, has not carried out the dogmatic method, and Renan would be likely to lose readers if he required them to understand the Gnostics.

Nevertheless, the avoidance of a keen political edge is a risk even to the most dispassionate and conscientious of writers. He does not see that in 1874 it would have been better not to dissolve before the budget ; he looks on the ballot as a medicine for corruption, not for the graver evil of pressure which makes men vote against their conviction, and always involves a lie ; and he does not clearly separate expenditure on insurance and defence from expenditure on the means of aggression. The danger to the student is that moral indifference in political thinking which Leroy Beaulieu homœopathically declares to be a very good thing as well as a very bad one : " Cette sorte de scepticisme, d'athéisme politique, est le grand péril, la grande difficulté de tous nos gouvernements, et en même temps c'en est le principal point d'appui : c'est à la fois le mal et le remède du mal."

XIX

A HISTORY OF THE FRENCH REVOLUTION.
By H. Morse Stephens. Vol. II [1]

Mr. Morse Stephens's *French Revolution* owes its success to an immense body of accurate detail. He has been the first of our countrymen to consult the whole recent literature of France, including tracts, reviews, and provincial publications. If he has left in comparative neglect the dusty and discoloured prints of the time itself, he may be trusted as a master of the newest knowledge and of the facts as they now are. His clear, plain, unpretentious narrative seldom rises above an even level, unbroken by perspective or reflection, and the reader, who is never stirred or dazzled or distracted, feels that he has got at last behind the north wind of fine writing and calculated pathos. The reserve and moderation of language, the directness of the appeal to reason, constitute a very real advance.

The difficulty has been to select from the mass of information, and of course there are not two men who would choose alike. At times the author indicates, and seems to announce, something which we should be glad to know, and then disappoints us. Vergniaud, he says, was a far more profound thinker than his associates. This is a good opening. For Vergniaud has been allowed to pass for no more than a superb rhetorician, and everybody would wish to learn what his profound

---

[1] *English Historical Review*, vol. vii. 1892.

thoughts were. But they do not appear. If the sentence upon him is unfair to any associate it is to Buzot, of whom Mr. Stephens dimly affirms that he had a system of his own, but leaves us to find out, when the dogs are devouring his remains, that he was a federalist. The fact is no doubt true, in theory as well as in policy ; but, as it has been questioned by the high authority of M. Taine, there was room for more, and the ugly word used in referring to the relations between Buzot and Madame Roland ought to be corrected or made good. Again, we are told that the iron safe furnished fresh arguments against the king. But it is not stated what they were. Now it chances that they were very serious arguments indeed, and they have been slurred over by so respectable a royalist as Barante. The list of omissions might be prolonged ; but, although the author's French is not entirely above reproach, inaccuracies are extremely rare. There is hardly anything in the Argonne that can fairly be called a mountain pass ; and Leopold of Tuscany is not fitly described when he is called one of the benevolent and intelligent despots of that epoch. The thing that distinguishes him from the rest, that distinguishes him favourably even from the King of England, is that, without necessity or even pressure, he desired to diminish his own despotic power. Following Lanfrey, Mr. Stephens has the courage to say that Carnot was no better than the rest ; and he follows still more illustrious examples when he calls Sieyès a shallow theorist. If he holds the supposed opinion of Burke, and means that in politics a theorist is shallow of necessity, because politics are insoluble by theory, the idea has a right to pass unchallenged in these pages ; otherwise it ought to be remembered that in the little band of true theorists, composed of Harrington and Locke, Rousseau and Jefferson, Hamilton and Mill, the rank of Sieyès is very far from being the lowest.

The philosophy of the Revolution, its causes in the region of thought, its long ancestry, its connection with like events, and its position in the series are not things to be inquired for from a writer absorbed in the difficult labour of discovering the event as it has come to appear under the fostering hand of a new republic. We may well be grateful for what we have got, for the most minute and careful account in the language of all that led to the establishment of the Reign of Terror. But the comfort derived from the praiseworthy avoidance of emotion and abuse is tempered by the fact that the author's moderation is not all due to self-government, but apparently to a rare and remarkable ethical indifference. Urbanity towards Robespierre and Marat is unquestionably meritorious. But the repose of reading about them without nickname or epithet is spoilt, when it appears that, if they are not treated like monsters at a show, it is because the author does not think them so very monstrous after all, but knows a good deal that may be said in their favour. He rightly holds that the royalists were often no better than their exterminators, and that the monotonous and interested representations of conservative writers call for redress. He is more shocked at their exaggerations than at those of Michelet or Hamel, and his sympathies with the latter lead him when he goes astray. He judges that the plot for seizing Strasburg justifies the decrees of the legislative assembly against the *émigrés*. In point of time the decree preceded the plot. It was vetoed by the king, and was renewed afterwards. Still the assembly was committed to the cruel policy before the transaction by which Mr. Stephens summarily justifies it. He is sorry for the king, and judges him, on the whole, equitably. But he insists that he was kindly treated in prison, and he calls attention to an item of twenty-two *livres* for the queen's washing. For her, indeed, he has little to urge, and he asks whether she would have been merciful had she conquered.

From the massacres of September the book degenerates. First, we are assured that the prisoners arrested on 30th August were men who, from their position, naturally disliked the progress of the Revolution. Afterwards it appears that they were murdered for fear they should break out and destroy their enemies, and that any one who was not a priest or a forger was able to save his life if he kept his wits about him. The massacres were not much minded at Paris, but were disapproved in England by the aristocracy. Political murder is, no doubt, a regrettable circumstance ; but it is common to all revolutions. " There is an apology for the great revolutionary leaders who ought to have interfered, but who yet confidently believed the death of a thousand poor creatures who were foully murdered in the prisons of Paris would pave the way for a stronger and more glorious France." There were two thousand victims at Lyons ; yet, terrible as this severity may seem, it must be remembered that it attained its object. Robespierre is described as a highly moral man, and an opponent of bloodshed who had a sincere love of liberty. He did not much care whether the king was guilty, but he held it clearly expedient that he should die. Like Marat, he had his faults ; but he was very nearly a great man. As to Marat, it is true that he libelled many innocent men and encouraged the Parisians to shed blood ; but at other times his words were full of the wisdom of the statesman. Another personage worthy of honour is Maillard, for it was he who gave to massacre the consecrating forms of law, and he saved quite as many lives as he destroyed. At last one is not in the least surprised to read that life was nowhere more happy and gay than in the prisons of Paris. Once, it is true, Mr. Morse Stephens encounters a deed of violence which he cannot palliate, a delinquent for whom he feels no compassion. A generous indignation stifles his love of mercy, and he admits that Charlotte Corday was only a cold-blooded murderess.

It is agreed that a critic says very much less than he means, and with this provision against misconstruction and the perils of understatement I may safely say that the methods of this book would be fatal to history. Our judgment of men, and parties, and systems, is determined by the lowest point they touch. Murder, as the con-

ventional low-water mark, is invaluable as our basis of
measurement.   It is the historian's interest that it shall
never be tampered with.   If we have no scientific zero to
start from, it is idle to censure corruption, mendacity, or
treason to one's country or one's party, and morality and
history go asunder.

XX

WILHELM VON GIESEBRECHT [1]

WHEN Giesebrecht died, on 18th December last, there
was no difficulty or difference in fixing his place amongst
his peers. His rightful rank was ascertained and undisputed. He never became a European classic, like
Ranke and Mommsen alone of the German historians.
He was neither the head of a school, like Waitz, nor the
chief of a party, like Sybel. Disciples of Baur knew
more than he about the growth of doctrines, and disciples
of Richter about ecclesiastical institutions. Sohm and
Gierke were superior to him in politics and law ; Ficker
and Denifle were more powerful originators. He did not
speak with authority of the things that came before Clovis
or after Manfred. Nobody turned to him for explanation
of the fitful slumber of the civil code, the rise of universities, the philosophy of Abelard, or the significance
and proportion of Citeaux. His limitations were distinctly
marked, and they were part of his strength. He spent
a long life of labour in mastering a single epoch and
writing a single book. But among all his countrymen
employed on the Middle Ages no one was more widely
known, and read, and trusted ; and his *Kaiserzeit* was the
nearest mediæval equivalent of the *Römische Geschichte*
and the *Zeitalter der Reformation.*

He gave himself up, until he was near forty, to the
occult studies of the critic, and acquired an almost faultless
knowledge of the sources, in print and manuscript, down
to the thirteenth century. His training and skill were

[1] *English Historical Review,* vol. v, 1890.

such that he succeeded in reconstructing a lost chronicle
from its derivatives, and the discovery of the forgotten
text afterwards proved the fidelity of his work.   He
depended, perhaps, more on chronicles and biographies
than on acts and letters, and was more entirely familiar
with the German and Italian publications than with French
and English.   In those early days, when no great reliance
could be placed on editions and collections, it behoved
the serious explorer to hew his own material, to decide
upon texts and dates, authors and authorities, for himself.
As national studies succeeded classical, this work has
been taken up by a swarm of zealous students ; essays
and dissertations have poured down from every quarter ;
and the reigns of the earlier emperors have been examined,
year by year, by the most solid historians in the land.
Giesebrecht accomplished this, the first part of his duty,
so well that Böhmer, in his day, considered him the
soundest of mediæval scholars, and Steindorff, coming after
him, declares that he leaves little to glean.   The preparation was so thorough, the gestation so prolonged, that his
account of Frederic of Hohenstaufen, where he is a pioneer,
and few preceding micrographers have broken the clods
and sifted the sands, is scarcely inferior to the Gregorian
volume, commodiously composed by the light of countless
rivals.   His tried methods and vast experience made him
slow to follow the lead of enterprising juniors.   In his
youth he had witnessed the crash of falling fables and
credulities, and had learnt the ways of the new learning ;
but he was guarded against historical iconoclasm, and
belonged, as a critic, to an epoch of reconstruction.   Criticism, in his hands, was an instrument not of scepticism
but of certainty.   For plain reasons, the newest surprises
the farthest innovations, have been connected with religion
Giesebrecht, though no theologian, was a deeply religious
Lutheran, an enthusiast in his royalism of so strict a
temper that he would never visit Paris, the seat of revolution and corruption.   He was not a man to be attracted
by audacity in negation and rejection.   All the doubt
which is cast on statements and documents by the desire

2 K

to remove an obstacle and promote a purpose was unknown to him.   No fact was unwelcome, no proof
traversed any favourite view ; for he inherited no tradition,
cultivated no prejudice, cherished no legend.   He felt the
pathos, not the passions of the past.   His profound
research into the literature of history left him inclining to
conservatism ; and he was tender of destroying, not from
deficient acuteness but from unswerving integrity.

The revolutionary year 1848 roused him from the
somewhat obscure and silent pursuit of evidence.   The
dream of empire was dispelled by the predestined emperor ;
the German people were humbled and dispirited by
failure.   Giesebrecht resolved to disclose to them what
the reality had been.   It was the resolve of a good
citizen to revive the fading faith, to remind his countrymen of the time when they were the foremost nation,
when their monarch wore the highest earthly crown, and
seemed to rule the world.   He called up the ages between
the Othos and Frederic as a loyal Frenchman revels in
the century between Vervins and Ryswick.   A finer
occasion, a happier inspiration, can scarcely be found in
literature.   Men of his standing, as able as himself, came
to the front just then, taking up the Roman republic, the
French revolution, the reign of Napoleon, the policy of
Prussia.   Some had no real contact with the topic of the
day ; others were in so close a contact as to damage the
serenity and security of impartial writing.   Giesebrecht's
subject, containing neither a Protestant church nor a
Prussian state, was at a safe distance from practical
politics, involved no controversy, and was legitimately
popular.   Before his book was half finished the empire he
believed in was restored, and he doubted for a moment,
under the altered conditions, whether it was worth while
to continue labours made superfluous by success.   He
almost seemed to ask himself whether, in fact, he was a
scholar making use of an incomparable opportunity, or an
astute patriot applying ancient forces to arduous conjunctures of the day.

With unexampled constancy he worked for forty years

at the five volumes which carried the imperial history to the end of Frederic Barbarossa. It was the first time that the highest scholarship was united, in German history, with the lighter elements of popularity. In early life, when Ranke asked him what he meant to be, he had answered that he wished to become a dramatist. "Nonsense," said his master; "you will be a historian." The literary taste and faculty survived the extinction of the poet; and besides the literary faculty there was the warm patriotism, the afterglow of 1848, the notion of history, neither philosophic nor cosmopolitan, but national.

The first part established his reputation, but did not display him at his best. Beyond all scholars of his rank and resource he was averse from the mechanical parade of inanimate erudition. He would have liked to quote nothing, but to present a compact and convincing narrative, without tags of proof, to a contented public. By degrees he modified his plan, to the advantage of serious readers. When no evidence is required he offers none. We miss the familiar and obvious passages with which the followers of Waitz rejoice to load the foot of the page. He only annotates when he has something particular to tell, some difficulty to explain; so that every note adds to the information in his narrative. When, as director of the Perthes collection of European histories, he invited Brewer to complete the work which Pauli had abandoned, he was bountiful as to space; but while he allowed the continuator ten or a dozen volumes he desired to restrict the notes, and did not like to be reminded that his own fill two hundred pages in a volume. In truth, they contain the most penetrating and instructive discussion of authorities to be found anywhere in modern literature, and there are readers who hold them to be a richer prize than the text which they illustrate.

To exact learning, sound criticism, and real literary power Giesebrecht added the rarer virtue of sincerity. Born and bred at Berlin, he went from Königsberg to Munich, and there spent the effective evening of his honoured and prosperous life. Those who complained of

Hyperboreans, bringing with them to the South the spirit of a Melanesian apostolate, found it hard to fix reproach on this high-minded and generous North German. From the beginning of Sybel's *Historische Zeitschrift*, which opened with his inaugural lecture, and from the Ghibelline controversy which, about the same time, brought the Prussian philosophy of history into high relief, it was apparent that he held aloof from the views of many men who were his comrades and friends. All of course would agree that the past must be interpreted and tried by some standard that does not vary, not by the view which each man may have made his own. But then there is the fixed standpoint of manifest destiny. If the past is not judged by the present, it must be judged by the event, which is the verdict of the power that governs the universe. Our view must be based not on theory but experience. History conveys no wisdom to men who refuse to verify and register its conclusions. Failure is always deserved, and that which perishes perishes by its own fault. Nothing in the memory of mankind broke down more disastrously than the scheme of ruling Western Europe by the combined Empire and Papacy. It brought upon the German and Italian people a long succession of sorrows and humiliations ; and its end, like that of ancient Rome, of ancient France, is among the solemn portents of the world. The judgment of ages impresses and imposes itself alike on royalist and republican, Christian and pagan, whose several sympathies have nothing to do with the manifest facts of science.

Giesebrecht was less definite in asserting his opinions, and practised a larger charity. Not being a divine, a canonist, a politician, but a narrator of events, he left it to experts of every kind to moralise, to generalise, to eliminate permanent truths from the succession of causes and effects. Papacy and Empire were the shape in which Germans of the twelfth century understood religion and policy ; he resolutely makes the best of pope and emperor. The hierarchy does not make him an enemy by crushing the liberties of Rome ; and when the emperor puts out the eyes of his prisoners he goes on with unabated interest to tell the rest of his story. In accordance with this easy amenity, made up, in unequal parts, of generosity, indifference, and calculation, he assigns a qualified credit to writers seldom treated seriously, such as Damberger and Sugenheim; so that he was sometimes accused of favouring the Jesuit and sometimes the Jew; and when Gfrörer assailed him in the tone of Landor or Carlyle he continued to cite him with respect. His extreme discretion and reserve, the absence of fixtures and of edge, made him fortunate in the limits of his work. He laid down his pen between the pacification of Venice and the third crusade, before the Sicilian marriage which wrecked the empire. If it had come down to the struggle for life or death which destroyed the house of Hohenstaufen and broke up the nation, his studious neutrality would have suffered a painful trial.

His eminent qualities, moral and intellectual, obtained an extended acceptance not given to harder men like Waitz and Dümmler, whom scholars prefer and few but scholars read. Outside of his domain, beyond the two centuries which were essentially his own, he was an excellent teacher and adviser. Every office of literary trust was forced upon him, and the inevitable corre-spondence explains the prodigious fact that only six months ago he was patiently labouring at a book begun before the middle of the century. He had been one of Ranke's earliest pupils, and remained one of the most faithful and representative observers of the direction which his master gave. He did not entirely escape that habit of the seminary of Berlin to dwell so long on the literary preliminaries that, as in the instance of his friend Koepke, the analysis of writers almost precluded touch with events. But, like his teacher, he wrote not for the school but the nation. Like him he believed that the true knot lay in the mingled fortunes of the Teuton and the Latin, of the race whose portion was the empire and the race that held the priesthood. And it was in the same genuine spirit that he was a gracious and merciful judge of men, forgetful of himself, and deemed it his true function to describe events, committing ideas, institutions, and principles to those whom they professionally concern. His fame will rise or fall with the authority of the school which still reigns supreme.   If, taking other examples and other methods into account, historians occupy themselves with all that goes to weave the web of social life, then the work of Giesebrecht, like the work of Ranke, will appear neither sufficient nor efficient, but characteristic of a passing stage in the progress of science.   But if politics and history are one, so that the historian has only to record, in absolute purity, the action of organised public forces, then he deserves to be remembered, among the best men of Germany, as one who during his lifetime was unsurpassed in mediæval narrative.

APPENDIX

By the kindness of Mrs. Creighton we are enabled to publish the following extracts from Acton's Letters to Creighton on the subject of the article on vols. iii. and iv. of the *History of the Papacy* contributed by Acton to the *English Historical Review*, reprinted here pp. 426-41. Acton's curiously naïve view of the situation is disclosed in the original covering letter to Creighton as Editor in which he describes the article as " the work of an enemy." We do not quote the letters in full but only such portions as serve to bring out more clearly perhaps than anything else which he wrote, the uncompromising rigidity of Acton's canons of judgment. They mark the gulf which divided him alike from the sympathetic writer, who excuses everything by a facile reference to the moral atmosphere of the age he is representing, and on the other hand from the " scientific " historian, whose ideal is to state facts and observe causes, but never to pronounce sentence.

After arguing, first, that the high absolutist theory of the Papacy was the real cause of the breach with Luther, and, secondly, that the Popes were individually and collectively responsible for the policy of persecution in the thirteenth and fourteenth centuries, Acton goes on as follows :—

The same thing is the case with Sixtus IV. and the Spanish Inquisition, what you say has been said by Hefele Gauss and others. They, at least, were, in a sort, avowed defenders of the Spanish Inquisition. Hefele speaks of Ximenes as one might speak of Andrewes or Taylor or Leighton. But in what sense is the Pope not responsible for the Constitution by which he established the new tribunal ? If we passed a law giving Dufferin powers of that sort, when asked for, we should surely be responsible. No doubt

the responsibility in such a case is shared by those who ask for a
thing.   But if the thing is criminal, if, for instance, it is a licence to
commit adultery, the person who authorises the act shares the guilt
of the person who commits it.   Now the Liberals think Persecution
a crime of a worse order than adultery, and the acts done by Ximenes
considerably worse than the entertainment of Roman courtesans by
Alexander VI.   The responsibility exists whether the thing permitted
be good or bad.   If the thing be criminal then the authority
permitting it bears the guilt.   Whether Sixtus is infamous or not
depends on our view of persecution and absolution, whether he is
responsible or not depends simply on the ordinary evidence of history.

Here again what I have said is not in any way mysterious or
esoteric.   It appeals to no hidden code.   It aims at no secret moral.
It supposes nothing, and implies nothing but what is universally
current and familiar.   It is the common, even the vulgar, code I
appeal to.

Upon these two points we differ widely, still more widely with
regard to the principle by which you undertake to judge men.   You
say that people in authority are not to be snubbed or sneezed at from
our pinnacle of conscious rectitude.

I really don't know whether you exempt them because of their
rank, or of their success and power, or of their date.   The
chronological plea may have some little value in a limited sphere of
instances.   It does not allow of our saying that such a man did not
know right from wrong, unless we are able to say that he lived
before Columbus, before Copernicus, and could not know right from
wrong.   It can scarcely apply to the centre of Christendom 1500
after the birth of our Lord.   That would imply that Christianity is a
mere system of metaphysics which borrowed some ethics from elsewhere.   It is rather a system of ethics which borrowed its metaphysics elsewhere.   Progress in ethics means a constant turning of
white into black, and burning what one has adored.   There is little
of that between St. John and the Victorian era.   But if we might
discuss this point until we found that we nearly agreed, and if we do
agree thoroughly about the impropriety of Carlylese denunciations
and Pharisaism in history, I cannot accept your canon that we are to
judge Pope and King unlike other men, with a favourable presumption that they did no wrong.   If there is any presumption it is the other
way, against the holders of power, increasing as the power increases.
Historic responsibility has to make up for the want of legal responsibility.   Power tends to corrupt, and absolute power corrupts
absolutely.   Great men are almost always bad men, even when they
exercise influence and not authority, still more when you superadd
the tendency or the certainty of corruption by authority.   There is
no worse heresy than that the office sanctifies the holder of it.   That
is the point at which the negation of Catholicism and the negation
of Liberalism meet and keep high festival, and the end learns to
justify the means.   You would hang a man of no position like

Ravaillac ; but if what one hears is true, then Elizabeth asked the gaoler to murder Mary, and William III. ordered his Scots minister to extirpate a clan. Here are the greatest names coupled with the greatest crimes; you would spare those criminals, for some mysterious reason. I would hang them higher than Haman, for reasons of quite obvious justice, still more, still higher for the sake of historical science.

The standard having been lowered in consideration of date is to be still further lowered out of deference to station, whilst the heroes of history become examples of morality, the historians who praise them, Froude, Macaulay, Carlyle, become teachers of morality and honest men. Quite frankly, I think there is no greater error. The inflexible integrity of the moral code is, to me, the secret of the authority, the dignity, the utility of History.

If we may debase the currency for the sake of genius, or success, or rank, or reputation, we may debase it for the sake of a man's influence, of his religion, of his party, of the good cause which prospers by his credit and suffers by his disgrace. Then History ceases to be a science, an arbiter of controversy, a guide of the Wanderer, the upholder of that moral standard which the powers of earth and religion itself tend constantly to depress. It serves where it ought to reign ; and it serves the worst cause better than the purest. . . . My dogma is not the special wickedness of my own spiritual superiors, but the general wickedness of men in authority— of Luther and Zwingli, and Calvin, and Cranmer, and Knox, of Mary Stuart and Henry VIII., of Philip II. and Elizabeth, of Cromwell and Louis XIV., James and Charles and William, Bossuet and Ken.

The following series of canons formed a postscript to the letter :—

ADVICE TO PERSONS ABOUT TO WRITE HISTORY—DON'T

In the Moral Sciences Prejudice is Dishonesty.

A Historian has to fight against temptations special to his mode of life, temptations from Country, Class, Church, College, Party, Authority of talents, solicitation of friends.

The most respectable of these influences are the most dangerous.

The historian who neglects to root them out is exactly like a juror who votes according to his personal likes or dislikes.

In judging men and things Ethics go before Dogma, Politics or Nationality. The Ethics of History cannot be denominational.

Judge not according to the orthodox standard of a system religious, philosophical, political, but according as things promote, or fail to promote the delicacy, integrity, and authority of Conscience.

Put conscience above both system and success.

History provides neither compensation for suffering nor penalties for wrong.

The moral code, in its main lines, is not new, it has long been known, it is not universally accepted in Europe even now, the difference in moral insight between past and present is not very large.

But the notion and analysis of conscience is scarcely older than 1700 ; and the notion and analysis of veracity is scarcely older than our time, barring sacred writings of East and West.

In Christendom time and place do not excuse—if the Apostles' Code sufficed for salvation.   Strong minds think things out, complete the circle of their thinking, and must not be interpreted by types. Good men and great men are *exvitermini*, aloof from the action of surroundings.   But goodness generally appeared in unison with authority, sustained by environment, and rarely manifested the force and sufficiency of the isolated will and conscience.

The Reign of Sin is more universal, the influence of unconscious error is less, than historians tell us.

Good and evil lie close together.   Seek no artistic unity in character.

History teaches a Psychology which is not that of private experience and domestic biography.

The principles of public morality are as definite as those of the morality of private life ; but they are not identical.

A good cause proves less in a man's favour than a bad cause against him.   The final judgment depends on the worst action.

Character is tested by true sentiments more than by conduct.   A man is seldom better than his word.   History is better written from letters than from histories ; let a man criminate himself.

No public character has ever stood the revelation of private utterances and correspondence.

Be prepared to find that the best gives way under closer scrutiny.

In public life, the domain of History, vice is less than crime. Active, transitive sins count for more than others.

The greatest crime is Homicide.   The accomplice is no better than the assassin ; the theorist is worse.

Of killing from private motives or from public, from political or from religious, *eadem est ratio* ; morally the worst is the last.   The source of crime is *pars melior nostri*, what ought to save, destroys ; the sinner is hardened and proof against Repentance.

Faith must be sincere, when defended by sin it is not sincere ; theologically it is not Faith.

God's grace does not operate by sin.   Transpose the nominative and the accusative, and see how things look then.

History deals with Life, Religion with Death, much of its works and spirit escapes our ken.

APPENDIX · 507

The systems of Barrow, Baxter, Bossuet higher spiritually, constructively, scientifically, than Perrin.

In our scales his high morality outweighs them. Crimes by constituted authorities worse than crimes by Madame Tussaud's private malefactors.

Murder may be done by legal means, by plausible and profitable war, by calumny, as well as by dose or dagger.

INDEX

INDEX

and its conditions, 99; his studies in Holland and change of faith at Hamburg, a royal witness, 99; he joins the Society of Jesus, in Rome, 100; is sent for by his father, who promises, later, to acknowledge him, 101; another change of name, 102; altered prospects suggested by Charles, 103; his brief stay in England, 103; he disappears from history, 104; is personated by the English husband of Teresa Corona, 104; is shut up in Gaeta, and pronounced an impostor, 105; set free, goes to France, returns, and dies, 105-6; the impersonation discussed, 106-8; inquiry into the probable history of the real de la Cloche, 108-15; what became of him? 108 et seq.

Coburg, Duke of, cited on Prince Albert, 478

Colbert, French ambassador to Charles II., 116 note, 117
why replaced, 121

Colebrooke, 345

Coleridge, Samuel Taylor, inspired Byron's Address to Ocean, 287

Cologne, George Eliot's meeting with Strauss at, 281

Colombière, La (priest), 111

Colonna, Cardinal, and the election of Clement VII., 13

Comines, 70

Commercial treaty, Talleyrand's defence of, 400

Commission of Clement VII. on the Divorce of Henry VIII., granted, 40; suspended, 53-5

Commune of Paris, 262
civil war due to, 271

Comte, A., anticipated by Fries, 287
belief of, in immediate retribution, 286
credited by Buckle with raising the standard of history, 332
ignored by Herbert Spencer, 283
influence of, on George Eliot, 283; its extent, 280; that of his later works, 300
praise of De Maistre, 301

Concordat, the Austrian, 186, 188

Condorcet, Sketch of the Progress of the Human Mind, 327

Confederacy, its one advantage over single Republican States, 135

Confederacy, the American, on what idea established, safeguards planned

by, the one omission, 141; what might have resulted, 142

Confederate proposal for conquest of Mexico and Canada, 162

Confederates refused leave to settle in Mexico, 163

Conne, 94

Conquestadores in Mexico, privileges and property of, 144

Conscience, liberty of, 467

Considérant, 391

Consistency versus justice, a Boston view, 132

Conspiracy bill, introduced by Cavour after the Orsini affair, 190

Constabili, on the Lewis XII. medal, "Perdam Babylonis nomen," 71
on the death of Pope Alexander VI., 431

Constance, Council of, 71

Constitution Civile, Talleyrand's share in, 407; the ruin of the Revolution, 444

Constitution, federal, of the United States, 124, 127; views on, of its founders, 128 et seq.
an omission in, 137, and what it implied, 141

Contarini, 41

Corday, Charlotte, character of, 494

Corona, Teresa, and her husband the pseudo Jacobus de la Cloche, 104-6

Correspondant, Le, criticism on Ranke, 358

Cortez, Hernando, 144

Cotta, 335

Council of Basel, 71
of Constance, 71
of Pisa, Creighton on, 435
proposed, to judge Pope Alexander VI., 67-9
of Trent, decrees of, accepted by Charles II., 95

Coup d'état, the, by whom carried through, 209

Cranmer, his anxiety for the marriage law, 23

Creighton, M. (afterwards Bishop of London), History of the Papacy during the Period of the Reformation, 426; see also Appendix, 503
method of compiling history, 428; authorities consulted by, 427; warning against credulity in historical research, 431-2; rank, skill, and style of, as an historian, 426-41
over-estimation of Sanuto, 433

Francis I., accusation by, of Wolsey,
1529., 54
betrothal of his son to Mary Tudor,
16
efforts of, to secure English friendship, 4
schemes for the subjugation of Italy,
11
Francis Joseph, Emperor of Austria,
and Napoleon III., 208
and the proposed Austro-French campaign in Germany, 211, 212 ; his
responsibility for the war, 225
relations of, with his brother Maximilian, 154-6, 164, 165, 171
Franco-Prussian War of 1870., 226
causes of the same (see also Ems
affair), 205
contribution of France to the problem, 204-13
contribution of Germany to the
same, 213-17
personal share of Bismarck, 204,
218 et seq.
personal share of the Empress
Eugénie, 205, 208, 213, 218,
219-20
summarised, 226-37, 484-8
declaration of, immediate preliminaries, 223-4, 226-37 ; sequence
of events in, 238
British intervention, Bismarck's action
as to, 240
German proceedings, July, plan of
the invasion, 240 ; armies exe-
cuting, operations of, 240 et
seq.
terms of peace, 251-4, 271
after the fall of Sedan, 254 et seq. ;
effects of prolongation of (see also
Paris, siege of), 271 ; after-
results of, 271-2
results of, on Germany and on
France, contrasted, 272
Fransecky, 268
Freedom of conscience, why not established in Charles II.'s time, 121
Freeman, E. A., on historic fairness,
373
History of the Norman Conquest, by,
385
Free-shooters, French, 257
Free-will not incompatible with fixed
law, 313-15
rejection of belief in, by Buckle, 310-
14
renders application of inductive process to human actions impossible, 321
French alliance, desired by Charles II.,

116 ; his aim, 117 ; Parliament's
attitude to, 120
army, re-organisation of, by Niel,
207
its lack of initiative and the
causes, 240, 242 ; position of,
end of July and after, 241 et seq.
three chief teachers of, 1870., 241
Constitution of 1791, effects of, 183
demands, as to the Spanish Crown,
232, 233 ; as explained by De
Gramont, 234
government and people, war spirit
of, 1870., 221, 227, 232-3
governments, during war of 1870—
Imperial, 243 et seq. ; its downfall,
247-9
Government of National Defence,
250
historians, tribute to, by German
writers, 385
hopes from Southern Germany, base-
lessness of, 213, 227, 238
military position before the war of
1870., 229-30
peasantry, conduct of, to the wounded,
257
preparations for possible war with
Germany, two forms of, 207 et
seq. ; no treaties concluded, 217
prisoners taken at Sedan, 246
troops recalled from Rome, 238
wars of Henry VIII., Wolsey's attitude to, 5 ; in relation to the
Divorce, 38-9
French Republic, proclaimed 1870.,
249 ; its military weakness, 252 ;
the majority averse to peace,
254
French Revolution of 1789, effect of,
on political spirit of old State,
Tocqueville on, 182 ; view verified in Piedmont, 183 ; History
of, 491-5 ; one of its causes,
127 ; principles of, those of
Cavour, 159
Freytag, George Eliot's supposed debt
to, 287
Friedländer's Sittengeschichte, German
history of art, 391
Fries, Comte anticipated by, 287
Fronde, the, 90
Frossard, with Bazaine, 259
Fuentarabia, supposed place of Charles
II.'s abjuration of Protestantism,
90
Fustel de Coulanges, M., 345

Gallenga, on Cavour's administration,
203

INDEX

Galway, Lady, sister of Lord Houghton, devoted care of his last days, 424

Gambara, the Nuncio, 21, 22, 23, 38

Gambetta, escape of, from Paris, position of, and operations of, 255 *et seq.* ; his view of Bazaine's surrender, 259 ; operations thereafter, 263 *et seq.* ; his resignation, 270

Gandia, Duke of (Juan Francisco de Lânço y Borgia), murder of, 72

Ganganelli, spurious letter of, 363

Gans, 357

Gardiner, Stephen (afterwards Bishop of Winchester), 21, 22

mission of, to Rome, its aim and result, 36-9

Garibaldi, Guiseppe, in the Franco-German war, 256, 260, 267

work of, in aid of Italian monarchy and unity, 198-9

Gattinara, 12

Gemistus Pletho, *Laws of*, editions of Alexandre and Schulze, 427

Creighton's omission in citing, 436

Genoa, Duke of, and the offer of the Spanish Crown, 217

Germain, *cited*, 464

German army in Franco-Prussian War, causes of its success, 256 ; gradual deterioration in disciplined chivalry of, the cause, 257-8 ; cavalry of, in 1870., 243 ; invading forces, leaders' dispositions and operations, 1870., 240 *et seq.* ; operations, after Sedan (*see also* Paris, siege of), 253, 256 *et seq.* ; position after withdrawal of Prince Leopold, 221

contribution to the problem of the causes of the war of 1870., 213-17

Empire, the Austrian treaties as factors in establishing, 206-7

the King of Bavaria and the erection thereof, 204-5

prospects in the war of 1870, erroneous official views on, in England, 218

Schools of History, 344-92

admission by, of value of English and other writers, 385

Berlin historians, 378, 379, 380

preconception of ideas a defect of, 382-4

comparative humility of later writers, 385

historical scepticism in, how far prevalent, 364, 365

honesty in research characteristic of leaders of later movement, 372, 373

influence of scientific era (*c.* 1850) on history, 386

mediæval studies promoted by Ranke and Pertz, 375

nineteenth-century era, 376

rise of, 345

and the romantic Renaissance, 346

study of pantheism, 368 ; of symbolism, 366, 367 ; of theology, 367-70

a typical scholar of the old school, 370, 371

writers on history of art, 391

works by, on the Middle Ages, 351 ; on Rome and Greece, 348, 349, 350

writers of, on history of civilisation, 392 ; on political economy, 388

strategy, why superior to tactics, 1870., 241

unity, Ollivier's views on, 227

Germanic Confederation, after war of 1866., 227

Germany (*see also* Southern States of), date of development of political economy in, 388

fall and rise of, between death of Frederic and overthrow of Napoleon, work on, by Häusser, 376

French invasion of, intended, 1870., 240

historical believers of supremacy of Prussia in, 378, 379

History of, by Treitschke, 380

influence of, on all branches of knowledge, 388 ; examples cited, 388

monarchy as understood in, 251-2

population of, increase of, in 1866, menace of, to France, 207

proposed Austro-French campaign in, 209 *et seq.*

Germany and France, effects of the war of 1870 on, contrasted, 272

Gervinus, 378 ; critic of Ranke, 357

History of the Nineteenth Century, by, 376

Gfrörer, 359, 501

Ghinucci, share of, in the Divorce of Henry VIII., 11, 22

Giberti, the *Datario*, Bishop of Verona, minister of Clement VII., his advances toward England, 5, 10, 13 ; his (presumed) views on Henry's Divorce, 14 *ante*

Mexican Empire, the, the rise and fall
of, 143
Mexico, area, climate, 143 ; fertility,
147 ; and mineral wealth of, 143,
148 ; its drawbacks, 143 ; its
history under Spanish rule, 144 ;
the rise of the Republic, its difficulties, 144-5 ; overwhelming
influence of the Church, 145 ;
how dealt with by the Democrats,
146, 148, 149 ; civil war, 146 ;
the rival leaders, 146-8 ; state of
affairs in 1861., 148-9 ; repudiation of payment on European
loans, 149-50, 153 ; intervention
of the interested Powers, 149-50 ;
the campaign under Prim,
claims of the Powers, 150 ; the
French claim, 150-51; the French
in Mexico, 151 ; their reasons
for expecting success, 153 ; progress of the war, 153-4 ; the new
government, the throne offered
to Maximilian, 154-6 ; and accepted, 156 ; story of his reign,
156 et seq., and see Maximilian
Mexico city, entered by the French
(1863), 154
Michelet, J., exaggerations of, 493
ignorant of Spencer's views, 283
Michiel, Cardinal (Venetian), death of,
432
Mickiewicz, reputation of, 282
Middle Ages, historical literature of,
Buckle's insufficient acquaintance
with, 333
Raumer, German writer, on, 351
Military science, its first axiom, 6 ; and
see re Sieges, 266
Mill, James, views of, anticipated by
Talleyrand, 400
Mill, John Stuart, political theorist, 492 ;
coldness of George Eliot's atti-
tude towards, 288 ; and Comte,
287
Milman, Dean, 332
Milnes, Pemberton, father of Lord
Houghton, 414-5
Milnes, Richard Monckton, see Hough-
ton, Lord
Milton, John, George Eliot's preference
for, 283
Minio, Marco, cited on cardinals' con-
spiracy of 1517., 434
Mirabeau, 488 ; and Talleyrand com-
pared, 402
Miramar, home of Maximilian, 155
Miramon, Miguel, career of, 146 et seq. ;
his financial methods, 147 ; and
their consequences, 149-51 ; he

offers his support to Maximilian,
165 ; the last campaign, 166-7 ;
his defence, 169
Maximilian's last courtesy to, 172
Minghetti, coaches Cavour, at the Congress of Paris, 189
Moabite antiquities, purchase of, 365
Modena, Mary Beatrice of, Queen, wife
of James II., 109
Möhler, 367
Molé, and Baron Werther on
Franco-Prussian War, 486 ; and
Napoleon's reason for Russian
campaign, 443 ; records of
Napoleon, 442
Mollien, Talleyrand's respect for, 398
Moltke, Count von, appointed Chief of
Staff, 229
and Bernhardi, 214
and Bismarck, feud between, 266
and the Franco-Prussian War, 204,
206, 216, 217, 218, 223
control by, over German strategy,
1870., 241
quality of troops used against the
army of the Loire, 256
refuses the armistice to Paris, 260
and the army of the Loire, 265
drives Bourbaki into Switzerland,
268
Mommsen, 383, 385
George Eliot's indifference to, 297
defect of, as historian, 382
rank of, as historian, value, 496
value of his work, 349
rejection of Neapolitan inscriptions,
364
Monarchy, danger of, 133
and Democracy, crimes of, 193-4
German view of, 251-2
the sole hope of Mexican Conservatives (1846 and after), 146
Monita Secreta, fabulous documents,
364
Monmouth, Duke of, his title less good
than that of de la Cloche, 85,
103
Mont Avron, fort on, near Orleans, 265
Montégut, tribute from, to George Eliot,
303
Montesquieu, 332
Talleyrand's studies of, 403 ; and
acceptation of, 400
Montezuma, 154
Montpensier, Duke de, a candidate for
the Spanish crown, 213, 230
Mademoiselle, and Charles II., pro-
posed marriage of, 87
Monumenta, The, connection of German
mediæval school with, 375

THE END

Printed by R. & R. CLARK, LIMITED, *Edinburgh.*